Hartwig Eckert and William Barry

The Phonetics and Phonology of English Pronunciation

A Coursebook with CD-ROM

specifically for German-speaking learners
with exercises in phonetic transcription,
ear training and pronunciation,
with numerous illustrations, diagrams and tables,
with traditional limericks
and new ones illustrated by Carlos Yanez

W0173281

Hartwig Eckert and William Barry

The Phonetics and Phonology of English Pronunciation

A Coursebook with CD-ROM

Wissenschaftlicher Verlag Trier

Eckert, Hartwig; Barry, William:
The Phonetics and Phonology of English
Pronunciation. A Coursebook with CD-ROM /
Hartwig Eckert, William Barry. –
2., verbesserte Auflage
Trier : WVT Wissenschaftlicher Verlag Trier, 2005
ISBN 3-88476-740-2

Umschlaggestaltung: Brigitta Disseldorf

Gedruckt auf säurefreiem und alterungsbeständigem Papier

WVT Wissenschaftlicher Verlag Trier
Postfach 4005, 54230 Trier
Bergstraße 27, 54295 Trier
Tel.: (0651) 41503, Fax: 41504
Internet: http://www.wvttrier.de
e-mail: wvt@wvttrier.de

0. Table of contents

I. Is this book for you?

A young woman was buying potatoes from a farmer at his market stall. They were unsuccessfully trying to get ten kilograms into her shopping bags.

"That's never going to work. I think you are wasting your time",
said a helpful German tourist, "why don't you try sex instead?"

(Had he read this book, he would have known how to pronounce "sacks".)

An English tourist on holiday in Germany had caught a cold and had lost his voice, so he went to see a doctor. *"No problem"*, said the German doctor with a sinister grin, *"ve hef vays of making people tok."*

If you vant, sorry, *want* your English to be the source of such amusing tales in Britain, simply shut this book and go ahead. If not, read on.

The problem of identity

If a fairy came along and said to you: *"You've saved my life. One good turn deserves another. I'll wave my magic wand to give you a perfect English accent"*, you would love that, wouldn't you. Would you really? How would your fellow students react if you said *shock* and it did not sound like *Schock* any more, and everytime you said *little children* the <l> sounded ever so dark, and above all, your voice had changed: you sounded a bit more nasal than most speakers of German and your voice went up and down in an un-German sort of way. Wouldn't you feel just a teeny weeny bit self-conscious, a little bit worried about your friends' reactions? *"Am I not overdoing it? Am I making a fool of myself? Will the people in my peer group admire me or will they smile and ask: `Who are you trying to impress?´ Wouldn't it be safer if I kept talking like the rest of them?"*

We believe that a foreign accent is not only a problem of articulation. If your hearing is normal, you will be able to perceive all the different sounds as we draw your attention to them. And since your speech organs have mastered your first language, there is no real reason why you should not be able to get your tongue and lips in the right positions for English sounds. We feel there might be social and psychological reasons why people are reluctant to sound really foreign. The way we move our speech organs to produce words is part of our personality, it is us. Some people are more reluctant to depart from these habits than others. There is – as we said – also the fear of overdoing it and making a fool of oneself. And there is peer-group pressure: you don't want to sound too different from the others in your group, so everybody goes for a compromise of not too strong a German accent but at the same time of not sounding like a different person and being the odd one out in the peer group. This phenomenon is known as **accommodation language.**

"You can take a horse to the water, but you cannot make him drink."

This old British proverb raises the question of motivation. Of course, if the horse is thirsty, he will drink. We have often been amazed by students and pupils who were almost immune to phonetic corrections but who we then heard singing English popsongs during the break with next-to-perfect pronunciation in a convincing imitation of their idols. Or we were flabbergasted by students who simply would not pronounce the dark <l> in *children* and who insisted: *"Oh, I can never get it right"*, but who thoroughly enjoyed imitating the German accent of English speakers: *"Sleep well in your little Bettge-stell"*, and there it was, the dark <l> in *well* and *Bettgestell*, as if the fairy had waved her magic wand. If you can do an impersonation of an English speak-er´s German accent, i.e. if you can speak German with English sounds, you have no phonetic excuse for not using these sounds in your impersonation of an English speaker speaking English!

Digging your heels in

And yet learners do make excuses. The following are the most frequently heard reactions to the teacher´s attempt to correct a non-English pronunci-ation:

1. *"I can't distinguish between [s] and [z] because I'm Bavarian/ Austrian/ Swiss/ Danish etc."* There is nothing wrong with where you come from, but it is a feeble excuse for not bothering. Ask anybody to make the sound of a bumble bee and they will all give you a voiced *"zzzzzz"* and they will never get it mixed up with a snake´s voiceless hiss like *"sssss"*. So there goes your excuse for not distinguishing between *plays* and *place*.

2. *"I can't pronounce the ˋth´ (the ˋw´/the ˋa´ ...) properly today because I have a cold."* Of course learners know perfectly well that this is not the real reason, because native speakers of English with a cold sound like English speakers with a cold. They do not develop a German accent.

3. *"Yes, yes, yes, I know, I have always pronounced it like that."* As if they wanted to tell the teacher: *"Will you never learn? Now remember, I belong to that group of people who pronounce ˋfish´ like ˋfüsch´."*

4. *"No, I can never get this right."* Meaning: *"You can take me to the water, but you can´t make me drink."*

5. *"But my British frients alvayß tell me my English is wery goot."* Yes, presumab-ly it is, but remember: They are probably being polite, and are, in any case, very grateful that you are talking to them in English.

What people mean by 1. to 5. is basically, *"Please leave me in peace, I do not wish to change my pronunciation."* If this were not the case, they would say things like, *"Oh I see. So how do you say it? Let me try again. Better this time?"*

Why does the German farmer keep his kettle in the meadows?

At an international conference on EU policies an Italian speaker talked about how universities could coordinate their courses, but to the amusement of the audience she pronounced *courses* like the English pronounce *curses*. After she had talked at length about postgraduate curses, the effectiveness of double curses, and French curses on European Law, she was nicknamed *"the Italian witch"*. The German participants found this frightfully funny. The next speak-er was a German talking about agricultural policies, and this time non-

German participants were amused by his accent, asking themselves: *"Why does the German farmer keep his kettle in the meadows?"*, which sounds like children´s joke questions. When the cause of amusement was explained to the Germans they declared the difference in pronunciation between *courses* and *curses* to be much greater than that between *kettle* and *cattle*. When we listen to other foreigners speaking English, we immediately register the "Italian-ness" or the "French-ness" in their English, whereas our German accent in English sounds so familiar to our ears that we do not register it. This is why most Germans – when confronted with a French and a German student speaking English – will be convinced that the German sounds more English than the Frenchman. This is a very natural and understandable way of looking at things, but in this book we want to de-familiarise you with accommodation language, i.e. the German pronunciation of English that you have come to consider good, or at least good enough.

Fun-netics

We would have liked to call this book "fun-netics", because phonetics does not have to be as tedious as Jerome K. Jerome described it a century ago:

> *I also think pronunciation of a foreign tongue could be better taught than by demanding from the pupil those internal acrobatic feats that are generally impossible and always useless. This is the sort of instruction one receives: "Press your tonsils against the underside of your larynx. Then with the convex part of your septum curved upwards so as almost – but not quite – to touch the uvula, try with the tip of your tongue to reach your thyroid. Take a deep breath, and compress your glottis. Now, without opening your lips, say 'Garoo'." And when you have done it they are not satisfied.*

So how can we persuade the horse to drink? How can we get you to stop digging your heels in? How can we coax you into allowing your lips, tongue, jaws etc. to produce English sounds? Here are a few suggestions.

1. Fall in love with an English speaker.

2. Think of phonetics as a kind of role play, a sort of drama activity. *"Could you try and sound like an old witch, an arrogant princess, a helpul nurse, an English disc jockey?"* Of course it is not you, you are acting, and while you are at it, try overdoing it: sound really arrogant, enormously helpful, typically English.

3. Talk to native speakers of English who have just begun to learn German, and listen to the way they pronounce, for example, *Heiterkeit*. Listen carefully to the Englishness of the "ei" in that word, and then, afterwards, when they are not within earshot any more, imitate their English accent in German. This exercise will give you a good idea of, and even a feeling for, the differences of the two languages. We have yet to meet a German speaking student who was unable to give a convincing performance of an English accent in German.

4. When you are on your own, put on a CD of your favourite English pop star and join in. If you can, use earphones, like they do in the studios. Shut your eyes and gradually become that pop star in front of a rapturous audience.

Of course, it is not *just* a matter of finding the right motivation. Earlier on we said that you are capable of pronouncing English correctly because you can pronounce German correctly. That is, in fact, a very good reason why you *cannot* slip smoothly into correct English pronunciation. Your mouth is finely adjusted to the German movements, and there are not only *new* movements to learn for the English sounds that do not occur in German, there are also just slightly different movements for the sounds that are *similar but not identical* to German ones. That is why, in this book, we have tried to motivate, explain, and give examples and exercises to help you capture the English accent that has been eluding you. We also try to explain what is going on in your mouth in terms of articulatory phonetics, what needs to be modified, and give you detailed instructions on how to achieve this.

This book deals with the pronunciation of **Southern British English (SBE)**, i.e. the pronunciation which is common among educated speakers in Southern England, though it is spoken by many people from other parts of Britain too if, for family or social reasons, or because of the school they attended, they have not acquired the regional accent. It is the type of English often referred to as RP (Received Pronunciation) or BBC English, though we would rather not use these terms. The first, because RP is too narrowly defined, and the second because the BBC is consciously extending the pronunciation varieties used by its speakers, so that "BBC English" is misleading as a term for a particular type of pronunciation. As an accent of English, SBE is certainly not better than American, Australian, South African, or any of the other widely spoken varieties of English. But it is the variety that most German schools take as their teaching goal. It would also be confusing to try to teach more than one accent in a book that attempts to combine theory with practice.

A further restriction to the aim of this book which we must make clear at the outset is our exclusion of intonation (speech melody). This is not because there are *no* differences between Standard English and Standard German intonation, though they are mostly rather subtle, but because the topic would require a book of its own. To deal with intonation superficially, as if it was an unimportant detail, is – at least for German learners of English – worse than not dealing with it at all. We have therefore concentrated on the *stress patterns* of words and phrases so that you can get the *rhythm* of the utterances correct. And since we stress careful listening throughout, we feel sure that in imitating the way the words are pronounced in phrases you will also be able to replicate the melody of the phrases.

II. How to use this book

Nobody learns a subject by reading twenty-four chapters about the theory first and then applying it in chapter 25. This book is organized to help people learn. So we do not start by telling you everything about your speech organs and by teaching you the whole of the phonetic alphabet before we let you open your mouth.

[əʊ ˈdʒʌst‿ɔːdəˈrenɪθɪŋ jukən prəˈnaʊns]

We *will*, however, as you see, make use of phonetic symbols right from the start. This should not alarm or confuse you, because we believe that:

1. you will have been exposed to the phonetic alphabet at school (even if you have never written anything in phonetic transcription yourself and even if you have forgotten most of it),

2. you will have consulted dictionaries to find out how a word is pronounced, and anyway:

3. we have provided you with an overview of the phonetic symbols and examples at the back of the book for quick reference. When you start you may wish to take advantage of these aids, but as you progress, try to read and write the phonetic alphabet on your own. Remember, when reading an English passage you may always be led astray by English orthography; you may be tempted to make *marriage* and *carriage* three-syllable words instead of the correct two syllables: ['mærɪdʒ], ['kærɪdʒ]. It is only by getting used to the phonetic alphabet with its one-to-one correspondence of sound to symbol that you will get away from the spelling pronunciation which is typical of learners of English. Give it a try right now and read the following joke in phonetic transcription. If you are having difficulties use the chart of phonetic symbols to decipher it.

We only see and hear what we know and what we are familiar with.
[wi‿əʊnli ˈsiːən ˈhiːə wɒt wi ˈnəʊ‿ən wɒt wiə fəˈmɪliə wɪð]

[ðəˈhʌzbəndz ˈkʌmɪŋ ˈhəʊm frəm ˈwɜːk | hɪz ˈwaɪf sez |
ˈdɑːlɪŋ | dʒə ˈnəʊtɪs‿enɪθɪŋ‿əˈbaʊt mi |
ðə ˈhʌzbənd ˈlʊksətɜːrən ˈsez | jesəf ˈkɔːs | nju ˈʃuːz |
nəʊ |
ɜːːːm | nju ˈmeɪkʌp |
nəʊ |
aɪ gɪˈvʌp |
ˈdɑːlɪŋ | ʃi ˈsez | aɪm ˈweərɪŋə ˈɡæsˌmɑːsk]

Infobox

Apart from the sound symbols themselves, we employ a number of conventions to focus your attention on other aspects of English pronunciation which are perennial stumbling blocks for German learners:

[dʒu ˈnəʊtɪs‿enɪθɪŋ‿əˈbaʊt mi]: Horizontal braces (‿) remind you to link words.

[lʊksət ˈhɜːrən ˈsez]: Linking is also indicated by writing words and their elements (e.g. articles, prepositions: *looks at:* [lʊksət] in one block]).

[jesəf ˈkɔːs]: The influence of words on one another means that they may differ from the dictionary pronunciation (e.g. *of* as [əf] not [əv]).

[nju ˈmeɪkʌp]: Stressed and/or accented syllables are marked with ˈ.

[gɪˈvʌp] for *give up*: Linking sometimes entails reorganising the syllables.

Of course what happened to the husband here could not possibly happen to us. Or could it? Well, put it to the test and read the following sentence aloud and record it on a cassette as you might like to listen to it afterwards:

E 1: Read (and if possible record) the following:

> *In London we went to Harrods to buy knives and spoons and forks and so on. In the evening we saw the two films Animal Farm and Kiss me Kate.*

We have experienced situations where an English assistant or lektor discusses a trip to England for an hour, always saying ˌAnimal 'Farm, ˌKiss me 'Kate and ['lʌndən] for *London*, and the students wrongly pronouncing these words 'Animal Farm, 'Kiss me Kate (with the stress on the first syllable) and *Londn* ['lʌndn̩] almost as if they wanted to correct the English speaker. But of course, they were not trying to be awkward, they just had not noticed the difference.

Infobox

The **asterisk** (*) is used to indicate that the example that follows is **wrong**.

You are familiar with the last three words of the first sentence in E 1, you have heard them dozens of times, but the vast majority of German speakers put the stress on the last word, wrongly pronouncing it *"and so ˈon"* instead of the usual English stress pattern *"and 'so on"*. And as far as *evening* is concerned, many German speakers use a spelling pronunciation, making it a three-syllable word instead of the correct pronunciation: ['iːvnɪŋ].

This is why we have to draw your attention to these phenomena and why we have to increase your language awareness generally, so that you *will* notice the gas-masks. (N.B. If you got the two sentences of E 1 right you can pat yourself on the shoulder: you belong to the 0.1% of German speakers who spotted the gas-mask, oops, sorry, the different stress patterns.)

Try not to ignore the theoretical parts of this book. Why? Well, first of all, like all teachers and lecturers, we find our subject fascinating and cannot think of anything more important in life than phonetics! Secondly, because "listen and repeat" exercises are extremely useful, but they need to be supported by some understanding of how the language works. When we first introduce a technical term it will appear in bold print. For easy reference we have provided an index.

We have consciously avoided presenting the phonetic theory in one indigestible block, preferring to deal with the points as they arise. You will also (we hope) notice that important matters are dealt with more than once, in different contexts, in different sections. This is entirely intentional!

III. Sound examples

For this chapter we have chosen the various sounds that may be represented by the letter <l> as examples of consonants, and the two sounds /e/ and /æ/ represented by the letters <e> and <a> respectively as examples of vowels. This will give you an idea of what to expect in chapters IV. and V. where we deal with consonants and vowels systematically.

We have devoted section III.3 to the explanation of the difference between letters (as units of the written medium) and sounds (as units of the spoken medium). The importance of the distinction between sounds and letters should not be underestimated, and the problems arising from the confusion of these two media and their respective symbols often require years of remedial teaching. Just pause to think for a minute and answer the following questions:

E 1: a. Name the vowels of English and German.
      b. How do you pronounce <ng> in English and German?
      c. How do you form the regular plural in English?

If you answered a. by giving the answers aloud, did you pronounce the vowels like you pronounce the <u>letters</u> of the alphabet: [eɪ], [aɪ] and [əʊ]? If you did it in writing, did you jot down <a>, <e>, <i> etc.? In either case you were not talking about sounds but letters. Now what might be the possible use of dividing the <u>letters</u> of the German and English alphabets into vowels and consonants? Check your list: Did you include <ü> in it, and if so, did you also include <y>, because in German that letter is pronounced like <ü>, and in English it is pronounced like <i>. Did you include the most frequent of all English vowels in your list, the so-called schwa sound, the symbol of which is [ə] and which you get at the end of *butter* in English? If you did not include <y> and [ə], could it be due to the fact that you were thinking in terms of letters, in terms of the written medium, where the distinction between vowels and consonants does not make much sense? Did you mention in E 1b. that German *Finger* does not rhyme with English *finger*? (see VII.1.3.) And did you answer E 1c. by saying "You add an `s´, as in *cups* and *saucers* and *bridges*", i.e. did you confine your answer to the written medium, instead of the spoken medium, where the regular plural is formed by adding [s], [z] and [əz] depending on the previous sound? (see VII.1.2.)

As you know, language is made up of sounds. Would you be able to answer the simple questions: "What is the function of these sounds? Is the distinction between any two sounds in English equally important?" Should you have any difficulties with these questions, you may find III.4. useful.

III.1. [l], [ɫ], [l̩] and silent <l>:
The sounds that make the difference

In Britain a white square with the red letter <L> for *Learner* must be displayed when you are taking driving lessons, so we thought the various pronunciations of the letter <L> might be an appropriate choice for your first pronunciation lesson in this book.

1   a. *Learners should use an L-plate.*

In this section we will demonstrate that the letter <l>, which occurs three times in 1., is pronounced differently in each case, i.e. has three different phonetic representations. We will teach you

- how to perceive them,
- how to produce them,
- which organs of speech are involved in their production,
- how to write them down as phonetic symbols,
- and how to predict which of these three varieties you have to choose.

C 1: Listen to these speakers and pay particular attention to their <l>-sounds. Repeat their sentences and try to imitate their accents.

a. a speaker from the Rhineland
b. an English person speaking German
c. an English person speaking English
d. a German person speaking English

You will have noticed the different ways of pronouncing the letter <l>. English, as opposed to standard German, has two very distinct /l/-sounds, often referred to as "clear l" and "dark l". Let us introduce two different phonetic symbols for them: **[l] for "clear l"** and **[ɫ] for "dark l"**. In C 1, examples a. to d., you heard the dark [ɫ]. If you can successfully imitate the English learner´s accent with [ɫ] in C 1 (c), where the [ɫ]-sounds were in the wrong places, you should have no difficulty pronouncing them in the next exercise in the *right* places:

C 2: Listen and repeat:

a. [l]: *Leave him alone, Liz; he´s trying to learn his English lessons.*

b. [ɫ]: *Jill, how much milk is there in that small bottle? - One pint. And a pint of milk a day is all you need to keep you healthy. - Did they tell you that when you were in hospital? - No. But, after I was ill, I had trouble with my weight. So I joined a self-help group and they told me.*

The clear [l] should not have caused you any serious problems because standard German has only clear [l]. But listen critically to your own pronunciation in C 2 a. above to judge whether your [l] is even "clearer" than the English speaker's. There are some regions of Germany - Northern Germany in particular - where the [l] is very [i]-coloured.

The dark sound quality of [ɫ] is particularly obvious in songs when it is lengthened. In the following lines from songs, pay particular attention to the /l/-sounds in the italicized words:

C 3: Listen (and join in, if you like):

a. *Michael, row the boat ashore*   b. *There were ten green bottles standing on the wall*

c. *You make me feel mighty real*   d. *Jingle bells*
e. *as she wheeled her wheelbarrow   through streets broad and narrow crying, "Cocklllles and mussellls alive, alive-oh."*

How to produce the /l/-sounds

For both "clear l" and "dark l" in English and German the tip of the tongue is pressed against the **teeth ridge.**

> *Infobox*
>
> The technical term for the teeth ridge is the **alveolar ridge,** pronounced [ˌæɫvi ˈəʊlə ˈrɪdʒ], or [ˌæɫˈviːələ ˈrɪdʒ] (with the stress on the second or third syllable of *alveolar*). This refers to the area above and behind the upper front teeth. The air escapes round the sides of the tongue. This is why the /l/ is called a **lateral sound** ("lateral" meaning "at the sides"). One way to get a feel for this is to put your tongue tip in the alveolar position for [l] and then breathe in and out forcefully. You should now be able to feel air streaming past the inside of your cheeks and the sides of your tongue. So the [l] in *leave* can be described as **alveolar** and **lateral.**

> The part of the "roof" of the mouth right behind the alveolar ridge is called the **hard palate.** If you move your finger along the roof of your mouth you will be able to feel that further back the bony structure ends where the hard palate gives way to the **soft palate** or **velum.** The area opposite the hard and soft palate is referred to as the **dorsum**, the **front** of which approaches and makes contact with the hard palate, the **back** of which moves up to the soft palate.

But what *is* it that distinguishes the clear [l], which German speakers are familiar with, from the so-called *dark* variety, which presents particular difficulties to many German speakers?

Pronounce a long [u:]-sound (as in *Kuh*). The back of your tongue, the dorsum, should be raised now. Prolong this sound, and then – while you are producing the [u:]-sound – put the tip of your tongue against the alveolar ridge. You should now be producing a dark [ɫ]-sound. The vowel [u:] (as opposed to [i:]) is often referred to as a dark vowel, and since you hear the characteristic dark vowel quality through this type of /l/, it is called the "dark l".

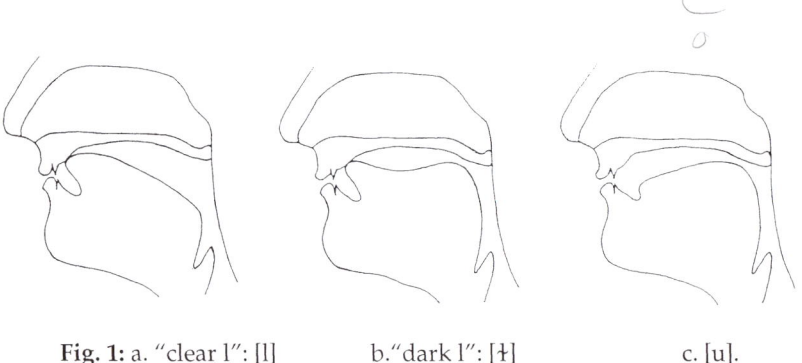

Fig. 1: a. "clear l": [l]   b."dark l": [ɫ]   c. [u].

> *Infobox*
>
> Notational convention for brackets: When we write the phonetic symbol for a particular sound we put it in **square brackets**. This allows us to distinguish between the "clear" and the "dark l" in phonetic transcription: **[l] vs. [ɫ]**. But sometimes we may find it convenient to talk about what these lateral alveolar sounds have in common. In these cases, where we choose to ignore some features, for instance the difference between the clear and dark lateral sounds, we use **slash marks** in generalized statements: "All **/l/** sounds are lateral sounds." When we wish to talk about letters, we use **angled brackets**: "The letter <l> in English may be pronounced as a velarized lateral."

As you can see, what both /l/-sounds have in common is that they are alveolar laterals, and this description refers to their **primary articulation**. The difference between the two sounds lies not in what the tip of the tongue is doing but rather in the shape of the rest of the tongue, as illustrated in fig. 1. This is a difference in what is known as their **secondary articulation**. If it helps, you might like to think of your articulation of the dark [ɫ] as the production of two sounds at the same time: an /u/-sound and an /l/-sound.

If you wanted to write a sad poem you would choose words with dark vowels like *gloom* and *doom*, both because of their meanings and their sounds, whereas you would choose a phrase like *"fit as a fiddle"* for a "happy" poem. Up till now we have been referring to the two lateral sounds as "dark and clear /l/". These are impressionistic terms, which attempt to descibe what we hear and the impressions that they create. We can also use a terminology which describes the *articulation* of the sounds. Sounds produced with a vowel quality akin to /i/, such as the lateral found in English *leave* and German *lieben*, are said to be **palatalized** (corresponding to *clear*), because of the tongue's proximity to the hard palate (cf. fig.1). Sounds in which the back of the tongue is raised up towards the velum are said to be **velarized** (corresponding to *dark*).

To illustrate the similarity between the sounds of figures 1b and 1c, we want you to listen carefully to the following sentence, spoken in a southern, non-standard dialect:

C 4: Listen carefully to the recording and try to identify what the difference between this dialect and standard English is.

> *Those poor people had no money, so the milkman gave them two pints of milk today for free.*

You may have noticed that – as well as there being different vowel qualities from standard English – there was something odd about this speaker's /l/-sounds. As a matter of fact, he did not pronounce an /l/-sound in *milk* at all (though it is still in *people* before *'ad*). Instead, it sounded more like: "*Those poor peopullad no money, so the meukman gave them two pints of meuk today for free.*" In this dialect the primary articulation of [ɫ] is lost: the sound is not an alveolar lateral sond any more. The dark back vowel sounds sufficiently similar to the dark [ɫ] to be able to replace it in this dialect. As a matter of fact, [mɪɫk] and [mɪuk] sound so similar that many people do not even hear the difference, whereas the difference between [mɪɫk] and *[mɪlk] is very obvious to every English listener. You may like to try and imitate the speaker in C 4 to get the feeling for that tongue position which so many German learners of English do not use in words like *fulfil* and *children*. And, in case you think how strange the English must be to leave out /l/-sounds, just consider the following advertisement on a tram in Bern. In Bavaria too, the /l/, in this case a clear /l/, also often becomes a vowel, as the following attempt at dialect orthography reflects: *Des iss nit ois Goid, wos glänzt.*

Fig. 2

The pronunciation [mɪʊk] is so common in England that you have to be familiar with it in order to understand peopu, sorry, people. However, since we are teaching Southern British Standard in this book and since you should not mix different dialects, we suggest that you use [ɫ]-sounds in these contexts all the time.

You will now appreciate the pun in the following headline, based on the title of the well known book:

Fig. 3: a: *The eagle has landed*   b: *The ego has landed*

The pun is based on the fact that in some dialects *eagle* and *ego* sound almost the same. The *ego*, i.e. the self-assured boxer Chris Eubanks was taken aback because a stranger did not recognise him when he had landed in Africa: *"Realising the man had no idea who he was, the … champion looked at him with a mixture of surprise and concern, like a missionary scrutinising some unfortunate primitive who has never heard the name of the Saviour."*

Devoiced [l̥]

When you pronounce the letters <p> and <b> you will find that the sound for the former is voiceless (as if you were whispering) and the latter is voiced. In *plate* you switch on your voice midway through or even after the /l/ so that it does not sound exactly like the /l/ in the word *late*. We call this /l/-sound devoiced (partially devoiced) and the phonetic symbol for it is [l̥]. You get it after voiceless sounds like /p, k, f, s/ as in *play, clay, fly* and *slight*. Luckily you get this type of [l] in German too, so it should not cause any problems.

If you do not use the dark [ł] in the appropriate places, native speakers of English may still understand you, but if you do not wish to have a strong foreign accent (as demonstrated in C 1 c. and e., you will have to master both sounds).

C 5: Exercises for dark [ł]. Listen and repeat:

> *"Hallo, Walton Carpets, how can I help you?" - "My name is Doddle. You advertised a Special Sale." - "That's correct. It's the final day today, Mr. Doddle." - "And what carpets are on sale?" - "Oriental rugs. Oriental 100% Wool Roll Runners. At very reasonable prices." - "Do you also sell fitted carpets?" - "Yes we do, Mr. Doddle. You should come and see our special wall to wall carpet sale." - "Are all carpets cheaper now at Walton's? Even small ones?" - "Yes indeed. We won't be undersold!" - "Well, it sounds good. I'll think about it."*

Now work with a partner and read the passage as a dialogue.

Discrimination: When do you use which /l/?

1. You get a dark [ł] at the *end* of a word

    a. if nothing follows, as for instance at the end of a sentence or when you say a word in isolation.
    Example: "Are you married or single?" - "Single."
    N.B.: Ignore the letter <e> at the end of *single*. These rules are phonetic rules, i.e. we are talking about sounds here, and *single* ends with an [ł]-sound;

    b. if the next word begins with a consonant. *Example: "The channel ferry".*

2. Within a word, you get a dark [ł] when it is followed by a consonant:

    a. at the end of a syllable, as in *fulfilment, shellfish,*   or
    b. post-vocalically within a syllable, as in *milk, myself, children* and *silver.*

3. At the beginning of a word, you always pronounce the letter <l> as a clear [l]-sound, as in *liberty, lap top, Labour Party, leggings.*

4. An /l/-sound within a word is clear if it is followed by a vowel, as in *blow, glitter, fellow, killing, mileage, Daily Telegraph, alone, butler, silly-billy.*

5. In connected speech, an /l/-sound at the end of a word becomes a clear [l] when it is linked to the following word, if that word begins with a vowel, as in *"Go tell it on the mountain.", "That goes for all of you.", "Don't forget to fill up the tank."*

6. After the voiceless sounds /p, t, k, f, s/ you get devoiced [l̥].

For didactic reasons we have listed *six* rules here for the distinction between [l] and [ɫ]. Theoretically you could merge them into just one: You never get dark [ɫ] before a vowel. Rule 3 is only a corollary of the fact that in English /l/ in word-initial position must always be followed by a vowel. But it will be worth your while learning those six rules so that you can apply them directly.

The phonetic transcriptions in dictionaries (even in specialised English pronunciation dictionaries) are of no help to you when it comes to the distinction between clear [l] and dark [ɫ], as they use only one symbol. They do so, because the type of /l/-sound you have to use is predictable. But of course it is only predictable if you know how to apply the rules. So here we go:

Examples of the application of these rules:

1. *Fly Singapore Airlines and collect AIR MILES.*
   fly: [l̥] (rule 6); *Airlines*: [l] (rule 4); collect: [l] (rule 4); MILES: [ɫ] (rule 2b); once again: ignore the letter <e>, because the [ɫ] here is followed by the sound [z], which is a consonant: [maɪɫz].)

2. *You´ll agree – this gift is essential for travelling in style.*
   You'll agree: [l] (rule 5); *essential for*: [ɫ] (rule 1b); *travelling*: [l] (rule 4).

3. *The Royal Bank of Scotland: Royal Bank*: [ɫ] (rule 1b); *Scotland*: [l] (rule 4)

4. *The Royal Airforce*: [l] (rule 5)

5. *Travel* [ɫ] (rule 1a) [ˈtrævəɫ] → *travel agent* [l] (rule 5).
   The change from [ɫ] to [l] makes sense only when you link the second word to the first. It helps if you think of the compound as *trave lagent* [ˈtrævə ˌleɪʤənt]. If you pronounced it as two words with a pause or a typically German hard onset of *agent*, there would be no reason for the change from dark [ɫ] to clear [l]. More on linking in section VI.1.

6. *In the middle* [ˈmɪdɫ̩] (rule 1a); but *in the middle of Austria* [ˈmɪdləv] (rule 5).

7. *Alcohol*: first <l>: [ɫ] (rule 2a); second <l>: [ɫ] (rule 1a); *alcoholic*: first <l>: [ɫ] (rule 2a); but second <l>: [l] (rule 4); [ˈæɫkəˌhɒɫ] vs. [ˌæɫkə ˈhɒlɪk]

8. *Love´s Labour´s Lost* (rule 3)

9. *Little bottle*: first <l> in *little*: [l] (rule 3); second <l>: [ɫ] (rule 1b); *bottle*: [ɫ] (1a)

C 6/E 1: First listen to the following two passages. Then mark each <l> as [l], [ɫ] or [l̥] as appropriate. If you can, work with a partner. One partner works on passage a. and the other passage b. When in doubt, consult rules 1 to 6 or listen to the passage again. Then swap your books and check your partner´s results. When you have agreed on all /l/-sounds read your passage aloud to your partner.

If the Clinton plan becomes law, a powerful seven-member National Health Board will sit down to work out the fine details for a medical information highway. This electronic health data network would over time enable regional health alliances, insurers and federal, state and local health officials and researchers to assemble and exchange information about each citizen covered (the plan will ultimately include everyone). Every American will also carry a plastic card with a patient identification number, which some privacy groups fear could turn into a de facto national identification card.

Certainly, a health information network offers clear, even compelling, benefits. Through it clinicians could quickly retrieve information about patients from anywhere in the country. Redundant medical tests could thus be avoided. Health claims could be speeded.

For years Hopkins had struggled in shadowlands of his own. First it was the shade of Richard Burton, who came from the same small town in Wales. Burton was both his role model and his phantom rival, the man whose reputation always eclipsed his own. At the National Theatre, Hopkins was known as Olivier's understudy. The young and angry actor hated authority figures and was too fond of the bottle. His wife of 21 years, Jenni, who prefers to stay in London, attests to his transformation. "He's quite fascinated with the changes one can make on oneself. He uses himself as a sort of guinea pig. He went about doing what was necessary to lighten himself up, to take life less seriously."

Restless: An avid reader, he will walk around with six books.

a. from *Scientific American*

b. from *Newsweek*

The silent <l>

Finally, we must draw your attention to a number of words whose spelling is misleading, since the <l> is silent, i.e. you do not pronounce this letter. You will just have to try and memorise the most important of these:

> *should, could, would* [ʃʊd] [kʊd] [wʊd]
> *walk, talk* [wɔːk], [tɔːk], *folk songs* [fəʊk]
> *palm* [pɑːm], *psalm* [sɑːm], *calf* [kɑːf], *half* [hɑːf], *halve* [hɑːv],
> *salmon* [ˈsæmən],
> *Lincoln* [ˈlɪŋkən], *Holborn* [ˈhəʊbən]

You are now familiar with the four different realizations of the letter <l> in English. Let us go back to our first example sentence, which illustrates these four possibilities, given here in phonetic transcription:

1   b. *Learners should use an L-plate.* [ˈlɜːnəz ʃʊd juːzəˈneɬ pleɪt]

E 2: Indicate the phonetic symbols for all occurrences of <l> in this sentence:

The cloisters of Lincoln Cathedral.

E 3: Pair work. At the record shop. Example: You are given two titles: *"Heal the World"* by Michael Jackson and *"Black or White"*. You and your partner use them for a dialogue according to the following pattern:

A: *Have you got "Heal the World" by Michael Jackson?*
B: *No, I'm sorry, but we've got "Black or White". That's Michael Jackson, too, and I think you'll like it."*

a. *"Michelle, ma belle"* and *"She's leaving home"* by The Beatles
b. *"Head Over Heels"* and *"Separate Lives"* by Phil Collins
c. *"Nothing Else Matters"* and *"Wheel of Fortune"* by Ace of Base
d. *"Sometimes I feel like a motherless child"* and *"Go tell it on the mountains"*, spirituals
e. *"Jingle Bells"* and *"Rudolf the red-nosed reindeer"*, Christmas carols
f. *"The first Noel,"* and *"Hark the herold angels sing"*, Christmas carols
g. *"Hey diddle diddle, the cat and the fiddle"* and *"Twinkle, twinkle, little star"*, children's songs.

Not making the difference between [l] and [ɫ] can reveal speakers as foreigners. There is, however, a magic spell that solves this problem once and for all. It is the witches' spell in Macbeth, Act 4, Scene 1. It works if you can recite it properly:

Double, double, toil and trouble;
Fire burn, and cauldron bubble.

Infobox

For advanced students: Our explanations and rules for clear and dark /l/ are a good basis for acquiring the correct differentiation of /l/ variants in English. But if you have been listening carefully to the many examples in the exercises, you will have noticed that there is not an absolute dichotomy between the two categories. The dark [ɫ]s are not all equally dark, and the clear [l]s are not all equally clear. In the expression "toil and trouble" above, from Macbeth, the /l/ in *toil* /tɔɪl/, though word-final, is much clearer than all the other word-final /l/s in the couplet. This follows rule 5. However, in the expression "towel and flannel", the /l/ in *towel* /taʊl/ is relatively dark, although rule 5 again applies. The reason for this is the influence of the "dark" preceding /ʊ/ in *towel* compared to the "light" preceding /ɪ/ in *toil*. Because the tongue needs time to get from the position of one sound to the position for another, there is always a mutual influence of neighbouring sounds. The technical expression for this inevitable merging of sounds is called **coarticulation**. You may like to pronounce the expressions *"fill in"* and *"pull off"*, and try to stop yourself in the middle of the [l]. You should be able to observe that the two /l/s are very different; the /l/ in the first is very "clear" and the /l/ in the second is relatively "dark".

Smileys: Can you explain the pronunciation basis of the following jokes?

Q: *What is the most common illness among spies? –* A: *A code in the nose.*
Q: *What is meant by "illegal"? –* A: *A sick bird.*

III.2. /æ/ vs. /e/: *D'ye ken if ye can?*

Ken is Scottish for *know* (compare German *kennen*). So *do* you know if you can distinguish /æ/ and /e/?

Fig 1: from the *Daily Mirror*

If *you* can´t say *Dad*, you may have a grave problem! Read on ...

The above headline is about the vicar´s objection to the informal word *Dad* instead of using the more respectful word *Father* on the gravestone. Just imagine you were reading the above headline aloud and – like many German learners of English – you could not distinguish phonetically between *Dad* and *dead*. People would look at you as though you were from a different planet, because they would be wondering why the sentence *"You can´t say dead on a gravestone"* should make headlines.

Fig 2: The Fairer Sax

This poster uses the idiom *The fairer sex* as the basis for the pun *The fairer sax*, implying that this trio of female saxophone players may be prettier to look at than a male trio. As you will have noticed, both the newspaper headline and the poster take advantage of the difference between two vowels that are distinctive sounds in English (cf. III.4. for `distinctive sounds´): The phonetic symbols for the two sounds that distinguish the pairs *sax* and *sex* in the poster and *dad* and *dead* in the newspaper are /æ/ and /e/.

There is nothing wrong with telling your fiancée's parents that you enjoyed the performance of the sax trio you went to last night, as long as you get your vowels right. For German learners of English, this is one of the most important and, paradoxically, in practice most neglected distinctions.

Distinguishing between /e/ and /æ/ is important because there are a lot of words which are only distinguished by /e/ and /æ/. Consider for example

1. *bet* vs. *bat*   *kettle vs. cattle*   *bend* vs. *band*   *rack* vs. *wreck*
    pen vs. *pan*   *celery vs. salary*   *pecking order* vs. *packing order*
    ex-murderer vs. *axe murderer*

Making sure that people know whether you are inquiring about *pens* or *pans* in a department store is a criterion of making sense in conversations that should convince everybody.

In terms of articulation the two vowels /æ/ and /e/ are a long way apart.

A crash course on vowels

We will deal with vowels extensively in chapter V., but we will give you a brief introduction here, because the point of this "**Sound Examples**" chapter is to give you an overview of the activities of your speech organs and what phonetics and phonology are about. In the previous section we said that with /l/, which is a consonant, the tip of the tongue is in contact with the alveolar ridge. With vowels the (the centre of the) tongue is never in contact with any other part of the mouth. We had also introduced you to the position of /u/, where the back of the tongue was raised, which is why /u/ is called a high back vowel. Vowels are distinguished partly by the tongue and jaw position, partly by the lip position. Pronounce the vowels from the words *kühl* and *Kiel* carefully. You should be able to feel that the *tongue* position for the vowels in the middle of these words is the same: The front of your tongue body remains in a high front position (with the tongue tip – as with all vowels – down behind your bottom front teeth). It is only lip rounding for the pronunciation of <ü> and lip spreading for the pronunciation of <ie> that tells us which word is meant. As a matter of fact you can lock your tongue in that high front position and then alternate between lip rounding and lip spreading and you will get a long succession of <iiiüüüüiiiüüü>.

Please do not simply read these passages silently to yourself. It is important that you actually do this. Playing around with your speech organs will give you a feeling of where they are and what goes on and it will help you to lose any inhibitions and shyness you may feel.

Now pronounce the words *kühl* and *cool*. Your lips will be in a rounded and protruded position for both. What distinguishes these two words is the high front position for *kühl* and the high back position for *cool*. This time lock your lips in that rounded and protruded position, pronounce the long /u:/-sound of *cool* and then gradually change it to the vowel in *kühl*. You will hear and *feel* how your tongue moves forward and back and forward again.

If you pronounce the following German words carefully in standard German and in that order, you will feel that your tongue moves from a high front position to a low front position: *biete, bitte, Beet, Bett, Bad*. A similar row of front vowels in English is *beat, bit, bet, bat*.

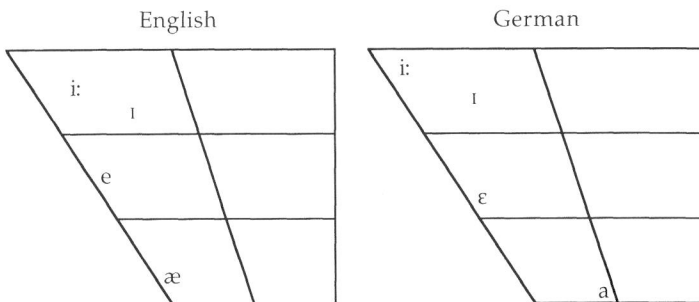

Fig. 3: Tongue positions for the English vowels in *beat, bit, bet* /bet/ and *bat* /bæt/ and the German vowels in *bieten, bitten, Bett* /bɛt/ and *hat* /hat/

Now back to [e] and [æ]:
Bed **bugs are** *bad* **bugs, but the doctor´s** *bad* **manners are not** *bed* **manners**

The tongue positions for [e] and [æ] are so different, you can easily *see* the difference. They are at least as far apart as the vowels in *bit* and *bet*, or as the German vowels in *fit* and *fett*. So why is the sound [æ] problematical and so difficult to master for Germans that it has become one of the stereotypical features of "German-English" (together with /v/ for /w/ and /z/ for /ð/ and the incorrect tag question), and is exploited by English comedians when they imitate German tourists:

2.   *Ve go kemping in ze velley, ja?*

In German, the /æ/-sound does not exist; it lies between the German /ɛ/ and /a/ sounds (as in *Deckel* and *Dackel*), as you can see in fig. 3. Strangely, Germans hear the difference between English /æ/ and German /a/, and avoid that confusion. A contributory factor to the confusion could also be the fact that, in German spelling, both the letters <e> and <ä> represent the short vowel /e/ – as in *Kelte* and *Kälte*. And since German speakers are aware that /æ/ is a "funny sort of ä", they may be tempted to think that the distinction between /e/ and /æ/ in English is also irrelevant.

Another point is surely that a considerable number of English words with /æ/ have found their way into German, where they are – naturally – pronounced in a German way. Thus *lap top* becomes [ˈlɛp tɔp] and *camping* becomes [ˈkɛmpiŋ] and *cash* [kæʃ] becomes [kɛʃ]. When Peugeot introduced a new van the advertisement in German newspapers was:

3.   *DER PEUGEOT 806. VAN SCHON, DENN SCHON*

exploiting the fect, sorry, the fact, that *van* as a loanword in German sounds like *wenn*, and not like the English word [væn]. And when Greenpeace had a battle with Shell about an oilrig, a German newspaper headline read:

4.   *Greenpeace siegt. We Shell overcome*

This is a nice pun and coincides exactly with the pronunciation of the Pete Seeger song as sung by many Germans. This is perfectly all right in German, but we should not believe that if we can order tickets in Germany for Webber´s musical [kɛts] (instead of [kæts]) this would be an acceptable pronunciation in London. For English speakers the two sounds /e/ and /æ/ are as different as /ɛː/ and /aː/ for Germans. Imagine your surprise if a foreigner asked you *"Was hast du für Kram im Gesicht?"* when she meant *"Was hast du für Creme im Gesicht?"*

Of course, there are dialects in the English speaking world where the /æ/ does *not* sound as open as in RP. But in these dialects, all the other vowels sound different as well, and the opposition between *bend* and *band* is still maintained, even though both sounds may be different from what you are used to. But if you pronounce *bend* as [bend] like the English do, you have to pronounce *band* as [bænd].

C 1: You may accept all this but still be afraid that you might exaggerate the /æ/and make a fool of yourself. Rest assured, there is no such danger: Just sit bæck and relæx, and enjoy this song from "Cæts":

> *Bustopher Jones is not skin and bones,*
> *In fact, he´s remarkably fat.*
> *He doesn´t haunt pubs – he has eight or nine clubs,*
> *For he´s the St. James´s Street Cat!*
> *He´s the cat we all greet as he walks down the street*
> *In his coat of fastidious black:*
> *No commonplace mousers have such well-cut trousers*
> *Or such an impeccable back.*

C 2: The following limerick is read to you by a native speaker. After each line there will be a pause just long enough to repeat it at the same speed. Try and pick up the speaker´s rhythm and vowel sounds.

A conceited blonde lady from Ham,	[ə kənˈsiːtɪd blɒnd ˈleɪdi frəm ˈhæm
Jumped hastily onto a tram.	dʒʌmpt ˈheɪstɪliˈɒntuə ˈtræm
As she swiftly embarked,	æz ʃi ˈswɪftli ɪmˈbaːkt
the conductor remarked,	ðə kənˈdʌktə rɪˈmaːkt
"Your fare, Miss." She said, "Yes I am."	jɔː ˈfeə mɪs ʃi ˈsed jesˏaɪˈæm]

C 3: Listen and repeat:

1. *The cat got in through the cat flap.*
2. *With my new lap top I can easily make back-up copies.*
3. *Golf news: Chapman captures Grand Slam.*
4. *Flapjacks, a tasty snack.*
5. *The cat crept into the crypt, crapped and crept out again.*
6. *The snack shack is at the back.*
7. *Don´t let the fat cats grab all the money.*
8. *Benn defies broadcast ban on Sinn Fein*

After these exercises we are sure you will find the following anecdotes as amusing as the British find them.

5. *An ice hockey player told his German friend he had fallen during a match and a piece of one of his front teeth was broken off. "Have they kept it?" asked the German. "Not much point in that, is there? We don´t collect them." (What the German had meant to ask was "Have they capped it?")*

6. *Susan: "What do you use for cooking here?" - Klaus: "Guess." - Susan: "Electricity?" - Klaus: "No, I told you!"* (What Klaus had been trying to say in answer to the first question was *gas*.)

7. *At an international conference, a German speaker explained how the Russian economy had to try and catch up with the west. He referred to this as the "ketchup strategy".*

8. *A young German girl told her elderly British landlady, "I went to see `Flesh Gordon´ and loved every bit of it." (`Flesh Gordon´ was a pornographic film; she meant the science fiction movie `Flash Gordon´.)*

9. *An English teacher said to a German assistant in England, "I´m Pat Anderson, just call me Pat." The next morning the young German man waved to her and shouted across the staff room, "Hallo, pet." (pet = `an animal kept in the home as a companion´,* often used by lovers or parents as a term of affection.)

E 1: Pair work: dictating newspaper headlines. There is a possible alternative with /æ/ for every sentence with /e/ and vice versa. Partner A starts dictating sentences, saying which number he/she is reading. Partner B writes down which of the two alternatives, e.g. 1a *or* 1b he/she has heard. At the end of this exercise, compare the dictation with what has been put down in writing. If you agree, everything is fine. If not, it may be due either to the wrong pronunciation by partner A, or to B having misheard the relevant sounds. In that case you should discuss both alternatives.

Partner A dictates:
  1   a. *You can´t say `dad´ on a gravestone.*
        b. *You can´t say `dead´ on a gravestone.*

2   a. *Tan Leather Gloves stolen.* (*tan*: yellowish brown)
      b. *Ten Leather Gloves stolen.*
3   a. *Britain's latest champion is as flashy as Chris Eubank*
      b. *Britain's latest champion is as fleshy as Chris Eubank*
4   a. *Selling coins and gems can be a sticky business* (*gems*: precious stones)
      b. *Selling coins and jams can be a sticky business*
5   a. *Wilder Grants Clemency to Men in Iverson Case*
      b. *Wilder Grants Clemency to Man in Iverson Case*
6   a. *Santa Claus Finds a Wife: Merry Christmas!*
      b. *Santa Claus Finds a Wife: Marry Christmas!*

Now swap roles and Partner B dictates:
7   a. *Charles confesses: I love Ellen*
      b. *Charles confesses: I love Alan*
8   a. *Ban on smoking ads*
      b. *Benn on smoking ads*
9   a. *Mothers Worried about Crash Kids*
      b. *Mothers Worried about Creche Kids*
10   a. *Dollar capped* (FT Jan15, 1994)
      b. *Dollar kept*
11   a. *Controversial play switched to new venue as backer quits.*
      b. *Controversial play switched to new venue as Becker quits.*
12   a. *Texas survival guide*
      b. *Taxes survival guide*

/æ/ and <a>: The former is a phonetic symbol, the latter is a letter

In many cases <a> is pronouced /æ/, but there are, as always [ˈɔːɬweɪz], exceptions *always* being one, with [ɔ:] like *also, although, altar, alternative, alderman, Aldershot, Aldous Huxley*. By analogy the following words are often incorrectly pronounced with an [ɔ:], but they should start with [æ]: *Albert Hall* [ˌæɬbət ˈhɔ: ɬ], *Alsation* [æɬˈseɪʃən], *Albania, Albion*. In Southern British English the words *dance, plant, grant, glass, grass* and *France* are pronounced with a long [ɑ:]. You will often hear American [dæns] for *dance*, but if you have decided on SBE you should not mix different accents.

In *"Dead men don't wear plaid"* plaid is pronounced [plæd] (a thick material with a particular pattern). *plaits* (*Zöpfe*) may be pronounced [plæts] or [pleɪts].

Many and *any* have an <a> but are pronounced: [ˈmeni], [ˈeni], not *[ˈæni]. For the different pronunciations of *can* and *have* see section VI.3.

Smileys:

"What happens when two French prams collide?" - *"You 'ave a crèche, Monsieur."*

a. *No photography at weddings. Vicar opposed to the pleasures of the flash*
b. *No photography at weddings. Vicar opposed to the pleasures of the flesh*

III.3. *A letter is a letter and a sound is a sound*

Fig. 1: /iː/ for /aɪ/ and /ef/ for /fɪʃ/?

Do you remember how they taught you to write at school?

1. *Oma: o wie Ofen, m wie Mama, a wie Apfel: Oooommmaaa.*

It was an attempt to relate sounds to letters. But this method only works if you pronounce the letter <m> as [m] and not as [em], because if you did, the combined pronunciations of these letters would sound more like *Oh Emma* than like *Oma.*

One way of readjusting our way of thinking about English sounds and letters is to do what school-beginners do in England. At that stage they know how to pronounce the words they use, but they certainly do not know the strange spelling conventions that exist to make their learning to read and spell so tortuous. They start learning to spell by pronouncing *ABC* as /æ bə kə/ rather than /eɪ biː siː/ so that the word *cab* would be spelled out loud as /kə æ bə/, and not /siː eɪ biː/. Of course this only works for certain words where <a>, <b> and <c> etc. are pronounced more or less like /æ/, /bə/, /kə/; in a word like *babe*, the two /bə/ letters still correspond to the sound, but the sounds /æ/ and /e/ (which the children learn to say for the letters <a> and <e>) do not help them to link <babe> to the word /beɪb/ that they know. The problem with many spelling systems is the lack of a one-to-one relationship between a particular letter and a particular sound.

You may consider the reminder that **letters are not sounds** tedious and unnecessary, but there is a difference between rationally accepting that statement and *automatically* thinking about the difference between a sound structure and the particular orthographic sequence representing it orthographically. There are many traps one can fall into by not being aware of this distinction. In the oldest public school in the USA, the Latin School in Boston, we came across an early attempt to teach reading and writing in 1635 (see fig. 1 above). They put <F> next to the picture of fishes. So far so good. But then <E>

was paired with the picture of an eye. This was the children´s first encounter with this letter. But if you pronounce the beginning of *eye* /aɪ/ slowly you will hear that it begins with an [a]-sound and this does not enable learners to predict /e/ for *end*. Similarly they used the picture of an owl to teach the letter <o>, an unfortunate choice because *owl* (like *eye*) begins with an /a/-sound.

Consider another possible pitfall. In section III.1. we had used the Guinness advertisement, where one chap is slow to get up, revealing the letter <l>, so that *Guinness* reads *Guinnless*, suggesting that he will be without a pint of Guinness. What makes the difference here, is the letter <l>. If we now ask you, how it is pronounced *in this context*, you should pronounce the clear [l]. But you pronounce the letter <l> with a dark [ɫ] ([eɫ]). You spell the new word *Guinn-less*: [ʤi: ju: aɪ en en eɫ i: es es]. These nine units are letters. The sounds of [ˈgɪnləs] are just these six sounds. The first one should be referred to as [g] (or rather [gə] because [g] is not really pronounceable by itself) and not a s [ʤi:]. When we asked our students which *phonetic symbol* made the difference between [ˈgɪnəs] and [ˈgɪnləs], they very often said: "[eɫ]", which showed that they confused letter and sound. The letter in this word is pronounced [eɫ] and is represented as <l>; the sound is pronounced as a single consonant (just like children who did not know the alphabet yet would refer to it) and it is represented by the phonetic symbol [l]. This knowledge is part of what is called **language awareness,** and being fully aware of the fact that <l> represents three different sounds or may, indeed, be silent, is the first step towards mastering the English pronunciation of lateral sounds.

These examples illustrate that one of the most persistent problems in learning a foreign language is coming to terms with the different relationships between letters and sounds that become established in different languages. Our native language *naturally* has a more logical link between letters and sounds. (Please reread that last sentence with *heavy irony* in your mind, because of course the relationships are, ultimately, arbitrary.) Why should Greek write <αρενα>, Bulgarian and Russian write <арена>, and English write <arena> for a word which clearly has a closely related sound structure and has an equivalent meaning in the four languages? There may be historical reasons, but certainly no logical ones why English uses <sh> and German uses <sch> for the sound represented by the IPA-symbol /ʃ/ (IPA: International Phonetic Association), or why, in English, <ch> is usually pronounced /tʃ/, as in *choose*, but not in *Chicago*, and why, in German, the same letters <ch> in e.g. *Chemie* are pronounced [ç] as in *ich* in the North but as [k] in the South, and why the same sound [ç] may be represented by <ch> or by <g>, as in *König*, but of course not in the South of Germany, where it is pronounced as [k], but then only at the end of a word. Imagine how confusing this interrelationship between sounds and letters must be for foreign learners of German!

We have accepted the irregularities of our native-language orthography during the course of our education (except where we still use our "own" spellings for certain words, which the teachers call "mistakes"!). Therefore we view any deviation from those native conventions (and exceptions) that we see in the spelling conventions of other languages as being something totally bizarre and illogical.

2. *I heard this young girl in the choir,*   [aɪ ˈhɜːd ðɪs jʌŋ ˈgɜːlɪn ðə ˈkwaɪə]
    Whose voice rose hoir and hoir,   huːz ˈvɔɪs rəʊz ˈhaɪərən ˈhaɪə
    Till it reached such a height,   tɪlɪt ˈriːʧt sʌʧə ˈhaɪt
    It was clear out of sight,   ɪt wəz ˈkliːraʊtəv ˈsaɪt
    And they found it next day on the spoir. ənðeɪ ˈfaʊndɪt neks ˈdeɪ‿ɔnðə ˈspaɪə]

NB: the correct spellings are: <choir>, <higher>, <spire>.

One unfortunate result of our familiarity with our own spelling conventions is the continuing temptation to see the orthography as representing the sound structure directly, to see letters and sounds as being the same thing. But we must stress again, however obvious it might seem to you while reading these lines: *it is important to keep the concepts of letters and sounds apart.* For instance, if you say: *"In English, the regular plural ending is formed by adding an `s´ or `es´ to the noun.",* you are teaching grammar through the medium of writing, i.e. spelling or orthography, and the basic units of this medium are *letters*. In that case you have only two units to consider for the regular plural endings: the letters <s> or <es>. If, on the other hand, you say: *"In English, the regular plural ending is formed by adding /s/, /z/ or /ɪz/.",* you are talking about the spoken medium, and the basic units of this medium are *sounds*. In this case you have three units to consider for the regular plural endings. (See also section VII.1.2. on confusing the written and the spoken medium.)

The common claim that "English has a lot of words with silent consonants" – referring to things like the <p> in *psychology,* the <b> in *lamb,* the <l> in *palm,* or the <g> and the <h> in *thought* – is a typical example of the way in which letters and sounds are confused. A consonant is a sound, so it cannot be silent. What is meant is that a *letter* which usually represents a consonantal sound actually has no sound correspondence in that particular word. For example, the <b> in *lamb* does not have a sound corresponding to it. For convenience we call it a "silent letter". There are many more words where letters that normally represent consonants are not pronounced.

E 1: Identify the "silent" letters in the following words:

a. *bomb, womb, tomb*   b. *bought, fought*
c. *psychosis, pneumonia, psalm*   d. *knight, know, knit*
e. *gnome, gnash, gnarled*   f. *palm, almond, alms*
g. *scene, scent, scion*

Sometimes even native speakers seem to have problems! *When the actress Jean Harlow met Margot Asquith she asked her: "Is the `t´ in `Margot´ pronounced or not?", to which Asquith replied: "No, the `t´ is silent – as in Harlow."*

Note: *harlot* [ˈhɑːlət], means *prostitute*.

Wrongly pronouncing silent letters is referred to as **spelling pronunciation**. Typical examples of English learners' spelling pronunciations are the incorrect three-syllable pronunciations of *[ˈmæ.rɪ.ədʒ] and *[ˈiː.və.nɪŋ] for *marriage* and *evening*, instead of the correct [ˈmærɪdʒ] and [ˈiːvnɪŋ], and you may have noticed learners of German saying *[ʃteːhən] instead of [ʃteən] for *stehen*.

Although both English and German are certainly not "regular" (Spanish is often cited as being a language where the orthography is most closely related to the sound inventory), English is considered to be less regular than German. Or perhaps we should just say that it has more rules, each covering fewer words, so that we see them as exceptions rather than rule based. So, for example <gh> can stand for /f/, /x/, for no consonant at all, or for /gh/:

3.   a. /f/ as in *cough, tough,*
     b. /x/ as in *lough* (an Irish lake, pronounced almost like German *Loch*)
     c. Nothing, as in *though, bough, thought, taught*
     d. /gh/, but only in compounds! As in *doghouse, leghorn.*

Of course, vowels as well as consonants have the many-to-one relationship from letters to sounds, and from sounds to letters. Some vowel variation is easy to remember, like the *babe* example discussed above; so *cat* has /æ/ but *Kate* has /eɪ/; *pet* has /e/ but *Pete* has /iː/; *bit* has /ɪ/ but *bite* has /aɪ/, *rot* has /ɒ/, but *rote* has /əʊ/; *bud* has /ʌ/ but *Bude* has /juː/. However, there are some letter combinations where the different vocalic pronunciations are not at all predictable. For example, the "regular" alternation between /ʌ/ and /juː/ just quoted is spoilt by the fact that *bud, pus, putt* and *budding* are pronounced with /ʌ/, while *bull, pussy, put* and *pudding* are pronounced with /ʊ/. And just by providing examples for the <gh> problem, we presented <ou> in *six* different words and with *five* different pronunciations!

4.   a. /ɒ/ in *cough* and *lough*   b. /ʌ/ in *tough*   c. /əʊ/ in *though*
     d. /aʊ/ in *bough*   e. /ɔː/ in *thought*

Let us take these problems of the interrelation between the written and the spoken medium one step further and beyond the individual sound. Have you encountered those horses that come from Blumento, and things that hold your leg? Native German speakers see *Blumento-pferde* and *bein-halten* as silly jokes though for English learners of German the recognition of letter groups in compound words is part of the process of learning the relationship between the written and the spoken form. A similar example in English is *misled*, which is sometimes jokingly mispronounced as /ˈmaɪzəld/ instead of /mɪs ˈled/. Whether it is *Blumento-pferde* or *Blumen-topf-erde* is a problem that staring at the letters cannot solve for you.

E 2: Crossword puzzle: *part of a building: r_ _ m*. The teacher was trying to help and said: *"It's a word with two vowels."* Is that statement correct, and if not, what is wrong with it (in the light of what we have written in this chapter)?

E 3: What type of mistake are the mispronunciations of the following words? If you are not sure look up the correct pronunciation. (* = wrong!)

carriage *[ˈkærɪʤ]   *basically* *[ˈbeɪsɪkæli]   *shepherd* *[ˈʃephɜːd]
casualty *[ˈkæʒʊæɫti]   *every* *[ˈeveri]   *gnome* *[gnəʊm]
gnaw *[gnɔː]   *extraordinary* *[ˌekstrəˈɔːdɪnəri]

E 4: Correct the spellings of the rhyme words of the following limericks:

a. *There was once a choleric colonel*
   Whose oaths were obscene and infolonel.
   And the Chaplain, aghast,
   Gave up protest at last,
   But wrote them all down in his jolonel.

b. *Have you heard of the lady from Slough,*
   Who went for a ride on a cough?
   The brute pitched her off,
   When she started to coff.
   She refuses to ride on it nough.

c. *A jealous young fellow from Gloucester*
   Found his wife had eloped with Fred Foucester.
   He traced her to Leicester
   And tried to arreicester,
   But in spite of his efforts he loucester.

Summary:

- Do not expect a one-to-one relation between letters and sounds.
- The phonetic symbol [ɫ] is pronounced [ɫ], and the letter <l>, when referred to in isolation, is pronounced [eɫ].
- A letter is a letter, i.e. a unit of the written medium. A sound is a sound, i.e. a unit of the spoken medium. A phonetic symbol is a symbol which refers to sounds.
- In a word the letter <k> may be pronounced [k], as in *collapse*. When we say the <k> is silent in *knee*, we mean the letter is not realised as a sound. It does not make sense to say: *"The [k] is silent."
- Explain the spoken medium in terms of sounds, and the written medium in terms of letters. "Add an <s > or <es> in the plural" is an instruction of how to write it. "Add /s/ or /z/ or /ɪz/" is an instruction of how to pronounce plural endings.
- The term "spelling pronunciation" refers to mistakes made by speakers who try to represent all letters by sounds, as in *[ˈmærɪ əʤ] and *[ˈɫiːvənɪŋ].

III.4. Phonology: *Sound functions*

Phonetics is the study of speech sounds. When we describe how a sound is produced, namely in terms of its *voicing*, its *place* and *manner* of articulation, as in "a voiced alveolar lateral frictionless continuant", we put the phonetic symbol for that sound in square brackets: [l].

Phonology is the study of the function of these sounds in a particular language. As a sound like [l] has neither a meaning in itself nor a grammatical function, its purpose in life must be something else. It is the rather modest task of being different from the other sounds of English. If you have the sound sequence [_end], this may be preceded by a number of different sounds, i.e. [b], [f], [l], [m], [s], [t] and [v], and in each case you get a different word with a new meaning: [bend, [fend], [lend], [mend], [send], [tend], and [vend]. As the context in which these sounds occur is always the same, i.e. [_end], the only way we can *distinguish* between them must be the difference between the sounds at the beginning. That is why they are called **distinctive sounds**. This statement is a phonological one, because it says what the *function* of these sounds in English.

We define the linguistic units that actually co-occur in a word or an utterance as a **syntagmatic field** (the word "syntagmatic" has the element "syntagm" in it, which comes from the Greek for putting things together). In the word [lend] these four sounds constitute a syntagmatic field. In the above example we played around with this syntagmatic field and tried to see how many sounds of the English language could be substituted in the first position for the [l]. All the sounds that can be substituted in a particular position of a syntagmatic field constitute a **paradigmatic field** (the Greek element *para-* means *against*, so all the sounds are in opposition to one another in that position).

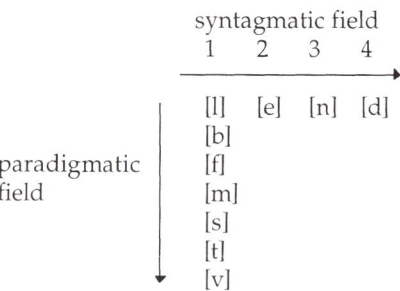

Fig. 1a: The syntagmatic field [lend] (horizontal dimension) of co-occurring sounds with four positions; and the paradigmatic field (vertical dimension) of possible substitutions in the first position.

If we now proceed to the second position we see that [e] may be replaced by [æ] to give us *land* [lænd], [əʊ] to give us *loaned* [ləʊnd], [aɪ] to give us *lined* [laɪnd] or [ɜ:] to give us *learned*.

$$\begin{array}{cccc} 1 & 2 & 3 & 4 \\ [l] & [e] & [n] & [d] \\ & [æ] & & \\ & [əʊ] & & \\ & [aɪ] & & \\ & [ɜ:] & & \end{array}$$

Fig. 1b: The paradigmatic field in the second position of [lend].

So the paradigmatic field of the second position of [lend] consists of only five items. But all you need to establish a sound as distinctive is a paradigmatic field of two items. The only difference between the two different words [lænd] and [lend] is that between [æ] and [e]. Such a pair of words with only one phonetic difference is called a **minimal pair.** You can now select any two items from fig. 1a to obtain minimal pairs such as [lend] vs. [bend] or [send] vs. [mend].

In section III.1. we said that the letter <l> in English can be pronounced as [l], [ɬ], [l̥] or [ʊ], or not at all, i.e. what is often referred to as "the silent <l>". Let us consider the first three variants first. Even though native speakers of SBE never fail to make these distinctions when pronouncing words, most of them are not aware that the three "l"s are different. In the minds of English speakers these three sounds belong together. This is our reason for saying that the three different sounds constitute one linguistic unit (more specifically one *phonological* unit). But what sort of unit and what shall we call it? Since we are concerned here with the spoken medium, we must not appeal to the letter <l>. We could simply give it a number and call it, say, "unit 23", but that would have a serious drawback: it would be difficult to remember that "23" was related to these sounds. And secondly, and more importantly, it would fail to indicate that these three sounds are phonetically similar: all three of them are alveolar lateral sounds. And thirdly, the choice between these three sounds is not arbitrary but rule-governed.

Before we proceed, we want to introduce one of the most basic principles of linguistics at this point: **meaning implies choice.** If a dictator forces his people to vote, but on the ballot paper they find only one name, i.e. his name, the "election" is meaningless, because they do not have a choice. If you leave out the last word in the syntagmatic field *"She had beautiful, straight, long, blond ..."*, no meaning in the sense of information content is lost, because the word *hair* is entirely predictable. You do not have a choice here, as the paradigmatic field *in this context* consists of only one item. If somebody told you *"She had* *beautiful, straight, long, blond hair."* and you missed the last word you would not say something like *"Sorry, I have no idea what you´re talking about, I didn´t understand the last word."* or *"Sorry, did you say `hair´ or `bear´?"* In this context *hair* and *bear* cannot be in opposition to each other.

The rules that govern the distribution of [l], [ɫ] and [l̩] in standard English allow you to predict which one will occur, provided you know the context. If we give you the instruction: Select the alveolar lateral for position 1 of the syntagmatic field [_end], you do not have a choice: it has to be the "clear" [l]. If on the other hand we ask you to select the alveolar lateral for the last position of [be_], it has to be the "dark" [ɫ], and in [p_eɪ] (*play*) you have to insert [l̩] (see section III.1. for details). In standard English there are no such minimal pairs as [beɫ] vs. *[bell], or [pl̩eɪ] vs. *[pleɪ], or [lɪv] vs *[ɫɪv], where the only phonetic difference is that between [l], [ɫ] or [l̩]. The possibility of the occurrence of one of these sounds in English excludes the possibility of occurrence for the other two. This type of distribution is called **complementary distribution**.

In summary, we can express this fact in several different ways (all meaning essentially the same):

The three English sounds [l], [ɫ] and [l̩]

  a. never occur in the same context,
  b. their distribution is different,
  c. they are in complementary distribution,
  d. they never constitute a paradigmatic field,
  e. they never help to constitute a minimal pair.
  f. As – in a given context – you do not have a choice between these three,
     they are **non-distinctive sounds**.

So what has happened to what most laymen refer to as the "l-sound"? The <l>-sound does not exist, as you cannot pronounce it. You can pronounce [l], [ɫ] or [l̩], but not all three at the same time. If we wish to say these three sounds constitute a linguistic unit because that is what they are in the mind of the native speaker, or because there is a rule governing their distribution, then this unit must be abstract. It is, therefore, useful to call this abstract unit a **phoneme**. And to distinguish it from the phonetic unit, we put the corresponding symbol in slashes. /l/ represents the abstract unit that stands for what alveolar lateral consonants have in common.

As you will recall from section III.1., there are two more representations of the letter <l>. One of them is the so-called silent <l>. This simply means the letter <l> has no corresponding sound as an alveolar lateral. This is important information on how to pronounce words like *palm, salmon* and *Lincoln*, but it has nothing to do with the phoneme /l/.

There remains a fifth possible realisation of the letter <l>. In III.1. we gave you the recording of a speaker who pronounced the letter <l> in 1a. not as an alveolar lateral consonant (i.e. not as an /l/-sound), but as a vowel, so that it sounded more like the pronunciation of 1b.

1a. *Those poor people had no money, so the kind milkman gave them two pints of milk today for free.*

1b. *Those poor peopu had no money, so the kind miukman gave them two pints of miuk today for free.*

Our pseudo phonetic transcription in 1b. represents only certain varieties of English. The substitution of a sound similar to [ʊ] (the sound you get in *put* and *book*) in these varieties is restricted to the dark [ɫ]. Let us assume that speaker A uses standard SBE pronunciation with only the three non-distinctive sounds [l], [ɫ] and [l̩], but that speaker B uses two language varieties: he uses SBE pronunciation when talking to his clients at the bank where he works and then pronounces the words *people* and *milk* with a dark [ɫ]: [ˈpiːpɫ] and [mɪɫk]. But when he goes *"for a pint with the lads"* he switches to his local dialect and says [ˈpiːpʊ] and [mɪʊk]. These speech habits are referred to as his two **sociolects.** We can now make the following observations about the distribution of [ɫ] and the [ʊ]-like sound in this speaker's English.

a. From a *sociolinguistic* point of view speaker B is not free to choose, because this change of language varieties or sociolects is dictated by the situation, the subjects talked about or the people talked to.

b. From a purely *phonological* point of view this speaker does have a choice: in all positions, where the dark [ɫ] occurs he may replace it by a sound similar to [ʊ]. (This replacement must be defined asymmetrically, i.e. it works only in one direction. We cannot say that all his [ʊ]-sounds may be replaced by [ɫ]-sounds, as the replacement of [ʊ] by [ɫ] does not occur in words like *soak* and *ego* ([səʊk] and [ˈiːgəʊ].)

c. If this speaker chooses to make the replacement from [ɫ] to [ʊ], the meaning of the word does not change. Both [mɪʊk] and [mɪɫk] are phonetic representations of the word *milk*. As [ɫ] and [ʊ] occur in the same context but do not change the meaning of the words, they are non-distinctive sounds (in that context). They are said to be in **free variation**.

Free variation in phonology usually goes hand in hand with a change of sociolect or regional dialect. The word *butter* for instance, is pronounced [ˈbʌtə], but the [t] may be replaced in some sociolects or dialects by a glottal stop [ʔ] (German: **Knacklaut** as in the middle of *Verein*): [ˈbʌʔə]. So whether you ask for *"a pound of* [ˈbʌtə]*"* or *"a pound of* [ˈbʌʔə]*"* says something about you as a speaker, about where you grew up, your social status etc., so from this point of view your pronunciation makes a difference, but you will be sold the same thing. Phonologically speaking, [ʔ] and [t] are in free variation in the context of [ˈbʌ_ə] and are thus non-distinctive sounds.

An abstract unit can only be in opposition to another abstract unit. The phoneme /l/ is in opposition with the phonemes /b/, /s/, /m/ etc. At the level of phonological analysis we are concerned with phonemes, i.e. with abstract units. If one now asks how these phonemes are pronounced, one refers to their phonetic realisations, and these are called **phones**. So the phoneme /s/ is represented by the phone [s], and in the word *lend* the phoneme /l/ is realised by the phone [l], i.e. the sound of the clear [l]. When there is more than one realisation for a particular phoneme, as in the case of /l/, it has been found convenient to refer to these as **allophones in** order to indicate that they constitute a phonological group. To illustrate this by the examples used so far, we can say that the minimal pairs /send/ vs. /lend/ and /lend/ vs. /tend/ yielded the phonemes /s/, /l/ and /t/. /s/ is realised by the phone [s]. /t/ is realised here by the phone [t] and /l/ by the phone [l] (i.e. the clear lateral approximant). As we saw that /t/ also has other representations, we can refer to these as allophones: [ʔ] and [t]. They are in free variation in certain contexts, they are non-distinctive sounds or the allophones of /t/. And the phoneme /l/ is realised by the allophones [l], [ɫ] and [l̥], which occur in complementary distribution in Southern British English:

phoneme   /l/

allophones   [l]   [l̥]   [ɫ]

Fig. 2a: phonological representation of the phoneme /l/ for speaker A

If a speaker, like speaker B in our above example, switches between [ɫ] and [ʊ] without a change of meaning, then these two sounds are - phonologically - in free variation in his speech habits. If you pause to think for a moment about speaker B´s allophones [ɫ] and [ʊ], you will see that they belong together because of their distribution. We are faced here with exactly the same phenomenon as with speaker A´s three allophones that led us to establish the abstract unit /l/. By analogy we have to establish an abstract unit for [ɫ] and [ʊ]. But what do these two sounds have in common? Phonetically it is their velarisation, as the back of the tongue is close to the velum in both sounds. And phonologically speaking their distribution is that of free variation. Strictly speaking we have to postulate three hierarchically ordered levels of analysis for speaker B: the phonemic, allophonic and the level of variants of allophones, which we can perhaps call "allo-allophonic", though this is, of course, not an established term.

The schema for the allophones given above acquires another level:

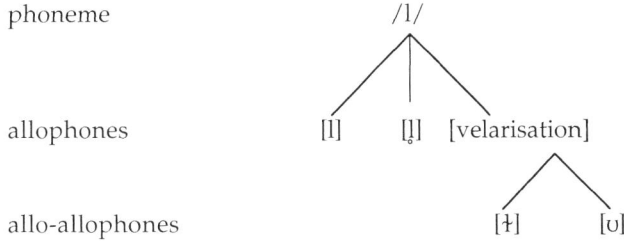

phoneme   /l/

allophones   [l]   [l̥]   [velarisation]

allo-allophones   [ɫ]   [ʊ]

Fig. 2b: phonological representation of the phoneme /l/ for speaker B

Now consider the following schema for determining the phonological status of sounds you identify in spoken words of a language (in this case English).

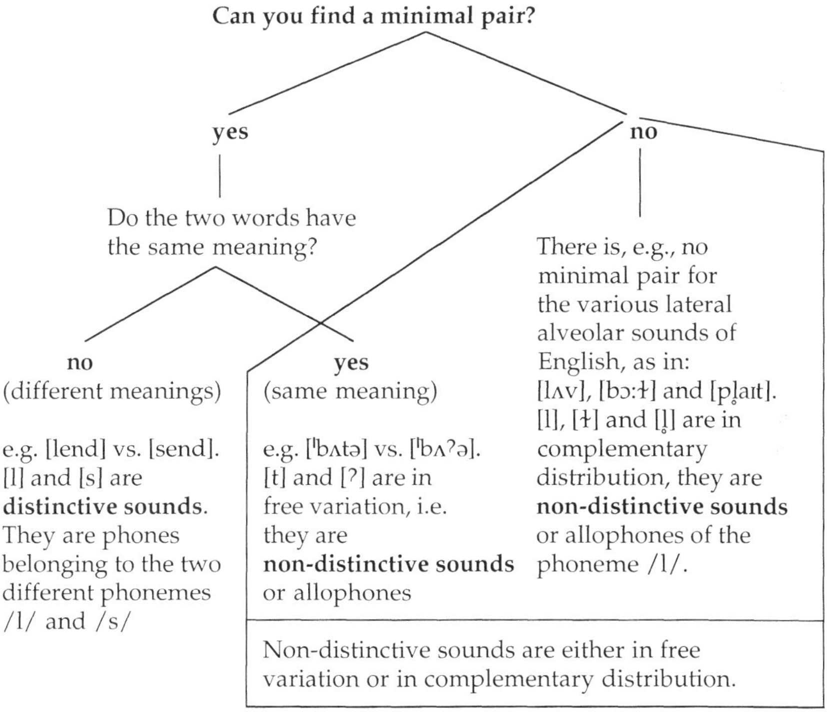

Can you find a minimal pair?

yes   **no**

Do the two words have the same meaning?

no (different meanings)	**yes** (same meaning)	There is, e.g., no minimal pair for the various lateral alveolar sounds of English, as in: [lʌv], [bɔ:ɫ] and [pl̥aɪt]. [l], [ɫ] and [l̥] are in complementary distribution, they are **non-distinctive sounds** or allophones of the phoneme /l/.
e.g. [lend] vs. [send]. [l] and [s] are **distinctive sounds**. They are phones belonging to the two different phonemes /l/ and /s/	e.g. [ˈbʌtə] vs. [ˈbʌʔə]. [t] and [ʔ] are in free variation, i.e. they are **non-distinctive sounds** or allophones	
Non-distinctive sounds are either in free variation or in complementary distribution.		

Fig. 3: How to establish allophones: a flow chart

IV. Consonants: *Sounds you can feel*

Fig. 1. Read her lips: What part of this utterance has she reached? It could be the [m] in *my* or the [p] in *lips* but certainly not the word [ri:d].

After the example chapters on the consonant /l/ and the vowels /æ/ and /e/ in Sections III.1. and 2., in this chapter we are going to concentrate just on consonants. The reason for doing this is that consonants are easier to think about because you can *feel* where in your mouth you are producing them – and *see* the articulation if the lips are involved, as the woman in the whiskey advertisement nicely demonstrates. As her mouth is almost closed with a tiny opening in the middle our guess is that she has just reached the final consonant cluster [ps]. And since our aim with this book is not only to get you to *sound* better, but also to understand *why* you sound better, we are keen to treat things in a way that will let you absorb the background phonetic knowledge.

Obstruents and sonorants

Basically, what makes a consonant in contrast to a vowel is some sort of barrier to obstruct the air flowing through the mouth. This is the reason why the technical term for an important group of consonants is **obstruent** – you can see the link to the word "obstruction" in the name.

Infobox

There are different classes of *obstruents*, distinguished by the way in which the airflow is obstructed – this is called "**the manner of articulation**".

Plosives, or *stops* are consonants that are produced by stopping the airflow completely somewhere in the vocal tract – [p] at the lips, [t] behind the teeth, and [k] further back in the mouth. Then it is released with a small explosion. Clearly "stop" and "plosive" are two words for the same thing, but the two words pick out different aspects of the articulation – the holding part and the releasing part.

Fricatives are sounds that are produced without complete closure, just with a narrowing, a constriction somewhere in the vocal tract. The air flowing through the constriction becomes turbulent, which is heard as a friction sound – [f], formed between upper teeth and lower lip, and [s] produced with a narrow groove in the tongue tip against the teeth ridge, are two examples of fricatives.

A third category of obstruent is the *affricate,* which is like a stop followed by a fricative. Instead of "exploding" the stop, the stoppage is opened just a bit, so that the escaping air causes friction – [ʧ] as in *chair* is an affricate. Because they behave like other single consonants, and because they are produced in the same period of time as a single consonant they are considered a sound *unit* in a particular language and are given a special name (with a special unitary symbol), rather than "stop + fricative" – [tʃ].

If you look on p. 287, at the back of the book, you will see the IPA consonant chart. The stops and fricatives are three of eight manners of articulation in the table (there is a lateral fricative that is given a row all to itself!), and the affricates are not even mentioned because they are considered to be a single sound consisting of a sequence of two manners of articulation (stop followed by fricative) at the same place of articulation. Notice that there are always two symbols in the box representing each place of articulation, a so-called "voiced" sound and a voiceless sound.

Those consonants that are *not* obstruents are often referred to as *sonorants.* This is because they are naturally voiced, i.e. they are produced with the vocal folds vibrating. This means that as far as sonorants are concerned there can be no distinctions that depend on voicing differences. You can see that they occur singly in the boxes of the IPA consonant chart, in contrast to the obstruents, which – as we stated above – are arranged in pairs, voiceless on the left, and voiced on the right.

The "voiced/voiceless" distinction in the obstruents is an important one, and although both German and English use the distinction phonemically – i.e., to distinguish words (read III.4. again if you have forgotten what phonemes are)

– there are important differences in their use, which of course is the source of problems (e.g. [z] vs. [s] in *lose* vs. *loose*; *seize* vs. *cease*, [d] vs. [t] in *bed* vs. *bet*). We shall be discussing the voiced-voiceless problems in this section and dealing with them more extensively in the next two sections (IV.2. & IV.3.).

Infobox

Sonorants are also subdivided into different classes according to their manner of articulation. What they have in common is that the articulatory obstruction which could potentially stop the airflow is *either* (i) bypassed as in [m], *or* (ii) it is too short in duration as in the Italian trill [r] or the German [R] (see IV.3.2.), *or* (iii) it is incomplete so that no friction is produced, as in [j] or [w].

(i) The **nasals** (e.g. [m] and [n] have a complete oral closure, just like a stop, but the soft palate – the velum – is lowered, and the air can escape through the nasal cavity.

(ii) The repeated brief contact of the **trills,** Italian [r] or German [R], and the very short contact of the **taps** or **flaps** as in Spanish *pero* ['pɛɾɔ].

(iii) The **approximants** [j] and [w] have too wide a constriction to cause friction, and the **lateral approximant** [l] allows the air to escape round the sides of the tongue.

A first look at voiced and voiceless

Before concluding this introductory look at consonants, we must return briefly to the question of voicing and lack of voicing, which is mentioned above in connection with obstruents. The voiced-voiceless opposition is often treated too simplistically, and this often leads to confusion. We would like to avoid that confusion right from the start.

We need to remember that we have pairs of sounds like /p/ and /b/, /f/ and /v/, /s/ and /z/ that are in opposition to one another and distinguish words by being different, e.g. *pat - bat, rip - rib; fat - vat, life - live* (adj.); *Sue - zoo, rice - rise*; etc. One of the ways in which the members of these pairs *can* differ is by one of them being "voiced" (i.e. being produced with the vocal folds vibrating) and the other being "voiceless" (being produced with the vocal folds pulled apart (**abducted**) so that they cannot vibrate).

Because of this *potential* difference in the way they are produced, they are usually given the label "voiced" and "voiceless". But the way the members of the pairs are produced *differs in several other ways* too:

a. The closure for /p/ and the friction in /f/ or /s/ are *longer* than for /b/ and in /v/ or /z/, respectively.

b. The explosion of /p/ and the friction of /f/ and /s/ are *stronger* than the explosion of /b/ and the friction of /v/ and /z/.

c. Measurements have shown that the muscular energy involved in producing /p/, /f/ or /s/ is also greater than for /b/, /v/ or /z/.

So it is really rather arbitrary to call the sounds involved in the opposition "voiced" and "voiceless". They could just as aptly be called "long" and "short" or "strong" and "weak".

In fact, in both German and English, the presence or absence of vocal fold vibrations is less important than the *relative strength* of the obstruent. The so-called "voiceless" obstruents are stronger than the "voiced" ones. The technical terms for this relative strength of articulation and the consequent difference in duration of the consonants, and the difference in their relative acoustic energy are "**fortis**" for the stronger "voiceless" ones and "**lenis**" for the weaker "voiced" ones.

This does not mean that the lenis consonants never have accompanying vocal fold vibration. They *do* tend to be voiced to a greater extent than the fortis consonants. But whether the vocal folds vibrate or not is influenced by the context in which the obstruents occur. *Lenis* obstruents between vowels and sonorant consonants (e.g. /d/ in *stand up*, /v/ in *move along* etc.) are often fully voiced, whereas *fortis* obstruents (e.g. in /t/ in *felt ill*, /f/ in *laugh easily*, etc.) are not. In that sort of context, the terms "voiced" and "voiceless" reflect the phonetic difference quite accurately. On the other hand, following or pre-ceding other obstruents, the lenis consonants are more likely not to have vocal fold vibrations (we often say "**devoiced**" because their potential voicing is not achieved), for example /d/ in *get down*, [get d̥aʊn], /v/ in *leave town* [li:v̥ tʰaʊn], /z/ in *lose touch*. [lu:z̥ tʰʌtʃ]. But, what is important is that the strength and duration difference remains; *get down* does not become *get town*, nor does *lose touch* become *loose touch*!

We shall come back to the so-called "voiced"-"voiceless" opposition in IV.1. and IV.2., and you will see again that the activity of the vocal folds is really the least important of the differences that you need to pay attention to.

IV.1. Example sounds /t/ vs. /d/: *Is your tea strong enough?*

1.   *I knew an old man from Dundee*   [aɪ ˈnjuːənəʊɫd ˈmæn frəm dʌnˈdiː
     Whose hobby was drinking strong tea.   huːz ˈhɒbi wəz ˈdrɪŋkɪŋ strɒŋ ˈtiː
     But hiss goot olt frient Hermann,   bət hɪs ˈgʊt əʊlt frent ˈhɜːmən
     (Who was of course German,)   huː ˈwɒzəf kɔːs ˈʤɜːmən
     Mate hiss D just ass strong ass hiss T. meɪt hɪs ˈdiː ʤəstəs ˈstrɒŋəs hɪs ˈtiː]

Fig. 1: *Hermann the German* [ˈhɜːmən ðə ˈʤɜːmən]

In this section we use /t/ and /d/ as example sounds, because if you understand how differently the opposition between these two sounds works in English and German you will have learned general rules and principles that you can then easily apply to a number of other distinctions as well (like /p/ and /b/, /k/ and /g/, /f/ and /v/ and others.

Place of articulation:

When you pronounce /t/ and /d/ the tip of the tongue moves to the **teeth ridge** (= **alveolar ridge** [ælˈviˌəʊlə ˈrɪʤ]) in both English and German. As we referred to consonants as "sounds you can feel", we suggest that you play around with different types of /t/ and /d/, starting with a dental position. Then, as you keep producing these sounds, keep retracting your tongue tip so the tip moves from the teeth via the alveolar ridge to the palate. If you say the sentence *"Don't pay ten dollars. Toni can get a gun for you for two dollars"* with a dental [t̪], you will sound like an Italian Mafia boss in an American film, and if you say it with the tip of your tongue curled up and backwards, touching the palate, you will sound like some speakers from India. (This tongue position is called "retroflex"; cf. consonant chart at the back of the book.)

Manner of articulation:

When you say *ten* you block the airstream with your tongue, allow the pressure to build up and then suddenly release it by pulling the tongue down for the /e/ position in *ten*. Between the /t/ and the /e/ you get a burst of air that you can hear, feel, and even see if you put powder on a piece of paper right in front of your lips. The effect would be even stronger if you said *pen*. The powder gets blown away as if you had caused a miniture explosion, and this is why all sounds with this kind of sudden release are aptly called **plosives**.

The powder gets blown away by the air that is breathed out between the release of the /t/ and the onset of the voicing for the vowel. This process is called **aspiration**. If you carry out the powder experiment with *ten* and *den* and with *pen* and *Ben* you will realise that there is no aspiration with the words beginning with /d/ and /b/ respectively. Since place and manner of /t/ and /d/ are the same, the distinction between the two is often said to be that of a voiceless alveolar as opposed to a voiced alveolar plosive. But strictly speaking, this is not entirely correct. If you do the "powder" experiment with

2.   *tale, stale, dale; tan, Stan, Dan*

you will find that – contrary to what you would expect from the spelling – *stale* goes with *dale* (and *Stan* goes with *Dan*), because when a voiceless plosive is preceded by a fricative at the beginning of a word, the plosive loses the aspiration that follows it. And this aspiration is, in fact, the main distinction between /t/ and /d/. This is confirmed when one simply cuts off the [s] in [steɪɫ] (*stale*) on a digitally recorded version. The remaining part then sounds like [d̥eɪɫ] (*dale*) and not like [tʰeɪɫ] (*tale*). The following spectrogram (fig. 2) and the recording of the words *stale, tale* and *dale* illustrate this.

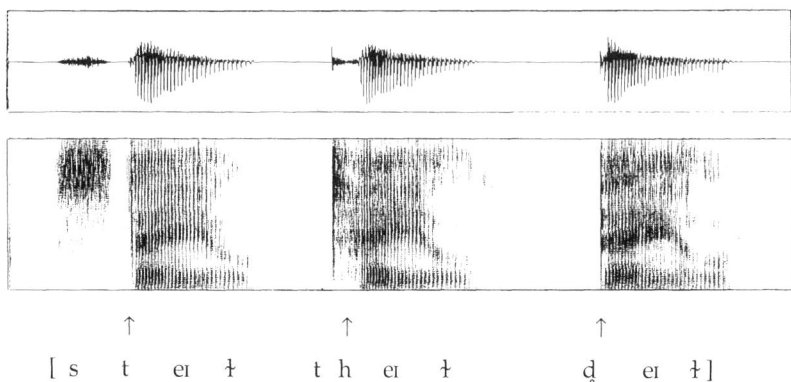

[s t eɪ ɫ t h eɪ ɫ d̥ eɪ ɫ]

C 1 / Fig. 2: Compare the degree of aspiration in *stale, tale* and *dale* (marked by ↑) in the above spectrograms with the recordings of those words (and with the 4th recorded word: *stale* with the [s] excised)

Luckily this rule also applies to German (compare *Tal, Stahl, Dahl*) and thus does not cause any problems. If the distinction is not entirely one of voiced and unvoiced sounds, what then are the other criteria? We will return to this question but first we want to draw your attention to the problems connected with plosives at the end of a word.

The biggest problem in dealing with /t/ and /d/ is not an articulatory one but one of distribution, or, put differently, a question of *when* to choose one or the other. Let us remind you of our friend Hermann the German in the opening limerick, who finds this problem notoriously difficult, especially when he is trying to find his way round in London, as the examples below confirm:

C 2 / E 1: Listen to the following sentences. In each of the written sentences there is a pair of street names which sound similar. In each case underline the street name the speaker is producing. As usual you will find the answers in chapter XII.

 a. *Excuse me, Fort Street/Ford Street is supposed to be around here somewhere?*
 b. *Excuse me, how do I get to Ratcliff Road, please/Radcliffe Road, please?*
 c. *Excuse me, is this The Mount/The Mound?*
 d. *Excuse me, I'm looking for Meat Road/Mead Road.*
 e. *Excuse me, you don't happen to know where Wates Grove/Wades Grove is, do you?*
 f. *Oh no, I think you want Richmount Gardens /Ridgemound Gardens.*

How did you get on? It is likely that you had problems identifying all the words on tape correctly. What is the problem? English differentiates the ends of words in different ways from German. In the German phrase *Hits für Kids* the two nouns [hɪts] and [kɪts] rhyme, but in the English version *Hits for kids* they do not: [hɪts] does not rhyme with [kɪdz].

/t/ is a *voiceless* and *strong* consonant. The technical term for *strong* is **fortis** (read the explanation in the previous section (IV) again if you have forgotten) and it was chosen to reflect the greater muscuar effort of the articulators. The production of /d/ requires less muscular effort, comparatively speaking, and this type of sound is referred to as **lenis**.

Although German and English both have a /t - d/ distinction, the opposition is distributionally incomplete in German because here all *syllable-final* obstruents are *voiceless* and *strong*. So irrespective of whether the spelling is <Bund> or <bunt>, the final sound is always /t/ because at the end of German words or syllables you never get /d/. *Bund* and *bunt* are **homophones**. Now pronounce the minimal pair *Bundes* and *buntes* with the syllable boundary after *bun-* , and you will hear that the only difference is that between /d/ and /t/, that is between voiced and lenis on the one hand and voiceless and fortis on the other. But when no vowel follows, these lenis consonants become fortis again. So we say *die Lieder* /di ˈliːdɐ/ but *das Lied* /das ˈliːt/. Incidentally, it is amusing to see that when the English term *lead singer* [ˈliːd sɪŋə] found its way into German and became a German loanword as *der Lead-Sänger* it was phonetically indistinguishable from *der Lied-Sänger*. And the name of the American car company *Ford* gave rise to silly jokes like this one:

Welches ist die älteste Automarke der Welt? Der Ford, denn in der Bibel steht: "Adam und Eva sündigten in einem Ford."(= in einem fort)

But it also has potential for commercial exploitation, as the advert by a local car dealer shows: *Meyer: Die Ford-Bewegung in Neustadt!*

Clearly, the automatic devoicing and strengthening of final voiced obstruents is a natural trap for German speakers of English to fall into. A German "fortis" version is established for foreign words with lenis final consonants that are borrowed, like "eine *life* Sendung" (although the English expression is "a *live* [laɪv] programme") or the neo-German word "Code". On its way from English to German *code* underwent a double adjustment: Firstly the diphthong of English [kəʊd] became simply a long [oː] and secondly the the final lenis sound became a fortis sound, so that the German loanword *Code* is pronounced the same as the historically more established but, socially speaking, less savoury word *Kot*. Speakers of German who have been pronouncing final obstruents as fortis consonants for as long as they have been able to talk, find it very difficult to "switch off" the commands to their articulators, even though they know they are speaking English. So in the last line of the limerick: "*Made his D as strong as his T*" the /d/ becomes /t/ and the /z/ becomes /s/: "*Mate hiss D ass strong ass hiss T.*"

Try doing it wrong first!

As with other problems where old habits have to be broken, you have first to *become aware* of the German habit. Try reading the following English phrases, first correctly and *then incorrectly*, i.e. with your German articulatory habits; we have included a wrongly spelt version to help you:

E 2: 1a. *Robin Hood was a good outlaw.* /ˈrɒbɪn ˈhʊd wəzə ˈgʊ ˈd‿aʊtlɔː/
       1b. *Robin Hoot wass a goot outlaw.* */ˈrɒbɪn ˈhʊt wəs ə ˈgʊt ˈaʊtlɔː/

       2a. *He robbed the rich and gave to the poor.*/hi ˈrɒbd ðə ˈrɪtʃən ˈgeɪv tə ðə ˈpʊə/
       2b. *He roppt the rich and gafe to the poor.* */hi ˈrɒbt ðə ˈrɪtʃ ən ˈgeɪf tə ðə ˈpʊə/

If the incorrect version felt as easy to pronounce as the correct version, or if you could not feel any difference between them, then you probably have not yet broken the German habit of final devoicing and strengthening. Of course, if you *have* learned to produce the weak (lenis) English final obstruents, making them strong (fortis) again will have felt and sounded very funny.

So what is special about English FVCs?

If you still have a problem with the weak or lenis English final obstruents (people often just call them **Final Voiced Consonants – FVCs** for short), it is important for you to know *what to concentrate on* to produce them properly.

You may have wondered why we talked about the error of applying the German habit of "final devoicing and strengthening to English", and why we stressed the fact that the English sounds are "weak". As we explained in the previous section, the actual voiced property that underlies the nominal opposition of "voiced" vs. "voiceless" used in phonological descriptions is perceptually much less important than the accompanying "lenis" (weak) vs. "fortis" (strong) quality of the sounds. English speakers do not *actively* produce voicing in obstruents; lenis obstruents tend to be voiced or devoiced in sympathy with the surrounding sounds. Between vowels, like the two [d]´s in *"Fred offered Anne the job"* [ˈfred‿ɒfəˈd‿æn ðə ˈʤɒb], they tend to be voiced, but before pauses (*"Look at Fred"*), or after voiceless consonants they are usually devoiced, like [d] in *"Get down"* [getˈ˺daʊn]. Putting it differently, it is much more important to make the /d/ in the word *card* weak to avoid the impression of *cart* than it is to make the /d/ properly voiced. In fact, if you *did* make it really voiced when pronouncing the isolated word it would not sound very English at all. ([tˈ˺] in the transcription of *Get down* signifies that the /t/ is not released.)

Let us assume you have not mastered the distinction between final /d/ and /t/, and when you mean to say *"Do you want a bed?"* native speakers of English think that you are offering them a bet: *Do you want a bet?* There is an easy solution to your problem: Lengthen the vowel! The word *bed* is longer than the word *bet*, and *beat* is longer than *bead*. This phenomenon of lengthening vowels before a lenis consonant is called **pre-lenis lengthening.** Because of the constant association between the lenis plosive and the slight lengthening of the preceding vowel natives speakers of English will expect a lenis sound and "hear" it even if you have not quite mastered the **lenition** (weakening) of the final /d/.

So part of the secret of making final obstruents like /d/, /b/ and /g/ sound weaker is to lengthen the vowel preceding it. Before the "voiced" plosives /b, d, g/ the vowels are consistently longer than before the voiceless plosives /p, t, k/. Just to reassure you, pre-lenis lengthening is not a peculiarly English thing. Many languages, including German, have longer sounds before "voiced" than before "voiceless" obstruents: E.g., the /aɪ/ in *leider* is longer than the /aɪ/ in *Leiter* and the /n/ in *Sonde* is longer than the /n/ in *sonnte*. It is as if the vocalic or sonorant part of the syllable is taking up more space in order to leave less space for the obstruent and thus make it weaker. But, German only has this phenomenon *word-medially*, never at the end of a word, and of course *that* is the source of the problem we are addressing.

Seeing is believing!

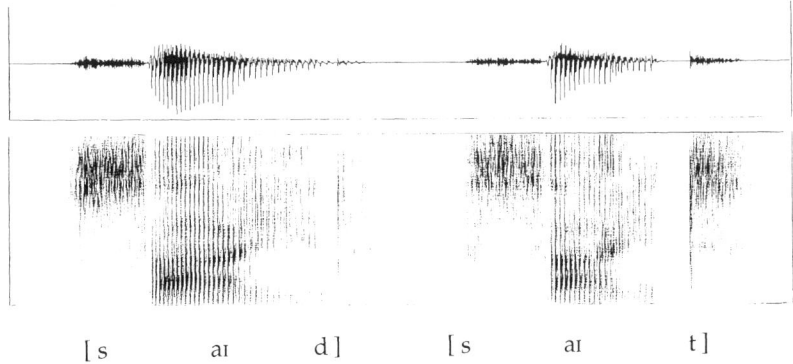

[s   aɪ   d]   [s   aɪ   t]

Fig. 3: Spectrogram of the words *side* and *sight* (cf. Infobox).

> **Infobox**
>
> In the study of speech, a spectrogram is a graphical representation of a particular analysis of the acoustic signal of an utterance (here it is a pair of words). It shows the **duration** from left to right, and the relative acoustic energy in the lower to higher **frequency** regions from bottom to top. The differences in energy distribution across the range of frequencies (the spectrum) are responsible for the different sound qualities of the speech sounds. The different degrees of energy present are shown here by different shades of grey. The darker it is, the more energy is present at that frequency. The relatively narrow bands of energy from left to right during the vowel part of the signal are called **formants**. The first two or three formants from the bottom have been shown to be sufficient to define the vowel we hear. In other words, all the linguistic information on the vowels is contained in the region below about 3000 Hz. The much more diffuse patches of energy (in the upper part of the spectrogram for the /s/ sounds here, but in different parts of the spectrum for other fricative sounds) are typical of fricatives. The gaps in energy are the consequence of the mouth being closed for the /t/ and /d/ closure phases, and the very short, spectrally broad bands at the end of the closures (almost like vertical lines) are the result of the explosion at the release of the closure.

The characteristic broad-band high frequency energy of the /s/ friction, the lower frequency energy bands (the "formants") of the /aɪ/, and the period without energy during the /d/ and /t/ closures followed by the broad-band impulse of energy at the release of the closure are easy to identify. A moment's scrutiny and you will recognise the properties we have been discussing:

a. The diphthong /aɪ/ is longer in *side* than in *sight*
b. The closure of the /d/ is shorter than the /t/ closure.
c. The burst of the /d/ is weaker than the burst of the /t/.
d. The /d/ closure is not fully voiced (the regular low frequency energy impulses – associated with the vibrating vocal folds – die out).

And now for some practice:

If we have succeeded in raising your *awareness* of the phonetic differences between word-final lenis and fortis obstruents, we can go on to the next stage of sensitivisation, namely to try and establish a permanent auditory picture of the different sounds. If you can *hear* the difference you stand more chance of listening critically to yourself *pronouncing* the sounds. Ultimately it is necessary to build up a connection between your feel for the articulation of the sounds and your auditory impression of them.

C 3: Listen to the following pairs of words (a.) and pay attention to the slight lengthening of the vowel before the lenis obstruent. Then play the sentences (b.) containing the same or similar examples, and try to imitate the difference in the length of the vowel and the strength of the final obstruent.

a. | | | |
|---|---|---|
| *wheat - weed* | *lout - loud* | *kit - kid* |
| *writ - rid* | *clout - cloud* | *hurt - heard* |
| *trite - tried* | *cart - card* | *lute - lewd* |
| *straight - strayed* | *plate - played* | *fright - fried* |

b. *That's not a weed, it's a wheat shoot.*
   If you don't rid yourself of the weapon, you'll be served a writ.
   Burt is very fond of his little bird.
   She sat there by herself looking rather sad.
   She realised that her boyfriend was a loud-mouthed lout.
   Their dogs never strayed far, and came straight back when called.
   Charles tried to be funny but it sounded very trite.

C 4: In the following list a similar lengthening can be heard, but this time it is in the sonorant consonant preceding the final obstruent (i.e. the longer /n/ in *bend* than in *bent*):

a. | | | |
|---|---|---|
| *bend - bent* | *felled - felt* | *found - fount* | *culled - cult* |
| *pined - pint* | *mauled - malt* | *fond - font* | *cold - colt* |

b. *When trying to catch a colt in the river, the cowboy only caught a cold.*
   After the lumberjack had felled the tree he felt much better.
   The secretary was particularly fond of the Times font.
   During the weeks of Lent he often pined for a fine pint of British bitter.

E 3: Read aloud:

An assistant professor named Ddodd	[ənəˈsɪstənt prəˈfesə neɪmˈdɒd
had manners arresting and odd.	hæd ˈmænəz‿əˈrestɪŋənˈdɒd
He said, "If you please,	hi ˈsed‿ɪf ju: ˈpli:z
spell my name with four d´s."	speɫ maɪ ˈneɪm wɪð fɔ: ˈdi:z
Though one was sufficient for God.	ðəʊ ˈwʌn wəz səˈfɪʃənt fə ˈgɒd]
An elderly lady named Rood	[əˈneɫdəli ˈleɪdi neɪmd ˈru:d
was such an absolute prude	wəz ˈsʌtʃəˈn‿æbsəlu:t ˈpru:d
that she pulled down the blind	ðət ʃi ˈpuɫdaʊn ðə ˈblaɪnd
when changing her mind,	wen ˈtʃeɪndʒɪŋə ˈmaɪnd
lest curious eyes should intrude.	lest ˈkjʊərɪəˈs‿aɪz ʃʊd‿ɪnˈtru:d]

E 4: Test yourself and your neighbour: And now go back to the sentences that you were listening to at the beginning of this section in C2/E1. But this time try reading the sentences to your neighbour, each time choosing *one* of the words from the pair without telling your neighbour which you have chosen. Make a note of the word you intended. Now compare your list of intended words with the list that your neighbour wrote down. And now swap roles.

The letters <t> and <d>

You will be familiar with the pronunciation of <t> as [ʃ] as in *pronunciation*, and [tʃ] as in *feature* and the combination <th>. But by and large it is fairly safe to assume that <t> is pronounced /t/ and <d> is /d/. You have to distinguish, however, semantically and phonetically between *used* [ju:zd] (German: *gebraucht*) and *used to* [ju:stə] (in the sense of *früher*: "I used to come here by bike." or in the sense of *gewohnt* as in "I´m used to it."):

3   a. `crikey´ is an expression that used to be used a lot by women.
     b. [ˈkraɪki‿ɪzən‿ɪksˈpreʃn̩ ðət ˈju:stə bi ˈju:zdə ˈlɒt baɪ ˈwɪmɪn]

The <t> is silent in all <stl> combinations, as in *bristle, thistle, whistle,* and also in *listen* and *Christmas.* In present-day English the words *soften* and *often* are pronounced without /t/.

If you speak a form of RP or Standard British English you should avoid pronouncing *butter* with an American flap as [ˈbʌɾə] or [ˈbʌdə]. After all, if you say *"putting on top"*, you do not want it to be understood as *"pudding on top"*!

C 5/E5: Listen to the introductory limerick (p. 40) and repeat. Enjoy your newly acquired ability to switch consciously from correct English to incorrect German final consonants.

Smiley:

Why do people brush their teeth regularly? - To avoid bad breath.
Why do vampires brush their teeth regularly? - To avoid bat breath.

IV.2. Other fortis vs. lenis oppositions

IV.2.1. /k/ vs. /g/: *Lug, lug, luggage*

Fig. 1: BA advert for Victoria Station check-in (*lug* = German *schleppen*)

If you tell someone about how you had to *lug your luggage* from one end of the terminal to the other, you are pronouncing words with **velar plosives in** them. [g] and [k] are velar plosives because you stop (and then release) the airflow between the back of your tongue and the velum (the soft palate). The following figure indicates how this contact is formed by raising the tongue right up to the velum, which is kept in a raised position to prevent any flow of air into the nasal cavities.

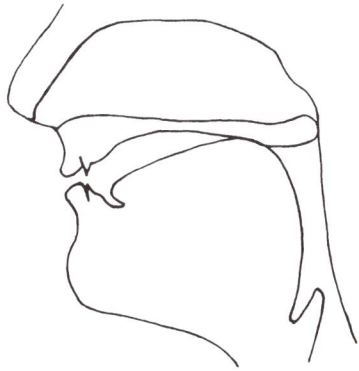

Fig. 2: Place of articulation for the velar plosives [k] and [g]

> **Infobox**
>
> The **velum** [ˈviːləm] or the **soft palate** [sɒft ˈpælət] (German: *Gaumensegel*) is the back part of the palate that can be seen when you stand in front of a mirror and open your mouth wide. In its relaxed state it obscures the back of your throat, the **pharynx** (German *Rachen*). The reason doctors ask you to say *"aaaah"* when looking into your mouth is that firstly you open your mouth wider than for other vowels (saying *"uuh"* would not be as effective) and secondly because [ɑ] is an **oral** sound as opposed to a **nasal** (see IV.4.6. &V.2.4.); you pull up the velum to make more air pass through the mouth instead of through the nose. And this allows the doctor to see whether your throat is inflamed. *"Say aaaah"* has proved much more useful than the request: *"Could you kindly raise your velum so I can see your pharynx better"*, but you, as budding phoneticians should know what is going on.

For German speakers there are no *articulatory* difficulties, as these sounds are basically the same in both languages. There is, however, the problem of *distribution*, i.e. which contexts require [k] and which require [g]. Everything we have said so far about fortis vs. lenis in general and [t] vs. [d] in particular also applies to the fortis plosive [k] and the lenis plosive [g]. So German *König* is pronounced *Könik* or (in the North) *Könich*, but in both *Könige* and *Königin* the letter <g> is pronounced [g], because it is not at the end of a syllable. This explains why English words are automatically adjusted phonetically when they become part of the German language: *logbook* becomes *Lockbook* or *Lockbuch* (with interesting connotations), and *gag* becomes *Gag* but undergoes two phonetic adjustments and is pronounced [gek]. How this may undermine simple everyday communication is illustrated in the following sketch:

A sketch: Hermann the German and his English landlady Meg

H: (coming in through the front door): *Hi Meck, I'm beck.*
M: *Hi Herman. Actually, it's "Meg".*
H: *That's what I said, isn't it?*
M: *Not quite.*
H: *I thought there'd be a sneck.*
M: *Look, if you're hungry ...*
H: *Oh no, I meant there'd be a difficulty.*
M: *Oh I see, you meant there'd be a snag.*
H: *That's what I said, isn't it? Anyway, I wouldn't mind a bite to eat and a cup of tea. Is this your muck?*
M: *I beg your pardon?*
H: *You don't mind me using yours, do you? I can't put my hands on my muck just now.*
M: *Well it's all over the place ... oh sorry, sorry, Herman, you mean mug, don't you?*

H: *Do I? By the way, it´s "Herrmann". Pass me the slice of cheese that I put in your paperback.*

M: *What?!*

H: *Uhm sorry: I mean "please".*

M: *Never mind about that just now, but if you need a bookmark I´d be most grateful if you´d use a piece of paper instead of a slice of Cheddar Cheese. Not in my books, anyway.*

H: *Who´s talking about books? I said pa - per - back.*

M: *Oh sorry, Herman, you mean "paper bag", that´s quite all right of course*

H: *I hope you don´t mind me asking, Meck, but, uhm, is your hearing ok?*

In this sketch we have taken advantage of minimal pairs that German speakers often find difficult to keep apart because of the habit of not using lenis consonants at the end of a word or a syllable. Hermann has not adjusted his hearing (or pronunciation) habits from German to English! If you want to say:

1. a. *The Greens do not object to people being issued with plastic bags as long as they can be recyled.*

you should not make it sound like:

b. *The Greens do not object to people being issued with plastic <u>backs</u> as long as they can be recyccled.*

as this might be interpreted as a major breakthrough in plastic surgery. Before you repeat the following sentences you should recall what we said about /t/ vs. /d/, which we repeat here with adjustments for [k] and [g]:

1) The diphthong [eɪ] is longer in *vague* [veɪg] than in *fake*.
2) The closure of the [g] is shorter than the [k] closure.
3) The burst of the [g] is weaker than the burst of the [k].
4) The [g] closure is not necessarily voiced.

C 1: Listen and repeat:

a. *She used a tack to fasten her name tag to her desk.*

b. *Have you seen my other clog? - No, but it´s half past seven. - No, no, I said "my other clog", not my other clock!*

c. *Sometimes I would like to hug Finn, but he´s always on the run. - Yes, a bit like his namesake Huck Finn.*

d. *We couldn´t climb any higher because of a large crack in the crag (crack = German Riß, Spalte; crag = German Fels).*

e. *Did you get a porter to help you with your luggage, granny ? - No such luck. I had to lug the suitcase all by myself.*

f. *How did Jack become so stinking rich? - He made expensive roof racks out of cheap scrap metal. - Ah, the old story: From rags to riches. - Ho ho ho, surely you mean "from racks to riches!"*

g. *Lovely animals! I´d like to buy one. Can I choose a pig? - By all means, go ahead, take your pick.*

The "sighlent" \<g\>

Smiley: *Q: What is a metronome? - A: A dwarf in the Paris underground.*
This joke question is based on the fact that a gnome in the metro, i.e. a *metro gnome* and a *metronome* are homophones. As a matter of fact, \<gn\> at the beginning and the end of a syllable is pronounced [n] as for example in:

gnaw, gnu, gnat, gnome; campaign, feign, reign, sovereign, foreign, sign, design, resign, Red Ensign [ˌredˈensɪn] (the flag of the British Merchant Navy), *consignment, assign, assignment, benign, malign.*

If \<gn\> is not part of the same syllable then it is pronounced [gn], as in *malignant.* The \<gn\>-rule in syllable final position also applies to \<gm\>: *diaphragm* (German *Zwerchfell*), and *paradigm* [ˈpærədaɪm], but *paradigmatic* [ˌpærədɪgˈmætɪk]. Examples of silent \<k\> are all words beginning with \<kn-\>, like *knee, know, knuckle, knapsack* with the exception of the foreign word *Knesset*.

\<g\> as [g] or [dʒ]

As this distinction does not normally cause problems we give you only the few words that our students occasionally got wrong:

[g]: *gimmick, gill* (German: *Kiemen*).   [dʒ]: *gibberish, gel*

\<x\> → [ks] or [gz] ?

The letter \<x\> is pronounced [ks] in most cases, as in *Mexico, ex-husband* and *taxes.* There are, however, a few instances of [gz] with a very high frequency of use, an example of which is *example,* [ɪgˈzɑːmpɫ] and that is why you have to memorise them. There is a rule: \<x\> before a vowel with primary or secondary stress is pronounced [gz], in other cases it is [ks]. This is why you get:

2. *exhibition* [ˌeksɪ ˈbɪʃən] but *exhibit* [ɪgˈzɪbɪt]
    execute [ˈeksəkjuːt] but *executive* [ɪgˈzekjʊtɪv]
    luxury [ˈlʌkʃəri] but *luxurius* [lʌgˈzjʊərɪəs]

As there are exceptions to this rule (like *hexameter*) and as there are only relatively few words with [gz] it is probably easier for you to just practice these rather than going by the rule book:

C 2: Listen and repeat:

I´m so exhausted. - Is it because of that one measly little exam you had to sit? - You know I absolutely hate being examined. - Oh come on, don´t exaggerate. Anyway, what was the exam about? - Phonetics. We had to think of exotic examples like: "She exhibits exemplary behaviour." - Well, yours certainly isn´t exemplary. We had to write about auxiliary verbs. - Auxiliary verbs? Should I have bought some for the garden? What are they? - You´ve just used two of them. They are verbs like "have" and "be", for example. You can´t talk without using them. - Well, that´s a bit of an exaggeration, isn´t it?

IV.2.2. /p/ vs. /b/: *Do you wear a bathrope?*

We shall deal with the *robe - rope* problem a little later, but first let us consider what sort of sounds [p] and [b] are. First of all they are **bilabial plosives**. The words *plosive* and *explosion* are in some ways onomatopoeic: The [p] in them sounds like what the words denote: an explosion, albeit a miniature one. If you repeat the *powder* experiment that we asked you to carry out with [t] and [d] in IV.2. by holding a piece of paper with some powder right in front of your mouth, you will see that it also works with [p] and [b]. If you use the words *pat, spat* and *bat* you will "see" (and by now hopefully also hear) that *spat* and *bat* go together, because the [p] in *spat* and the [b] are both unaspirated and sound the same (particularly if the [s] is removed electronically, see the example of *stale* and *dale* in IV.2.).

Against the background of this phonetic insight, you should now be able to explain the very slight phonetic weakness in the clever play on words (let us pray vs. let us spray) in the last line of the following limerick:

1. *An indolent vicar of Bray*   [æˈnɪndələnt ˈvɪkərəv ˈbreɪ
    His roses allowed to decay.   hɪz ˈrəʊzɪz‿əˈlaʊd tə dɪˈkeɪ
    His wife more alert   hɪz ˈwaif mɔr‿əˈlɜːt
    Bought a powerful squirt   bɔːtə ˈpaʊəfəɫ ˈskwɜːt̪
    And said to her spouse: "Let us spray." ən ˈsed tə hɜ ˈspaʊs letəsˈspreɪ]

Strictly speaking one should use the same phonetic symbol, namely unaspirated [p] for the plosive in *spat* and *bat*. We could now take advantage of the phonological principles outlined in chapter III.4. and say there is the phoneme /p/ which may be represented by at least two allophones, i.e. the aspirated [pʰ] in [pʰæt] and the [p] in *spat* [spæt] and *bat* [pæt]. As we have pointed out with obstruents generally, a fully voiced bilabial plosive normally only occurs between two vowels as in [ˈrɒbə] (*robber*) or between a sonorant consonant and a vowel, as in [ˈeɫbəʊ] (*elbow*) and the phonetic symbol [b] could be reserved for this particular case. You may rightly ask why this is not done and why we – in this book – follow the tradition of conventional dictionaries. The answer is that it would make life unnecessarily complicated in a field that does not cause any problems for most German learners of English, because the allophonic set-up in word-initial position is the same in German *Paten, Spaten, baten.*

We said "for *most* German learners". If, in your dialect, you do not distinguish between *Gebäck* and *Gepäck*, between *Griegs Ende* and *Kriegsende*, and between *die änderten die Schiffe* and *die enterten die Schiffe*, you need to acquire the English habit of aspirated [pʰ], [kʰ] and [tʰ] at the beginning of words.

Where German learners do encounter problems is the by now familiar problem of final "fortissification" (if you pardon the expression) of lenis consonants. As this is the gist of IV.1.&2. and IV.3.1. we would like to repeat what we said earlier on: The automatic devoicing and strengthening of final voiced obstruents is a natural trap for German speakers of English to fall into. After all, a German "fortis" version is established of foreign words with lenis final consonants that are borrowed:

2. | English | German | English | German |
|---|---|---|---|
| snob [snɒb] | Snob [snɔp] | mob [mɒb] | Mob [mɔp] |
| job [dʒɒb] | Job [dʒɔp] | lob [lɒb] | Lob [lɔp] |
| Bob [bɒb] | Bob [bɔp] | club [klʌb] | Club [klʊp] |
| pub [pʌb] | Pub [pap] | kids [kɪdz] | Kids [kɪts] |

One of our students meant to say 3a, which came out as 3b:

3   a. *He was stabbed to death.*
    b. *He was stepped to death.*

What happened here was an unfortunate accumulation of mistakes. Firstly, the vowel [æ] in *stabbed* was replaced by [e]. Secondly, the two consonants at the end were made fortis and voiceless: [pt], and thirdly, as a consequence of this the vowel was shortened. This last process is known as **pre-fortis clipping** and is correct in *stepped* [stept] but not in *stabbed* (where **pre-lenis lengthening** is required). What happens at the end of *stabbed* when you say it in isolation is this: The devoicing sets in as the lips are closing. The [b] is thus partly devoiced, and the [d] is fully devoiced, but lenis. In other words, the final burst of air should not be as strong as it would be with a [t] in, for example, [hɒt].

If the final consonant in *stabbed* and in *bulb* is not voiced, why do pronouncing dictionaries use the phonetic symbol [d] and [b] respectively instead of [t] and [d]? In order to appreciate this convention you have to be aware of the fact that phonetic symbols represent bundles of features. It would, of course, be possible to have a different symbol for each and every combination of features, i.e. we could have one for the bilabial voiceless lenis plosive (as the one in *stabbed*), one for the bilabial voiced lenis plosive (as the one in the middle of *blubber*), one for the bilabial voiceless fortis plosive (as in *hop on*), one for the bilabial voiceless aspirated plosive (as in *pat*), one for the bilabial unaspirated plosive (as in *spat* and *bat*), one for the bilabial plosive where the built-up pressure is not released (as for instance in *yep* (for *yes*), where one does not open open the lips after they have come together for the [p]), and so on. As a matter of fact, phoneticians do have symbols for the different sounds, but can you imagine how cumbersome this would make the reading of phonetic transcription for everyday use?

We considered it best to restrict the inventory of plosives to the minimum, because in word-initial position and in fully voiced intervocalic positions German learners do not normally have any difficulties. And what you have to remember for word-final position is that /b/, /d/ and /g/ should be lenis instead of their German fortis counterparts as demonstrated with English loanwords in German in 2. Another advantage of sticking to these symbols is that they will help to remind you of the rule of linking plosives: Even where the lenis plosive is devoiced as in the pronunciation of /b/ in 4a it becomes fully voiced when followed by a vowel as in 4b:

4   a. *He lost his job.*
    b. *He got a fantastic job offer.*

So the link in *got a* has a voiceless aspirated alveolar plosive, and the link in *job offer* results in a fully voiced bilabial plosive. The choice of the symbols /t/ and /b/ will remind you of this process, and any further symbols may make life for the learner unnecessarily complex.

C 1 / E 1: Spot the foreign accent. In this discrimination exercise we ask you to listen to sentences spoken by a native speaker of English and by a foreigner, but not always in that order. If for sentence a. you think you heard the native speaker of English first and then the foreign accent, write "a. E/F", if you think it was the other way round write "a. F/E". (Solutions in chapter XII.)

   a. *He grabbed the money and ran.*
   b. *She certainly has the gift of the gab but sometimes I wish she´d shut her gob.*
   c. *Let´s take a cab and go to a pub and have a drink or two.*
   d. *When my son joined the cubs they taught him to wash his cups himself.*
   e. *I still like fairy tales like "The Wolf and the Seven Little Kids" and "Little Red Riding Hood".*
   f. *He was stabbed to death.*

<s> for *psalm* or The silent <p> and the dumb <b>

The letter <p> is silent in all word-initial <ps-> and <pn-> combinations, as for instance in *psychology, psalm* [sɑ:m], *pseudonym* [ˈsju:dənɪm], and *pneumonia* [njuˈməʊnɪə]. Both <p> and <b> are silent in the <pb> and <bt> combinations in *cupboard* [ˈkʌbəd] and *subtle* [ˈsʌtɬ].

In words ending in <-mb> the <b> is always silent, even in their conjugated and derived forms like *climb* [klaɪm], *climbing* [ˈklaɪmɪŋ], *climbed* [klaɪmd] and *climber* [ˈklaɪmə], *bomb, bombing* and *bomber, beachcomb* and *beachcomber* [ˈbi:ʧ kəʊmə].

E 2: Say the following words out loud to yourself, bearing in mind the possibility of non-pronounced letters.

pseudo	*combing*	*psyche*	*fumbling*
psalm	*bombing*	*psi*	*womb*
psychological	*dumbly*	*Ptolemaic*	*door-jamb*
pneumatic	*entombed*	*pneumonia*	*Pnom Penh*
clamber	*plumber*	*lumber*	

As a fun exercise in decoding orthographical nonsense, you might like to read the following, and – if you follow the non-pronounced letter conventions – find it does make sense after all:

5.   *The pneu pseut was phar more than he could pay. Ptony psyed; he pneu he was dombed to pserve, and pnever to pnow phaimb or phortune.*

The following rather grim poem relies on the silent <b> for its rhyme:

6.

Beginnings and endings of every life   [bɪˈgɪnɪŋzəˈnendɪŋzəˈv‿evri ˈlaɪf

take place in cramped and narrow rooms   teɪk ˈpleɪsɪn ˈkræmptən ˈnærəʊ ˈruːmz

among much hassle and trouble and strife   əˈmʌŋ mʌtʃ ˈhæslən ˈtrʌblən ˈstraɪf

from wombs of hope to doom of tombs.   frəm ˈwuːmzəv ˈhəʊp tə ˈduːməv ˈtuːmz]

But let us not end this section full of gloom and doom. Here is a silly question to cheer you up:

[ɪfə ˈbrɪkleɪə kən leɪ ˈbrɪks ˈwaɪ kɑːntə ˈplʌmə leɪ ˈplʌmz]

IV.2.3. /s/ vs. /z/: *Ssserpentsss hisss, but beezzz buzzz*

The sounds that occur at the end of the words *hiss* and *buzz* are [s] and [z], **alveolar fricatives**: You can hear the friction of the air being squeezed through the narrow groove between the blade of the tongue and the alveolar ridge onto the front teeth (see section IV.1. to refresh your memory). Together with the [ʃ] and [ʒ] sounds (cf. IV.2.4) they form the class of **sibilants** (from the Latin word for *hiss*). They differ partly in that [s] is voiceless and [z] is voiced. Anybody trying to do an impression of Sir Hiss in Disney´s *Jungle Book* will produce the serpent´s (i.e. the snake´s) hiss as a prolonged [s:::::], and if you ask people to imitate the sound of a bee they will produce a prolonged [z:::::] with the vocal folds vibrating.

When we say the articulation of the two fricatives /s/ and /z/ does not cause any problems to native speakers of German, we simply mean that, unless they have a speech impediment, everybody can do the snake sound and the sound of bees. Their distribution as sounds in speech, however, and the realisation of these two phonemes is different in the two languages according to the phonetic contexts in which they occur. Let us assume the following head-lines appeared after the controversial count of votes in the USA for George W. Bush and Al Gore in the 2000 presidential elections:

1. Headlines:
    a. *New Precedent: Looser Rules after USA Election Recount*
    b. *New President: Loser Rules after USA Election Recount*

1a. says the rules for counting votes are now not as tight as they used to be, whereas 1b. claims that the candidate who actually got fewer votes has been declared president.

We have two minimal pairs here: In 1a., *Precedent* and *Looser* have the voice-less fricative [s]: [ˈpresɪdənt] and [ˈluːsə], whereas in 1b. *President* and *Loser* have the voiced [z]: [ˈprezɪdənt] and [ˈluːzə]. The [z] sounds are fully voiced in 1b because they occur between two vowels (i.e. intervocalically), so the vocal folds continue vibrating throughout the word *loser*. This applies also to [z] in *rules* as it follows a sonorant sound and gets linked to the initial vowel in *after*, so in spite of the word boundary, phonetically speaking the [z] in *"rules after"* [ˈruːɫzɑːftə] is between two sonorants. But now let us look at the phoneme /z/ in other positions:

2   a. *The best cause for us would be to fight starvation with peace.*
    b. *The best course for us would be to fight starvation with peas.*

Again we have two minimal pairs. If you look them up in a dictionary you will find the following phonetic transcriptions for them: *cause* [kɔːz] vs. *course* [kɔːs], and *peas* [piːz] vs. *peace* [piːs]. The phonetic convention here obscures the fact that the English alveolar fricative which is given the symbol /z/ is partly or even fully devoiced if not followed by a vowel or sonorant consonant. What distinguishes *peas* [piːz] from *peace* [piːs] is not primarily the phonetic difference voiced vs. voiceless, i.e. vibrating vocal folds vs. abducted, non-vibrating folds, but – as we pointed out in IV.1. and IV.2.1-2. – the longer duration of [iː] in *peas* [piːz] and the weaker muscular effort for [z], which is referred to as "lenis". A narrow phonetic transcription could be used to indicate the lack of vibration of the vocal folds by using a small circle under the [z] to indicate devoicing: *peace* [piːs] is voiceless and fortis, whereas the fricative in *peas* [piːz̥] is devoiced and lenis. In *fussy* ['fʌsi] the alveolar fricative is completely voiceless and in *fuzzy* ['fʌzi] it is fully voiced because it is in intervocalic position.

There are good didactic reasons for adhering to the notation of /s/ and /z/ in spite of the fact that /z/ does not always imply "voiced". First of all, there are no minimal pairs like /piːz/ vs. /piːs/ in German, and the trap that German speakers tend to fall into is to make the pronunciation of *green peas* sound more like *Greenpeace*. So the /s/ vs. /z/ notation serves as a constant reminder of the distinction in English. And secondly, when it comes to linking, /s/ remains voiceless, but /z/ becomes fully voiced.

C 1.: Listen and repeat:

a. *seal - zeal; zip - sip*

b. *fussy - fuzzy; looser - loser; rules* [z̥], *loser rules after election* ['ruːɬz̥ɑːftə]

c. *Zorro's sorrows were over after he had rescued Sue from the zoo. - Was her going to the zoo part of this Greenpeace campaign? - Yes, they claim these campaigns against the ozone hole are a race against time in the fight against dangerous rays. - She joined them even though she's afraid of fierce animals, but what actually happened there exceeded her worst fears. - Yes, they were treated like animals by the police. - Please, spare me the gory details.*

d. *Any luck with the little Miss you wanted to take to "Close encounters of the third kind"? - You mean Ms Bonzo, don't you. - Oh yes, the little Miss that Bruce is dating. - Ms Bonzo, to you, Les, if you please. - Okay, okay, did you and Ms Bonzo see the film? - Well, it came to close encounters of the third kind, but actually before the film. - Oh, is that how Bruce got his bruise? - Yes, Les. The show-off had borrowed Roy's Rolls Royce and beat me to it. - And then you beat him? Did he lose any teeth? - No, he just had a few loose teeth. - Oh dear. Let's face it, you're going through a difficult phase. - Not really. Liz, I mean Ms Bonzo, realized that it was Roy's Royce and she allowed me to take her out for a meal. - Did you get on well? - Yes, very well. She was just talking about Shakespeare's plays when the fish arrived and I asked innocently "Your plaice or my plaice?" She must have misunderstood me.*

E 1: Write the symbols [s], [z] or [z̥] below the letters <zz>, <z> and <s> as appropriate:

a. (from "Winnie-the-Pooh") *That buzzing noise means something. You don't get a buzzing-noise like that, just buzzing and buzzing, without its meaning something. If there's a buzzing noise, somebody is making a buzzing-noise, and the only reason for making a buzzing noise that I know of is because you're a bee."*

b. *If a man has ten sons and each son has a sister, how many children has he altogether? - Eleven, because the daughter is each son's sister.*

E 2: Pair work. Choose any of the following four phrases and dictate them to your partner, keeping track of the order in which you read them out loud and then compare notes to make sure that she or he wrote down the intended version.

1. a. *Keep your eyes on the prize.* 2. a. *The price of peace.*
  b. *Keep your eyes on the price.*   b. *The prize of peace.*
  c. *Keep your ice on the prize.*   c. *The price of peas.*
  d. *Keep your ice on the price.*   d. *The prize of peas.*

Difficult words

We would like to remind you of some "favourite" mistakes, first of all with a verbal expression we touched on in IV.1. The good students, who have mastered the fortis/lenis distinction correctly say:

3 a. *We use* [juːz]*Word 6 on our computers./ We used* [juːzd]...

But the verb *to use* (G. *benutzen*) is phonetically different from *used to* (G. *früher*), where the fricative is fortis:

 b. *We used to use Word 6* [ˈjuːstə juːz]*, but now we only use* [juːz]*Word 7.*

The noun *use* also has the fortis fricative so, again, the vowel is much shorter:

 c. *What's the use of it?* [wɒts ðə ˈjuːsəvɪt]

It is a good idea to learn and teach these words only as phrases, as in 3 b. and 3 c., and never in isolation.

As most Germans tend to make the mistake of saying *[wi ˈjuːst ɪt ə ˈlɒt] instead of [wi ˈjuːzdɪtə ˈlɒt] for "We used it a lot.", the incorrect voiced pronunciation of *the use* and *used to* is a case of hypercorrect pronunciation: the student has become too good and has to unlearn the voicing with these two forms. The same applies to *has*, which – in its strong form – is pronounced [hæz], but *has to* in the sense of obligation is [hæstə]:

4. *Has he got access to e-mail? - Oh yes, he has* [hæz]*. He has to use it for his job.*
 [hi ˈhæstə ˈjuːzɪt fərɪz ˈdʒɒb]

Incidentally, the same rule applies to *Yes, I have* ([hæv]) as opposed to *I have to do it.* ([ˈhæftə]).

60   /s/ vs. /z/

Fig. 1: Housing advertisement

The change from a lenis fricative in the verb (*to use*) to a fortis fricative in the corresponding noun can also be observed in the pairs *advise* (vb) vs *advice* (n) and *house* (vb) (G. *für eine Wohnung sorgen*) and *house* (n). In figure 1 the pronunciation has to be [haʊz] as *house* is the verb here. So *House our youth* is a homophone of *How's our youth?*

Another case of hypercorrection is the wrong voiced ending of *cease*, which has to be kept distinct from *seize*:

5. *My teenage daughter never ceases* [ˈsiːsɪz] *to surprise me. At times she does not seem to take an interest in anything at all, and at other times she seizes* [ˈsiːzɪz] *every opportunity.*

Some other facts you simply have to learn are that *geese* [giːs] does not rhyme with *cheese* [ʧiːz], and that *dissolve* as in *Sugar dissolves in water* is pronounced [dɪˈzɒɫvz], despite the <ss> and despite its connection to *solve*.

Spelling

/s/ can be represented orthographically as:

<s> *song, bus, cats*   <ss> *chess, missing*
<c> *cent, magnificent; France*   <sc> *scissors, omniscient,*
silent <s> *Calais* [ˈkæleɪ], *chamois, debris* [ˈdebri], *patois, isle, aisle, island*

/z/ can be spelt:

<z> *zero, lazy*
<zz> *buzz, fuzzy*
<x> *Xerox* [ˈzɪərɒks], *xylophone*
<s> *Archimedes, Socrates, Muslim, Israel, Islam,* and all words ending in *-ism*
<ss> *scissors, dissolve, Missouri* [mɪˈzʊəri]
<ex> /gz/*executive, example* (see IV.2.1, in particular C 2)

Smileys:

1. [aɪ ˈjuːstə bi ˌɪndɪˈsaɪsɪv bət ˈnaʊ̯ aɪm nɒt sə ˈʃʊə] Boscoe Pertwee (eighteenth century wit).

2. Q. *How many psychiatrists does it take to change a lightbulb?*
   A. *Only one, but the lightbulb <u>has to</u> want to change.* (cf. "have to")

3. Graffiti: *Lethargy rulezzzzz*

For a discussion of the pronunciation of <-s> and <-es> as grammatical endings see VII.1.2.

To conclude, we hope our account of alveolar fricatives has not put you to sleep...........

IV.2.4. /ʃ/ vs. /ʒ/ and /ʧ/ vs. /ʤ/: *Rouge on your ruche or lipstick on your collar! Is that a choice for Joyce?*

If we were living in the sixteenth or seventeenth century we might possibly be worried about incriminating signs of *rouge* on our *ruches* (German: *Halskrause*), though, today, neither that sort of adornment to our clothing nor the cosmetic use of rouge is particularly common. And with smudge-proof lipstick, men no longer even have to worry about marks of secret "socializing". The significance of the phrase is, however, not that it signals a change in fashion, but that these two words together with *Confucian* vs. *confusion* represent about the only minimal pairs which support the classification of /ʃ/ vs. /ʒ/ as a phonemic opposition (cf. section III.4).

Infobox

The number of words that are distinguished by a particular phonemic opposition is called its **functional load**. With only two pairs of words depending on the /ʃ - ʒ/ opposition, its functional load can safely be classed as low!

As far as the articulation of the sounds is concerned, neither should cause a problem for most German speakers. In German /ʃ/ occurs in all positions: Word-initially in *Schuh*, *Ski* and *Schein*, word-medially in *Pascha*, *tuscheln* and *Kirsche*, and word-finally in *lasch*, *Busch* and *Fisch*. /ʒ/, on the other hand, only occurs in loanwords from French, word-initially as in *geniert*, *Genre* and *Gendarme*, and word-medially as in *Blamage*, *couragiert* and *Staffage*. Like all other voiced obstruents, it cannot occur word-finally because of the German "final devoicing" rule. It is in the word-final position that it is most likely to cause problems.

But is it worth making a fuss? /ʒ/ is a very rare sound in English, not just in terms of minimal pairs, but in terms of general occurrence. In English it also appears mainly in loanwords from French, like *largesse* /ˌlaːˈʒes/, *garage* /ˈgæraːʒ/, and *mirage* /ˈmɪraːʒ/, and even then it is optionally replaced by /ʤ/, viz. /ˌlaːˈʤes/, /ˈgærɪʤ/, and /ˈmɪraːʤ/. For that reason we decided to treat /ʃ/-/ʒ/ and /ʧ/-/ʤ/ together. So, like Joyce in the limerick in 1., you always have a choice!

But the choice does not really help because although /ʤ/ exists in German – again in foreign words (*Dschinn*, *Dschungel*, *Maharadscha*) – it is also a voiced obstruent and causes the same problems in word-final position as /ʒ/. Also, to actually *have* a choice you need to know which words can be pronounced with /ʒ/.

1. *The famous astronomer Boyce*
   Neglected his lovely wife Joyce.
   While he searched in the stars,
   She frequented the bars,
   Claiming there she´d a much greater choice.

   [ðə ˈfeɪməs̩ əsˈtrɒnəmə ˈbɔɪs
   nɪˈglektɪdɪz ˈlʌvli waɪf ˈʤɔɪs
   waɪli ˈsɜːtʃtɪnðə ˈstɑːz
   ʃi frɪˈkwentɪd ðə ˈbɑːz
   kleɪmɪŋ ˈðeə ʃiːdə ˈmʌtʃ greɪtə
   ˈtʃɔɪs]

E 1: Read and note the following /ʒ/ words:

1. Words of vowel + <-sure> and vowel + <-sion> ⟹ (compulsory /ʒ/)

a. *measure*	[ˈmeʒə]	b. *leisure*	[ˈleʒə]
c. *treasure*	[ˈtreʒə]	d. *pleasure*	[ˈpleʒə]
e. *closure*	[ˈkləʊʒə]	f. *embrasure*	[ɪmˈbreɪʒə]
g. *intrusion*	[ɪnˈtruːʒən]	h. *evasion*	[ɪˈveɪʒən]
i. *erosion*	[ɪˈrəʊʒən]	j. *elision*	[ɪˈlɪʒən]
k. *cohesion*	[kəʊˈhiːʒən]	l. *decision*	[dɪˈsɪʒən]

2. There are also <-zure> words with compulsory /ʒ/):
   a. *seizure*   [ˈsiːʒə]
   b. *azure*   [ˈeɪʒə] or [ˈæʒə]
3. Words of the *French* <g> class (optional /ʒ/ or /ʤ/):
   a. *garage*   [ˈgæraːʒ], [gəˈraːʒ] or [ˈgærɪʤ]
   b. *massage*   [ˈmæsaːʒ] or [ˈmæsaːʤ]
   c. *mirage*   [ˈmɪraːʒ] or [ˈmɪraːʤ]
   d. *largesse*   [laːˈʒes] or [laːˈʤes]
   e. *liege*   [liːʒ] or [liːʤ]
   f. *prestige*   [presˈtiːʒ] or [presˈtiːʤ]

But the following words seem not to have given in to /ʤ/ pressure yet and are only pronounced with /ʒ/:

   g. *beige*   [beɪʒ]
   h. *potage*   [pəʊˈtaːʒ] (German: Gemüsesuppe)

Using [ʒ] instead of [ʤ] does have certain social connotations though. Such matters may appear anachronistic in this egalitarian day and age, but it may be of interest to our readers to know that [ʒ] speakers used to be considered more educated and solidly Middle Class. Then the effects of more equally distributed educational opportunity led to increased contact and verbal communication between members of previously separated social groups. So the [ˈgæraːʒ] or [gəˈraːʒ] and [ˈmæsaːʒ] pronunciation of *garage* and *massage* spread – and the new prestige [preˈstiːʒ] pronunciation by those who wished to keep themselves distinct from the aspiring masses became [ˈgærɪʤ] and [ˈmæsaːʤ] – the same as the "working classes" (if they ever had cause to use such words)! And of course, aspiring to use [ʒ] brings the danger of using it wrongly. There are some words like *homage* and *dotage*, which seem special and rare enough to have retained some pronunciation traces of their French origins, but which are pronounced [ˈhɒmɪʤ] (German: *Huldigung*) and [ˈdəʊtɪʤ] (German: *Altersschwäche*) and nothing else!

/ʃ/ or /ʒ/?

In E 1.1. above we gave a number of <-sure> and <-sion> words as examples to illustrate the compulsory [ʒ] pronunciation. They contrast with <-ture> words, which are pronounced [tʃ] (*nature, feature, future*) and <-tion> words, which are compulsorily pronounced with [ʃ] (*nation, lenition, contribution*).

So far so good! But you will presumably have been learning English long enough to expect nothing to be quite that simple. Words like *censure, tonsure, mansion, pension, emulsion, expulsion* are pronounced with [ʃ]. Can you think of a reason why? Before you say *"There are always exceptions"*, pause for a second and try and work out why. If they were chance exceptions, it would mean that an English speaker would have had to learn whether each individual <-sion> word – and there are over 200 of them – is pronounced with [ʃ] or [ʒ]. That not only seems an unnecessary burden on the memory, it also fails to explain why no-one forgets, nor why they get a new word, say a word like *dissension*, right the first time.

Did you work out the rule that "after /l/ and /n/ the <-sure> and <-sion> are pronounced with [ʃ]"? That is certainly correct, but it misses the generalisation that they are pronounced [ʃ] if the preceding syllable ends with any letters that may be pronounced as consonants . This applies to <l> and <n> in *emulsion* and *tension*, but can also include other consonant-letters.

The phrase "letters that may be pronounced as consonants" is important for the generalised rule above because we then have an explanation why *conversion*, *excursion* and *mission* are also pronounced with [ʃ]. Of course, after section "III.3. *A Letter is a Letter and a Sound is a Sound*", you might protest that a /ʒ/ should be predicted for these words because the <r> in *excursion* is a *letter* that is not pronounced postvocalically (in standard English), so there is no consonantal *sound* preceding the <-sion>, and that the same goes for *mission*, because phonetically you get a vowel before the [ʃ]. You are absolutely right, but the solution to this apparent contradiction lies in the fact that the spelling and the pronunciation are - historically speaking - out of phase. The <r> in *excursion* used to be pronounced as /r/ in this position (and still is in many dialects of English), and even though it has disappeared as a sound in SBE, the [ʃ]-rule still applies. It is like someone still bending down when walking past a tree even though the low branch was removed some time ago. And if you think of the <sure> in *pressure* as being preceded by <pres>, the rule for [ʃ] works for all letters preceding <sure> and <-sion> that may be pronounced as consonants. So this rule also covers *pressure* and *fissure*, *session* and *mission* being pronounced with [ʃ] while *treasure* and *lesion* and *vision* are pronounced with [ʒ]. And as you would expect with an out-of-phase state, there may be movement within the system: Words like *conversion* and *excursion* can *also* be pronounced with [ʒ] (to practise [ʒ] see the limerick on p. 68).

Common or garden /ʤ/:

The gradual suppression of potential [ʒ] pronunciations by [ʤ] is probably due to the frequent use of [ʤ] in English words that are not clear loans from French. There are many words that are spelt with a <dg>, where the [ʤ] pronunciation is unambiguously signalled. Consider the following examples:

2.	*edge*	*ridge*	*lodge*	*cadge*	*fudge*	*stodge*
	budget	*badger*	*codger*	*lodger*	*widget*	*midget*

Word-initially, a /ʒ/ only occurs in very clearly French words like *gendarme* or *genre*, and the spelling of a lot of English [ʤ]-words with <g> as well as with the unambiguous <j> will presumably have contributed a lot to [ʒ] suppression. The following examples are just a few of the hundreds of words with initial [ʤ] spelt with <g>:

5. German   *gel*   *gelatin*   *gem*   *geminate*   *gender*
   gene   *general*   *Geneva*   *generate*   *generous*   *genius*
   gentle   *geology*   *George*   *germ*   *gerund*   *giant*
   gin   *ginger*   *gipsy*   *giraffe*   *gibberish*   *gist*
   gym   *gymnastics*

Please note that not all words beginning with <gi>, <ge> and <gy> have [ʤ]: Apart from the obvious *get* and *give* there are a few you may like to memorise, as, e.g. *gills* [gɪɫz] (German *Kiemen*) and *gynaecologist* [ˌgaɪnəˈkɒlədʒɪst] (but *gyroscope* [ˈʤaɪrəskəʊp]).

Though the sound [ʤ] does exist in the standard pronunciation of some German loan words like *Dschungel*, *Marahadscha* and *Dschinn*, there is strong evidence from the mouths of unspoilt "Bundesbürger" that [ʧ] is a much preferred variant. Just consider the pronunciation of the Japanese word *Fuji* in German and English: Germans say [ˈfʊʧiː] while the English say [ˈfʊʤiː].

Fig. 1: Jeep or cheap imitation?

This means that like the closely related [ʃ] and [ʒ], mentioned above, and unlike the other sound distinctions dealt with in IV.2., the problems of [ʧ] vs. [ʤ] may not be restricted to syllable-final position. To reassure yourself that you have no difficulties in identifying [ʧ] and [ʤ], we will first give you a short listening test:

C 1/E 2: Listen to the following examples and write down whether the words are pronounced correctly with [ʤ] or incorrectly with [ʧ].
   a. *John*   b. *cage*   c. *raging*   d. *jury*   e. *stagecoach*
   f. *alleged*   g. *German*   h. *refuge*   i. *germain*   j. *revenge*

You probably did not have much trouble in distinguishing the sounds. Check your answers with the solutions given at the end of the book. If you *did* make a mistake or two, we predict that they will have occurred in the words where [ʤ] is in syllable-final position. That is the position we have concentrated on in these sections dealing with the fortis-lenis opposition. The following exercise will give you further opportunity to practise the production of this opposition with the [ʧ] vs. [ʤ] sounds:

C 2: Listen and repeat the following word pairs, paying attention to the length of the vowel preceding [ʧ] vs. [ʤ], and to the strength of the affricate.

a. *surge - search*   b. *cadge - catch*   c. *edge - etch*   d. *age - aitch*
e. *Marge - March*   f. *Madge - match*   g. *purge - perch*   h. *ridge - rich*
i. *wadge - watch*   j. *large - larch*   k. *badge - batch*   l. *"veg" - vetch*

Now listen to some of the word pairs in phrases and repeat them:

m. *Poor man! He was no match for Madge.*
n. *The mansions of the rich had all been built up on the ridge.*
o. *That antique badge arrived in the last batch.*
p. *You don't spell "age" with an aitch.*
q. *The treasure spot was marked by an extremely large larch.*

E 3: Exercise in length of the vowel preceding [ʧ] vs. [ʤ]. Read aloud:

The dirge from the church
[ðə ˈdɜːʤ frəm ðə ˈʧɜːʧ]

Young Sue, in a birch by the church,
[jʌŋ ˈsuːʷɪnə ˈbɜːʧ baɪ ðə ˈʧɜːʧ]

Had an urge to jump from her perch.
hædəˈnˏɜːʤ tə ˈʤʌmp frəmə ˈpɜːʧ

"Down there is my Sarge
daʊn ˈðeərɪz maɪ ˈsɑːʤ

getting married to Marge,
getɪŋ ˈmærɪdˏtə ˈmɑːʤ

leaving me with young Reg in the lurch!"
liːvɪŋ ˈmiː wɪð jʌŋ ˈreʤɪn ðə ˈlɜːʧ]

Some English [ʧ] words have [ʃ] equivalents in German:

6. *Charlie*: [ˈʧɑːli] vs. [ˈʃɑːliː]
   English chickens go cheep cheep; Deutsche Küken machen schiep schiep
   There are chimpanzees in British zoos; im deutschen Zoo sind es Schimpansen
   In Britain people have cheque cards; in Deutschland sind es Scheckkarten.

Of course the problem becomes no easier when you discover that *Chicago* is pronounced [ʃɪˈkɑːgəʊ] and not *[ʧɪˈkɑːgəʊ], as the <ch> spelling would lead you to expect. *Chute* and *parachute*, too, are exceptions to the [ʧ] for <ch> rule.

Smileys:

   a. On which day do lions eat people? - On Chewsday.
   b. "I am going to make you a parachute jumper." - "Gee, sergeant, that´s great! I didn´t even know you could knit."

Captain Lurch was the cause of derision,	[kæptɪn ˈlɜːʧ wəz ðə ˈkɔːzəv dəˈrɪʒn̩
Unable to make a decision,	ʌˈneɪbɫ tə ˈmeɪkə dəˈsɪʒn̩
When he saw a bright light,	weni ˈsɔːə braɪt ˈlaɪt
He said: "Right! ... Left! No! Right!"	hi sed ˈraɪt | left | nəʊ ˈraɪt
Which lead to a head-on collision.	wɪʧ ˈled tuə ˈhedɒn kəˈlɪʒn̩]

IV.3. Other consonants

IV.3.1 /v/, /w/ and /f/: *Why wild vines make fine vintage wines*

Say the words *weasel* and *violent* and try to pay particular attention to the sounds at the beginning of these words. Look in the mirror: How would you describe the difference you see? If you are pronouncing the words correctly, for the initial sounds your mouth should have:

a. rounded and slightly protruding lips at the beginning of *weasel*
b. slightly spread lips, top teeth resting on your bottom lip in *violent*.

The difference between [v] and [w] is not merely between different configurations of the lips and teeth. In addition to rounding your lips for [w] you also need to raise the back of your tongue towards the soft palate, as if you wanted to pronounce an [u]. That is why it is called a **labial velar approximant**.

E 1: You should be able to arrive at a good [w] by trying the following:

a. Pronounce *weasel* with a long [u] at the beginning: [u::::::i:zəɫ]. This will give you a good feel for the way your tongue and lips should be.

b. Keep pronouncing *weasel*, gradually shortening the [u] at the beginning. By the end the [u] should be so short that it is no more than the place that your tongue and lips start from when you pronounce the rest of the word.

When you come to think of it, the rounding and the protruding of the lips at the beginning of the word *weasel* is not really what you would expect. Just pronounce the words *keep* [ki:p] and *caught* [kɔ:t] and you will find that the two /k/ sounds are different, because at the same time as you pronounce them your lips get ready for the following vowel. So you pronounce the /k/ in [ki:p] with lip spreading and the /k/ in [kɔ:t] with lip rounding. The [k] in [kɔ:t] is classed as a velar sound, but not as a labial sound, because what you do with your lips is determined by the following sound. You might expect the same sort of anticipation with *weasel* and *water*, but even with /w/ followed by [i] (a vowel with lip spreading) the lips will be rounded in careful pronunciation. This is why [w] is classed as a bilabial sound. Admittedly, in fast speech you may not have time to round your lips properly, but you still have to narrow them to get the sound that is typical for [w]. But whatever you do, avoid the labio-dental fricative [v]. Rounding the lips with [w] is never wrong and it has the great advantage for German learners in that it keeps the lower lip away from the upper teeth, which is one of the reasons why we asked you to practice the pronunciation of *weasel* as [u::::::i:zəɫ].

Pronouncing [w] as [v] is not likely to bring you the fame and fortune it brought Frank Abelson (The Guardian on how the singer got his stage name):

"When he first went into show business, his agent ... declared that Frank Abelson wasn't going to see his name in lights. Frank remembered that his grandmother always called him – in her Russian Jewish accent – my number vawn grandson. So he took her at her word and became Frankie Vaughan."

To summarise: [w] is a voiced labial velar approximant:

Voiced, because the vocal folds vibrate.
Labial, because the lips are rounded and protruded.
Velar, because the back of the tongue raised towards the velum (like an [u]).
An approximant, because the constrictions – either at the lips or at the velum – are not narrow enough to cause friction.

When you pronounce the [v] in *violent* ['vaɪələnt] you put your lower lip against your upper teeth, switch on your voice and hear the air squeeze through teeth and lips. Or put differently: **[v]** is a **labio-dental voiced fricative**.

It is similar to the first consonant in *weil* and *Wasser* as pronounced by speakers in the North of Germany. Similar, but not identical, because in English you use more energy. We suggest you press the lower lips against the upper teeth harder than usual and say [vvvvv], and then practice it in the phrase *very violent behaviour*, making sure you can clearly hear the friction of the [v] in all the three words. Do not be afraid of overdoing it at the beginning. The danger for Germans – particularly in the southern parts of the country – is to pronounce the [v] so weakly that the English do not recognize it as a [v].

Fig. 1: Anthony Hopkins´ lip position:

a. for [v]   b. for [w]

In the first illustration you see Anthony Hopkins pronouncing a [v] sound. The lower lip is tightly pressed against the upper teeth. Have a close look at the region around the corners of his mouth and you can actually see the tension, the muscular effort that goes into the production of this fricative. The connection between hearing and seeing sounds was well-put by Joost van Vondels, who said to Rembrandt: *"... paint Cornelis' voice. If one wants to see Anslo, one has to hear him."*

In an attempt to emphasize a statement, the English often repeat the adverb *very*, as in *That´s very very interesting*. Now if you do that without any muscular effort for the [v], your pronunciation works in the opposite direction and the statement sounds as funny as the German remark: *Die deutsche Sprache hat richig Saf´ un´ Kraf´*.

Fig. 2: [ændə'nʌðə 'seɪfti ˌfi:tʃə ðət wiv dɪ'veləpt ǀ ə 'verɪ 'verɪ wi:'kendʒɪn] ("Pick of Punch", Punch Publications Ltd.)

Listen to the following production exercises (C 1 - C 3) and then pronounce them yourself. Try to imitate the speakers as closely as possible. If you are still not sure that your lips are doing the right thing use the mirror again.

C 1: Listen and repeat

A lively young man from the West,   [ə 'laɪvli jʌŋ 'mæn frəm ðə 'west
loved a woman called Vickey with zest.   lʌvdə 'wumən kɔ:ɫd 'vɪki wɪð 'zest
So hard did he press her   səu 'hɑ:d dɪdi 'presə
to make her say, "Yes Sir",   tə 'meɪkə seɪ 'jes sə
she squashed the cigar in his vest.   ʃi 'skwɒʃt ðə sɪ'gɑ:rɪnɪz 'vest]

C 2: Listen and repeat

What are you reading now, Vivien? - I finished "Oliver Twist" last week and I am now reading "The Vicar of Wakefield", it´s a novel by Oliver Goldsmith. - Wow, you seem to be devouring these fat volumes. Personally, I prefer William Wordsworth´s verses; they are shorter! - Why don´t you try a short novel, Walter, like "The Wind in the Willows" or Virginia Woolf´s "The Waves", or... - Vivien, you read a novel every week. Why don´t you go to university and study literature? Getting a university degree is a tremendous advantage these days. - What kind of university course would you suggest, Walter? - What about English Language and Literature at Warwick University? - Why Warwick? - It´s very close to where your relatives live . - Well, that could very well turn out to be a disadvantage. - Ok, what about Coventry, Liverpool or even Inverness?

C 3: Listen and repeat

Who is your internet provider? - My provider is Compuserve, and I use Netscape Navigator to get into the world wide web. - Isn´t the world wide web a waste of time? We were investigating Victorian values last week, and the web was a complete waste of valuable time. - Well, sometimes it´s well worth your while. - So what were you looking up in the world wide web? - I want to know what school leavers do after they´ve taken their A-levels. - What´s an A-level? Is it a kind of university entrance qualification? - Yes, it stands for advanced level and is a school leaver´s certificate. -

Wery vell, said Hans, *or*
The Sad Case of The Man Who Knew too Much (Part I)

Even when German learners have managed to articulate English [v] and [w] correctly, they often make mistakes like poor old Hans in the heading of this subsection. The reason for this is simple: German beginners tend to be hypnotised by the letters, and when they see the word *weather* they may pronounce the letter <w> as they have learned to say it in German: *[ˈveðə]. The teacher corrects them every time by saying: *No. It´s not* [ˈveðə], *it is* [ˈweðə]. So eventually the learner breaks the old habit, and every time he feels tempted to press the lower lip against the upper teeth he anticipates the teacher´s comment and corrects himself by rounding the lips for a beautiful [w]. Everytime. And that´s where the hidden trap is. Next time he wants to say [ˈverɪ] he remembers the teacher´s words: *It´s not* [v], *it´s* [w], and corrects himself by beautifully but wrongly pronouncing the word as *[ˈwerɪ]. This is a perfectly normal transitional stage on the way to perfect pronunciation. The pupil simply has become too good. Making a mistake in the attempt to avoid it, i.e. the application of a rule to an instance where it does not apply, is called **hypercorrection**.

Another source of mispronunciation of [w] are English loan words, where the native speaker of German may have to unlearn using a [v] for the letter <w>:

1.	German [v] in:	English [w] in:	German [v] in:	English [w] in:
	Hardware	*hardware*	*quick*	*quick*
	Software	*software*	*Queen*	*queen*

If Roosevelt were alive he´d turn in his grave, *or* The problem of In All the Right Places.

No matter whether the last letter of a German word is <w>, <v> or <f>, (as in the Russian name *Kirov, Kirow* or *Kiroff*) they are always pronounced [f], because there are no lenis consonants, like [v], at the end of a German word (cf. sections IV.1. and IV.2. on fortis-lenis). This explains why the English word [laɪv], as in *The match was broadcast live* is pronounced [laɪf] when it is used as a loanword in German: *Das wird heute live gesendet.* This is perfectly all right, and you would sound pretty arrogant if you pronounced it as [laɪv] in a German sentence, i.e. with a much longer syllable and a lenis ending. As loan words *live* (adj.) and *life* are not distinguished phonetically.

When O.J. Simpson's murder trial was in the media there were two questions: would the trial be broadcast *live*, and if found guilty, would he get *life*? Look at fig. 3 and imagine the implications of not distinguishing between the two.

Fig. 3: Live or life?

Practise speaking the following word pairs, concentrating on the length of the vowel preceding [v] and the weaker friction in [v] than [f].

2a. *serve*   *surf*   *five*   *Fife*
     live   *life*   *leave*   *leaf*

There are some alternations between verb and noun (2b) and between the plural and singular forms of nouns (2c):

2b. *believe*   *belief*   2c. *lives*   *life*
     calve   *calf*   *thieves*   *thief*
     prove   *proof*   *wives*   *wife*
     relieve   *relief*   *wolves*   *wolf*
     shelve   *shelf*   *knives*   *knife*

With the above plural forms you have to be aware of the fact that the [v] here triggers off the lengthening of the vowel and the voicing of the plural ending. The noun *hoof* has two alternative plural forms, written *hoofs* and *hooves* respectively. They are pronounced [hu:fs] and [hu::vz]. As we explain in the chapter on morphophonology, this is a phonetic rule of assimilation that goes for all three grammatical endings with the letter <s>, i.e. genitive ´s, plural s and third person singular. That is why you can hear the contrast between voiced [vz] on the one hand, and voiceless [fs] on the other, even with phonetic pairs of a verb form and a noun form like:

3.   *He believes* [bɪˈliː::vz] vs. *his beliefs* [bɪˈliːfs]

C 4: Listen to the following limerick and repeat

An eccentric old man of St. Ives,   [ən ɪkˈsentrɪk əʊɬd ˈmæn frəm sənˈtaɪvz
Who callously murdered his wives,   hu ˈkæləsli ˈmɜːdədɪz ˈwaɪvz
Said, "It's not quite the thing,   sedɪts ˈnɒt kwaɪt ðə ˈθɪŋ
But I thought it would bring   bətaɪ ˈθɔːtɪt wəd ˈbrɪŋ
Some eventfulness into their lives."   sʌm‿əˈventfʊɬnəˈsɪntəðɛ ˈlaɪvz]

The Sad Case of The Man Who Knew too Much (Part II)

So you do not make mistakes like *Dafe and I hef twelfe oliffss* and you proudly announce this progress by saying: *One doesn't have to have a foreign accent*, where you pronounce the part in the middle: *[ˈhævtəˌhævə]. Nice try, as they say. But it is wrong, because the correct pronunciation for *have to have a* ... is [ˈhæftəˌhævə]. As this form is used so frequently you will [ˈhæftə rɪˈmembərɪt].

This is a rather special case of how words change depending on the sounds in the words around them (see "chapter VI. Putting sounds together" for a thorough treatment of how words are linked together). In this case, the very frequent expression *have to* has become like a single word *haveto*. In a word-medial sequence of fricative + plosive it is usual to have both voiced or both unvoiced, but not a mixture of voiced + voiceless or vice versa. Here, the voiceless /t/ has affected the /v/ of *have* and we end up with [ˈhæftə].

Since you have also mastered the difference between *surfer* and *server*, you may be tempted to pronounce the phrase *the Church of England* as *[ðə ˌtʃɜːtʃəf ˈɪŋglənd]. But in spite of its spelling the preposition *of* has a voiced ending, both in its weak and its strong form (see VI.3. for details):

4.   [ðə ˌtʃɜːtʃəˈv‿ɪŋglənd]
     [ðæts wɒt juv gɒtəbi‿əˈweərɒv] *That's what you've got to be aware of.*

This keeps it apart from the word *off* [ɒf].

Problems with spelling and pronunciation

Problems with spelling? You are in good company:

> *Mr. Weller spelled with a `wee´.* (Ch. Dickens)

> *Why do Chelsea girls love BMWs and VWs? - Because they are the only car makes they can spell.*

Possible spellings for /w/ are:

> *- witch, which, quilt, choir, language, suite [swiːt], one, Kuala Lumpur.*

The letter <w> is not pronounced as [w] but as [h] in, e.g.: *who, whom, whole, whore*, and in the following letter sequences it is merely part of the ortho-graphic representation of the vowel: <-aw> like *saw* and *dawn*, <-ow> as in *How now brown cow?*, <-ew> as in *few*, <-iew> as in *view*, and in *ewe* [juː] (female sheep).

The letter <w> is also not pronounced, i.e. it is silent, in all words beginning with <wr->, as for example: *writing, wrap, wrestler, wreck, Wrexham*; and it is also not pronounced in a number of proper names after <r>, as in:

> *Harwich* [ˈhærɪtʃ],   *Norwich* [ˈnɒrɪtʃ]
>
> *Warwick* [ˈwɒrɪk],   *Berwick* [ˈberɪk]

The /v/ sound is represented orthographically by <v> with the exceptions of:

of, which is pronounced [əv] or [ɒv]
Stephen is pronounced like *Steven*.

Show Off! Tongue Twisters for the Advanced

E 2: Read the following passage at normal speed:

The cheese and wine party in Walt´s vaults:
Gosh, it´s very stuffy in Walt´s vaults. - Well, that´s not my fault. - Where is Walt, anyway? - He went to check the air vent five minutes ago. - Again? He can never leave well alone, can he? - Oh stop whining, will you? Would you like another glass of wine? - Yes, please, I´d love one. - Why don´t you try this vintage wine. - I think there are only twelve wines in the whole wide world worth sampling. - Sorry, did you say `twelve vines´? - No, `twelve wines´. They are really very fine wines. - I suppose you have to have them delivered to your wine cellar. - Oh look, Vickey Willerby has just arrived. She´s a VIP in the media world. - Yes, I´ve read her article `Why women are not allowed at the wailing wall´ in The Village Voice. - She got an award for that from Woman´s Own Voice. Have you ever won a prize? - Yes, I once won one in Vawn Wannemaker´s Wonderful One Woman Show. - Wow!

E 3: Give a phonetic transcription of each word containing <v> (the solution is given in chapter XII):

Man: *I´ll have apple-pie without custard please.*
Waiter: *Sorry, sir, we don´t serve it with custard. You´ll have to have it without cream.*

Smileys:

A German host said to his English guest, who was obviously not enjoying his meal: "I´m sorry you don´t like our food, but I´m afraid the wurst is yet to come."

Vivien, you know this vase you were worried I might break? - Yes, Wendy, what about it? - Well, your worries are over.

Waiter, have you got frog´s legs? - No, Sir, I always walk this way.

Q: What do you call snakes on your car windscreen?
A: Windscreen vipers.

A verbal contract isn´t worth the paper it´s written on.

IV.3.2. /r/: *I'm tewwibly sowwy!* or chameleon R

The apology in the title is of course a trick to attract your attention to one of the funny varieties of /r/ that are found in English – perhaps you can remember the pronunciation of *Brian* in the Monty Python film; it should really have been called *Life of Bwian*! Phonetic variety is the hallmark of the /r/ sound. It is the most varied sound in German, though most people are not aware of it and in English too, there are a number of varieties. Some of them even overlap with the German varieties, though unfortunately the area of overlap contains the varieties that are considered non-standard in English. So you are faced with the problem of mixed accents if you go for a non-standard /r/ because it will not fit in with the other English sounds you have learned.

You have no doubt forgotten your many weeks of intensive articulation practice in German (you were, after all, less than a year old!), and have been happily using the result of that practice ever since, without giving a moment's thought to it. So you have probably not considered the complexities of the /r/ sound. Let us introduce you to the delights of the R-world. We hope the information on German /r/ will help you to realise which sorts of /r/ you use yourself, and that should prepare you for hearing the different English /r/ sounds.

Fig. 1: GRRRAHAM'S PORT

The wonders of R

Many /r/ varieties – whether English or German – are dependent on the context in which they occur. In German, after a vowel, particularly syllable- and word-finally, the /r/ often weakens so much that it becomes a vowel [ɐ].

E 1: Pronounce the following German words and listen whether you produce a vowel-like /r/ or a consonantal (fricative or rolled) /r/:

> *vor*, [foːɐ], für [fyːɐ], *leer*, [leːɐ], *Lauer*, [laʊɐ], *bitter* [ˈbɪtɐ], *Mutter* [ˈmʊtɐ]

In Southern British English the post-vocalic /r/ disappears completely (*Shah* [ʃɑː] and *far* [fɑː], *saw* [sɔː] and *four* [fɔː] are perfect rhymes). After a /p/, /t/ or /k/ the /r/ loses its voiced quality in both languages (compare also /l/, section III.1)

E 2: Pronounce the following German and English word pairs and listen to what happens when you release the stop closure:

> *Brei - Preis,*   *Droge - Troge,*   *Greis - Kreis or*
> *bray - pray,*   *dray - tray,*   *grow - crow*

But in German there is also a free choice (it is only theoretically free, as we shall explain in a minute) between a front /r/ – apical/r/ – using the tongue tip (apex) against the alveolar ridge, behind the upper front teeth, and a back /r/ – uvular /r/ – where the uvula vibrates against, or produces friction with the raised back part (dorsum) of the tongue. The phonetic symbols are [r] and [ɾ] for multiple taps (trill) and a single tap or flap of the tongue tip, respectively. For the back /r/, the symbol for the tap, trill or roll is [ʀ], and for the fricative it is [ʁ] .

C 1: Listen to the words *Preis, Brei, Karren, hart* pronounced with different apical and uvular /r/ sounds.

> a. apical trill   b. apical tap   c. uvular roll   d. uvular fricative

These are the basic choices, and they determine the nature of most other con- textual variants. However, the *choice* of one of these free variants is really only a pseudo-choice because it is determined to a large degree by the region you grow up in and/or by the accent spoken by your parents. In the regions in which Austro-Bavarian or North-German Plattdeutsch dialects are spoken, you are likely to grow up using a front /r/, even if your predominant lan- guage is Hochdeutsch rather than the regional dialect. Outside those regions, you will be more likely to use a back /r/.

Infobox

Varieties of R. The back /r/ itself has two distinct varieties, a rolled (or trilled) variant /ʀ/, where the **uvula** (/ˈjuːvjələ/; Deutsch: **Zäpfchen**) actually vibrates in the airstream, and the fricative variant /ʁ/, where the tensed uvula forms a narrow gap causing friction as the airstream passes through.

In English, there is practically no choice between the back and front varieties; English nearly everywhere uses a front /r/, a tongue-tip or tongue-blade variety (some South African varieties use a uvular /r/, [ʁ], and there *is one* small dialect enclave in England, on the Humber estuary in North East England, that is reported to have a uvular /r/). So if you have the back /r/ in German you are faced with a radical change in the articulator you use for English /r/. The automatic upward movement of the tongue dorsum whenever a word has an /r/ has to be suppressed, and you have to persuade the front of the tongue to become active. As we have stressed with other problem sounds, the difficulty of eradicating an articulatory habit and developing a new one is *not* to be underestimated!

Life is unfair!

German speakers with a tongue-tip /r/ obviously have a big advantage to start with, because they are at least using the correct part of the tongue. However, if they just transfer their German apical trilled or tapped /r/ to English, they will be using a sound that is non-standard though common in many areas of Scotland and Ireland. The standard /r/, transcribed phonetically as [ɹ], is produced with the tongue tip and blade raised, but without any tap. It is called an approximant because the articulator (tongue tip and blade) is brought *close* to the place of articulation without making contact, and it is not close enough to cause friction (see the Infobox on different classes of consonants in section IV). Fig. 2 gives you an idea of the position and shape of the tongue.

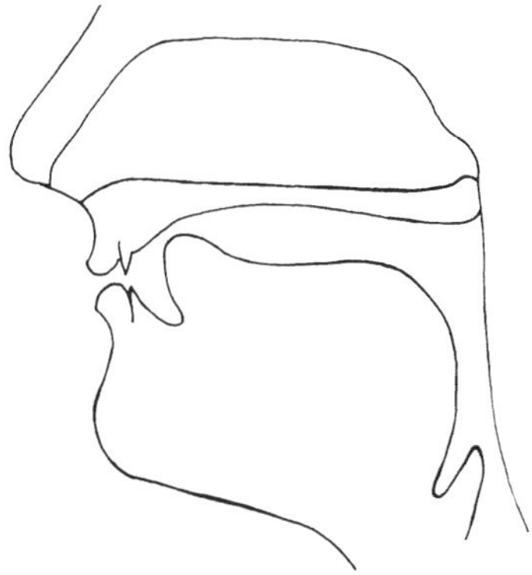

Fig. 2: Tongue position for the English approximant [ɹ]

C 2: Listen to the English (post-)alveolar approximant [ɹ] in different contexts:

    a. Word-initial: *reed, wreck, raft, rose, room*
    b. Intervocalic: *weary, merry, carry, sorry, fury*
    c. Initial cluster: *priest, Brie, press, bread, pram, bracket, proof, bruise*

If you are a person who likes to mimic speakers with other accents, you will have probably already mastered [ɹ], the English approximant /r/. If not, you need to start playing with your tongue tip and trying to persuade your tongue dorsum to stay still!

Exercises for those who have (almost) given up trying!

We suggest you work through the text of these graded exercises, carefully trying them out, and then listen to the examples on the tape all together at the end.

We can best start with an intervocalic [ɹ] as in *hurry*. Start with a long [ə:::::::::] (a sort of hesitation sound) and – while you are producing it – move your tongue tip slowly *upwards* and slightly *backwards*, (as if you were trying to touch the middle of the roof of your mouth; but only take it *half way* there), and then back to the [ə:::::::::]. Do that several times, trying to get gradually faster with your tongue tip movements, and *listen to yourself* while you are doing it. You should hear two syllables, a sort of [ə:ɹə:]. While you are moving your tongue tip up and back, you can make the [ɹ] sound stronger and more English by *slightly* rounding your lips at the same time.

Now try it between other vowels, moving your tongue tip slowly at first and then speeding up. You can then move onto proper words like *berry, very, Arran, carry, hurry, curry, sorry, lorry, fiery* (/ˈfaɪɹi/), *fairy*. Listen to yourself as you are saying them, and when you repeat the exercises at the end of this section, compare your own production with the recordings to make sure they sound English.

You are now ready to take up the [ɹ] position before you speak, and then produce an initial [ɹ], moving from that position as you start to speak to the sounds for the rest of the word: *reap, real, red, wrecked, rapid, rattle, rather, rascal, run, root,* and again compare your pronunciation with the recorded version when you repeat them at the end of the section.

The last stage is to combine the [ɹ] with other consonants in clusters like /br, dr, gr/ etc. It is best to start with lip consonants /p, b, f/ because the [ɹ] has to be formed at the same time as the other consonant and the lips do not get in the way of the tongue position for [ɹ]. Say the words *brown, bread, brag, price, prove, praise, fry, freeze, fraught* and check at the end of the section with the recorded versions. Then progress to the back consonants /k/ and /g/ because the tongue tip is still free to get into the [ɹ] position while these sounds are being formed. Say the words *grown, Greek, crag, creek, grove, graze, cry, crawl,* and compare your pronunciation with the recordings. Now try the tongue-tip clusters /tr, dr, ʃr/, which are the most complicated because the tip and blade have to form a compromise between the first consonant and the [ɹ]. For /tr/ and /dr/ the stop closure, and for /ʃ/ the groove, are formed a bit further back than usual, in preparation for the slightly turned back shape needed for the [ɹ]. Try saying *trade, dread, shrug, trice, drove, shred, try, dream, shriek,* and again compare your auditory impression of your own production with the recordings.

Finally, try the /θr/ cluster. This time, you will notice that as you pull your tongue tip back from the interdental position it flaps against the alveolar ridge. This is quite normal, and this is the one context where standard Southern British English actually has an apical tap or flap /θɾ/. Practise with the following words: *three, through, throw, threaten, thrilling,* and just to make it difficult *thrice* and *thrash.*

C 3:   Listen and repeat the example words practised above.

a. Intervocalic [ɹ]
berry, very, Arran, carry, hurry, curry, sorry, lorry, fiery (/'faɪɹi/) *fairy*

b. Initial [ɹ]
reap, real, red, wrecked, rapid, rattle, rather, rascal, run, root

c. [ɹ] in consonant clusters
i) labial consonants
brown, bread, brag, price, prove, praise, fry, freeze, fraught

ii) velar consonants
grown, Greek, crag, creek, grove, graze, cry, crawl, cruel, group

iii) alveolar and post-alveolar consonants
trade, dread, shrug, trice, drove, shred, try, dream, shriek

iv) <th> with /r/ ([ɾ])
three, through, throw, threaten, thrilling, thrice, thrash

Having used the [ɹ] and [ɾ] symbols to represent the phonetic properties of the English /r/ variants in different contexts, to simplify matters we shall now revert to the basic [r] symbol for any transcriptions containing /r/.

Sorry or sowwy?

Returning to the labialised /r/ illustrated in the title of this chapter: It is a fairly rare, but frequently satirised variety which, strangely, seems to be more common among the higher social classes. A number of very prominent politicians have sported it, with no disadvantage to their career. We are now in a position to describe it as well, after discussing the articulation of a standard /r/. It is not really a [w] – the people who use it make a systematic difference between *red* and *wed*. It is a very weak [ɹ] gesture with the tongue blade augmented by stronger than usual lip-rounding gesture. We are not asking you to practise this variety of /r/ – unless you wish to become a prominent British politician! But you might like to experiment with the degree of lip-rounding and the degree to which you turn your tongue tip back.

The /r/ that comes and goes!

While we are dealing with /r/, we would like to bring to your attention what happens to words ending in the missing postvocalic /r/ when they are combined with other words beginning with a vowel. Compare *She bought a pair* /ʃi ˈbɔːtə peə/ with *She bought a pair of shoes* /ʃi ˈbɔːtə peərəv ˈʃuːz/. In the chapter on linking (section VI.1) we have stressed how important it is to run the words together. The final /r/ helps to run words together.

We can perhaps best understand the process in English if we think of the /r/ as *really being there*, with a rule which says that:

If a consonant or a pause follows the /r/, the /r/ sound is deleted (or it turns into [ə]).

We shall finish this chapter on /r/ by alternating phrases with the deleted postvocalic /r/ and phrases with linking /r/ (you will have other examples to practise in the chapter on linking (section VI.1)), and with a silly little limerick which has the formulaic spelling of <Rt. Rev.> for "Right Reverend", the title used for a bishop, which is transferred in the subsequent lines onto expressions which are not abbreviated in that way. This gives you the task of reconstructing the expressions to rhyme with "Right Reverend" (but note that the second and fifth line do not rhyme perfectly with the first). All the expressions give you /r/-practice.

C 4: Listen and repeat, paying attention to the linking [r]

Come here!	*Come here and talk to me.*
He bought four.	*He bought four of them.*
Don't stare!	*Don't stare at me!*
Pour me a cup of tea, please.	*Pour a cup of tea, please.*
The choir sings well.	*The choir always sings well.*

C 5: Now reconstruct the text of the following limerick and recite it, then listen to the recording as a check.

The sermon our Bishop Rt. Rev.	[ðə ˈsɜːmən‿aʊə ˈbɪʃəp raɪt ˈrevrənd
Began, may have had a rt. clev.,	bɪˈgæn meɪəv ˈhædə raɪt ˈklevərend
But his talk though consistent,	bʌtɪz ˈtɔːk ðəʊ kənˈsɪstənt
Kept the end so far distant	keptðiˌˈend səʊ fɑː ˈdɪstənt
That we left since we felt he mt. nev.	ðət wi ˈleft sɪns wi ˈfelti maɪt
	ˈnevərend]

IV.3.3. /j/ (yod): *Yes, yes, yes! The problem with /j/*

C 1: Listen to the following limerick and repeat.

A delightful young lady from Trier	[ə dɪˈlaɪtfʊɫ jʌŋ ˈleɪdi frəm ˈtriə
Said her yearning had lasted a year	sedə ˈjɜːnɪŋəd ˈlɑːstɪdə ˈjɪə
And if her young yuppie	ænˈdɪfə jʌŋ ˈjʌpi
Didn't give her a puppy	dɪdnt ˈgɪvərə ˈpʌpi
She would yearn for it year after year.	ʃid ˈjɜːn fərɪt ˈjɪɹ‿ɑːftə ˈjɪə]

Apart from the spelling difference between English and German for the sound /j/ (in English it is <y> as in *yoghurt, yacht* and *yodel*, in German it is <j> as in *Joghurt, Jacht* und *jodeln*) you might think that there is nothing to worry about. Of course, even spelling differences are a bit more complicated than they might appear at first glance: In words like *ubiquitous, unit, urology, useful, eulogy, euphemism, Eugene,* and when <u> and <ui> are preceded by letters other than <y> – as in *duty, pure, nuisance* etc., there is no individual letter to represent the /j/ at all.

Infobox

The /j/ before /uː/ is not usual in US-English when the word begins with an alveolar consonant. So *suit, duty, nuisance, lewd* are pronounced [suːt], [ˈduːd̪i], [ˈnuːsəns], [luːd]. In Britain, this loss of "yod" (the name used for [j]) is also common in some words, e.g *suit, absolute.*

However, even at the articulatory level there are problems lurking. As so often, we have to point out that regional accents in German can be an advantage *or* a disadvantage in their influence on your English. If you have grown up in the North of Germany, you may have a very strong /j/, with noticeable friction: The IPA symbol for a fricative variant of /j/ is [ʝ]. Your rendering of the limerick at the beginning of the section might sound more like:

C 2: Listen to the wrong version of the limerick in C 1 with "North German" fricativised /j/ ([ʝ]). If this incorrect version sounds right to you, go back to C1 and practise that version again.

So the first warning is: Keep the [j] nice and soft, avoiding friction noise. It is after all a **palatal approximant**, and approximants are sounds where there is a narrowing of the passage through the oral cavity at the place of articulation, but the constriction is not narrow enough to cause friction.

Infobox

Before the 1989 changes to the IPA symbol set, the [j] sound was called a "vowel glide" because it is produced by moving from a very close [i] vowel position to another vowel quality. It is also often called a "semi-vowel" because, on the one hand, it is a sound that fulfils the phonetic criteria for a vowel: It is voiced and produced without audible friction, with an unhindered airstream passing through the centre of the oral cavity. On the other hand, it functions as a syllable onset, i.e. as a consonant, not as a syllabic nucleus like other vowel sounds (i.e. you get *hobby* [ˈhɒbi] but not *[ˈhɒbj]). A reminder of the letter/sound distinction with the "invisible yod" in words like *uniform* and *unit*: Although written with the letter <u>, these words have a consonantal onset, namely [j]. It is therefore, "*a uniform*" and not *"*an uniform*" as in *"an uncle."*

You can practise the non-frictional [j] by consciously replacing the [j] by a short [i] (this is similar to the exercise for /w/ using /u::/ in section IV.3.1):

E 1: Speak the following words slowly and carefully (but please avoid a hard glottal onset as in *Ver*[*?*]*ein*). Start with a long <ee> as in *bee* and go smoothly into the second part of the word,

ee-ess	⟹	*yes*	*ee-ellow*	⟹	*yellow*	*ee-ard* ⟹ *yard*
ee-oung	⟹	*young*	*ee-ore*	⟹	*yore/your*	

Now repeat them several times, gradually speeding up, until you are left with the "vowel glide" that constitutes the /j/.

Infobox

If the /j/ is no more than a glide from an [i] vowel, you may ask how /j/ is pronounced in *yeast*, and what the difference is between *east* and *yeast*? Strictly speaking, English /iː/ is [ɪi] (see section V.2.1., p.112), so the [i] onset that forms a [j] starts with a higher tongue position and there is still a slight glide from [j] to [ɪist] in *yeast*. In *east*, [ɪist], there is no on-glide, of course.

Having given you the basic warning that English /j/ is a vowel glide in contrast to the tendentially fricativised German /j/, we must immediately point out that there *are* also two *fricative* variants of the /j/ variants in English (*allophone* is the technical term, explained in III.4.). There is a weaker, voiced one which is very like the German fricative [ʝ]. This occurs in words like *due, duty, dew*, and in word combinations like *"did you?", "good year"*, etc. It can also occur after /b/ and /g/ if the word or syllable is emphasized (though it is only unstressed after /g/ and therefore not likely to be emphasized). So expressions like *"How beautiful!"* and *"Don't argue!"* are pronounced [haʊ ˈbʝuːtɪfʊɫ] and [dəʊntˌˈɑːgʝuː].

A stronger, devoiced fricative, very much like the German *Ich-Laut* [ç] occurs after voiceless obstruents (defined in section IV. *"Sounds you can feel"*), i.e. in words like *tune, pew, cue, few*, and word combinations like *not yet, that year, look young, stop yawning* etc. (compare the consonant table inside the front cover).

Generally the voiceless variant should not be difficult for German speakers of English because the exclamation *Tja* and the expression *"Es geht ja"* have the same sound, and anyway, there is the *Ich-Laut*. The voiced variant is more problematical though, particularly in word combinations like *"did you?"*, because if you make the final [d] of *did* voiceless this is likely to cause the correct [..dʝuː ...] to be pronounced *[..tçuː ...].

One case of the voiceless variant which does remain problematical is the one which is represented orthographically by <h> in words such as *Hugh, hue, hew* and *huge*, which are assumed to be /hjuː/ and /hjuːdʒ/ phonemically, and are pronounced [çuː], [çuː], [çuː] and [çuːdʒ], respectively. In theory, they should present no difficulties (except for the final consonant in *huge*) because [ç] occurs initially in words like *Chemie, China* (if you use a fricative for these words rather than a /k/). But there are no [ç] + /u:/ sequences in German, so *huge* is often wrongly pronounced as *[ju:dʒ] (or even more likely as *[ju:tʃ]).

Infobox

Danger! Regional differences! In saying that English /hj/ as in *Hugh, hue, hew* is like the German *ich*-sound, we must warn you that this is only true for German speakers whose *ich*-sound is a mid-palatal /ç/. Many speakers in the Rhineland, in Hesse and the Southwest of Germany use a pre-palatal version of /ç/, which we would transcribe as alveolo-palatal [ɕ]. If you are not certain whether your /ç/ is truly palatal or not, ask an English speaker whether he or she can accept your /çu:/ as an acceptable rendering of *Hugh!*

A variant of /t/ + /j/ in fluent speech given in the literature – and even indicated in tabloid newspaper headlines – is the affricate /tʃ/ (the sound in *choose, chain, chuckle*). If someone says "Bet you!", which we transcribe as [ˈbetçə], it can become [ˈbetʃə], and may be spelt <betcha> in normal orthography.

Betcha Blair won't win my £20,000

Fig. 1: A newspaper headline challenge to Blair

You may well hear this variant in very casual or stylized casual speech, but we do not recommend adopting it as your normal speech style because it covers a rather restricted social range. In fact, using it at all is dangerous; it is a bit like swearing in a foreign language. There are all sorts of subtle accompanying features which take many many years to master.

C 3: Listen to, and imitate the socially neutral and socially restricted versions of the following phrases.

a. *You must cut your losses.*   b. *Annie get your gun.*   c. *Sit yourself down.*
d. *Shut your mouth!*   e. *Put your money where your mouth is.*

E 2: Having heard these variants, read the little ditty **Why be good?** and decide which of the above versions it has to be read in to make "poetic" sense.

Decent parents never let you
Ever be a dirty lecher.
And they surely will not put you
In their will if you're a butcher.
Be a good boy, go and sit you
Down in peace and you'll be richer!

A quick summary:

We have advised you to be careful to avoid the German fricative /j/ in vocalic and sonorant contexts (*Are you...*, *When you...*, *While you...* etc.). A fricative /j/ is required after /p, t, k/ and /d/, and after /b/ if the word is emphasized. The fricative after /p, t, k/ should be the palatal [ç] ([pç, tç, kç]), which also serves for the pronunciation of initial <hu...> (phonemic /hju:/) sequences (*hue, Hugh*, etc.). The over-casual realisation of /tj/ as [tʃ] is not recommended unless you are very confident of the situation, the context, and that you can produce it with the necessary confidence.

More about letters

We have been discussing the "yod", which is a sound, not a letter. As we said at the beginning of the section, the /j/ is commonly represented by <y> orthographically. However, <y> is also used to represent a vowel – it occurs perhaps most frequently at the end of words in *very, happy, really, mightily, sorry,* etc., and is either pronounced as a short unstressed [i], or as [ɪ], depending on the variety of English spoken (see section V.2.1). It also occurs for the sound /ɪ/ in stressed syllables, mainly in words that have been taken over from Greek, as in *mystery, myth, nymph, lyrical, martyr.* Otherwise, the vocalic <y> in stressed syllables stands for /aɪ/, as in *fly, why, cry,* etc.

The <y> in Greek words is a notorious stumbling block for German learners of English because the German and English words are so clearly related. So German speakers are easily tempted to transfer their <y> pronunciation from German (*Lyrik* /ˈlyːrɪk/, as if it were spelled <Lürik>) and *myth* comes out as [myθ]. The problem is exacerbated to some extent by the fact that the /ɪ/ vowel is often pronounced as if it was indeed written <ü> when it occurs before /ʃ/ (*Füsch*), particularly if it is also preceded by a labial consonant. Some very common German words, e.g. *Fisch, Tisch, mischen* are often pronounced [fyʃ, tyʃ, ˈmyʃn̩] instead of the standard [fɪʃ, tɪʃ, ˈmɪʃn̩]. This can result in an insensitivity to the /ɪ/ - /ʏ/ distinction.

C 4/E 3: Listen to the following recordings of near-homophones in English and German. Some of them have been read as English words, some as German words. Can you tell the difference?

1. *Yuppie*	2. *Yoga/Joga*	3. *New York*
4. *Yiddish/Jiddisch*	5. *Yamaha*	6. *Yeltsin/Jelzin*
7. *Yankee*	8. *Yen*	

IV.3.4. /θ/ vs. /ð/ (plus /s/ and /z/ revisited):
If you love Beth, don´t propose to Bess

1. *A lisping young lady named Beth*   [ə ˈlɪspɪŋ jʌŋ ˈleɪdi neɪmd ˈbeθ
    was saved from a fate worse than death   wəz ˈseɪvd frəmə ˈfeɪt wɜːs ðən ˈdeθ
    seven times in a row,   sevn̩ ˈtaɪmzɪnə ˈrəʊ
    which unsettled her so   wɪtʃ ʌnˈsetɫd hɜ ˈsəʊ
    that she quit saying "no" and said "yeth". ðət ʃi ˈkwɪt seɪŋ ˈnəʊən sed ˈjeθ]

Pronouncing the <th> is easy, as it is a sound that you can feel and sometimes even see. Laymen may be tempted to refer to these fricatives as a lisp,
but not any lisp is a lithp. Most speakers, when asked to imitate a lisp, exaggerate and put their tongue between their teeth so it becomes visible. This is
one way of pronouncing the <th>, but by no means the most common. Native
speakers of German do not normally show you their tongue in normal
conversation, and neither do most native speakers of English. When they pronounce the <th>, they usually have the rim of the tongue in contact all the
way round with the lower edge of the upper front teeth and then allow the air
to escape through a slit between the tip of the tongue and the front teeth, as for
instance, in the pronunciation of *teeth* and *thin* and *breathe* and *thus*. This way
of pronouncing the <th>, i.e. putting the tongue tip behind the upper teeth, is
referred to as a **postdental fricative**. Admittedly, when watching dubbed
American films in German, some German viewers find it very odd to actually
see the tongue tip when an actress says *danke*. The simple explanation is, of
course, that in the original version the word is *thank you*, and here the speaker
used the **interdental** variety of the <th> pronunciation, which is possible, but
not common. The accoustic difference between these two tongue positions is
negligible, but the sounds that we want you to practise here in most cases are
the two **postdental fricatives: voiceless [θ]**, as in *thin* [θɪn], and **voiced [ð]**, as
in *thus* [ðʌs].

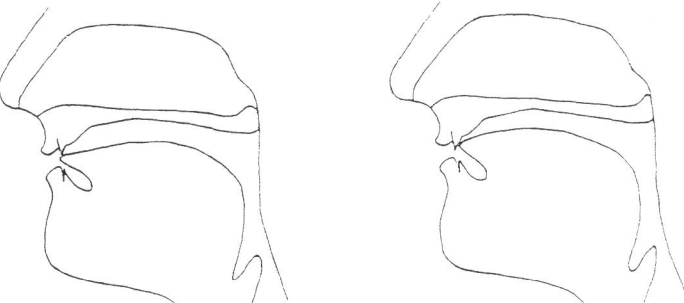

Fig. 1: interdental vs. postdental

It is interesting to have a look at the alternatives that various speakers use for the <th>. In Disney´s *"The Little Mermaid"* , the crab is a Caribbean speaker, where the [ð] is replaced by [d], as for example in his famous song *"You want to kiss de girl"*. Cockney speakers replace the dental fricatives by labio-dental fricatives, so *"three o´clock"* becomes *"free o´clock"*, and *"don´t bother"* becomes *"don´t bovver"*. When Germans use English words in German, it is common to stick to German sounds, as you might appear to sound pretentious if you used perfect foreign pronunciation in the middle of a German sentence. So it is perfectly alright to say *"Wir haben im Fernsehen einen Sriller gesehn"* and to talk about *"Meggie Setcher"* and *"St. Martin in ze Fielts"*. NB: in *German* contexts. For reasons explained in the introduction to this book, we do not recommend a cockney accent to German learners of English, but as far as per- ception is concerned, those learners who cannot, or do not want to, pronounce the sound [θ] would be better advised to say *Jonafan* rather than *Jonasan*.

Having said that we hasten to add that in standard English the sounds [θ], [ð] [s] and [z] are distinctive sounds, as in *think*, *sink* and *zinc*, and in *breathe* and *breeze*. So we will start you off by practicing [θ] and [ð] in words where they should not cause any articulatory problems:

C 1: Listen and repeat:

> *"A penny for your thoughts." - "Oh, I was just thinking of this, that and the other, you know, nothing in particular." - "Well, that´s good. I thought you were worried about Jonathan and Keith getting into trouble again." - "Me worried about those two? They´ll help each other. They stick together through thick and thin." - "You´re right, they´re like brothers, aren´t they?" - "They are, indeed. Better than some real brothers. I mean, think of Kenneth and Bruce, for instance." - "Oh God! Those two are always at each other´s throats."*

This exercise, we trust, was fairly easy, with perhaps the exception of the last two words, where you may have found the sequence [zθ] in [ˈʌðəz ˈθrəʊts] difficult. What may be causing problems is not the production of the individ- ual sounds [θ] and [ð] and [s] and [z], but the combination of these fricatives. You will have to practice the quick change from voice to voiceless and vice versa and from the slit fricatives [θ] and [ð] to the groove fricatives [s] and [z]. Say *"you want to kiss the girl"* aloud, first with the interdental fricative for *the*, and then with the postdental fricative. We trust you will find the transition from [s] to [ð] in *"kiss the"* slightly easier to pronounce with the postdental variety of [ð], as the tip of your tongue does not have to travel as far as with the interdental one. The same goes for all the other examples where a slit frica- tive and a groove fricative occur next to each other.

E 1: We suggest that you read the following nine combinations slowly and re- peatedly until you have built up sufficient confidence to handle them a bit faster in everyday conversation. Read aloud:

[sð]: ... *you want to kiss the girl.*
[zð]: *Does that mean he won't come?*
[sθ]: *You'll pass through several villages.*
[zθ]: *She was thin.*
[θs]: *Jonathan Griffiths and his friend Kenneth study maths.*
[θð]: *The drugs were hidden beneath the floorboards.*
[ðz]: *The poor woman had to feed so many mouths.* [mavðz]
[ðs]: *The doctor wants you to breathe slowly.*
[ðθ]: *When you breathe thin air you soon get out of breath.*

C 2: Listen and repeat:

Have you heard of the spinster in Harrow,   [həv ju ˈhɜːdəv ðə ˈspɪnstərɪn ˈhærəʊ
whose views were exceedingly narrow?   huːz ˈvjuːz wərˌɪkˈsiːdɪŋli ˈnærəʊ
At the end of her paths   æt ðiˈendəvə ˈpɑːθs
she had two different baths   ʃi hæd ˈtuː dɪfrənt ˈbɑːθs
for the two different sexes of sparrow.   fə ðə ˈtuː dɪfrənt ˈseksɪsəv ˈspærəʊ]

C 3: Listen and repeat:

> *"Were you at Thelma's birthday party?" - "At her thirtieth birthday party?*
> *Yes, I was. We were both there, remember?" - "Of course, and Beth Simpson was*
> *there, too, and so was Bess Thornton." - "Was that the girl that got drunk?" -*
> *"No, I'm afraid that was me. Scotch whisky, with or without soda, always gets*
> *me." - "I normally loathe the taste of whisky, but when you're up there in the*
> *North, in Rothesay [ˈrɒθsɪ], in that cold weather ..." - "Oh come off it, Dorothy,*
> *you could have had a hot Scotch broth instead."*

"/ð/ or /z/?" - "I can't remember exactly, but it's on the tip of my tongue."
or: **Elision and Assimilation**

If you took your time in this last exercise and pronounced every <th> as either
[ð] or [θ] you can't have gone wrong. But we would now like to take you
through a number of phrases and words where even native speakers seem to
find the rapid succession of [θ] and [ð] and [s] and [z] a bit of a mouthful and
where they often cut corners to make life at the tip of the tongue a bit easier.

A very useful phrase for the foreigner travelling in Britain is:

2a.   *Excuse me, is this seat taken?*

It is possible to pronounce the words *"is this"* as [ɪzˈðɪs], but if you listen carefully to native speakers of English asking you this question you will usually
hear 2b, where [ð] has disappeared: it has been **elided** (the noun is: **elision**).

2b.   [ɪzɪs ˈsiːtˌˈteɪkŋ].

In the question

3a.   *Is this the train to Plymouth, please?*

the "correct" careful pronunciation is

3b.   [ɪzˈðɪsðə ˈtreɪn tə ˈplɪməθ ˈpliːz],

but here you have the change from [z] to [ð] in "*Is this* ... " and also the change from [s] to [ð] in "... *this the* ... ". It is this double switch which results in greater suppression of [ð] in *this* than what is likely in the previous example. So pronounced at normal speed, 3a will usually be pronounced as

3c.   [ɪˈzɪsðə treɪn tə ˈplɪməθ ˈpliːz].

and in faster speech possibly even as

3d.   [ɪˈzɪsz̥ə treɪn tə ˈplɪməθ ˈpliːz]. ([z̥] indicates a devoiced /z/)

You will recall that we described /z/ as an alveolar fricative. In 3c and 3d you may find that it is slightly fronted, but does not go as far as the front teeth, let alone between the teeth. The tip of the tongue moves forward from its usual alveolar position of /z/ in a gesture that seems to say: " *Yes I know there should be a dental or interdental fricative here but I'm in a bit of a hurry.* "

The irony of it all is that it may be precisely the advanced students, i.e. the ones that have mastered the difficult cluster of 3b, who will find it difficult to "unlearn" the careful pronunciation and adopt the simplified version of casual speech. But you should not be unduly alarmed about the varieties under 3, because all three are possible and acceptable.

We would now like you to pronounce the word *Monday* slowly and feel where you put the tip of the tongue for the sound [n]. You will have touched the area just behind the front teeth, which makes this sound alveolar. If you now pronounce the word *month*, you will find (and feel) that the position for the [n] has changed, because you anticipate the postdental (or interdental) sound [θ], and it is, of course, a lot easier to pronounce the last two sounds if you make the [n] a dental (or interdental) sound too. This process is called **assimilation**, and a narrow transcription of *month* is, therefore, [mʌn̪θ], where the bridge under the [n] signifies that here this sound is pronounced as a dental sound. The two final sounds of *month*, which – when pronounced in isolation – are alveolar and postdental respectively, now have the same place of articulation. The technical term for this is: [n̪] and [θ] are **homorganic**.

Infobox

Additional symbols that you use for further specification of a sound, like the [̪] under [n] in [mʌn̪θ], or [̥] under [z] (in 3 d. above), are called **diacritics**.

If you now compare the /t/ of *at* in 4.

4.   *He saw it at a glance.*

with the /t/ of *at* in 5a.

5a.   *He likes being at the centre of attention.*

you will find assimilation at work again, because in 4 the /t/ will be heard and felt as an alveolar sound, as opposed to a dental sound in 5a due to the following voiced postdental (or interdental) fricative [ð]. So you get

5b.   [hi ˈlaɪks ˌbiːŋətðə ˈsentrəvəˈtenʃən].

Dental plosives are also used in *breadth* and *width*.

If you compare the /l/ sounds in *hell* and *health* you will find the same principle at work, with an alveolar lateral sound in the former, and a post-dental (or, depending on your preferences, an interdental) lateral in the latter:

6.   *The National Health Service* [ðə ˌnæʃnəɫ ˈheɫθ ˌsɜːvɪs]

Practise postdental laterals also in the following words: *wealth, commonwealth, stealth, filth* and *filthy*.

There is a teacher-induced mistake that has been haunting English lessons in Germany for decades: It is the pronunciation of *clothes*, which is either [kləʊðz] or [kləʊz], but it is never a bisyllabic *[ˈkləʊðəz]. Similarly the third person singular of the verb *breathe* [briːð] is *breathes* and it looks like it wants to masquerade as a bisyllabic word, but don't be fooled, it is a monosyllabic [briːðz].

Fractions of a <th>

7.   Question: *Are you good at maths? Okay then, how many haystacks is seven tenths of a haystack plus eight sixths of a haystack?*
     Answer: *One haystack.*

What exactly are the adjustments that the speech organs have to make in the transition from [n] to [θ] when you say *"one tenth"*?

Read the following description and compare it with the schema in figure 2. below. Since the [n] is a nasal sound (lowered velum) and the [θ] an oral sound (raised velum), the state of the velum has to change. When you raise it, to close off the nasal exit, the air pressure in your mouth increases, and the air pushes its way between tongue tip and front teeth for the fricative [θ]. As the two sounds are homorganic, due to assimilation, the place of articulation remains the same, but a slight relaxation of the tongue tip pressure against the teeth guarantees the fricative escape of air, and avoids a plosive [t̪]. The second critical adjustment is the state of the glottis as you change from the voiced [n] to the voiceless [θ].

If the velum closes and the tongue tip closure remains tight, you get [n̪t̪θ], with an inserted plosive, which is due to the untimely increase of air pressure in the mouth (and which, by the way, is called an **epenthetic** plosive because it is not part of the planned sound structure, but just arises as a result of the asynchrony).

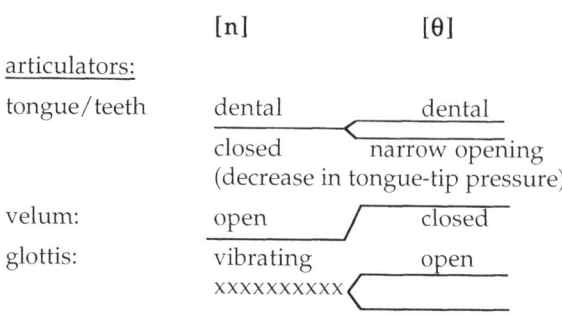

articulators:

tongue/teeth

Fig. 2: Schema of articulatory change from [n] to [θ] in *tenth*

tenth is always pronounced with a [θ]: i.e. [tenθ], both in *one tenth* and in *the tenth of December*. But let us take the plural of *one tenth*, as in our above example of *seven tenths*: here you have the choice between [tenθs] and [tens]. In the latter case this fraction may be a homophone with *tense*. The most difficult of all fractions is the one in our example 7: *sixths*: [sɪksθs], at the end of which you have a consonant cluster of four consonants with the tricky transition from groove to slit to groove fricative. So it is hardly surprising that even native speakers simplify matters here and often say [eɪt ˈsɪks]. And the same goes for the film title *"Sixth Sense"*, where you have the same sequence of fricatives, i.e. either [sɪksθˈsens] or [sɪksˈsens]. And you may be pleased to know that you cannot go wrong with the plural of *month*, because both the careful pronunciation [mʌnθs] and the one where you elide the [θ] as in [mʌns] and even [mʌnts] are acceptable.

C 4: listen and repeat:

I bought this camera at Woolworth´s, and look at the results: Judith is okay, but Edith and the two Merediths are out of focus. Is this the sort of thing you´re expected to put up with with a cheap camera? - It´s not the camera´s fault. It´s the problem of the depth of field. You took the photograph with a thousandth [-ntθ] of a second and a large aperture. Try a sixtieth of a second [ə ˈsɪkstiəθəvə ˈsekənd] and a small aperture and you´ll get the right depth of field.

A word of warning:

So you now have a near-native command of English and after having pain-stakingly mastered all the difficult possible combinations of /θ/, /ð/, /s/ and /z/, you have gone one step further and unlearned some of them to sound convincingly English in everyday conversation. You now say [ten ˈmʌns], [kləʊz] for *clothes* and [ɪˈzɪszə treɪn tə ˈplɪməθ ˈpliːz]. But please remember that these are the exceptions, and that *maths* never becomes *mass*, *deaths* never *dess*, *this thing*, pronounced [ˈðɪs θɪŋ], never rhymes with *Miss Sing*; and however casually you may wish to introduce Mr. Griffiths, the sooth-sayer, he reliably remains [ˌmɪstə ˈɡrɪfɪθs ðə ˈsuːθseɪə].

E 2: Read aloud:

Why's the baby crying? - Teething problems, I think. - Oh, poor thing. How many teeth has she got now? - Only three teeth so far, but the fourth tooth's coming through up there. - Is that the one that's causing the problem? - Yes, and to make matters worse, she's got a cold. - Shall I go and get some medicine to soothe her sore throat? - No thanks, I don't think it's worth it, she sleeps through the night and breathes [briːðz] regularly. - Perhaps I should bathe her then. A hot bath will do her good and in the meantime you can watch "Young Mothers and Birth Control". - Oh, stop teasing me, I've got enough with the baby teething. - Okay, no more teasing problems, hohoho. Sorry darling, I couldn't resist that one.

E 3: Exercise for *seize, sees, seas, cease, seethe.*

a. Which of these five words are homphones?
b. Which word should be pronounced with a shorter vowel than the others?
c. Now read the following sentence and write the appropriate phonetic symbols for all occurrences of the letters <s>, <z> and <th>:
Real sailors seize every opportunity to travel the seven seas, where one sees, in dark and stormy nights, how the waves seethe, and where, in the deep blue sea, wonders will never cease.

E 4: Give a narrow transcription (with diacritics) for /n/, /l/ and /t/:

a. *October is the tenth month of the year.*
b. *Could I borrow your Shakespeare anthology.*
c. *It's not in the interest of the public.*
d. *Does the National Health Service apply to all Commonwealth countries?*
e. *At the moment*

In our section on the distinction between fortis and lenis we pointed out that the most important difference between *bet* and *bed* is the longer duration of the vowel in *bed*. This is certainly also true of the opposition between what we described as voiceless [θ] and [s] on the one hand, and voiced [ð] and [z] on the other, because at the end of a word [ð] and [z] are usually devoiced, which means that the distinction between *teeth* and *teethe* and *mouth* (n) and *mouth* (vb), and that between *bus* and *buzz* rely heavily on the longer vowel duration before [ð] and [z]. So in addition to the articulatory problem of distinguishing between these fricatives, one has to be careful to distinguish between short and long vowels. And to drive home this message we have concocted the following poem, the only purpose of which is to illustrate their distinctiveness by using the minimal pair *grace* vs. *greys*, and the minimal triplet *face* vs. *faith* vs. *phase*: As you read this poem, take care to make the vowels in the words with the lenis ending [z] (i.e. *greys* and *phase*) longer than those with the fortis endings [s] and [θ] (i.e. *grace, face, wraith* and *faith*). (E. *wraith* [reɪθ] = G. *Gespenst, Geist*).

E 5: Read aloud:

When he asked this young girl to say grace,
this old priest, I´m afraid, he lost face,
for her face went through all shades of greys:
"I´m going through a difficult phase."
"Why? Dear girl! You look like a wraith!"
"Well, last night, as you know, I lost faith."

[weni‿ˈɑːskt ðɪs jʌŋ ˈɡɜːɬ tə seɪ ˈɡreɪs
ðɪsəʊɬd ˈpriːst‿aɪm əˈfreɪdi lɒst ˈfeɪs
fə hə ˈfeɪs went θruˈbːɬ ʃeɪdzəv ˈɡreɪz
aɪm ˈɡəʊɪŋ θruːə ˈdɪfɪkəɬt feɪz
waɪ dɪə ˈɡɜːɬju ˈlʊk laɪkə ˈreɪθ
weɬ lɑːsˈnaɪtəz ju ˈnəʊʷaɪ lɒst ˈfeɪθ]

E 6: Give the phonetic symbols for the letters <s>, <z> and <th>:

a. *seize/sees/seas* vs. *sis* vs. *cease* vs. *seethe*   b. *breath* vs. *breeze* vs. *breathe*
c. *size/sighs* vs. *scythe*   d. *teeth* vs. *teething, teethe* vs. *tease*
e. *wreath* vs. *wreathe*   f. *loath* vs. *loathe*
g. *close (adj.)* vs. *close (vb)* vs. *cloze* vs. *clothe*
h. *The Norsemen in the North of Scandinavia observed northern lights, which the Southerners in the South of Sweden never see.*

E 7: Dictate this passage to a fellow student.

> *The general was leading his troops up the path to where the enemy blocked the pass in the mountain range, where he saw the snow thaw in the sun. When the general heard the enemy shout "Cease fire" he asked himself, should he seize the opportunity? But did they mean it? Was this the truth? Could it really be the truce he had sought to achieve and he had thought he'd never live to see? In his youth there had been no use talking to him about negotiating, but now he had learned that war brings force and brutality, and peace brings forth clemency and prosperity.*

Now compare his or her text with the original. If there are discrepancies, try to work out whether it was due to your pronunciation or his/her lack of listening skills.

Spellings and sounds:

Words ending in [ð]:

a. spelling <-the>: *bathe, lathe, scathe, soothe, seethe, sheathe, swathe, lithe, blithe, writhe.*
b. spelling <-th>: *smooth* [smu:ð], *mouth* (verb), *bequeath* and *booth* [ð] or [θ].

<th> as [t]: *Thames, Thomas, Thomson, thyme, Thai.*

Smileys:

How do mice save a drowning mouse? - By mouse to mouse resuscitation
(People do it by mouth to mouth resuscitation.)

Cogito ergo sum. I think I exist; therefore I exist, I think. I think I think. Therefore I think.

[ðə ˈsɔːnə bɑːθəˈtendənt sed tə ˈsuːzən | ˈsɒri aɪ dɪdnt ˈrekəgnaɪz ju wɪð jɔ ˈkləʊðzɒn]

Tongue twisters (not for serious practice)

The sixth sick sheik's sixth sheep's sick.

Can a speech synthesizer synthesize "Thelma Thistlethwaite received thirty-six hyacinths on her thirty-sixth birthday"?

IV.3.5. /h/:
The sound /h/ and the problems of not pronouncing it

The letter <h> is pronounced [eɪtʃ] when you *spell* words or abbreviations (like [ˌen eɪtʃ ˈes] for *NHS: National Health Service*), and is usually pronounced [h] when you *use* words. It sounds exactly like the German /h/, so we can safely say that words like *head* and *hip* do not pose any articulatory problems for learners of the German speaking area. (Here you have an advantage over French and Spanish or Italian learners of English.)

But if you now read the following limerick (pay attention to the rather unusual rhythm!) you will understand what sort of difficulty we alluded to in the title of this section:

1.	*She was peeved and called him "Mr.",*	[ʃi wəz ˈpiːvdən ˌkɔːɫdɪm ˈmɪstə
	not because he came and kr.,	ˈnɒt bɪkəzi ˈkeɪmən ˈkɪstə
	but because, just before,	bʌt bɪˈkɒz dʒʌs bɪˈfɔː:
	when she looked in at the door,	wen ʃi luːˈkɪnətðə ˈdɔː:
	this same Mr. kr. sr.	ðɪs ˈseɪm ˈmɪstə ˌkɪstə ˈsɪstə]

Here *mister* and *sister* rhyme with *kissed her*. The question that arises is: what is the effect if you do not omit the [h]-sound in *kissed her*? If you always pronounce the /h/ as you did when you learned the citation form of *her* [hɜ:] in isolation, then it will sound too prominent (accented) and you will be saying something you do not mean. The general rule is that with the personal pronoun *he* and the possessive pronouns *his* and *her*, the /h/ is not pronounced when the pronoun is unaccented and when it does not occur in sentence-initial position or after a word-final vowel:

2. a. *What´s he doing here?* [ˈwɒtsi ˈduːɪŋ hɪə];
    b. *He saw her running away.* [hi ˈsɔː hə rʌnɪŋəˈweɪ];

If on the other hand you kow perfectly well what he is doing but you are very surprised, possibly even annoyed to see that he turned up at your party, *he* becomes the focal point of your utterance; it is accented and does not lose the /h/:

3. *I invited her, but what´s he doing here?* [aɪ ɪnˈvaɪtɪd ˈhɜ: | bət ˈwɒts ˈhi: duːɪŋ hɪə]

Pronouncing the [h] with these three function words (*his, her, he*) implies emphasis, contrast or - if somebody did not understand you and you repeat your statement - greater precision. These three criteria do not apply if you use the idiomatic expressions *what´s-his-name* and *what´s-her name*, as in

4a. *Oh look, here comes what´s-his-name.* [ˈwɒtsɪz neɪm]

When using idiomatic expressions you should take great care to get the pronunciation right, because it would sound very silly if you said

4b.   *Oh look, here comes what is his name. *[ˈwɒt ɪz hɪz neɪm]

Omitting the initial [h] means, of course, that these pronouns then start with a vowel and consequently they should be linked like other words beginning with a vowel:

5   a. *Pour him a drink.* [ˌpɔːrɪmə ˈdrɪŋk]
    b. *Where were her parents at the time?* [ˈweə wərə ˈpeərəntsət ðə ˌtaɪm]

The intrusive [r] is optional, but even if you yourself do not use it, you should be able to analyse

6   a. [aɪ ˈsɔːrɪm]   as
    b. *I saw him.*

There is also a limited number of content words where the letter <h> is not pronounced in standard English, as for instance: *hour, heir, honour, vehicle* [ˈviəkɫ], *exhaust* [ɪɡˈzɔːst], *exhibit* [ɪɡˈzɪbɪt], exhibition [eksɪˈbɪʃn].

Ear we go again!

The omission of [h] in words like *honour* is not the same as what is usually referred to as "h-dropping", which only occurs in certain dialects. In a world heavyweight title fight Tyson bit off part of Holyfield´s ear. When reporting the possibility of a rematch the British daily "The People" could not resist a pun and wrote: "Ear we go again", which is homophonic with "Here we go again" in h-dropping dialects. We do not recommend this kind of omission of [h], because you would then have to make numerous other adjustments in order to be consistent. In a Northern English dialect, for instance, *my husband* would be [miˈuzbənd]. As h-dropping is widespread, you should have a passive knowledge of it so as to understand it when you ear it – sorry, hear it. So look at these jokes and work out what they're based on:

Jokes for h-dropping

a. *From Our Bookshelf: The Return of the Prodigal Son by Gladys Back*
(*the prodigal son:* German: *der verlorene Sohn. Gladys Back = glad he is back.*)

b. *What do you get when it rains beer? - An ale storm.*

c. *Which detective used to be an electrician? - Sherlock Ohms.*

d. *Who looks after sick gnomes? - The National Elf Service.* (*Elf* is the Cockney pronunciation for *Health* with h-dropping and [f] for /θ/.)

e. As the following poem may cause offence, we quote it here in phonetic transcription and leave the deciphering of it to your discretion:

[ʃi ˈmeɪdɪməˈnɒfə
hi ˈɒnədəˈrɒfə
əˈnɔːɫ θruː ðə ˈnaɪt
iwəˈzɒnərəˈnɒfə]

f. A limerick illustrating h-dropping in the function word *her*:

A fearsome old bulldog named Caesar	[ə ˈfɪəsəm‿əʊɫ ˈbʊɫdɒg neɪmd ˈsiːzə
Sees a cat and decides just to taesar;	siːzə ˈkætən dɪˈsaɪdz ʤʌstə ˈtiːzə
But she scratches and spits	bʌt ʃi ˈskræʧɪzən ˈspɪts
Till the big bulldog quits:	tɪɫ ðə ˈbɪg bʊɫdɒg ˈkwɪts
Now Caesar just saesar and flaesar.	naʊ ˈsiːzə ʤʌst ˈsiːzərən ˈfliːzə

(In case you had difficulties decoding the "modified" spelling used for all the [-iːzə] words, we repeat them here in standard spelling: *taesar: tease her; saesar: sees her; flaesar: flees her.*)

/h/ before /uː/

When a word starts with the letter <h> and the following vowel is [uː], the accepted phonetic transcription is [hjuː]. As the initial sound of *hew, heuristics, human, humid* is like a weak version of the final sound of German *ich*, one could also use the symbol for this palatal fricative [ç]. This has been dealt with in more detail in section IV.3.3., so please refer back to it if you are still not sure.

Infobox

A common variant of /h/: [h] is produced by narrowing the vocal folds sufficiently to cause the noise that you hear when the air squeezes through the glottis. As the vocal folds do not vibrate, /h/ is a voiceless glottal fricative. In intervocalic position, as in *ahead, behave*, however, there is not enough time to fully abduct the vocal folds, so they continue to vibrate, albeit with a lot of accompanying friction. So intervocalic /h/ is usually voiced, as it is, for example, in German *aha*. It is a voiced glottal fricative, and the symbol for this variant is [ɦ]: [aˈɦaː].

IV.3.6. Nasals: /m/, /n/ and /ŋ/; nasality and denasality

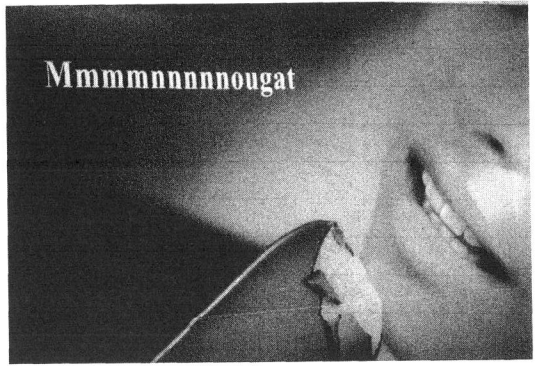

The defining characteristic of **nasals** is that the air from the lungs escapes through the nose. As you pronounce *mmmmmmnnnnnougat*, i.e. the prolonged sound [m:::] (which is the paralinguistic expression for *delicious*) immediately followed by the pronunciation for the sweet [ˈnuːgɑː] you will discover that – as you reach the [uː] – the airflow switches from "through the nose" to "through the mouth" (i.e. from **nasal** to **oral**).

In addition to [m] and [n], there is a third nasal sound in English: [ŋ], as in the final sound of *ring*. Prolong this final sound of *ring* and put a mirror under your nose and you will "see" the nasality as the warm airstream from the nostrils causes condensation on the glass. So even though the lips and the teeth are apart, and you may feel as if your mouth is open, your oral passage is in fact closed at the back and the airstream coming from your lungs is redirected through your nose.This [ŋ] is produced in the following way: The velum (or soft palate) is lowered and rests on the raised tongue dorsum. This opens the entrance to the nasal cavities and closes off the passage through the mouth (see fig. 1).

To sum up: You can prevent the air flowing through the mouth
a. by putting the lips together as in **[m]**, which is, therefore, called a **bilabial nasal**;
b. by putting the tongue against the alveolum (or teeth ridge), as in **[n]**, which is called an **alveolar nasal**, or
c. by doing what we asked you to do in section IV.2.1. with the velar plosives /k/ and /g/, where you stopped the airflow between the back of your tongue and the velum. If you do not release this closure, you get the prolonged **velar nasal /ŋ/**, as for instance at the end of the word *ring* (see section VII.1.3.).

But when you are trying to blow out a candle and you want all the air from the lungs to flow through the puckered lips, how do you stop part of the air escaping through the nose? It is the velum at the back of your mouth that acts as a valve that blocks off the nasal cavity (in its raised position) or allows you to direct air into the nasal cavity (in its lowered position).

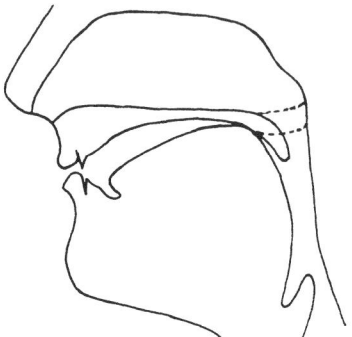

Fig. 1: The velum in its lowered position for [ŋ]. The dashed line shows it in its raised position for [g] and [k].

Homorganic sounds are those that are produced at the same place of articulation. The three groups of sounds [p], [b] and [m]; [t], [d] and [n]; and [k], [g], and [ŋ] are homorganic. The title of this section teaches us that nasals – as opposed to their plosive homorganic counterparts, i.e. [p], [b] and [g] – can be prolonged. What happens if you pinch your nose or if you have a cold and the nasal cavity is blocked? Try it and you will find that – due to the resulting air pressure – the intended [m] or [n] sound like the corresponding plosives [b] or [d] as you open the lips or release the tongue tip closure. This relationship is the basis of the following poem:

1.   *The Dodo*

The dodo had a cold in its nose,   *So maybe the dodo*
Or rather, its beak,   *Was really a*
And could hardly speak.   *Yes-yes,*
When a man said,   *Or could be a*
"I thought you were dead,"   *Nono?*
Said the dodo,
"Oh dodo,
I've just got a code id de head."   (The Puffin Joke Book, p. 55)

This kind of "cold-in-the-head" voice quality is – phonetically – referred to as **denasal**. The opposite would be a nasal voice quality, where the velum is often in a lowered position. You may have noticed that some RP speakers often pronounce vowels as nasalised sounds. This is noticeable with open vowels as in [kæt, kɑːt, kɒt] and particularly in vowels preceding a nasal:

2   a. *I can't stay long, I have to catch the last train home.*

The words *can't, long, train* and *home* all have nasals, and in anticipation of the nasal the speaker lowers the velum during the preceding vowel (sometimes even at the beginning), which is why this phenomenon is called **anticipatory nasality**. Using the tilde as the diacritic for "nasalisation" we can transcribe 2a as

2   b. [aɪ kã:nt steɪ lõŋ | aɪ hæftə ˈkæʧ ðə lɑ:s ˈtreɪ̃n ˈhə̃ʊ̃m]

What this teaches us is that the classification of English sounds into the three nasals [m], [n] and [ŋ] as opposed to all other sounds as non-nasal sounds is a phonolological classification, i.e. an either-or classification. At the level of phonology this makes sense, as there is no minimal pair where [kã:nt] means *"not able to"* and [kɑ:nt] means something else. Phonetically, however, nasality is often a question of degrees, of more or less, and it is often a feature of sounds that have been classified as "oral" at the phonological level.

Let us examine the word *on* in some detail, in the following interchange:

3. *"Do you want the light on or off?" - "On."*

What are the phonetic features that might give away a speaker with a strong German accent in the answer *"On"*? To begin with, the hard onset or glottal stop at the beginning of the word (a problem that we will look into in the next sections). Secondly, the vowel quality may be wrong (see V.2.5.). Thirdly, there is not likely to be the strong anticipatory nasality that some English speakers use. And fourthly, the [n] may sound wrong in spite of the fact that the blade of the tongue is in the correct alveolar place of articulation. Please recall what we said in III.1. about the so-called clear and dark "l": Both sounds have the same primary articulation with the tip of the tongue against the alveolum, but differ in their secondary articulation, i.e. the shape of the rest of the tongue. The dark "l" was said to be velarised, as the back of the tongue was raised towards the velum. By analogy, we can distinguish between the clearer and the darker /n/. There is a tendency for many German speakers to articulate the clearer /n/ (a slightly [i]-coloured /n/) <u>independent</u> of the preceding vowel, whereas the English /n/ is more neutral (an [ə]-coloured /n/) but this makes it more prone to contextual influence. That means that *"in"* has a clearer /n/, causing no problems of German accent, and *"on"* has a much darker /n/, which makes a German /n/ stand out strongly.

C 1: practice for nasals and nasality. Listen and repeat:

> *Sandra, do you want the light on or off - On. It's getting dark and I can't find anything. - Oh come on, you're not looking for your free samples of CD-ROMs again, are you? - As a matter of fact, I am. The one for advanced learners of English, for example. Can you help me find it? - No, I'm sorry I can't. I've got to mow the lawn before it gets really dark. - Oh Sam, can't that wait until tomorrow morning?*

We called section III. "Sound Examples", and many of the phenomena that we described there apply here as well. We said that the letter <l> could be represented by: [l], [ɫ], [l̥], as syllabic [l̩], and silent <l>. The letter <n> may be represented, as we saw in the preceding paragraph, as palatalised or velarised, as devoiced in [sn̥æʧ] and ['sn̥uːpi], and as syllabic [n̩], in *fish 'n chips*, and *button*.

<-mn> at the end of a word is always pronounced as [m]: *damn, condemn, solemn, column* and *autumn. him* and *hymn* are homophones: both are pronounced [hɪm].

<mn-> is an example of "silent" <m> in *mnemonic* [nəˈmɒnɪk].

When <n> is followed by <f>, as in *conference* and *information*, there are three possibilities: a. you pronounce the <n> as [n], which sounds very formal. b. in a process of assimilation you anticipate the labiodental [f] and pronounce the nasal as a labiodental sound as well ([ɱ]), pressing the lower lip against the upper teeth: [ˌɱfə ˈmeɪʃn̩], or c. you pronounce the nasal as a bilabial [m] prior to forming the [f]. This is similar to the way many Germans pronounce the word *fünf*: [fʏmf].

In Southern British English you cannot have the consonant cluster nasal + plosive + nasal, so *Clinton, London, Camden* and *Wellington* are pronounced with a schwa sound before the final consonant: [ˈklɪntən], [ˈlʌndən], [ˈkæmdən] and [ˈwelɪŋtən], but not *[ˈlʌndn̩], whereas [ˈeɫtn̩] for *Elton* is correct, as the [tn̩] cluster is not preceeded by a nasal. (In American Eng. [ˈlʌndn̩] is acceptable.)

Cross references: For other sections related to <n>, <m> and <ng> see: section VII.1.3. for [ŋ]; for *gnash* : see plosives; for sonorants: see section IV.

See section IV.3.4. for *tenth month* etc.

Syllabic [m̩] under "assimilation": *happen* → [ˈhæpm̩], *open the door* → [ˈəʊpm̩ ðə ˈdɔː].

IV.3.7. [ʔ] glottal stop: *With a li´le bi´ of luck*

The **vocal folds** are muscular folds inside the larynx. We will consider here only three of their different states for three different functions: Firstly, they can be together (**adducted**) and vibrate when the air passes through them. This is called **phonation** or **voicing**, and sounds produced with them in that state are referred to as **voiced**. Secondly, the vocal folds can be apart (**abducted**), as they are when we breathe. And thirdly, they can be tightly shut, like when we hold our breath to lift something heavy, for instance. Try breathing out forcefully and then suddenly holding your breath. In the process of stopping your breath you will feel the **glottal stop**, symbolized by [ʔ]. It is obviously a "stop" because you stop the airflow, and it is "glottal" because this is the adjective for "**glottis**", which refers to the space between the vocal folds.

In standard German, the word *Verein* has a glottal stop in the middle, and the two words *verreisen* and *vereisen* differ in that the former has a /r/ sound and the latter a glottal stop in the middle. Say *Verein* in standard German, but pause at the end of the first syllable and you will feel the shutting of the glottis. Hold your breath in the middle of this word for a second or two, and if you now continue and suddenly release the built-up air pressure you will hear the bursting open of the vocal folds at the beginning of the second syllable: -*ein*. This sound is, of course, a plosive similar to /t/ and /d/. It would make sense to refer to the noise produced by the sudden closure of the vocal folds as a glottal stop and the sudden release as vocal plosive, but the term "glottal stop" has come to be used for both.

We would now like you to put on your thinking caps and ask yourselves: *Why are there two symbols for all plosives with the same place of articulation, as for /t/ and /d/, /k/ and /g/, and /p/ and /b/ but only one for the glottal stop?* The answer is that these distinctions refer to the opposition between voiced and voiceless, i.e. the question of whether the vocal folds are involved or not. The glottal stop refers to the activity of the vocal folds, and you cannot have a glottal plosive or "vocal fold plosive" without the vocal folds being involved.

The glottal stop is not often thought of as a real consonant because it is not represented anywhere in the orthography, either in English or in German. But it is something that can make the difference between sounding English or not (and it is just as important for English speakers learning German) because it is simply used differently in the two languages. In German, you will also have got used to marking the onset of (accented) words beginning with a vowel by using what is often called a "**hard onset**" (harter Einsatz). This is in fact a glottal stop released abruptly into the vowel. So you might say

1. *Alle Autos ärgern mich!* as [ˈʔalə ˈʔaʊtos ˈʔɛɐɡɵn mɪç]

In standard German it is normal to have a glottal onset, at least with accented words, although often in continuous speech the vocal folds do not stop completely, because there is insufficient time for the muscular constriction to take effect properly, or it is not strong enough, but the slowed, irregular vocal fold vibration has the same auditory effect, and we hear the word onset clearly.

In English, a word with a vowel onset has to be pronounced rather emphatically before it is likely to be given a glottal onset. Compare 2a. (unemphatic) with 2b. (with emphatic *ALWAYS*):

2   a. *I've always adored onion soup!*   [aɪˈvɔːɬweɪzəˈdɔːˌdʌnjən ˈsuːp]
    b. *I've ALWAYS adored onion soup!*   [aɪv ‖ˈʔɔːɬweɪzəˌdɔːˌdʌnjən ˈsuːp]

Note that *I*, *adored*, and *onion* also begin with a vowel, but they are not pronounced with a glottal onset; in fact *adored* and *onion* are **linked** to the final consonant of the preceding word. You may, as so many German speakers of English do, find it difficult to "switch off" the glottal onset and to link the words smoothly. We want to point out here that reading an unknown text is the worst possible phonetic exercise for German speakers as far as the overuse of hard onsets is concerned, firstly because reading slows you down considerably, and secondly because one tends to be hypnotised by the visual gaps between words and tends to respect word boundaries phonetically in a totally unenglish pronunciation. This is why we recommend the *"Listen and Repeat"* exercises and also reading phonetic transcriptions as in 2a. We deal with "linking" extensively in section VI.1.

We do not recommend the glottal stop that replaces [t] in *butter*: [ˈbʌʔə], as it is not the variety of English which we are aiming at in this book. You will, however, have to get used to another difference in the use of the glottal stop between English and German, which is the greater frequency of **glottal reinforcement** in postvocalic plosives in English, when another consonant follows the [t]. So in a word like *football*, a glottal stop is produced at the same time as the closure for the [t], so the pronunciation [ˈfʊtʔbɔɬ] (or even [ˈfʊʔbɔɬ]) is quite common. Similarly *department* may be pronounced [dɪˈpɑːtʔmənt] or [dɪˈpɑːʔmənt], whereas [dɪˈpɑːtʰmənt] would sound pedantic and stilted.

C 1: Listen and repeat:
    a. German *Verein, vereisen, verreisen; Alle Autos ärgern mich.*
    b. *I've always adored onion soup!*   [aɪˈvɔːɬweɪzəˈdɔːˌdʌnjən ˈsuːp]
    c. *I've ALWAYS adored onion soup!* [aɪv ‖ˈʔɔːɬweɪzəˌdɔːˌdʌnjən ˈsuːp]
    d. The following words will be said three times in this order: 1. glottally reinforced, 2. glottaly replaced 3. non-glottalised. We recommend the first version:
    football, department, Gatwick, street-map, catmint, petshop, whitewash

Although the glottal *replacement* of a plosive is restricted to [t], the glottal *reinforcement* of the other plosives – [p] and [k] – is very common. As with [t] it occurs before another consonant rather than in other contexts.

C 2: Listen to the glottally reinforced and non-glottalised versions of the following words: *stepmother, laptop, stopgap, pickpocket, tape-measure, brakelight.*

V. Vowel sounds

In this chapter we introduce you to the vowels of English, explain potential problems and give you practice in hearing and speaking them.

The first section deals with the basic phonetics of vowels, explaining what sort of sound they are, i.e., what they all have in common. But it also tells you how the differences between them are described so that you can follow our explanations in the subsequent sections of the (sometimes rather subtle) differences between English and German vowels.

But we do not expect you to be experts in these differences immediately, without any practice, so of course, in the sections that follow we also give you exercises in listening to and in producing the vowels. We hope that, in consequence, you will not only acquire a skill and a confidence in pronouncing the vowels of the standard pronunciation that we are dealing with in this book, but that you will also develop an interest in the varieties that occur in different regional accents.

You may not have thought very deeply about vowels before, perhaps merely in terms of their orthographic representation as <a, e, i, o, u>, so you may be a little surprised to see that we have 21 vowel sections and subsections! We have organized these into groups so as to bring the vowels together that share related problems.

V.1. Are vowels important or: *Cn w d wtht thm?*

Vowels are funny things in two very different ways. Firstly, they are always produced with your vocal folds vibrating and, in contrast to most consonants, without any obstruction from your tongue or lips. When you pronounce a vowel, as for instance, a very long [i:::], the air escapes freely between tongue and palate. If, however, you move your tongue higher while pronouncing the [i:::] you begin to feel the point of obstruction as the friction sets in and it becomes a [ʝ:::] (the sound in an emphatically pronounced German *jjjeder*), and you will be able to feel the air as it squeezes through the narrow gap. In IV. we described consonants as "Sounds you can feel". By analogy we might describe vowels as "sounds you don't feel". The lack of much direct tactile information with vowels makes it rather difficult to explain to learners how to produce foreign vowel sounds. Secondly, there is a huge discrepancy between their contribution to your *understanding* of an utterance and how much you *notice* them. First we shall look at this aspect of the vowel´s prominence, and then we shall return to how they are produced, and consider the problem of learning new vowels.

Vowels are the bits of a sentence that stand out most because they carry the syllables along. On the other hand, they are relatively unimportant for the comprehensibility of a sentence. Just think of the children´s singing game: *"Drei Chinesen mit dem Kontrabaß"*, where you produced the whole verse on one vowel (say: *"Dro Chonosen mot dom Kontroboß"*) and then swapped over and produced it on another vowel. Great fun, and it *did* sound very strange, but you could still follow the words without any difficulty.

So what function do vowels have? Of course they do help to keep words apart; a *cat* is not a *cut* or a *coot*. The following little poem shows that vowels are really not totally irrelevant:

E 1: Read the phonetic transcription of it and rewrite it in normal orthography (and turn to the chart of phonetic symbols with example words if you have any problems):

> [ˈswɒn ˈswæˈm‿əʊvə ðə ˈsi:
> ˈswɪm ˈswɒn ˈswɪm
> ˈswɒn ˈswæm ˈbæk‿əgen
> ˈwel ˈswʌm ˈswɒn]

Vowels vary a lot from dialect to dialect, so we are very used to *"being flexible"* about vowel quality. Quite generally, because of all the distractions going on while we talk and listen, we make use of the context to understand the words. This means, too, that we can adjust for variation of vowels within the correct consonantal frame. Those of you who saw the English comedy series *"'Allo 'allo"* can probably remember the Englishman disguised as a French policeman who simulated talking bad French by exchanging the vowels of some words in each sentence. So his stock phrase as he came on the scene was *"Good moaning"* with [əʊ] instead of [ɔ:]. It was funny because we knew what he meant, despite the wrong vowel, and the new word created by the wrong vowel did not fit.

The variation of vowels with regional dialect indicates a very important secondary function that they have in verbal communication. They give very weighty signals about the geographical and social background of the speaker. Even a single syllable like *"No"*, given in answer to a question can brand the speaker for the rest of the dialogue.

C 1: Demonstration of *"no"* in different accents. Listen to the examples paying attention to the different vowel qualities. Most native speakers of English would have a fairly good idea of these speakers' background.
Question: Do you come from Edinburgh? Answer: No.

a. Scottish   b. Northern English
c. Advanced RP   d. North American
e. French   f. German

Any concern to acquire an acceptable English pronunciation must therefore be a concern with the quality of the vowels. Even though you will probably be quite comprehensible with "bad" vowels, you will be sending out signals of foreignness and not caring about the people whose language you are using.

The other strange thing about vowels that we mentioned at the beginning of the chapter – that they are produced without any clear contact between the articulators – means that they cannot be learned in the same way as consonants. It is not possible to give instructions like "place your tongue tip against the edge of the upper front teeth" (as you might when learning the English "th"). The position of the tongue *is* just as important, but it does not rest against anything as it mostly does with consonants.

Concentrate on the body of your tongue while you pronounce a long vowel like [i::::] (like in a stretched *viele*), [y::::] (like in *fühlen*) [a:::::] (like in *Phase*) and [u:::::] (like in *Fuge*). It is not the tongue tip, which you should be paying attention to, although that is much easier to feel! Sometimes, particularly when first starting to register things happening in the mouth, people are distracted by what is happening to the tongue tip and are not aware of the changes in the tongue body. With the four vowels we have just selected, you will notice that the *body* (not the tip) of the tongue moves:

up and down with the jaw (go slowly from an [i:] to an [a:] and back); here we talk about "tongue height", or "close"(= high tongue position) "mid-close", "mid-open", "open" (= low tongue position) and vowels.

backwards and forwards (go slowly from [y:] to [u:] and back); we talk of "front", "central" and "back" vowels.

And the lips can change shape from being spread to rounded (go slowly from [i:] to [y:] and back).

Infobox

Traditionally the up-and-down and the backwards-forwards positioning of the tongue is shown graphically on the International Phonetic Association (IPA) **Vowel Chart**:

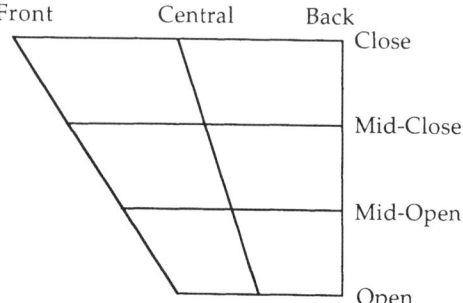

The key points are defined as **Cardinal Vowels**, which are reference vowels, against which the vowels of any language can be defined. The Cardinal Vowels (CV) themselves do not occur in any language.

Three of the CVs, [i, u, ɑ] are defined articulatorily, by the **friction limit** which turns a vowel into a fricative, while the intermediate vowels between them were defined by the English phonetician Daniel Jones as **perceptually equidistant**. The friction limit for [i] was mentioned at the beginning of the section; [u] has a similar limit. If the back of the tongue dorsum is raised higher than CV [u] the velar fricative [ɣ] results. Similarly, if the tongue is lowered and retracted beyond the CV [ɑ] limit, the root forms a constriction with the back of the pharynx, resulting in the pharyngeal fricative [ʕ]. The following schematic sagittal cross sections of the oral cavity with the tongue positions for these three vowels illustrate the friction limits:

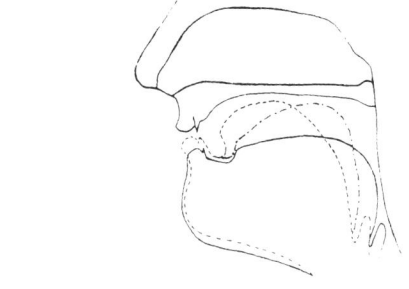

What is important about the vowels is their "timbre", "colouring" (we usually say "vowel quality"). Of course you have to do the right thing with your tongue and lips to get the vowel quality you need, but it is difficult to follow instructions as you might with a "th" and get the right sound automatically. It is really a matter of trial and error, matching the things you do with your mouth to the sound that you hear. So you have to listen carefully and get a clear picture in your mind of the sound you need to produce. You can be fairly certain that the first time you do the right thing and get the right sound, it will feel strange because your mouth is just not used to doing it, and is sending indignant signals to your brain to say that it is in an unusual position. So there will be conflicting information going to your brain. Your ears will pick up the sound and – if you have made yourself familiar with the vowel you want to learn to produce properly – send a positive message, while your vocal organs will be protesting.

Infobox

When you read this, you may think: "I have no idea what they are trying to say!" One of the many problems with learning pronunciation is the change of perspective that is necessary. You start thinking about things that you have taken for granted. Part of the aim of this book is to give you some guidance in how to think (and listen, and feel). Observing your vocal organs and listening to the sounds produced may not come easy, but do not give up. Keep trying to fit what you observe yourself with what we are trying to express.

To put it another way: If you pronounce the English words *star*, *shock* and *band* – which have all been imported into German (*Star*, *Schock*, *die Band*) – and your English pronunciation feels familiar and comfortable, then *your alarm bells should be ringing*, because this is an indication that you are not modifying your articulation to make the *phonetic* distinction between the English and German pronunciation, and you are almost certainly producing them with a German accent!

So, we can say that your ears lead the way when you learn vowels, and your mouth has to be persuaded to do the right thing!

V.2. Monophthongs: *Hold your tongue!*

Is a *Mailbox* a *Mehlkiste*? Of course not! *Kiste* is a possible translation of *box*, but *Mehl* is not *Mail*. For Germans, the English vowel /eɪ/ in the loanword *Mail* has turned into the German vowel /e:/ because (standard) German does not have an /eɪ/. This makes the pronunciation of *Mail* and *Mehl* the same. No problems for Germans using the loanword in Germany, of course, but they have to remember to pronounce /meɪl/ when using the word in an English context. An English speaker may possibly not be able to pronounce /me:l/ for German *Mehl* because there is no /e:/ in English (of course there is a further difficulty with the postvocalic /l/, as you know from section III.1.).

C 1: Listen to the following recordings of *Mailbox* and *Mehlkiste*, *laser printer* and *Laserdrucker* spoken first by a German and then by an English speaker. The difference between the two speakers is that the German has learned to keep his tongue still when producing a long [e:] vowel, while the English speaker has learned to move his. Neither habit is inherently wrong, of course, but as you probably judged for yourself, it *is* wrong to keep your tongue still when the language demands that you move it, and it is wrong to move it when you should keep it still! A similar problem occurs for Germans and English learners with the German [o:] vowel and the English [əʊ] vowel. So the English loanword *dufflecoat* has become /ˈdafəlko:t/ in German, and German *...oder so* is likely to be pronounced /əʊdə ˈzəʊ/ by an English learner.

A vowel that has no change of quality is called a **monophthong**. It is often said that the tongue does not move during the articulation of the vowel (hence the little allusion in the title of this section to keeping your tongue still). But of course the tongue *does* move at the beginning and end. It *has* to move from the preceding sound to the vowel position and then on to the next sound. But these movements are not heard as changes of vowel quality, and they are very different from the movement *during* the vowel. This is heard as a change of quality, and the vowel is then called *diphthongal*. A **diphthong** has a sequence of *two* distinct positions and the tongue body moves from one position to another. (We will deal with diphthongs in V.3.)

There are clear differences between some German and English monophthongs, of course, and we deal with them as thoroughly as we can. But there are a lot of similarities – some vowels are deceptively similar but subtly different, which may not be serious for beginners since they cause no comprehension problems at all, but they are a challenge to advanced learners. These we deal with also, and try to make the subtle differences clear.

A comparison of the vowel charts with the monophthongs and the two English diphthongs /eɪ/ and /əʊ/ (see fig. 1) gives a quick reference to consult. Remember, the vertical axis represents the degree of jaw opening and tongue-body lowering, while the horizontal axis represents the backwards-forwards position of the tongue *body*. Finally, the two dots after a vowel symbol indicate a long vowel, which is distinctly longer than a short vowel (compare *bieten* with [iː] and *bitten* with [ɪ] in German).

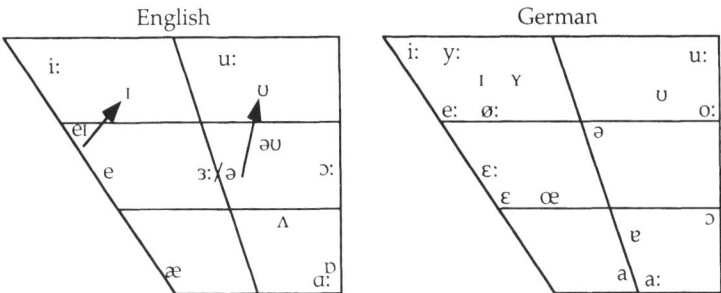

Fig. 1: Vowel qualities in English and German

The first thing that must strike you is the existence of a whole series of front vowels that exist in German but not in English. They are the front vowels with liprounding: [yː] as in *fühlen*, [ʏ] as in *füllen*, [øː] as in *Höhle* and [œ] as in *Hölle*. They are a problem for English learners of German, and only cause problems for you because they interfere with your attempts to perfect a vowel like English [ɜː] (as in *shirt*), which does not exist in German. You can see it just below the middle of the English chart. You will learn more about it in V.2.8. The lack of correspondence for the German [eː] and [oː] monophthongs is also clearly visible, and their substitution for (and by) /eɪ/ and /əʊ/ has been discussed above.

Another English vowel that has no clear correspondence in German is the well known [æ] which has already been introduced to you in III.2., the rest can be linked – for better or for worse – to German equivalents. One that seems not to have an equivalent is the English [ɔː] as in *sport, caught*. However, for many German speakers the [ɔʁ] sequence in *vorne* is pronounced as a lengthened [ɔː] rather than [ɔʁ], and this provides a tempting substitute for the proper English [ɔː]. If you compare the charts, you will see that the English [ɔː] and German [ɔ] are some distance from each other. Similarly, the English and German [uː] have radically different tongue positions (see V.2.4. and V.2.2.).

To sum up: German has more monophthongs than English, and there appear to be rough German equivalents for most of the English monophthongs – all except /æ/ in fact – as you found out in III.2. However, as the vowel chart shows, the actual *phonetic values* of these roughly (or shall we say *temptingly?*) equivalent vowels can be considerably different. In the next part of the book we devote a short section to each of the English vowels.

V.2.1. [ɪ], [i] and [iː]: *Say "Cheese"*

"Say `cheese´", is what you hear when someone wants to take a photograph of you with a smile on your face. In terms of phonetics, [iː], as in [ʧiːz], is a vowel with lip spreading. At the same time it is a high front vowel. (As a matter of fact, as we wrote in V.1, you cannot really get it much higher and further to the front without your tongue getting so close to the hard palate as to turn it into the fricative [ʝ].) Let us assume you had done something really nasty and somebody shouted [biːst] at you, should it be possible to tell whether you had been addressed in English or in German, i.e. whether the word was intended as *beast* or *Biest*?

The good news is: the two /iː/-vowels are very similar in English and German, but English /iː/ tends to be slightly lower and it also tends to be slightly diphthongal. With *knee* the tongue starts with a slightly more central position and then moves up and to the front (see Fig. 1).

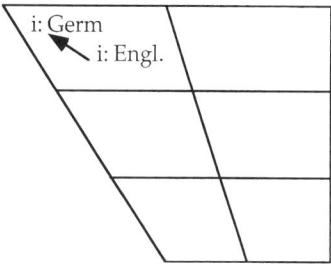

Fig. 1: German /iː/ and the slightly diphthongal quality of English /iː/

In the following exercise with **cross-language near homophones,** i.e., phonetically similar English and German words, we would like you to listen to the recorded words and put a "G" behind the appropriate number if you think the German word was spoken, and an "E" if you think it was the English one.

C 1/E 1: Discrimination exercise. Listen and identify the language

   1. *beast* vs. *Biest.*   2. *beat* vs. *Beat*   3. *flee* vs. *flieh*
   4. *she* vs. *Ski*   5. *knee* vs. *nie*   6. *beaten* vs. *bieten*
   7. *fee* vs. *Vieh*   8. *lee* vs. *lieh*

There are two short varieties of high front vowels: one of them is not only shorter than /iː/, it also has a lower and less fronted postion. The symbol for it is /ɪ/, as in *fit* /fɪt/. The German word *fit* is, to all intents and purposes, identical with its English counterpart, and in accordance with the philosophy of this book we will leave well alone and move on to the *other* short English variety: It has the same place and lip position as its long counterpart and has, therefore, been given the same symbol, but of course without the diacritic for lengthening: [i]. In present-day English many speakers use it at the end of a word, as in

1   a. *Don´t worry, Lily, I´ll be back in a jiffy.*
      b. [ˈdəʊnt ˈwʌri ˌlili | aɪɫbi ˈbækɪnə ˈdʒɪfi]

Please note that in the words *Lilly* and *jiffy* you have both varieties of short high front vowels. In refined and conservative RP as well as in some dialects in the North of England you will also hear [ˈlɪlɪ] and [ˈdʒɪfɪ], but it is important for you to be consistent and we suggest that you go for the pronunciation of 1.b., which ties up with the type of English that we have decided on in this book. As part of your ear training we will demonstrate the two varieties on tape:

C 2: listen:

> *I´m very happy to say that philosophy has been made obligatory at this university in our lovely city.*

   1. Refined RP: [ˈverɪ, ˈhæpɪ, fəˈlɒsəfɪ, əbˈlɪgətrɪ, juːnɪˈvɜːsətɪ, ˈlʌvlɪ, ˈsɪti]
   2. SBE: [ˈveri, ˈhæpi, fəˈlɒsəfi, əbˈlɪgətri, juːnɪˈvɜːsəti, ˈlʌvli, ˈsɪti]

"Füsh n Shüps" vs. [ˌfɪʃn̩ ˈʃɪps]

It is true, the articulation of English high front vowels does not cause any major problems for German speakers, but it is also true that old habits die hard, and if you happen to belong to the group of Germans who tend to pronounce these sounds with lip rounding (*Tüsche, Füsche*), you will have to abandon the lip rounding in English. (Remember: in German lip rounding is often used paralinguistically to indicate that you do not have strong feelings on a particular issue and are willing to go for a compromise, as in *"Joh, Füsch un Schüps üs schon ün Ordnung"*. But this paralinguistic feature is not used in English.) The temptation to use the sound of <ü>, the phonetic symbol for which is [ʏ] or [y] is particularly strong in words that contain the letter <y>, which in German is pronounced [ʏ] or [y], i.e. just like the <ü>, as in German

Dynastie and *zynisch*. In English, however, the lip rounding for [ɪ] in words with <y> must be avoided at all cost:

2   a. *dynasty* [ˈdɪnəsti], *cynical* [ˈsɪnɪkɬ], *dyslexia* (G: *Legasthenie*), *dyslectic*

     b.   *Here´s a limerick on young Lady Smith,*   [hɪəzə ˈlɪmrɪkɒn ˈjʌŋ leɪdi ˈsmɪθ
          Whose virtue was mostly a myth,   huːz ˈvɜːtju: wəz ˈməʊstliə ˈmɪθ
          She said: "Try as I can   ʃi sed ˈtraɪəzaɪ ˈkæn
          I can´t find a man   aɪ ˈkɑːnt faɪndə ˈmæn
          Who it´s fun to be virtuous with.   huˍɪts ˈfʌn tə bi ˈvɜːtjuəs ˈwɪð

"Don´t feed these obese Chinese geese with cheese."

We have to admit that this is a silly sentence, but try and read it aloud all the same. There are five words ending in *-ese* in the above subtitle, and did you notice that the pronunciation [-iːz] alternates with that of [-iːs]? The phonetic transcription of 3a. is 3b.:

3   a. Don´t feed these obese Chinese geese with cheese.
    b. [ˈdəʊnt fiːd ðiːz əʊˈbiːs ʧaɪˈniːz ˈgiːs wɪð ˈʧiːz]

Once again we wanted to draw your attention to the fortis/lenis problem for German speakers in word- and utterance-final position. With many German speakers using the demonstrative pronouns *this* and *these*, it is difficult to tell whether the plural or the singular is intended until one actually hears the plural ending of the noun because their *these* is too short. In that case the listener might hear *"*this tables*". The plural of nouns ending in a vowel is formed by adding [z], so you might expect the lengthening of the preceding sound, which is basically true, but not to the extent that you get *[ˈsɪtiːz]. The plural of words ending in [i] is pronounced [-ɪz], i.e. with a high but short front vowel: *cities* [ˈsɪtɪz], *hillbillies* [ˈhɪɬbɪlɪz], *opportunities* [ˌɒpəˈtjuːnɪtɪz].

C 3: Even when you have mastered the different articulatory positions of the high front vowels, it is important that you practice the length of these sounds as it is determined by their phonetic environment. We have listed the words on a scale from short to long:

    a. *sit* < *Sid* < *seat* < *seed*
    b. *bit* < *bid* < *beat* < *bead*
    c. *fit* < *feet* < *feed*
    d. *sis* < *cease* < *seize*
    e. *this city* < *these cities; this opportunity* < *these opportunies*

"eeeeek" and other spellings

Even though the days of the week end in *-day*, they are usually pronounced [ˈmʌndi], [ˈsʌndi] etc., just like *yesterday* [ˈjestədi]; but [-deɪ] is also a possibility, as for instance in Beatles song: *Yesterday, all my troubles were so far away ...*, and *birthday* is normally pronounced [ˈbɜːθdeɪ].

We would like to draw your attention to a number of words from our list of **frequently mispronounced words** that you should memorise:

litre [ˈliːtə], *kilo* [ˈkiːləʊ] but *kilo-* [ˈkɪlə] as in *kilobyte* [ˈkɪləbaɪt] and [ˈkɪləwɒt]; *kilometre* may be pronounced [ˈkɪləmiːtə] or [kɪ ˈlɒmɪtə].

And in the following three words [iː] should *not* be used; they all start with [sɪə]: *serious* [ˈsɪərɪəs]; *series*, (sg. [ˈsɪərɪz], pl. [ˈsɪəriːz]); *cereal*: [ˈsɪəriəɫ], *serial* [ˈsɪəriəɫ]. N.B. in all three cases [ˈsɪə-] not *[ˈsiːr-]!

A rather subtle difference, but one an advanced learner needs to know is the pronunciation of <de-> at the beginning of a word as [di(ː)] or [dɪ]. In words like: *decentralize, deconstruct, decouple, decoke, declassify*, etc., where the <de-> element clearly means to reverse or "undo" the process expressed by the verb stem, the pronunciation is most commonly [di], sometimes with a second stress on the <de->, in which case it is lengthened to [diː].

In words like: *decree, default, deport, defunct* (German: (aus)gestorben), *department, depression*, etc, where no undoing of a process is implied, the pronunciation is most commonly [dɪ]. But beware! If a suffix is added which moves the stress from the second to the third syllable, then [dɪ] becomes [diː], as in: *deportation* [ˌdiːpɔːˈteɪʃən] and *departmental* [ˌdiːpɑːtˈmentəɫ].

Interestingly, in a few words, e.g. *deflate, decrease*, where the <de-> element *does* mean a reversal of a process, but where the verb stem alone does not convey the process being undone (*increase* not *crease*, and *inflate* not **flate* are being reversed), either [di(ː)] or [dɪ] appear to be equally acceptable.

V.2.2. /uː/: You and your /uː/
Is there room for improvement?

C 1: To answer the above question you should listen very carefully to the long [uː] sounds in *foolish, Peru, shoe* and *true* in the following limerick:

This foolish old man from Peru,	[ðɪs ˈfuːlɪʃˌəʊɫd ˈmæn frəm pəˈruː
who dreamt he was eating his shoe,	hu ˈdremti wəˈziːtɪŋɪz ˈʃuː
awoke in the night	əˈwəʊkɪn ðə ˈnaɪt
with a terrible fright,	wɪðə ˈterɪbɫ ˈfraɪt
and found it was perfectly true.	ən ˈfaʊndɪt wəz ˈpɜːfəktli ˈtruː]

You may have noticed that, compared to German, the English /uː/ is slightly diphthongised. By this we mean there is some tongue movement with a corresponding change in vowel quality. You may also have observed that the vowel in English *shoe* is further to the *front* than the one in German *Schuh*. In narrow transcription it is the difference between [u̟ː] and [ɵʉ] (the diacritics ˌ and ˍ mean that the vowels are further forward and further back, respectively, than the symbol alone signifies. For [ɵ] and [ʉ], see the IPA chart).

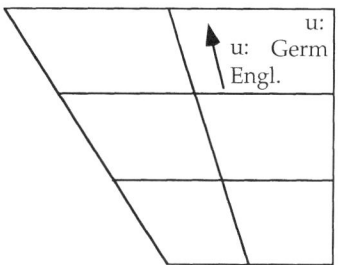

Fig. 1: English and German /uː/

We will now demonstrate what this visual difference means in auditory terms by contrasting a number of German and English /uː/ sounds:

C 2: **Cross-language near-homophones.** The German word will always be played first: listen and repeat:

German	English	German	English
a. *Schuh*	*shoe*	d. *Hindu*	*Hindu*
b. *Hut*	*hoot*	e. *Ruth*	*root*
c. *Wudu*	*Voodoo*	f. *muh*	*moo*

E 1: Work with a partner. Pick any of the words listed in C2 and ask your partner to guess whether it was meant to be an English or a German word. If after many attempts your partner keeps guessing your words were always the German ones, you should return to C 1 and C 2.

C 3: listen and repeat after each line:

An epicure, dining at Crewe, [ən ᵇʔepɪkjʊə ˈdaɪnɪŋət ˈkru:
Found quite a large mouse in his stew. faʊnd ˈkwaɪtə lɑːʤ ˈmaʊsɪnɪz ˈstju:
Said the waiter: "Don´t shout sed ðə ˈweɪtə dəʊnt ˈʃaʊt
and wave it about, ən ˈweɪvɪtəˈbaʊt
or the rest will be wanting one, too." ɔːðə ˈrestɫ bi ˈwɒntɪŋ wʌn ˈtu:]

C 4: Listen and repeat:

"Which films are on view now?" - "There´s `Room with a view´ and coming soon: `One flew over the cuckoo´s nest´." - "I like horror movies, like `The monster from the blue lagoon." - "And for children they are showing `Winnie the Pooh´ and `Dr. Dolittle´." - "And there's a selection of favourite cartoons, with Goofy and Snoopy."

E 2: Read these words making sure you distinguish between the two types of /u:/, i.e. the one with prefortis clipping and the one without, i.e. both *root* and *rude* have a long [u:], but in *rude* it is slightly longer:

institute , aptitude;	*route, rude;*	*newt, nude;*	*coot, cooed;*	*lute, lewd;*
loose, lose;	*suit, sued;*	*moot, mood*		

/u:/ before [ɫ]

So far we have avoided words containing /u:/ followed by /l/. The dark [ɫ] has a strong effect on the /u:/ for many speakers of English, giving it a distinctly retracted [u:] quality, much more like German /u:/. The vowel quality itself is therefore not a problem for German speakers, but of course it has to be linked with a correct dark [ɫ].The following recording contrasts the retracted [u:] with the normal English fronted and diphthongized [ɵʉ].

C 5: Listen to the different timbres of /u:/ in the following word pairs, and repeat:

cooed	-	*cool*	*crude*	-	*cruel*
poo-pooed	-	*pool*	*food*	-	*fool*
too	-	*tool*	*grew*	-	*gruel*
drew	-	*drool*	*Jude*	-	*jewel*
nude	-	*Newel*	*dew*	-	*duel*

"Shoes repaired while-u-wait"

U 2 will come a † ...... Sorry: you too will come across signs like these in shops, but spelling is not always that simple. With /u:/ in particular there are plenty of possibilities:

<oo> is generally pronounced as /u:/ and always occurs in the stressed syllable: *kangaroo* [ˌkæŋgəˈru:], *Sutton Hoo*, [ˌsʌtn̩ ˈhu:], *Waterloo*, *woo, room, boot, Winnie the Pooh*

But of course there are some exceptions, where <oo> is *not* pronounced [uː]:

a. <oo> before <d>: *food* and *mood* are pronounced regularly, i.e. as [fuːd] and [muːd], but *good* and *wood* have short [ʊ], and so does *hood* [hʊd] as in *Robin Hood* and *Little Red Riding Hood*. On the other hand *blood* [blʌd], *flood* [flʌd] have the more open unrounded vowel [ʌ].

b. <oo> before <t>: *boot, coot, loot, root* and *moot* all have /uː/, but *soot* [sʊt] has a short [ʊ] and thus rhymes with *foot* and is not a homophone of *suit* [suːt].

c. <oo> before <k>: All <oo> words before <k> have short [ʊ]: e.g., *book, brook, cook, hook*, (try and remember the idiomatic phrase: *by hook or by crook*; (German: *auf Biegen und Brechen*), *look, nook, rook, took* and *shook*.

d. <oo> before <l>: Most <oo> words with <l> are pronounced [uː] (compare C 5 above), but *wool* [wʊɫ] is an exception. Make a note of the idiomatic phrase: *"They tried to pull the wool over my eyes."* [pʊɫ ðə ˈwʊləʊvə maɪˈaɪz]

A unique pronunciation of <oo> as [əʊ] is *brooch* [brəʊtʃ] (German: *Brosche*).

Other spellings of [uː]:

<u> *with or without* <e>: *immune* [ɪˈmjuːn], *tribute* [ˈtrɪbjuːt], *brute, flute; dune, tune* [tjuːn] (but usually no long [uː] in *fortune* [ˈfɔːtʃən]); *Susan; Peru, flu, menu, tutu; glue, glued;*

<ui>: *recruit, fruit, suit, the pursuit of happiness*, but *biscuit* [ˈbɪskɪt];

<ou>: *blue bayou, caribou, Lou;*

<oe>: *canoe, hoopoe* and *shoe*, which are the big exceptions, because the other words ending in <-oe> are pronounced like *toe* [təʊ];

<om> *with and without* <b>: *womb* [wuːm], *tomb* [tuːm], *tombstone* [ˈtuːmstəʊn], but *honeycomb* [ˈhʌnikəʊm]; *Domesday Book* [ˈduːmzdeɪ ˌbʊk];

E 3: Read these words aloud and write them under the three headings given below: *wool, tomb, fortune, tribute, brooch, menu, brook, canoe*

[uː]   [ʊ]   other

Fun-netics:

Graffiti:

"To be is to do" - Sartre. *"To do is to be."* - Nietzsche.
"Dobedobedoo." - Frank Sinatra

- *What did the toothbrush say to the toothpaste? - Meet you outside the tube.*

Limerick:

There once was a very old gnu,
Who was used by a chef in some stew.
He should have been told
The gnu was too old:
For stews, only new gnus will do.

[ðə ˈwʌns wəzə ˈverɪ əʊɫd ˈnju:
hu wəz ˈjuːzd baɪə ˈʃefɪn səm ˈstju:
hi ˈʃʊdəv bɪn ˈtəʊɫd
ðə ˈnju: wəz tu ˈəʊɫd
fə ˈstjuːz‿ɔʊnli ˈnju: ˌnjuːz wɪɫ ˈdu:]

Now that you have mastered the /u:/ you may enjoy reading aloud the following poem by A. E. Houseman:

When I was one-and-twenty
I heard a wise man say,
"Give crowns and pounds and guineas
But not your heart away;
Give pearls away and rubies
but keep your fancy free."
But I was one-and-twenty,
No use to talk to me.

[weˈnaɪ wəz ˈwʌnən ˈtwenti
aɪ ˈhɜːdə ˈwaɪz mæn ˈseɪ
gɪv ˈkraʊnzən ˈpaʊndzən ˈgɪnɪz
bʌt ˈnɒt jɔ: ˈhɑːtəˈweɪ
gɪv ˈpɜːɫzəˈweɪ‿ən ˈru:biz
bʌt ˈki:p jɔ: ˈfænsi ˈfri:
bʌˈtaɪ wəz ˈwʌnən ˈtwenti
nəʊ ˈjuːs tə ˈtɔːk tə ˈmi:]

When I was one-and-twenty
I heard him say again,
"The heart out of the bosom
was never given in vain;
`Tis paid with sighs a-plenty
And sold for endless rue."
And I am two-and-twenty,
And oh, `tis true, `tis true.

weˈnaɪ wəz ˈwʌnən ˈtwenti
aɪ ˈhɜːdɪm ˈseɪəˈgeɪn
ðə ˈhɑːt‿aʊtəv ðə ˈbuzəm
wəz ˈnevə ˈgɪvn̩ɪn ˈveɪn
tɪz ˈpeɪd wɪð ˈsaɪzəˈplenti
ənd ˈsəʊɫd fəˈrendləs ˈru:
ənˈdaɪ‿əm ˈtu:ən ˈtwenti
ənˈdəʊ tɪz ˈtru: tɪz ˈtru:]

V.2.3. /ʊ/: *Yes I would, if I could*

The good news is, if you pronounce the English word *bush* like the German word *Busch* it will be good enough. German *Busch* tends to have slightly stronger lip rounding than *bush*, so try not to overdo the liprounding. Recall that with the high *front* vowels the short [ɪ] differed from its long counterpart [iː] not only in duration but also in its position, which was lower and more central (see V.2.1). With the two high *back* vowels only one of these aspects is true: in the Southern British English accent we are aiming at the vowel of *put* and *foot* has moved to a more central position and the short [ʊ] is certainly more open than its long counterpart. But since [uː] has been pushed forward (and is also slightly diphthongal), it is not necessarily further back than [ʊ]. The [ʊ] that we feel goes best with the other vowels that we recommend is shown in fig.1 and demonstrated in C 1. Notice the amount of variability that is acceptable for [ʊ] – indicated by the size of the ellipse in the diagram.

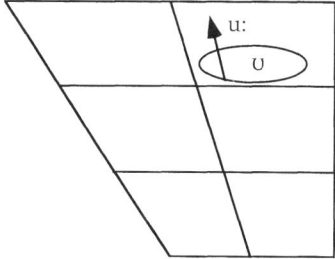

Fig. 1: Southern English [ʊ] in relation to [uː]

C 1: Listen and repeat (Southern English pronunciation):

> *"He told Woodcock he didn´t like books with footnotes." - "But look, Woodcock´s book is full of them." - "Yes, he shouldn´t have said that. He really put his foot in it." - "Well, I like the book. I think it´s very good."*

Advanced students may like to know that in Northern English dialects [ʌ] as in *love* is replaced by a fairly high [ʊ]. This means that SBE *putt* [pʌt] is pronounced [pʊt] and becomes a homophone of *put* [pʊt] for many Northern speakers of English. Consequently they often make "mistakes" when they try to change from their dialect to Standard English – which often happens in these days of professional mobility. In their attempt to sound like educated SBE speakers they may then use hypercorrect forms, pronouncing *cushion* as [ˈkʌʃn]. So it is not only poor German learners of English who may have problems with words like the following, which contain the letter <u>. After you have done the exercise, check your answers in chapter XII.

E 1: Indicate the correct pronunciation by placing either [ʌ] or [ʊ] above <u>:

puddle, pudding, budding, pulpit, culprit, putt, put, custard,

lucky, cushion, gushing, bud, pus, puss, courier, Fulham

As we said before, the vowel of *put* and *foot* has moved to a more central position in SBE. The word *good* is a very special case: with some speakers its vowel has been moved forward to such an extent that if people had not learnt how to spell this word and did not know that it has <-oo-> in it, i.e. if they just had to rely on what they actually hear, they would presumably spell it *gid*, because its vowel is closer to the shwa sound and even the [ɪ] than it is to [ʊ]. If you wish to sound really English your vowel in *good* should be further to the front than in *wood* and *put* (see fig. 1).

The modal verb forms *should* and *would* spoken in isolation, in stressed positions and at the end of a sentence are pronounced [ʃʊd] and [wʊd]. However, as they are function words, the vowel is often weakened, moving towards schwa or even disappearing altogether.

1   a. *I certainly would.* [wʊd]
     b. *I would certainly have a go at it.* [aɪ wəd ˈsɜːtn̩li]
     c. *I'd certainly give it a try.* [aɪd ˈsɜːtn̩li]

These weakening phenomena are treated more thoroughly in section VI.3.

They tried to pull [ʊ] *the wool* [ʊ] *over the poor* [ɔː] *fool's* [uː] *eyes*

Let us have a look at words ending in either [ʊ]+consonant or [uː]+consonant, like *proof* (and also *soothe*, because in spite of the spelling there is only one consonant at the end, i.e. [ð]). The spelling is a good guide here, as "-oo-" often indicates [uː]: *fool, foolproof, tool, room, broom, soon, booth, smooth, snooze* (see V.2.2). We should, therefore, have a look at <-oo-> words with short [ʊ], as there is the danger of overgeneralisation here, and indeed native speakers of German tend to wrongly pronounce *wool* as *[wuːɫ], based on the analogy with *school, cool, pool* and *fool*, instead of using the short vowel: *wool* [wʊɫ].

With words ending in <-ook> it is the other way round: they normally have the short [ʊ] vowel like *book, cook, hook, shook, look, took*, and the exceptions are *snook* [snuːk] and *snooker*, and *spook* and *spooky*. Foreigners often wrongly use the long vowel for <-ook>-words they are not familiar with, like *[bruːk] for *brook* and *[ruːk] for *rook*.

The same rule applies to <-oot>-words: most of them have the long [uː], like *boot, hoot, shoot, loot*, and *root*. Everybody is aware of the exception *foot* [fʊt], but most learners are not aware of the other one: *soot* (German: *Ruß*) [sʊt]. The words with <-ood> vary most. They can be pronounced with [uː] as in *food*, or [ʊ] as in *hood, Robin Hood, stood* and *wood*, or [ʌ] as in *flood* and *blood*. But, possibly because these are high-frequency words, learners do not seem to have so many difficulties with them.

Let us finish this section with a limerick, which you can first listen to and enjoy, then repeat.

C 2: Listen and repeat:

Was there something that Robin J. Hood,	[wɒz ðə ˈsʌmθɪŋ ðət ˈrɒbɪn dʒəɪ ˈhʊd
US taxman, had misunderstood?	juː es ˈtæksmæn həd ˈmɪsʌndəˈstʊd
"What I take from the needy	wɒt aɪ ˈteɪk frəm ðə ˈniːdi
I give to the greedy.	aɪ ˈgɪv tə ðə ˈgriːdi
Like my namesake that Mr. Rob Hood."	laɪk maɪ ˈneɪmseɪk ðæt ˈmɪstə rɒb ˈhʊd]

V.2.4. /ɑː/: *It's a hard path to start on!*

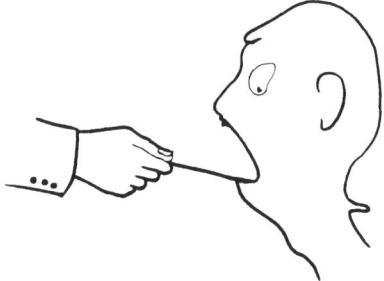

Fig. 1: Doctor: [seɪ ˈɑː]
Patient: [aːːːːː]
Doctor: [ˌfɜːðə ˈbæk]
Patient: [ɑːːːːː]
Doctor: [ˌnaʊ ˈðæts
wɒt aɪ kɔːlə ˈləʊ
ˌbæk ˈvaʊəɫ]

If you are keen to sound English, the vowel in three of the words of this section heading is something you have to make an effort with. Not that there is any chance of being misunderstood, because it is one of the sounds which has an unconfusable equivalent in German (*Staat, Bahn,* etc.), but it is just phonetically different enough to sound clearly German.

Imitate an English speaker (or the Hamburg harbourmaster!)

Just listen to the English speaker saying the phrase *"In the barn"* and compare it with the German speaker saying the same phrase but pronouncing *barn* in the same way that *Bahn* is pronounced. Then see whether you can imitate the English speaker, and make the *"ah"* sound *"darker"* (you speak it with your tongue pulled further back in your mouth). Alternatively, if you know how a real dyed-in-the-wool Hamburg speaker pronounces *Bahn*, try to imitate that. The symbol used to signify this more "retracted" long *"ah"* sound is [ɑː] as opposed to the more "fronted" quality, symbolised by the IPA symbol [aː]. The following vowel chart illustrates what we have just tried to describe.

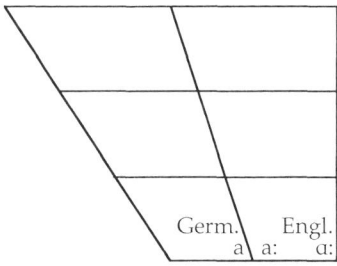

Fig. 2: Positions for German short /a/ and long /aː/, English long /ɑː/

Infobox

Let us remind you: Vowels can be described according to a) the degree to which the jaw and tongue are opened, b) whether the mass of the tongue body is fronted or retracted, c) whether the lips are rounded or not, and d) whether the vowel is long or short (relative to its context!).

C 1: Listen and repeat:

    a. Standard English: [ɑ:] *in the barn, at the start; barn, start*
    b. Hamburg dialect: [ɑ:] *in der Bahn, im Staat; Bahn, Staat*
    c. Standard German: [a:] *in der Bahn, im Staat; Bahn, Staat*

As the <u>standard</u> German and English *"ah"* sounds are different, it is useful to have different symbols to remind us. So we shall use [ɑ:] for the English vowel in words like *barn* and [a:] for the German vowel in words like *Bahn*. Remember, the *symbol* is only to remind you of the sound, and it is the *sound*, and the imprint of that sound in your auditory memory that is important.

E 1: Cross-language near-homophones: Select one word from each pair and say it aloud. Your partner or the rest of the class have to guess whether you intended it to be a German or an English word.

a.	i. *Carter*	ii. *Kater*	e.	i. *lava*	ii. *Lava*
b.	i. *barn*	ii. *Bahn*	f.	i. *party*	ii. *Party*
c.	i. *calm*	ii. *kam*	g.	i. *Guardian*	ii. *Guardian*
d.	i. *start*	ii. *Staat*	h.	i. *tart*	ii. *Tat*

A little practice

So, let us return to the standard English [ɑ:] sound, even if it *is "hard to start with"* [hɑ:d tə ˈstɑ:t wɪð].

C 2a: Listen to the following little conversation between a speaker of standard English and a German-English speaker, and familiarise yourself with the different quality of the two speakers' [ɑ:] and [a:] sounds.
    German speaker: *Is it far to Hyde Park?* English speaker: *Well, it's not far by car! -* G: *But where can I park my car? -* E: *In the underground car park.*

C 2b: These dialogues are between native speakers. Listen and repeat.

1. A: *Have we passed the farm?*
     B: *No, but it can't be far now.*
     A: *Is it after the barn?*
     B: *Yes, up the path and across the yard.*

2. A: *Where did you find the car?*
     B: *In "Exchange and Mart".*
     A: *Was it a bargain?*
     B: *Hard to judge yet.*

3. A: *We're having a garden party.*
     B: *When does it start?*
     A: *At half past two.*
     B: *Afternoon or morning?!*

4. A: *What can I get you from the bar?*
     B: *A half of lager, please.*
     A: *Harp or Carlsberg?*
     B: *Half and half!*

Spellings of [ɑ:]:

<ar>	*farm, car, Carl, hart,*	<er>	*clerk, sergeant, Derby,*
<ear>	*heart, hearth,*	<al>	*calm, qualm, calf, half, almond* [ˈɑ:mənd]
<a>	*lava, master, faster, last, bastard, basket, cast, caste, lager, Shaftesbury*		

Rare spelling: *Amman* [əˈmɑ:n]

Now practise [ɑ:] with our following variation on the "animal encounters" theme made famous by the limerick about the "Lady from Riga":

Famous last words

She jumped in the sea from a barque.	[ʃi ˈdʒʌmtɪn ðə ˈsi: frəmə ˈbɑ:k
"I did it", she said, "for a lark."	aɪ ˈdɪdɪt ʃi ˈsed fərə ˈlɑ:k
She returned to the barque,	ʃi rɪˈtɜ:ntə ðə ˈbɑ:k
having rued her remark -	hævɪŋ ˈru:d hə rɪˈmɑ:k
with a grin on the face of a shark.	wɪðə ˈgrɪn‿ɒn ðə ˈfeɪsəvə ˈʃɑ:k]

V.2.5. /ɒ/: *Why a Schock is not a shock*

Using German [ɔ] instead of English [ɒ] will never lead to a misunderstanding of the intended word, but will be heard as un-English. So we want you to start with ear training. The rhyming words in lines 3 and 4, i.e. *Block* and *shock* have German counterparts. Try and identify how the English words are different from their German equivalents.

C 1: Learn to listen (*He´s a chip of the old block = Er kommt ganz nach dem Vater*)

They buried a salesman named Phipps.   [ðeɪ ˈberɪdə ˈseɪɫzmən neɪmd ˈfɪps]
He married on one of his trips   hi ˈmærɪdɒn ˈwʌnəvɪz ˈtrɪps
A widow named Block,   ə ˈwɪdəʊ neɪmd ˈblɒk
Then died of the shock,   ðen ˈdaɪdəv ðə ˈʃɒk
When he found there were five little chips. weni ˈfaʊnd ðəwə ˈfaɪv lɪtɫ ʧɪps]

C 2/E 1: Discrimination exercise.

In this exercise of cross-language near-homophones we want you to listen to the recording of the numbered list of word pairs and decide whether each pair was pronounced in the order as written, or whether the order was reversed for the recording. Put "E/G" behind the appropriate number if you think the order was English and then German, or "G/E" if you think it was German and then English.

1. *otter* vs. *Otter*   2. *dock* vs. *Dock*   3. *got* vs. *Gott*
4. *flock* vs. *Pflock*   5. *block* vs. *Block*   6. *pop* vs. *Pop*
7. *shot* vs. *Schott*   8. *plotter* vs. *Plotter*   9. *shock vs. Schock*
            10. *Oppenheimer* vs. *Oppenheimer*

C 3/E 2: Analysis of English/German differences.

This exercise is a little more demanding in terms of analytic listening. We have selected English-German pairs that do not constitute minimal pairs because they display other differences as well as the different [ɒ]-sounds. We want you to comment on these differences, so you have the two-fold task: First identify which of the two similar words you hear is English and which is German, and then explain at least one further phonetic difference. <u>Example</u>: 1. *stock* vs. *Stock*. Let us assume that the order of the recording is reversed, so you write: "1. G/E and E [st-] vs. G [ʃt-]." (Underline the letters that are pronounced differently if you do not know the phonetic symbols.)

1. *stock* vs. *Stock*   2. *nonstop* vs. *Nonstop*
3. *Hongkong* vs. *Hongkong*   4. *Concord* vs. *Concord*
5. *Pavarotti* vs. *Pavarotti*   6. *job* vs. *Job*
7. *hot pants* vs. *Hot Pants*   8. *logbook* vs. *Logbuch*
9. *Tom Stoppard* vs. *Tom Stoppard* 10. *Oliver Cromwell* vs. *Oliver Cromwell*

E 3: Select words from C 2 and C 3 and say them aloud. After each word, your partner has to say whether you intended a German or an English word.

The "[hɒt] potato" exercise

Now that your ears have tuned into the audible difference between *Schock* and *shock*, your tongue dorsum has to learn a new position, lower and further back than the German [ɔ]. Also the lips need to be less rounded. Fig. 1 gives a schematic illustration of the difference in tongue position (though of course it cannot reflect the more relaxed lip-rounding of English [ɒ]):

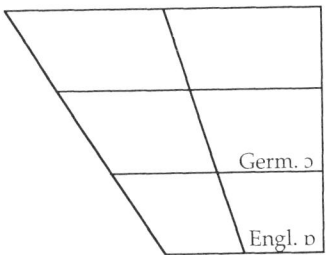

Fig. 1. German [ɔ] and English [ɒ]

In the vowel diagrams in V.2, you will see that the low right hand corner of the German chart has an empty space, whereas the English chart has two vowels: [ɒ] and [ɑ:], as in *pod* and *past*. That is the "lower and further back" position mentioned earlier. You will have to train your tongue to explore this "terra incognita". One light-hearted way of doing it is to imagine you have a hot potato in your mouth. That might help you to retract and lower your tongue in trying to avoid contact with it. Trying to say *hot* while doing that should make the vowel [ɒ] in [hɒt] sound convincingly English. Of course, the production of a low back slightly rounded English [ɒ] has to become an automatic gesture but the *"hot potato"* exercise is a good starting point.

Acquiring a good pronunciation is very much a question of one´s attitude. We suggest you enjoy saying [smɒk] as much as [hɒbz] in fig. 2.

Fig. 2: Calvin & Hobbes. *The Days are Just Packed.* (Warner Books 1993, p.98)

C 4: Listen and repeat. Remember that in addition to the different tongue position, you must also have weaker lip rounding when producing [ɒ]:

a. *Doc Holiday was shot and died on the spot.*
b. *The whole lot was auctioned off, lock, stock and barrel, at rockbottom prices.*
c. *"Did you enjoy Don Waddle´s latest novel `Shot in the Dark´?" - "I liked it a lot, especially the dialogues, but I thought the plot was a bit odd."*
d. *The college offered courses on phonology, morphology, photography. Bob, who had only ever taken holiday snapshots, chose photography as a soft option.*
e. *John toddled off, with a dog named "Spot", and promptly got lost.*
f. *The Wroxham Hot Shots´ song came second in Top of the Pops.*
g. *The doctor arrived at four o´clock on the dot. Yes, as always: spot on time.*

C 5: Listen and repeat after each line.

Parson Doddle was constantly mocked	[ˌpɑːsən ˈdɒdɫ wəz ˈkɒnstəntli ˈmɒkt
Because he was easily shocked.	bɪˈkəzi wəˈziːzɪli ˈʃɒkt
"I saw in my flock	aɪ ˈsɔː ɪn maɪ ˈflɒk
A girl with no frock ...	ə ˈgɜːɫ wɪð nəʊ ˈfrɒk
Uhm.. in jeans!" added he, and was mocked.	əːːm ǀ ɪn ˈdʒiːnz ǀ ædɪd ˈhiː ǀ ən wəz
	ˈmɒkt]

V.2.6. /ɔ:/: *Any port in a storm; all aboard*

The English vowel /ɔ:/, as in *"All aboard!"* is another deceptively "easy" one. At least for those speakers of German who pronounce *Portwein* without any /r/, i.e., just by lengthening the [ɔ], the temptation to substitute their German vowel in English words is difficult to resist. As with many other vowels, there is little if any danger of being misunderstood, and there are a number of English dialects – not to mention some varieties of Southern Irish and US English – that have a vowel that is similar in quality to a lengthened German /ɔ/. However, unless the German learner speaks one of those dialects in its entirety, he or she will be immediately recognised as foreign, and probably as a German speaker of English, because the vowel quality is much too open for Southern British English. The vowel diagram below (fig. 1) shows the quality of the Standard German /ɔ/ and the lengthened [ɔ:] of [ʀ]-less *Portwein*, compared to a standard Southern British English /ɔ:/.

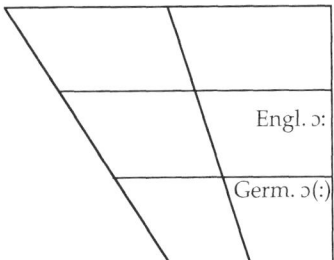

Fig. 1: Standard German /ɔ/ and [ɔ:] variant compared to a SBE /ɔ:/

Of course, the diagram will only start to mean something to you when you can actually hear and pronounce the difference. You will notice that the lips and jaw are more closed for the English sound than for the German one, which is why the position on the chart is higher. Of course, the tongue is carried by the jaw, so we speak of a "higher" or "more close" tongue position. "Close" means closer to the palate.

Being aware of this, and being able to hear that other German speakers are "doing it wrong" is the first step, but another danger lurks round the corner. As with any attempt to correct a bad habit, the tendency is to go too far the other way (you may have noticed that ex-smokers often become the most intransigent opponents of smokers!). Unfortunately there is a German vowel sound which is produced with a slightly closer tongue-jaw position than the English /ɔ:/, which may lure you into the over-corrected form. It is the /o:/ as in *Boot, Fohlen, Schot, Ton, tot,* even *Kot.* These German words all have corresponding English words to tempt you: *bought, fallen, short, torn, taught, caught.* You are sure to find other German-English *faux-amis* of the same kind.

So a second step in learning the English /ɔː/ sound must be to develop an auditory impression of the over-corrected version.

C 1: Listen to the examples spoken first by a German speaker, and then by a speaker of standard English. Some of the examples spoken by German speakers are the version which is influenced by the lengthened [ɔː] that can occur in *Portwein*, some of them are the over-corrected form influenced by German /oː/. This should help you to form an "auditory picture" of the vowel.

a. *She bought a horse.*
b. *She gave a short talk.*
c. *That´s a tall order.*
d. *Don´t fall for that story.*
e. *Turn Saul into Paul.*
f. *That orchestra´s awful!*
g. *He's fallen in the water!*
h. *Any port in a storm.*
i. *The orders were ignored.*
j. *There was sawdust on the floor.*

When you feel confident of the auditory image of the English vowel in contrast to the German sound, try saying the phrases yourself, and remember (see info box in section V.1.): Don´t be put off if it feels strange at first. Your mouth has to become accustomed to a slightly new shape.

Of course, eventually (and *please* don't think that means "eventuell"!) you have to reach the point where you produce the "new" sound automatically, and don´t slip back into either of the German versions of it. That is best done by practising the sound, consciously at first, in expressions that you will use frequently. So think – in English – about the things you do, routinely, as part of your everyday life, and see which of the words connected with them contain the vowel /ɔː/. Now work out short expressions containing those words, and practise them to yourself. The following examples may get you going:

1 a. *Good Morning.*
   b. *Your car's on the forecourt.*
   c. *The ball's in your court.*
   d. *Could you open the door for me please? - Yes, of course.*
   e. *Do you have any thoughts on the matter?*
   f. *I´ll give you a call.*
   g. *Are there any new orders?*
   h. *I shouldn´t have thought so.*

paw and pour, board and bored: Orthography can be very galling, or:
[ˈpɔː ən ˈpɔː | ˈbɔːd ən ˈbɔːd | ɔːˈθɒɡrəfi kəmbɪ ˈveri ˈɡɔːlɪŋ]

From the few example phrases under 1 a - h you will already have registered that there are many different ways of spelling the /ɔː/ sound. Some of the following examples represent /ɔː/ and nothing else, others are used for other vowels too – they are not unique to /ɔː/:

<or>: cord, sort, born, ford, lord, corn, morning, horse, torso
       but: *worse* ([ɜː]), *worsted* [ʊ].

<oar> *board, soar, boar*

<oor> *floor, door,* (but cf. V.3.6.3. on /ʊə/ for *poor* and *moor*)

<our>   *pour, court, courgette, mourn*, but: *tour, dour* [ʊə], and *sour* [aʊə].

<ar>   *war, warm, swarm, swarthy*; (otherwise [ɑ:])

<aw>   *awl, shawl, paw, lawn, bawl, jaw, pawn*;

<all>   *call, fall, gall, hall, mall, pall, tall, wall*

<al>   *Baltic, bald, alter, altar, alternative, alderman, alder, almanc(k)*;
         but: [æ]: *Alsation, altimeter, altitude, altruism*

<ough>   *bought, sought, brought, fought, nought, ought*;
         but: *plough, drought* ([aʊ]), *cough* ([ɒf]) *rough, tough* ([ʌf]);

<au(gh)> *caught, haughty, taught, distraught, cauldron, faulty, pause, vault*;
         but: *laughter* ([ɑ:f]), *cauliflower* [ɒ], and *vault* can also be [vɒɫt])

Rare spelling: *Sean* [ʃɔ:n]

Infobox

Did you notice that the first five spelling variants all involve an <r> which is not pronounced? But it is important to remember that words that end with that <r> do have an [r] in their pronunciation *if the next word begins with a vowel*. That is the phenomenon that we call "linking -r" (see VI.1).

V.2.7. /ʌ/: *Huts* [hʌts] *have roofs shaped like* [ʌ]

Fig. 1: [ə ˈdʌk ˈdrɪŋkɪŋ
aʊtəvə ˈbʌkɪt] (doodle from
The Puffin Joke Book)

We hope the duck-doodle will help you to remember the phonetic symbol for the vowel in *duck* [dʌk]. The [dʌks] tail sticking out of the [ˈbʌkɪt] clearly shows why English phoneticians chose this IPA symbol! Others claim it was because the [ʌ] resembles the roof of a *hut* [hʌt]. Take your pick!

C 1: Listen and repeat:

Beneath this stone,	[bɪˈni:θ ðɪsˈ stəʊn]
A lump of clay,	ə ˈlʌmpəv ˈkleɪ]
Lies Arabella Young,	laɪˈz‿ærəˌbelə ˈjʌŋ]
Who, on the twenty-third of May	hu‿ˈɒnðə twenti ˈθɜ:dəv ˈmeɪ]
in seventeen-hundred and seventy-one,	ɪn ˈsevnti:n ˈhʌndrɪdn̩ ˈsevn̩ti ˈwʌn
Began to hold her tongue.	bɪˈgæn tə ˈhəʊɫdə ˈtʌŋ]

Fig. 2: [gʊt lak]!

A German varnish company with a sense of humour, and presumably in keeping with globalisation, used the slogan *"Good Lack"*. You may or may not find it amusing, but it is a nice illustration of the fact that taking over English expressions does not mean taking over the English pronunciation. English *luck* does not have the same vowel as German *Lack*. [ʌ] as in [lʌk] is a mid-open vowel without lip rounding, but not quite as open nor as central as the German [a] in *Lack* as the vowel chart in fig. 3 illustrates:

When you have heard, produced and "seen" the sound, you should find our discrimination exercise easy.

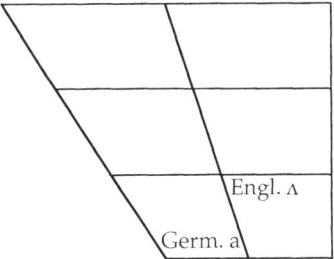

Fig. 3: The relative positions of English /ʌ/ and German /a/

As in previous sections on vowels, we offer you cross-language near-homophones. We would like you to listen to the numbered list of words and put a "G" behind the appropriate number if you think it is a German word, and an "E" if you think it is English:

C 2/E 1: Listen and identify the language:

1. *luck* vs. *Lack*
2. *hut* vs. *hat*
3. *putt* vs. *patt*
4. *bun* vs. *Bann*
5. *but* vs. *Bad*
6. *puck* vs. *Pack*
7. *mutton* vs. *Matten*
8. *done* vs. *dann*

C 3/E 2: Loanword or native English? Again, write "E" or "G" according to what you hear. NB: there may be more than one phonetic difference to help you with your choice.

1. *bubble gum*
2. *curry*
3. *comeback*
4. *button*
5. *pub*
6. *ketchup*
7. *butler*
8. *punk*

E 3: Discrimination exercise. Pair work or group work: Student A chooses an item from the above lists (C 2&C 3), and the others try to guess whether the English or the German word was intended. Take it in turns.

Where "*Ta, luv*" may mean "*Thank you, Madam*"
or: **When is an /ʌ/ not an /ʌ/?**

We would now like to make you familiar with a number of different sound shapes the standard English phoneme /ʌ/ takes on, and we are doing it for the following two reasons: Firstly it will help you to understand a greater variety of native speakers of English. After all, we cannot expect everybody in the English-speaking world to adopt the type of English that we advocate in this book. And secondly, we have found that learners who have been exposed to different dialects of English often pick up elements of these in a fairly unsystematic way. It is a bit like an Englishman saying in German "Mir kroxeln ieber de Bärche" in a mixture of accents from Bavarian to Saxonian, with an English accent on top of it. So the following paragraphs aim at passive knowledge for the more advanced student. You do not have to practice these varieties but it is an advantage to be aware of them.

In the North of England many speakers replace [ʌ] by [ʊ], so *love* [lʌv] becomes [lʊv]. In Manchester, for instance, you will often hear *"Ta, luv"*, where *ta* stands for *thank you* and where *luv* is used as a friendly form of addressing people. When the distinction between two sounds is lost, as that between /ʌ/ and /ʊ/ in this case, this is bound to give rise to homophones in that dialect which constitute minimal pairs in SBE. So in these northern dialects *luck* and *look*, *buck* and *book*, *putt* and *put* respectively are merged into [lʊk], [bʊk] and [pʊt]. There are not so many homophones, so communication is not affected.

Sometimes speakers of these northern dialects are aware of this phenomenon and try to avoid using [ʊ] in /ʌ/ words. This results either in cases of hypercorrection (['pʌ⁺pɪt] instead of ['pʊ⁺pɪt]), or a shifting of both /ʌ/ and /ʊ/ to a central, almost schwa-like vowel higher than [ʌ], but lower than [ʊ]. Younger-generation, educated northern speakers in particular often use a slightly lip-rounded [ə] for both /ʌ/ and /ʊ/. It also happens to coincide with a fashionable "mid-Atlantic" accent used by many British pop-stars. The phrase *"Feel like makin' lurve?"* in The Guardian was an attempt to capture this in normal orthography. If you are familiar with Elton John's *"You've got to lurve someone"* you will know what it sounds like.

In conservative RP the vowel in *putt* is produced further back and in an even more open position than in the SBE we are advocating. It could be this similarity which prompted the following cartoon a few years ago:

Fig. 4: "It's a putt of gold!"
The Observer, 8 Dec 96
(Nick Faldo was UK sport's top-earner in 1996 with £8 million)

This cartoon is based on the English saying: *"There's a pot of gold at the end of the rainbow"*, i.e. on ignoring the phonetic distinction between [pʌt] (*putt*) and [pɒt] (*pot*). In American English the vowel in *pot* [pɑt] is not far from British English *part* [pɑːt] and very close to that in conservative RP *putt* [pʌt].

The following vowel chart shows the different vowel variants used for /ʌ/ words that we have mentioned:

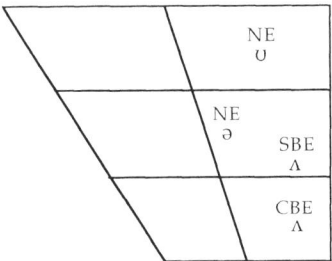

Fig. 5: Regional and social variants of vowels in /ʌ/ words
SBE: South. stand. Brit. Engl.; CBE: Conserv. Brit.Engl.; NE: Northern English

It is not important for you to master all these varieties of the phoneme /ʌ/. But it is important for you to be consistent, and we advise you not to pick up an American vowel here and a northern English vowel there, but to stick to one variety. That is why we recommend [wʌn ˈwʌndəz weðə ˈmʌŋks‿ən ˈnʌnz ʃʊd bi əˈlaʊd tə ˈlʌviːˈʧʌðə], which would sound like this in a northern English dialect: [wɒn ˈwɒndəz weðə ˈmʊŋks‿ən ˈnʊnz ʃʊd bi əˈlaʊd tə ˈlʊviːˈʧʊðə], but try not to mix the two.

A common mistake is the use of [ɒ] in the following words which should all be pronounced with [ʌ]:

> *one* [wʌn], *won* [wʌn], *wonder,* [wʌndə], *ton* [tʌn], *tongue* [tʌŋ], *monetary* [ˈmʌnətri], *worry* [wʌri], *mongrel* [ˈmʌŋgrəl].;
> but: *commonwealth* [ˈkɒmənweɫθ] (cf. also section V.2.5).

The inscription on the grave of Arabella Young (see C 1) may help you to remember that *one* and *tongue* have the same vowel as *Young.* And the following limerick may be used as a reminder that *worry* rhymes with *hurry.*

C 4: *A nervous young lady from Crewe*   [ə ˈnɜːvəs jʌŋ ˈleɪdi frəm ˈkruː
Said she wanted to catch the 2:2.   sed ʃi ˈwɒntɪd tə ˈkætʃ ðə tu ˈtuː
Said the porter, "Don't worry,   sed ðə ˈpɔːtə dəʊnt ˈwʌri
Or scurry or hurry,   ɔ ˈskʌri ɔ ˈhʌri
It's a minute or two to 2:2."   ɪtsə ˈmɪnɪtɔ ˈtuː tə tu ˈtuː]

Now that we have dealt with with the vowels [ʌ], [ɒ] and [ɔː] (sections V.2.5. - V.2.7.) we want to compare and contrast them.

[ʌ] vs. [ɒ]

C 5: There are a number of words where – because of the confusing spelling – learners of English tend to get mixed up between [ɒ] and [ʌ]. First repeat the words and then the sentences containing them:

a. *one* [wʌn], *won* [wʌn], *wan* (= pale) [wɒn] *ton* [tʌn]; *monetary* [ˈmʌnətri] *commonwealth* [ˈkɒmənweɫθ]; *mongrel* [ˈmʌŋgrəɫ]

b. *Only one of them can have won the jackpot.*

c. *We were in the middle of a meeting, when the new office boy just wandered in. He said he was wondering if he could leave early today. Off course, the boss came down on him like a ton of bricks.*

d. *Is that dog a collie? - No, I´m afraid it´s only a mongrel.*

e. *Will the Commonwealth go to pot because of the EU´s monetary union?*

E 4: Write the symbols [ɒ] and [ʌ] above the syllables that you think contain these vowels:

a. *one, won, wan, wandering, wondering, donkey, monkey, monk, monetary, commonwealth, ironmonger, scaremonger, mongrel, yoghourt, waddle, waffle, The Grapes of Wrath, trough, scones, tons, mongoose, monastery*

b. *"The boat was* chock-a-block *with people, all of them English. I spent the first quarter of an hour* wandering *around* wondering *how they had* got *there without getting filthy ..."* (Bill Bryson, *Notes from a small island*, p. 38. London 1996)

[ɒ] vs. [ɔ:]

As the "hot potato" exercise explains, English [ɒ] in *shock* is lower than German [ɔ] in *Schock*. On the other hand, English [ɔ:] in *short* is higher than German [ɔ] in *Schott* (see section V.2.6.).

Smileys:

[ˈhaɪ ˌʤɒn | dɪdju hævə ˈgʊd ˌmɔ:nɪŋɒn ðə ˈgɒɫf kɔ:s ˌɑ:sktɪz ˈwaɪf ˈmɒli | ˈnɒt ˈbæd sed ˌʤɒn | ænd ˈhu ˈwʌn | dɪdˈju: | ˈdəʊnt bi ˈsɪli | aɪwəz ˈpleɪŋ ðə ˈbɒs]

"Will you ever forget that lovely weekend we had together on the Costa del Sol?" the boss asked his gorgeous blond secretary. *"What´s it worth?"* she responded slyly.

"Mum, you know that vase you were worried I might break?" - *"Yes, what about it?"* - *"Well, your worries are over."*

"I was nearly christened ´glug-glug´. The vicar fell in the font."

The "Doctor! Doctor!" jokes provide reliable /ɒ/ exercises:

"Doctor! Doctor! I keep thinking I´m a donkey." - *"Come off it! You're taking me for a ride!"*

"Doctor! Doctor! I keep thinking I´m a dog." - *"What nonsense! Lie on the couch."* - *"Sorry, I´m not allowed on the furniture."*

"Doctor! Doctor! I keep thinking I´m a frog." - *"All right, hop on the couch."*

V.2.8. /ɜː/ as in "bird": /bɜːd/

Fig. 1: The turtle and the tortoise

C1: Listen and repeat:

"Let us swim", said Bertie the turtle
to a pretty young tortoise named Myrtle.
She didn´t return.
So what do we learn?
If a tortoise, don´t swim with a turtle.

[letəs ˈswɪm sed ˈbɜːti ðə ˈtɜːtɬ
tuə ˈprɪti jʌŋ ˈtɔːtəs neɪmd ˈmɜːtɬ
ʃɪ ˈdɪdn̩t rɪˈtɜːn
səʊ ˈwɒt du wi ˈlɜːn
ɪfə ˈtɔːtəs | dəʊnt ˈswɪm wɪðə ˈtɜːtɬ]

Question:

Should pretty young Myrtle
have averted the flirtle
with Bertie the turtle?

[ʃəd ˈprɪti jʌŋ ˈmɜːtɬ
hævəˈvɜːtɪd ðə ˈflɜːtɬ
wɪð ˈbɜːti ðə ˈtɜːtɬ]

Did you know that in the Old Testament there is an interesting passage about the correct pronunciation being a question of life and death?

Infobox

Shibboleth (Hebrew, ear of corn, flood). Password of the Gileadites under Jephthah, at a ford of the Jordan, during their war with the Ephraimites (Judges xii,6). The fleeing Ephraimites pronounced the word *sibboleth*, thus betraying their identity, and were subjected to great slaughter. The word is used for the watchword or pet phrase of a political or other party or class.

It is reported that the British used the word *Churchill* [ˈʧɜːʧɪɫ] as a shibboleth in the second world war when they captured men who claimed to be somewhere from the English speaking world. The British were pretty certain no German, however good his English might be, would be able to pronounce the name of the then Prime Minister correctly and convincingly. This is partly due to the dark [ɫ], and partly to the vowel [ɜː]. If we now Germanise the word in writing *"Tschörtschel"* everybody will say how silly and un-English it *looks*. But please bear in mind that a corresponding pronunciation *sounds* equally funny to a native speaker of English.

The tongue position of [ɜː] is similar to that of the schwa sound [ə], i.e., it is a central sound. It is similar to the sound English speakers use as a hesitation phenomenon, as illustrated by the following dialogue, which we hope you find mildly amusing, because the two people are talking at cross purposes:

> Lecturer to student: *Give me a mid-central vowel.*
> Student (who had been absent last time and is unprepared): ... *er* ...
> Lecturer: *Very good.*

Make sure you do not move your tongue forward as far as you would for the first vowel in German *Öfen* or *örtlich*. But what is really important about the vowel [ɜː] that German learners in particular have to bear in mind, is the lack of lip rounding. When people learn a new sound in a foreign language they tend to look for an equivalent in their own language, and German speakers tend to substitute the [ɜː] sound of *church* with a sound for the letter <ö> as in *Möhre* or *Mörtel*. The difference can be demonstrated in the pronunciation of words borrowed by English and German from French. In German, *Conoisseur* and *Masseur* are pronounced like *Frisör* with lip rounding, a feature that is totally absent from the RP pronunciation of [ˌkɒnəˈsɜː] and [mæˈsɜː]. We have found it useful to ask students who have problems with this sound to pronounce the words *absurd, terminal, church, German* etc. with excessively spread lips, as if they were smiling broadly while saying: *"That's absurd!"*

The following vowel chart illustrates the difference in tongue position, but remember that the presence or lack of liprounding, which cannot be represented on the vowel chart, makes an additional difference.

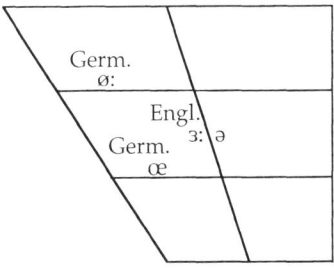

Fig. 2: Vowel chart with /ə/-/ɜ:/ and /ø:/-/œ/
(as in German: *Öfen, örtlich*)

Another pitfall for native speakers of German are the many English loan-words whose pronunciation has, of course, been Germanised when they are used in German, so that the pronunciation of words like *Terminal, Sir, Girls, Turn* (in *Segeltörn*) and *Birmingham* with lip rounding has become quite famil-iar, and as you know: old habits die hard:

> *Törminal thörteen? Over there, Sör? Thank you, but how on örth did you know I was Görman?"*

In the following sentences remember to avoid too much fronting of the tongue and to avoid lip rounding. In particular with the words *murderer* and *words*, as a result of the labial consonants, and in analogy with *Mörder* and *Wörter*, you may find it difficult to avoid rounding your lips. Especially with words that begin with a [w], e.g. *world, word, worse*, make sure that the lip rounding for [w] does not continue long into the [ɜ:].

C 2: Listen and repeat.

1. *We were going round in circles.*
2. *These surfboards are dirt cheap.*
3. *I just did it on the spur of the moment.*
4. *Germany urges Turkey to release Kurds..*
5. *These are just words, and words will never hurt me.*
6. *To all intents and purposes, it was a simple case of murder.*

C 3: Ear training. Listen to the following words that exist in both English and German. Mark those which are pronounced as English words with an "E", and those which are pronounced as German words with a "G".

1. *Terminal.*	5. *Guernsey*	9. *Gershwin*
2. *Flirt*	6. *Girls*	10. *Surfer*
3. *Churchill*	7. *Safety first*	11. *Server*
4. *Birmingham*	8. *Wordsworth*	12. *Surfboard*

C 4: Connected speech; a dialogue. Listen and repeat:

Susan: *I hate getting up early.*

Paul: *But it´s the early bird that catches the worm.*

S: *That´s certainly true, but if you are a worm sleep late, because it´s the early worm that gets caught by the early bird.*

P: *Well, I guess you worked late last night?*

S: *Yes, burning the midnight oil, as they say. It´s getting on my nerves. It´s certainly taken a turn for the worse. Why is it always me who has to do the dirty work?*

P: *You simply have to leave early before the others desert you, leave you in the lurch.*

S: *Do you think they´re doing it on purpose?*

P: *No, but it´s a vicious circle: the earlier they leave the longer you have to work. You´ve got to assert yourself. Be firm. So tonight you leave early and let them do the work. Let them learn it the hard way.*

S: *But my colleagues will curse me.*

P: *Sticks and stones will break your bones, but words will never hurt you. Just tell them you worked late for them last night and now it´s their turn. One good turn deserves another. And if the worst comes to the worst, your boss can employ a part timer.*

S: *You´re right, dear. I´ll be off to the office now and tell him right away.*

P: *But we haven´t cleared the breakfast table, darling.*

S: *I´ll be firm. I´ll assert myself. I´m off now, dear. I mustn´t shirk work. And I´ll be home early tonight.*

P: *Why is it always me who has to do the dirty work?*

C 5: Listen and repeat.

Shirley: *What´s the world wide web?*

Tina: *It´s part of the huge network called internet. Surfing in the internet is essential for research work. And if you have a mail-server you can even send e-mail messages.*

S: *Great. Could I send a message to Hermann in Germany. It´s his birthday today.*

T: *Look here, Shirley, first, you need a mail server secondly you need to know the server name, and thirdly you need a password. But I´ll let you use the terminal in my office. Okay?"*

S: *Perfect. So what do I do?*

T: *You simply write the happy birthday message in Word and I´ll copy it and insert it later as your e-mail message to Hermann.*

S: *I see. You don´t want me to know your password.*

T: *Don´t be absurd. I trust you, Shirley. Okay, insert my password where the cursor is. It is `Kermit´. And then press `return´.*

S: *And my message is: Happy birthday to you, happy birthday to you, happy birthday dear Hermann, happy birthday to you.*

T: *Perfect. And frightfully original. Hermann the German will be pleased!*

Fig. 3: *Häppy Börsday* (McDonald's)

Spellings:

murderer, church, curd, Kurd, curt, surge, cur, turn, burn, furl, curl, occur
blurred, occurred, purr, burr
Guernsey, infer, inter ([ɪnˈtɜ:] "bury"), *intern, term, germ, German, fern, tern,*
merge, her, sermon, inferred, interred, err,
third, stir, fir, sir, dirt, shirt,
words, world, worm, attorny,
heard, learn, earn, yearn

Unique spellings for /ɜ:/: *myrrh, journal, colonel*

Words that may cause problems:

1. *desert* [ˈdezət] (German: *Wüste*) vs. *to desert* [dɪˈzɜ:t] (German: *desertieren*)
vs. *dessert* [dɪˈzɜ:t] (German: *Nachtisch*); 2. *colonel* [ˈkɜ:nɫ].
So *colonel* is a homophone of *kernel*, but they are not homographs, whereas the
verb *to desert* and the noun *desert* are homographs but not homophones.

Smileys:

- There are three ingredients in the good life: learning, earning and yearning.
- Graffiti on a fur shop: Furs: The first wearer of your fur coat died in it.

E 1: Read the following joke aloud:

[ˈgɪnzbɜ:gˀ gəʊz tə ˈhærədz | aɪ ˈwɒntə baɪ maɪ ˌgɜ:ɫfrend ˈmɜ:tl̩ə naɪs ˈpen fə
hə ˈbɜ:θdeɪ | ˈɑ: | sed ðə ˈʃɒpəˌsɪstənt | ˈðætɫbi ə naɪs səˈpraɪz fɔ: hə | ɪt
ˈsɜ:tənlɪ ˈwɪɫ | sed ˈgɪnzbɜ:g| ʃi:ziks|pektɪŋə ˈwɜ:dˌprəʊsesə]

E 2: Read the following limerick aloud:

A certain Bert Burton from Lyme	[ə ˈsɜ:tn̩ bɜ:t ˈbɜ:tn̩ frəm ˈlaɪm
said he married three wives at one time.	sedi ˈmærid θri ˈwaɪvzət wʌn ˈtaɪm
When asked, "Why the third?"	weˈnɑ:skt waɪ ðə ˈθɜ:d
He said, "One is absurd,	hi sed ˈwʌnɪzəbˈsɜ:d
And bigamy, sir, is a crime."	ən ˈbɪgəmi ˌsɜ:rɪzə ˈkraɪm]

V.2.9. /ə/: schwa: *The centre of the vowel universe*

Schwa is a very special sound. In a way it is the "centre of the vowel universe", the vowel around which all other vowels gather. But schwa is also the least "colourful" of all the vowels, the vowel with the least "weight", because it can never be stressed. It is the vowel that would emerge if you were just vocalizing, not trying to produce any particular vowel; if you were struck in the stomach unexpectedly that would be the sound that just came out. It is the vowel you get at the end of *butter* [ˈbʌtə] and at the beginning of *about* [əˈbaʊt]. It is *the* neutral vowel *par excellence*.

Schwa's neutrality means that it does not serve to distinguish words in the same way as other vowels. The "sentences" in E 1, containing only schwa in the place of all the other vowels – whether short or long monophthongs or diphthongs – should illustrate this. Note that we have replaced stressed as well as unstressed vowels with schwa, something that cannot normally happen because – as already stated – schwa is, by definition, unstressed. We have done it here to illustrate the contribution of vowel quality to word recognition.

E 1: Read the following transcribed sentences silently. Sentence a. is easy because it is a well-known English proverb, but perhaps you can also decode sentence b.:

a. [əˈnəplə ˈdə kəps ðə ˈdəktər‿əˈwə]
b. [ðə ˈmən hə ˈlə‿ən ðə ˈrəd wəz ˈnət ˈsək bət ˈdrəŋk]

Were you able to reconstruct the sequence of words we had in mind when we wrote the transcription? Now read the sentences out loud and see whether you fare any better.

All the vowels we have dealt with in the previous sections of this chapter have had their distinct quality which allows them to distinguish words, and which often reflect the regional roots of the speaker (whether native English or non-English speaking). Trying to work out what the above sentences mean, where all the vowels are the same central schwa sound, will probably confirm for you that vowel quality is not without importance, particularly in single-syllable words (see section V.1. *Are Vowels Important?*).

Some of the words, like [ðə], and perhaps also [ət], [əv], [wəz] and [bət] were probably quite easy for you to identify, at least when you read the sentence out loud. This is because words of this kind are often pronounced with a schwa-like vowel (we call them "function words" – see VI.2&3. for a thorough treatment). On the other hand saying [də] for *day*, [kəps] for *keeps* etc. is throwing away all the vowel information that distinguishes *day* from *die, doe* or *dough, do, dare, dire, dour, door, dear* or *deer*, and *keeps* from *cops, caps, cups, coaps* or *copes, coops, corpse* etc.

Of course the single-syllable words are usually more difficult than poly-syllabic words. It is easy to understand *apple* from [ˈəpl̩], particularly in the context, because only *apple* and *opal* fit the "stressed vowel + /pl/" structure. *Doctor* is even clearer because there is no other word in English with the structure /ˈdVktV/ (where V stands for "vowel").

What about E1b.? It was unfair of us to choose only monosyllables. If we had given you:

1. [ðə ˈʤəntɫmən hə ˈlə ən ðə ˈpəvmənt ˈwəznt ˈənʤəd hə wəz ənˈtəksəkətəd]

you would probably have understood the word sequence immediately and laughed at the analogy with the children's chanting game:

2. *Dree Chehnehsehn meet deem Kehntrehbehs.*

Note, however, that substituting any other single vowel but schwa in the sentence underlying E1b (*The man who lay on the side of the road was not hurt but drunk*) would have changed *some* of the words into *other* words – something that did not happen with schwa. We illustrated this above for *day* (*die, doe* or *dough, do, dare, dire, dour, door, dear* etc.) and for *keeps* (*cops, caps, cups, coaps* or *copes, coops* etc.) in sentence a., but the lexical words, and some of the function words in b. also change their identity with changes of vowel. For example:

3. *road* can become *reed, rid, red, rod, roared, rude, raid, ride* etc.
    not can become *neat, knit, net, gnat, nut, nought, night.*
    sick can become *sec, sack, sock, Sark, suck, sake.*
    drunk can become *drink, drank.*

A very important rule of English pronunciation is: **schwa never occurs in stressed syllables.** If – say, for reasons of contrast – you want to stress the function words "a" [ə] and "the" [ðə] you have to change schwa into another vowel so it may carry stress:

4. [ɪts nɒt ʤʌst ˈeɪ bʊkɒn fəˈnetɪks ‖ ɪts ˈði: bʊkɒn fəˈnetɪks]

[ˈði: ʤeɪmz ˈbɒnd]?

[ˈjes ‖ ju ˈhɜ:d ‖ ˈði: ʤeɪmz ˈbɒnd ‖ ɑ: ju ˈtraɪŋ tə ˈteɫ mi aɪ hævə ˈneɪmseɪk] ?

Fig. 1: [ˈeɪ mɪstə bɒndɔ: ˈði: mɪstə bɒnd]

When we look at the pronunciation of English polysyllabic words we find that there are schwa vowels in many (but not all) of the syllables that do not bear lexical stress (see VI.2. and VII.2. for a systematic treatment of stress). This makes schwa by far the most frequent vowel in English because there are a lot of unstressed syllables that are pronounced with schwa and all the other vowels must share the stressed syllables between them! Consider the following polysyllabic words:

5. argument   [ˈɑːgjəmənt];
    believable   [bəˈliːvəbɫ];
    concession   [kənˈseʃn̩];
    injury   [ˈɪndʒəri];
    existence   [ɪgˈzɪstəns];
    conservation [ˌkɒnsəˈveɪʃn̩].

There are eight schwa syllables and only eight other vowels, three of which are [ɪ], one [iː], one [ɑː], one [e], one [ɒ], and one [eɪ]. We can also observe that related words change the position of the schwa with the changing stress pattern, so the schwa in the second syllable of the last example above: *conservation* [ˌkɒnsəˈveɪʃn̩] is replaced by [ɜː] when the second syllable becomes stressed in *conservatory* [kənˈsɜːvətri] and the [ɒ] in the first syllable is replaced by schwa because now it is unstressed.

This alternation of schwa with other vowels is both interesting for phonologists (some of whom regard any occurrence of schwa as one of the other "proper" vowels in disguise) and a problem for learners of English, particularly for German learners of English. In word pairs like *philosophy* vs. *philosophical; psychology* vs. *psychological* an English speaker will switch the position of schwa without any problem:

6. *English*: [fɪˈlɒsəfi] - [ˌfɪləˈsɒfɪkɫ] and [saɪˈkɒlədʒi] - [ˌsaɪkəˈlɒdʒɪkɫ]

whereas a German speaker is used to pronouncing the related words *Philosophie* and *philosophisch*:

7. *German*: [filozoˈfiː] - [filoˈzoːfɪʃ] and [psyçoloˈgiː] - [psyçoˈloːgɪʃ]

For German speakers it is counter-intuitive to reduce vowels represented by letters like <o> and <a> to schwa, and it has to be admitted that it makes spelling more of a problem for English people too. After all, to someone learning to spell it seems quite arbitrary for the word ending [-əri] to be spelled <-ory> in *history*, <-eri> in *scenery*, <-ury> in *injury* and <-ary> in *Hilary*.

Although in German the length of vowels varies with stress placement, the quality of the vowel does not change so radically from a full vowel to a schwa. No doubt you can appreciate that a transfer of this "full vowel habit" to English will result in a strong German accent, as English is partly characterised by schwa being its most frequent vowel.

Schwa: the neutral vowel

Clearly schwa does not have as big a burden to carry in the sound patterning of English as the other vowels. It is not really needed to distinguish words because at the lexical level it only occurs in words of more than one syllable, and pronouncing such words with a full vowel instead of schwa may sound strange – it is a sort of "spelling pronunciation" – but it does not change one word into another. Pronouncing *society* as *[səʊˈsaɪeti:] instead of [səˈsaɪəti] or *collectable* as *[kɒˈlekteɪbɫ] instead of [kəˈlektəbɫ] does not affect their identity.

However, as we saw above, multisyllabic words do have to be learned with the schwa vowel pronounced in the correct syllable. But this can normally be learned once and for all.

C 1/E 2: Mark the letters in the following words that are pronounced as schwa, and afterwards listen to the recording to check whether you are right.

a. *apparently*   b. *suggestively*   c. *resurrection*   d. *contagious*
e. *surgeon*   f. *remorseless*   g. *conspiracy*   h. *competition*
i. *parachute*   j. *conflagration*   k. *phonetics*   l. *semantic*

There are only relatively few words that have alternating schwa positions across morphologically related words, and there are even less words where accepted alternative pronunciations show a schwa shift, e.g.:

8. *controversy*   [ˈkɒntrəvɜːsi] and [kənˈtrɒvəsi]
   inventory   [ˈɪnvəntri] and [ɪnˈventəri]
   garage   [ˈgærɑːʒ] and [gəˈrɑːʒ]
   harass   [ˈhærəs] and [həˈræs]

Does your "eh" betray your origins?

Schwa is not only phonologically neutral, it is often also considered to be a "neutral vowel" in a more phonetic, articulatory way, because the sound we involuntarily produce when we vocalize when hesitating – our "eh" – is often very schwa-like (remember also the unexpected blow to the stomach mentioned in the introductory paragraph). Something like a schwa is what we relax into when we are not planning a specific sound. But if you listen to different people hesitating, particularly people from different language backgrounds, there seems to be a link between that neutral vocalization and their language. A popular example of this is the French person's tendency to hesitate with rounded lips - something which would be very unusual for an English speaker. French has more lip-rounded vowels than English, and they are usually produced with more extreme rounding. So it is plausible to see the "relaxation position" that influences the actual schwa quality as a product of all the articulatory gestures that comprise the sounds of a language or dialect (strictly speaking of each individual's **idiolect**). A technical term that has been coined to express such differences in the overall setting of a person's mouth when speaking (the tendency to speak with rounded lips, or to nasalize, or to keep the mass of the tongue body further forward, or further back in the mouth) is the **basis of articulation**. Admittedly it is a very vague term, which we have tried to make a little more concrete with reference to a "relaxation position", but it may help you to understand that getting an accent right is much more than being able to pronounce sounds right in isolated syllables.

Of course, hesitation phenomena are much too varied within a language for us to want to claim that schwa = hesitation = relaxed vocal tract. People do not have to hesitate with a schwa-like sound; [əmːː], [mːː], [aːː], [iːː], [eːː] are all possible transcriptions of different hesitation sounds, and you can probably think of other, quite idiosyncratic hesitation phenomena. However, we do know that there are systematic differences between standard German schwa in a word like *bitte* and standard English schwa in *bitter*. Also, German r-schwa with the symbol [ɐ] in German *bitter* [ˈbɪtɐ] is different from English schwa in English *bitter* [ˈbɪtə]. Phonetically we say that this r-schwa is more open/lower and more retracted than English schwa, and German schwa in *bitte* [ə] is closer/more raised (and sometimes slightly more fronted). This is illustrated in the following vowel chart:

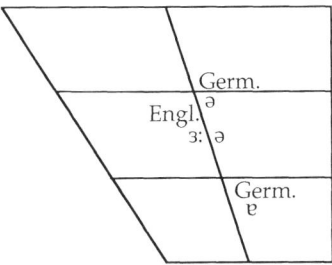

Fig. 2: Tongue positions of English schwa and German schwa and r-schwa.

C 2/E 3: Cross-language exercise. Listen to the following words and write down whether they are English or German (e.g. a. i, a. ii, or a. iii):

	i. E	ii. G	iii. G
a.	*bitter*	*bitte*	*bitter*
b.	*clipper*	*Klippe*	*Klipper*
c.	*locker*	*Locke*	*locker*
d.	*Linda*	*Linde*	*linder*
e.	*clever*	-	*clever*
f.	*fitter*	-	*fitter*
g.	*setter*	-	*Setter*

When you have checked your responses with the answers given in chapter XII listen to the recording again.

E 4: This time repeat the words, paying special attention to the differentiation of the English and German versions of the unstressed syllable.

C 3/E 5: Now listen to the following short poem, and then read it out loud, trying to hit the central vowel quality of the words ending in schwa (spelt <er>).

Whether the weather be cold,
Or whether the weather be hot
We'll weather the weather,
Whatever the weather,
Whether we like it or not!

And, finally, there is the well-known tongue-twister with a lot of schwas. Again, try to hit the central schwa quality, avoiding the more raised German schwa and the more open r-schwa:

E 6: *Peter Piper picked a peck of pickled pepper.*
If Peter Piper picked a peck of pickled pepper,
Where's the peck of pickled pepper Peter Piper picked?

V.3. Diphthongs: *Taam to chairnge* [ˈtɑːm tə ˈʧɛːnʤ] or *vowel movements!*

If you pronounced *time to change* like a Yorkshireman as *taam to chairnge* [ˈtɑːm tə ˈʧɛːnʤ] or *keine Augen im Kopf* as *keene Oogen im Kopp*, i.e. without altering the shape of your mouth or the position of your tongue during the vowel – although you certainly do have "time to change" your mouth shape – it would clearly sound odd, or at the very least non-standard; Yorkshire English and Berlin German are often imitated in this way.

The sort of vowel that clearly changes from one vowel quality to another as it is produced, is called a "diphthong" (pronounced [ˈdɪfθɒŋ]). Diphthongs exist both in German and English, but they exhibit clear differences in quality – and therefore also contribute to a foreign accent. As the name suggests ("mono" means "one", from the Greek, and "di-" means "two"), these are vowels that have *two* parts, in contrast to "monophthongal" vowels, for example /aɪ/ in English *light* and German *Leid*, /aʊ/ in English *lout* and German *laut*, /ɔɪ/ in English *boy* and German *Heu*. In Southern British English the diphthongs are long vowels, in fact, although it is not very noticeable, measurements have shown them to be even a little longer on average than other long vowels; this gives them the "time to change" that the title above hints at.

Another thing to remember is that even though a diphthong clearly has two parts to it, they form a *single* syllable, just as a long vowel does. A diphthong is therefore different from a sequence of two vowels forming two syllables, such as /aː/ + /ɔ/ in the German word *Chaos* (/ˈkaːɔs/). For this reason their monosyllabic nature is often signalled in the transcription by adding an additional diacritic, either a linking bar under the two symbols to show that the two parts belong together, e.g. [a͜ʊ] or by marking one element as being non-central to the syllable ("non-syllabic"), e.g. [aʊ̯]. However, similar to other books on pronunciation, we shall not use the diacritics when transcribing diphthongs in this book. The danger of interpreting a diphthong as two syllables, or vice versa, is minimal in English and German.

The approximate correspondences between the above three German and English diphthongs are misleading to learners and require the same sort of careful listening and articulatory practice that has been argued for in the case of the monophthongal or "pure" vowels that are similar but not identical in the two languages. They will be dealt with in more detail in the next few sections but it is perhaps useful (since we introduced the idea of "time to change") to think about the *relative time* spent on the two parts of the diphthongs. This tends to be different in English and German. Although both languages have so-called "**falling diphthongs**", i.e., they place *greater weight* on the first part of the diphthong, the duration of the first part tends to be even greater in English than in German. It is important to be able to hear and produce both the quality and the temporal differences.

Apart from the three diphthongs /aɪ/, /aʊ/ and /ɔɪ/ English has two other diphthongs which have no correspondence in German, namely /eɪ/ as in *bait* or *gate*, and /əʊ/ as in *boat* or *moan*, which we dealt with in our discussion of monophthongs in section V.2. As we saw there, the German sounds that are closest to these are the long monophthongs /e:/ as in *Beet* and /o:/ as in *Boot*. It is fairly clear where the problems arise in these pseudo-correspondences for learners of both languages. English learners of German are unable to stop their tongue and jaw moving during the long vowel, and consequently produce diphthongal *Beet*, *geht*, *Boot* and *Mohn* words, and Germans tend to produce monophthongal, or at least insufficiently diphthongal versions of the English *bait* and *gate* or *boat* and *moan* words. These diphthongs are dealt with in sections V.3.1. and V.3.2.

The following figure shows the general quality changes that are identifiable for the five English and the three German diphthongs.

English   German

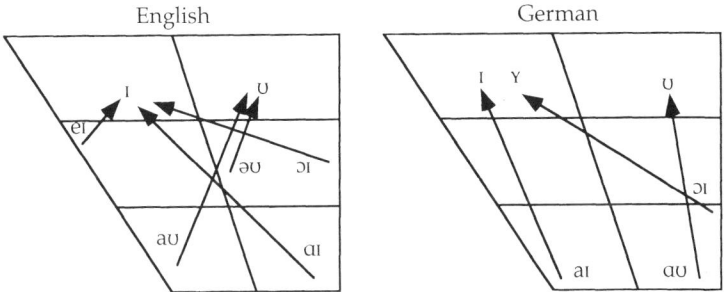

Fig. 1: Diphthong qualities in English and German

There are clear differences in the onset qualities of /aɪ/ and /aʊ/ in the two languages, the German diphthongs using the open-to-close dimension (and a change from unrounded to rounded in /aʊ/), whereas the English diph- thongs have an additional front-to-back and back-to-front movement. This will be treated in more detail, with ample opportunity to hear the differences in the subsequent sections.

Part of the difference in the German and English /ɔɪ/ is also an onset differ- ence, related to the difference between the mid-open German /ɔ/ and the closer English /ɔ:/ (cf. section V.2.6.). However, there is also a tendency for the German diphthong to retain some liprounding whereas liprounding disappears in English as the tongue moves forward. /ɔɪ/ is dealt with in section V.3.5.

You may begin to wonder whether the larger number of diphthongs on the English side of all these pseudo-correspondences reflects some more fundamental pronunciation difference between English and German. And your wondering would be by no means unfounded! Apart from the English *bait* and *boat* diphthongs with their German monophthongal *Beet* and *Boot* correspondences, English also has two very "impure" long vowels /iː/ and /uː/ as in *beat* and *boot* (cf. V.2.1. and V.2.2.). Despite their monophthongal transcription symbols, they are often spoken with a clear change of quality. They are said to be "diphthongised", which is really a way of saying that while they do not have two distinct vowel qualities like the other diphthongs, they still have a clearly audible shift in timbre.

May these few comments suffice for an introduction to "vowel dynamics". Our conclusion – that there is a greater tendency towards timbre shifts in long English vowels than in long German vowels – is more .... or less true, of course depending on what regional accents of English or German we are listening to. As far as Southern British English and standard German are concerned it is a useful generality. But more details and examples will be offered in the individual chapters to follow.

V.3.1. /eɪ/: *Make a date for eight, eh?*

C 1: Listen and repeat.

I know an old spinster named K8,   [aɪ ˈnəʊən̩ˌəʊɫd ˈspɪnstə neɪmd ˈkeɪt
Whose efforts to marry were gr8.   huːˈzefəts tə ˈmæri wə ˈgreɪt
But I h8 to rel8,   bʌtaɪ ˈheɪt̩ tə rɪˈleɪt
That K8's awful f8,   ðət ˈkeɪts̩ ɔːfʊɫ ˈfeɪt
Was to stay in a celibate st8.   wəz tə ˈsteɪ‿ɪnə ˈselɪbət ˈsteɪt]

(Can you locate the 9 [eɪ]s in that limerick?)

In V.2. we asked: "Is a *Mailbox* a *Mehlkiste?*" in our attempt to draw your attention to the fact that standard German does not have the English [eɪ], which – in loanwords – is replaced by the German vowel [eː] thus turning *Mail* and *Mehl* into homophones. Just knowing that English [eɪ] is *different* from German [eː] in *Beet* is not enough of course. But it does help to get a feeling of how different it is, and how unacceptable it is to substitute one for the other. A German asking *"Kenn vi mehk a deht at eht?"* is certainly no more acceptable than an Englishman asking *"Voh gate ez zoo dane laser-roymen?"* (*Wo geht es zu den Leseräumen?*).

Read the limerick at the top of the page again, this time using a German [eː] instead of English [eɪ] and then listen to it again being read with a Southern British English accent. You will no doubt begin to get a feel for the difference, and if the feeling is already strong in you, then simply enjoy the awareness of how strange your "German" version sounds.

You might like to recite another [eɪ]-limerick:

1. *An old mathematician named Haines,*   [əˈnəʊɫd mæθməˈtɪʃn neɪmd ˈheɪnz
   After endlessly racking his brains,   ɑːftəˈrendləsli ˈrækɪŋɪz ˈbreɪnz
   States that now he has found   steɪts ðət ˈnaʊ‿iəz ˈfaʊnd‿
   An alien sound   əˈneɪliən ˈsaʊnd
   That travels much faster than planes.   ðətˈtrævəɫz mʌʧ ˈfɑːstə ðən ˈpleɪnz]

As we explained in the introductory section on diphthongs (V.3.), English [eɪ] as in *Kate, great, hate, relate,* etc. gets reinterpreted by German speakers as [eː] as in *Beet.* So although English words like *Baby, Aids, After Eight, After Shave, Playmobil, Trainer, Inliner Skates,* and *Laser* have been absorbed into modern German they have not retained the English [eɪ] pronunciation any more than earlier German imports into English, like *Kindergarten* and *Übermensch* kept their [ar] and [yː] pronunciation of *-garten* and *Über-,* when they were *imported* into English. Of course borrowing words and anglicising or germanising them for use in your own language is different from learning to speak a foreign language, whether German or English, where you try to learn the correct pronunciation!

Since the English vowel [eɪ] as in *bait* has no diphthongal correspondence in standard German, the need for contrastive English-German listening practice may appear less pressing than for some other vowels. On the other hand, the first step towards learning a foreign-language vowel is based on an established mental picture of the vowel quality, in this case of the starting quality and the change of quality.

The two vowel charts below show the range of variation that might be expected for German [eː] and the onset of English [eɪ], with the standard English variant that we are aiming for marked as a solid arrow.

Even speakers of standard German vary to some extent from North to South, as you will immediately hear if you compare the phrase in C 2. 1. spoken by a number of speakers from different parts of Germany. Similarly, speakers of English can also vary considerably in the onset quality of their [eɪ]. More conservative RP speakers have a closer quality (it is pronounced with the bottom jaw and tongue body closer to the top jaw and palate) which can overlap in its onset with the standard German [eː] varieties, though, of course, it does not remain monophthongal. Less conservative RP speakers – and this is the quality we are aiming for – have a slightly more open onset [ɛɪ]. Speakers of the ever-expanding southeastern variety, popularly called "Estuary English", can have a much more open onset [æɪ]. Listen to the different examples in C 2. 2. The vowel diagram should help you to visualize the difference in tongue height as you listen.

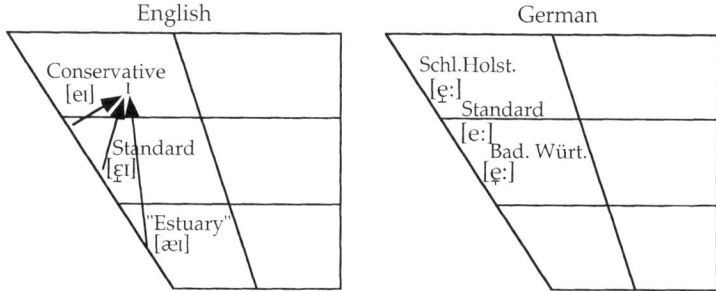

Fig. 1: English [eɪ] varieties and German [eː] varieties

C 2. Listen and try to imitate.
   1. *Der Wind weht den Schnee über den See.*
      a. Standard German;
      b. Schleswig Holstein German;

   2. *The rain in Spain falls mainly on the plain.*
      a. Southern British English; b. Conservative RP; c. "Estuary" English

Now practice the standard pronunciation for the following phrases:

2.   *Will you stay, in case the train 's late?*
Her face is amazing!
You can stake your claim now.
She had eight maids-in-waiting and eight pages at her wedding.
They stayed awake talking till very late.

The spellings of /eɪ/:

"Regular:"

reign, feign, deign, eight, weight, neigh, beige,
bait, strait (and *straight*), *fail, sail, mail, gain, main,*
age, ape, fame, mane, gale, male, gaze, lace, state,
alias ['eɪliəs], *amiable, behaviour, Mavis,* (but also: *ancient, angel, manger*)
ley, whey, and *lay, way*

Also, please remember that the prefix <a-> in the sense of *"not"* or *"non-"* is pronounced [eɪ]:

asymmetrical [ˌeɪsɪˈmetrɪkɫ], *agrammatical, atheist, amoral.*

Many Germans pronounce *Los Angeles* *[lɒs ˈeɪntʃələs], with an [eɪ] by analogy with *angel.* But in English it should be pronounced [lɒˈsændʒəlɪs], the same vowel sound as in *Angela* and *angelic* [ænˈdʒelɪk]. There are a number of other words that look as if they should be pronounced with an [eɪ], but do not fall into that trap; take note of **the non- [eɪ] list:**

Maya - [mɑːjə]; *mayor* - [mɛə]; *prayer* - [prɛə]; *maverick* - [ˈmævrɪk]; and there is also *sleight* = [slaɪt], used in the expression *"a sleight of hand"* for a quick action that deceives the eye.

We said at the beginning of this section that just as Germans tend to use the monophthong [eː] in loanwords (which makes *Laser* a homophone of *Leser*) so the English use [eɪ] in their loanwords which originally had an [eː], which gives rise to lines as in the Eartha Kitt song:

3.   *I like Chopin and Bizet*   [aɪlaɪk ˈʃəʊpæn̩ æn biːˈzeɪ
and the songs of yesterday   ænðə ˈsɒŋzəv jestəˈdeɪ]

So you have to avoid [eː] in English and pronounce *Las Vegas* as [læs ˈveɪɡəs]. French words ending in <é, et, er> etc. are pronounced [eɪ]: *buffet* [ˈbʊfeɪ], *foyer* [ˈfɔɪeɪ], *Bizet, ballet.*

V.3.2. /əʊ/: *Holy smoke!*

Fig. 1: *The Vicar of Stoke*

A vicar whose home was in Stoke
At breakfast would always invoke
The revered holy ghost
While burning his toast
In the hope it would be holy smoke.

[ə ˈvɪkə huːz ˈhəʊm wəzɪn ˈstəʊk
ət ˈbrekfəst wəˈdɔːɬweɪz ɪnˈvəʊk
ðə rɪˈvɪəd həʊli ˈɡəʊst
waɪɬ ˈbɜːnɪŋɪz ˈtəʊst
ɪn ðə ˈhəʊpɪt wəd ˈbiː həʊli ˈsməʊk]

It is logical to follow the /eɪ/ section with this section on /əʊ/. The mid-close long vowels /e:/ and /o:/ in the German system both have diphthongal equivalents in the English system, namely /eɪ/ and /əʊ/. The direct problem of interference for German learners is, therefore, the substitution of a German monophthongal [o:] for [əʊ]. With such unfortunate pairs as English *coat* and German *Kot* you would presumably not like to catch yourself saying "I left my [ko:t] in the [bo:t]".

Although the monophthong-diphthong difference is easy for most people to hear, there are some regional varieties of German that have a slightly diphthongal [ʊ] quality for the /o:/ phoneme, which can make it difficult for those speakers to hear the English-German distinction.

C 1/E 1: Just to make sure that you can hear the difference, listen to the recordings of words selected from the following list of cross-language pairs and mark whether the speaker is producing the English or the German word.

English or German?			English or German?		
lope	-	*Lob*	*Coke*	-	*Coke*
toast	-	*Toast*	*choke*	-	*Choke*
coat	-	*Kot*	*dope*	-	*Dope*
folk	-	*Folk*	*hope*	-	*hob*

If you are pronouncing the English sound correctly, you should be able to hear – when producing the sound in slow motion – that you do actually start near the central vowel [ə] which is used in the transcription symbol [əʊ], and move towards the back rounded vowel [ʊ] as illustrated in the chart below.

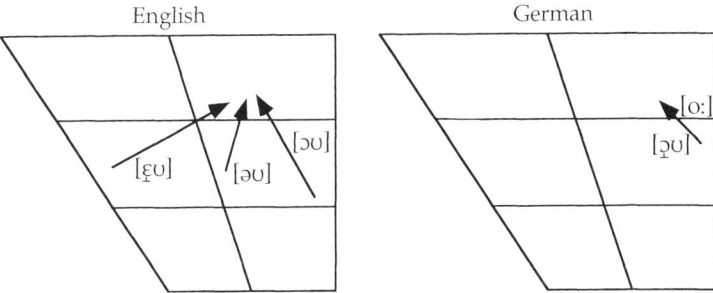

Fig. 2: Standard English [əʊ] and standard German [o:] with variants.

As with any vowel, of course, there are clearly marked regional and social variants of [əʊ], as the following recordings illustrate.

C 2: Listen to the quality of the onset (the quality at the start of the diphthong) in the recordings of *"Don't poke the goat!"* and check it against the corresponding arrow on the vowel chart in fig. 2. The phrase is spoken a. by a standard Southern English speaker, b. by an older generation, upper middle-class speaker, c. by a speaker from a southwestern English region.

You will probably have recognized that the older-generation upper middle-class speaker started the diphthong much further forward, closer to [e] , while the speaker from Southwest England started with a more retracted, rounded element, close to [ɔ]. You might find it amusing to try and imitate these different [əʊ] qualities, and the practice it gives you in keeping your articulators flexible is certainly useful training.

The [ɔʊ] variant is also found as an allophone of [əʊ] used by standard speakers, namely in words where [ɫ] follows the vowel: *coal, foal, hole, mole, pole, soul, toll, cold, fold, hold, mould, polled, sold, told* are often produced with an [ɔʊ] variant rather than [əʊ]. There is nothing better or worse about either of these two variants; both can be regarded as conforming to a standard southern English accent, so you can choose which comes more easily to you. In one case, ([ɔʊ]), you are allowing the following "dark l" (see III.1. for [ɫ]) to influence the diphthong quality, whereas in the other, ([əʊ]), the normal quality is maintained despite the "pull" of the [ɫ].

C 3: Listen to the following series of word pairs with and without postvocalic [ɫ], and concentrate on the difference in the quality of the diphthong. The words with [ɫ] will be pronounced once with a central, schwa-like onset and once with the more retracted onset. Try to imitate the two variants.

coat coal;	*folk foal;*	*host hole;*	*mope mole;*
post pole;	*soak soul;*	*toast toll;*	*coat cold;*
phone fold;	*home hold;*	*moat mould;*	*poke polled;*

C 4: Listen and repeat. Having practised a variety of [əʊ] types, go back and read the "Vicar of Stoke" limerick at the beginning of the section, and repeat it, trying to produce the same diphthong quality as the speaker.

Spelling

[əʊ] can be spelled in a variety of ways. In <u>open syllables</u> we find:

<o>: *go, hallo, so, no, quo, rho, Truro*   **<oe>**: *Coe, doe, foe, hoe, Joe, roe, toe, woe, Monroe;* and probably the most frequent:
<ow>   *bow, window, low, willow, mow, minnow, row, arrow, tow,*
a few words with: **<ough>** *dough, though, although,* and *furlough,*
and a small number of confusing exceptions: *sew (sewn), bureau.*

In <u>closed syllables</u> (ending in a consonant) standard spellings are

<o_e>   *bone, stoke, pole, rote, pose,* etc. (*rogue, brogue,* must be included too)
<oa>   *boat, road, goal, foam, shoal, toad, roast, poach,* etc.
<ow> in inflected forms of the <ow> open-syllable words mentioned above:
follows, followed, rows, rowed, flows, flowed, arrows, pillows, crows, blown, etc.
<o> when followed by [ɫ]:   *bold, cold, fold, gold, hold, roll, sold, told, toll, colt, dolt, volt, revolt, jolt,* but also: **<ou>** in *mould* and *moult.*

And to finish this section on [əʊ] another limerick:

There was once a confused little gnome,	[ðə wəz ˈwʌnsə kənˈfjuːzd lɪtɫ ˈnəʊm
Who regrettably tended to roam,	hu rəˈgretəbli ˈtendɪd tə ˈrəʊm
Once when he got lost,	wʌns ˈwenfi gɒt ˈlɒst
He found he had crossed	hi ˈfaʊndiəd ˈkrɒst
The road just a stone's throw from home.	ðə ˈrəʊd dʒʌstə ˈstəʊnz θrəʊ frəm ˈhəʊm]

V.3.3. /aɪ/: An "eye" for an "Ei"

Pardon our adaptation of the Old Testament quote "An eye for an eye", but we wish to draw your attention to the phonetic difference between German "Ei" and English "eye". To get used to the English diphthong /aɪ/ please listen to the following limerick:

C 1: Listen to the quality of the /aɪ/ in the following limerick:

I knew an old man who said: "Why	[aɪ ˈnjuː‿ənəʊɫd ˈmæn hu sed ˈwaɪ
can't I look in my ear with my eye?	kɑːntaɪ ˈlʊkɪn maɪ‿ɪə wɪð maɪ‿aɪ
I think I can do it	aɪ ˈθɪŋk‿aɪ kən ˈduː‿ɪt
if I put my mind to it	ɪfaɪ ˈpʊt maɪ maɪnd ˈtuː‿ɪt
You never can tell till you try."	ju ˈnevə kən ˈteɫ tɪɫ ju ˈtraɪ]

The English diphthong /aɪ/:

(a) It starts slightly further back in SBE (and many Southern dialects) than the corresponding German diphthong. It then moves up to a position for which most dictionaries use the symbol [ɪ], but in RP the target or end position of the tongue is usually slightly lower, i.e. it can perhaps be described as a centralised [e]. We will stick to the [aɪ] convention in this book, outside this section, but bear in mind that it is better not to aim for [ɪ] but to pronounce it [aḙ] rather than aiming at too high a position and wrongly pronouncing it [ai].

(b) As we said in the section V.3., diphthongs tend to be slightly longer than long monophthongs. German diphthongs differ from their English counterparts in the time spent on the first part of it. So when you lengthen diphthongs you should spend more time on the first part of the English diphthong, while the upward movement of the German diphthong starts sooner. This makes the [a] part of the diphthong in, for example, "Ei" shorter than in "eye".

In section V.2.4. we distinguished between German [aː] vs. English [ɑː]. To give you a symbolic reminder of these phonetic differences, in this section we will use [ae] for the English diphthong, and [aɪ] for the German one. So the title of this section: "An `eye´ for an `Ei´" can now be transcribed as: [əˈnae fərən ˀʔaɪ].

As a preliminary ear-training and articulation exercise we have compiled a short list of cross-language near-homophones, i.e. words that do not necessarily mean the same in both languages but that nearly sound the same. We will select only one item of each pair (i.e. either "eye" or "Ei"), and your task will be to repeat the word and then write down the number and [aɪ] if you think it was the German word, and [ae] if you believe it was the English counterpart.

C 2/E 1: Cross-language near-homophones: Listen and identify the language:

1. *eye* vs. *Ei*	2. *my* vs. *Mai*	3. *lime* vs. *Leim*
4. *mine* vs. *mein*	5. *shine* vs. *Schein*	6. *nine* vs. *nein*
7. *fine* vs. *fein*	8. *tiger* vs. *Taiga*	9. *lice* vs. *leis*
10. *mice* vs. *Mais*	11. *light* vs. *Leid*	12. *might* vs. *Maid*

If you found numbers 9 - 12 more difficult than the others there is a very good reason for it: the words of these last four examples end in voiceless sounds (here in [s] and [t] respectively), and voiceless sounds in final position have the effect of shortening the preceding vowel, making "lice" [laes] shorter than "lies" [laez]. With shorter diphthongs the task of discerning the difference in duration between the first part of English and German diphthongs becomes more difficult.

In certain dialects, in particular in America, we get a phenomenon that is often called **smoothing**, which means diphthongs become monophthongal. So "dime" is pronounced "daam", and "I" is smoothed to [ɑː]. We mention this phenomenon here for two reasons: firstly because it is a good exercise to pronounce these words with smoothing just to get used to lengthening the first part. And after you have said "aa don't have a daam", you can then repeat the phrase with exactly this long first part and then – just before the end of the vowel part – you slip in a short [e] to make it [dɑːem]. And secondly, because you will often hear this type of smoothing used by pop stars all over the world, irrespective of where they come from. Their English is referred to as "Mid-Atlantic English". This is fine if you are the lead singer in a band, but in order to be consistent you should not overuse smoothing in the type of English that we are aiming at in this book.

Fig. 1: A zoological example of "smoothing"

C 3: Listen to the following limerick and repeat each line separately:

This pretty young lady from Riga,	[ðɪs ˈprɪti jʌŋ ˈleɪdi frəm ˈraɪɡə
was smiling while riding a tiger.	wəz ˈsmaɪlɪŋ waɪɫ ˈraɪdɪŋə ˈtaɪɡə
They returned from the ride	ðeɪ rɪˈtɜːnd frəm ðə ˈraɪd
with the lady inside	wɪðə ˈleɪdi‿ɪnˈsaɪd
and a smile on the face of the tiger.	əndə ˈsmaɪl‿ɒnðə ˈfeɪsəv ðə ˈtaɪɡə]

"Aisle bayou a kight" or was it "I´ll buy you a kite"?
- Hints on how to reconcile your spelling with your pronunciation

E 2: Transcribe the last word of each line phonetically.

Often teachers are so strict,
making students work all night,
but still some students can´t predict
the pronunciation of "indict".

Now, luckily, the pronunciation [ɪnˈdaet] for *indict* (German: *verklagen*) is an exception to the other "-ict"-words. And you or your lecturers can decide on whether the word is important enough for you to memorise it.

But let us start with the more predictable spellings of the diphthong [ae]:

(a) Words with <i> and final <-e>:

slice, slide, fife, like, smile, slime, dine, vine, ripe, rise,
site, cite, dive, live (adj.), *size, die* (pl. *dice), lie, pie*

There are three exceptions where the <i> + <e> become two syllables with no [ae] in two of them:

recipe [ˈresɪpi] *Yosemite* [jəˈsemɪti] and the goddess *Aphrodite* [ˌæfrə ˈdaeti].

(b) with <y> with or without an <-e>:

bye, dye, rye, byte, recycle, fly, cry, spy, sly, sty and *stye, pylon, nylon;*

(c) words with <i> in the stressed syllable followed by another syllable:

Simon, lilac, Viking, timer, lining

(d) words with <-ind>:

bind, behind, find, hind, kind, mind, rind, wind (vb.)

(e) <i> followed by <gh> or <gn>:

tights, light, sigh, high, nigh, sign, align, malign, benign

(f) a few special words that you might like to remember:

wild but *wilderness* [ˈwɪɫdənəs], *mild* but *mildew* [ˈmɪɫdjuː];
climb (but *limb* [lɪm]); *hieroglyphics; irony; ion; hi; indict;*
and *aisle, isle* and *I´ll* are homophones.

And now let us have a look at some other letter-sound correlations:

Of all the <-eight> words, *height* [haet], *heighten* [ˈhaetn̩] and *sleight* [slaet] (as in "sleight of hand"), are the exceptions, because the others are pronounced [eɪ]: *eight, weigh, weight, freight, sleigh.*

(Of course you get <ei> as [ae] in words of German origin, like *Einstein* and *eiderdown.*)

Should you consider this last word sufficiently important, you may appreciate the following joke:

1. *In the middle of winter a young man's car breaks down near a farmhouse. The kind farmer offers him a room on the ground floor for the night. When they meet near the bathroom in the middle of the night the farmer says: "If you are cold, you can have our eiderdown." - "Thanks a lot", said the young man, "but she's been down twice already." Hint*: "Eider" and "Ida" are homophones. (*Eiderente*, the duck from which the best feathers for the eiderdown quilt originally came.)

Prefixes

There are a number of productive prefixes with the same spelling in German and English, which might cause interference. They are usually produced with a secondary stress, but occasionally have the main lexical stress in nouns:

<bi->   [ˌbae(-) ˈ-] in *bimeˈtallic, biˈsexual, biˈsect biˈsection, biˈweekly, biˈpartite;*
        [ˈbae-] as in *biplane, bivalve, biped, bicycle;*

<di->   [ˌdae(-) ˈ-] as in *diˈlute, diˈchotomy, diˈgest, diˈlate, diˈoxide;*
        [ˈdae-] as in *diphone;*

<hypo-> [ˌhaepə–] as in *hypochondriac* [ˌhaepəˈkɒndrɪæk], *hypothetical;*
        But: *hypothesis* [haeˈpɒθəsɪs], hypotenuse [haeˈpɒtənjuːz];
        and: *hypocrite* [ˈhɪpəkrɪt];

<hyper->[ˌhaepə–] as in *hypersensitive* [ˌhaepəˈsensɪtɪv], *hyperˈsonic;*

Now see if you get the following joke:

2. *A man went into a pub with a newt* (German *Molch*) *on his shoulder. "That's a nice newt," said the barman, "What's he called?" - "That's pretty obvious, isn't it? He's called Tiny," answered the man. - "Why on earth is it obvious that his name is Tiny?" asked the barman. The man answered, "Because he is my newt."*

If you did not get it, we'll give you a clue: "minute" [ˈmɪnɪt] (= 60 seconds) vs. "minute" [mae ˈnjuːt] (= very small).

The triphthong [aeə]

"Anyone who sees a psychiatrist [saeˈkaeətrɪst] *wants his head examined."*

The first syllable of *psychiatrist* contains the by now familiar diphthong [ae]. If you add schwa to the diphthong [ae] you get the triphthong [aeə], as in the stressed part of [sae ˈkaeətrɪst]. It is called a centering triphthong, because at the end of it the body of the tongue moves to the neutral central position in the mouth, which – in the vowel diagram – is occupied by schwa: [ə].

Earlier on we mentioned the phenomenon of smoothing, oberved in some speakers who smooth the diphthong [ae] of *bye* to a monophthong [ɑː]. This smoothing of diphthongs is not obligatory and we did not recommend it, but it is very common in triphthongs, where it has the effect of changing the triphthong into a diphthong: [aeə] → [ɑːə].

This ensures that in spite of the reduction of the triphthong there is still a phonetic difference between

> *tie* [tae] and *tyre* [tɑːə]
> *pie* [pae] and *pyre* [pɑːə]
> *fie* [fae] and *fire* [fɑːə]

We are drawing your attention to the smoothing phenomenon for two reasons: firstly, because you should be aware of this trend so you will recognise the sound sequence [ˈkwɑːə] – when you hear it – as the word *choir*. And secondly, because lengthening the first part of the vowel section and weakening the second part makes *choir* and *fire* monosyllabic words in contrast to the clear two syllables in the German word *Eier*. This distinction is so important that you should avoid a German triphthong – as in *Eier* – with its disyllabic structure at all cost. As a matter of fact, reducing a triphthong to a long first vowel followed by [ə] is probably the most effective way of adopting a convincing English accent.

George Bernard Shaw is said to have mockingly pointed out, triphthongal smoothing can even go as far as to become monophthongal, leading to confusion between [ɑː], [aeə] and [aʊə]: *"A tower of tyres on the tar"* can then be represented as [ə ˈtaːrəv tɑːz ɒn ðə ˈtɑː] after smoothing from [ə ˈtaʊərəv taɪəz ɒn ðə ˈtɑː]. But smoothing to diphthongal [ɑːə] or [aːə] does not really risk misunderstanding.

To round off this section on [ae] and [aeə], we repeat the limerick from III.3. (but with correct spelling this time) to illustrate the alternative rendering that smoothing offers:

C4: Listen to the two recordings, one with and one without smoothing of the diphthongs:

We loved the young girl in the choir,	[kwaeə] or [kwɑːə]
whose voice rose higher and higher,	[haeə] or [hɑːə]
till it reached such a height,	[haet]
it was clear out of sight,	[saet]
and they found it next day in the spire.	[spaeə] or [spɑːə]

E 3: Give a phonetic transcription of the following text:

> *My brother Clive was trying to buy a magazine on the Yosemite National Park for the archives of his library because his sisters Pauline, Irene and Isobel wanted to climb the spires of the five churches there with the fine carved choirs.*

Reminder: We are now returning to the use of [aɪ] for English /aɪ/.

V.3.4. /aʊ/: *How now, brown cow?*

After working through the previous diphthong sections, particularly the section on /aɪ/, you should find it relatively easy to come to grips with /aʊ/.

What English /aʊ/ and /aɪ/ have in common (together with other diphthongs) is (a) the relatively long duration of the first part and (b) the fact that the glide towards the second element does not normally reach the target area indicated by the second symbol, in this case [ʊ]. The [a]-onset of /aʊ/ differs from /aɪ/ by being more fronted, i.e., closer to [a] than [ɑ] (cf. V.3.3.) This difference in onset quality is the opposite of what is found for standard German, and is therefore a source of potential interference. The first vowel element in the German word *Haus* is further back than in the English word *house*, while it is further forward in German *-keit* than with English *kite* (at least in the varieties of the two languages that we try to aim at). In a *narrow* phonetic transcription we can use the fronted [a] in our transcription of English *brown* [braʊn], and the backed [ɑ] for our transcription of English *light* [lɑɪt]. In standard German this would be reversed: the first element of the German /aʊ/ diphthong in *braun* is best represented with the back [ɑ] ([bʁɑʊn]) while the first element of the German /aɪ/ diphthong in *Leid* is best represented with the front [a] ([laɪt]). German and English /aʊ/ also differ in *lip shape* for the second element. English has very little lip-rounding, whereas German has stronger lip-rounding. The following vowel charts illustrate the tongue-position differences, but cannot reflect the differences in degree of lip-rounding, of course.

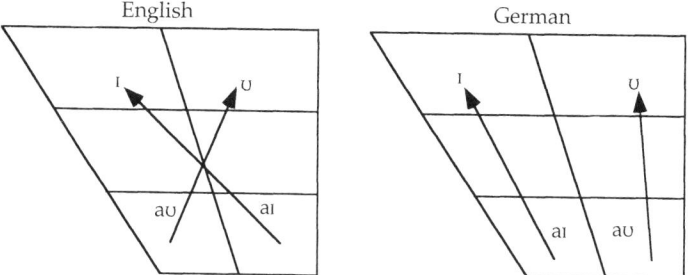

Fig. 1: Diphthongs /aɪ/ and /aʊ/ in English and German

C 1/E 1: As an ear-training and articulation exercise we have, once again, compiled a short list of cross-language near-homophones. You will hear only one item from each pair (i.e. either *house* or *Haus*), and your task is to repeat the word and then write down the language: "G" if you think it was the German word, or "E" if you believe it was the English one.

Example: 1. E. *how* vs. G. *hau;* You hear *how*; repeat it, making sure to imitate the long duration of [a:] before you start the glide up towards [ʊ]; then put an "E" for "*English*" after the "1". Now continue:

2. E. *house* vs. G. *Haus*   3. E. *mouse* vs G. *Maus*   4. E. *louse* vs G. *Laus*
5. E. *clown* vs G. *Clown*   6. E. *lout* vs G. *laut*   7. E. *clout* vs G. *klaut*

Before you start the next exercise remember the effect of pre-lenis lengthening: so you get shorter diphthongs before voiceless sounds, as in all except 5. in the above examples, but longer diphthongs in *cowboys, Brown, lounge* and *somehow*. The word *houseproud* contains two diphthongs, where the first is shorter, because of the following [s] giving you [haʊs], and the second is longer, because of the following [d] giving you [pra:ʊd]. So, in a narrow transcription the whole compound can be represented as ['haʊsˌpra:ʊd].

C 2: Listen and repeat: *The children wanted to play cowboys and Indians in Mrs. Brown's house. - Why in the house and not outside? - Well, the "Indians" wanted to hold a powwow. - What's a powwow? - It's a kind of council. - How did it go? - Mrs. Brown didn't want them in the house. She's ever so houseproud. And such an old sourpuss. - Now Mr. Brown is even worse. He's one of those down-and-outs without a job. He never leaves the house. He's a real couch potato. If he gets up at all, he slouches around the house grumbling and grousing. Mr. Brown couldn't agree with Mrs. Brown about whether the children should be allowed in the lounge. They had a tremendous row. It was embarrassing because he is so loud, and all the neighbours around their council house could hear him. He even called her a stupid cow. He's such a foul-mouthed individual.*

The numerous spellings of /aʊ/: Ho*w* [haʊ] do you kno*w* [nəʊ] when an <*ow*> is [aʊ]?

<**ow**>: A common spelling for [aʊ] is <ow>, but it is also common for [əʊ].

E 2: Read the following poem, making sure you get the rhymes right. Then transcribe the last word of each line phonetically.

At the Theatre

At first he just raised his right brow	1
when he saw she was in the wrong row,	2
but then the two had a big row,	3
when she found they were in the wrong show.	4

We hope you realised that line 1 rhymes with 3 and line 2 with 4, not 1 with 2 and 3 with 4. The vast majority of words which contain the letters <ow> are pronounced [əʊ], like *elbow, meadow, shadow, widow; window, show,* including the place-names *Glasgow, Moscow, Barlow, Krakow, Winslow*. But there are some important words where <ow> is pronounced [aʊ]: You are, of course, familiar with the high frequency words *how, now, town* and *allow*. But *row, bow* and *sow* may cause problems, because they are pronounced in two ways, with [aʊ] *and* with [əʊ]. The single *spelling* represents (at least) two different words, which makes them **homographs**. They are not, however, **homophones** (= words that have the same pronunciation irrespective of their spelling), because the two words are *pronounced* differently. We summarize them for you (with the equivalent German words) in the following table:

[aʊ]	[əʊ]
row [raʊ] = *Streit;*	*row* [rəʊ] = *Reihe*
	= *rudern*
bow [baʊ] = *Bug;*	*bow* [bəʊ] = *Bogen ("bow and arrow"*
= *sich verbeugen,*	and *"violin bow")*
("I bow to your greater experience.")	= *Schleife*
sow [saʊ] = *Sau*	*sow* [səʊ] = *säen*

Useful [aʊ] words are:

brow (brow of the hill; eyebrows), the *"animal group" fowl, owl, cow, sow; miaow, bow-wow,* the exclamation *wow!* and the verbs *to vow* and *to avow* (German *schwören*). *Endow* may not be a household term, but you might want to remember it since it figures prominently in the American Declaration of Independence, 1776: *"We hold these truths to be self-evident, that all men are created equal, that they are endowed* [en¹daʊd] *by their creator with certain unalienable* rights ... *"*

Use the diphthong [aʊ] in words that end in <-own>, like *clown, crown, down, gown* and *town* except for the verb *own* [əʊn] and all past participles ending with <-own>, which are pronounced [əʊ]: *blown, flown, grown, ingrown, known, shown, sown, thrown.* But verbal infinitives in <-own> are pronounced [aʊ]: *drown, frown.*

<ou> *house; douse; louse, blouse, mouse, spouse, rouse, arouse; carouse; grouse, renounce, trout, voucher, noun, rout,* but: *routine* [ˌruː¹tiːn]*, route* [ruːt]*.*

<-ough> The pronunciation of words ending in <-ough> is notoriously difficult to predict (compare sections III.3. and V.3.2.); remember *bough* [baʊ] (German *Zweig/Ast*), *plough* [plaʊ] (German *Pflug/ pflügen*).

Triphthong [aʊə] in *flowerpower*

All triphthongs in English have, as you know, a centering end movement of the tongue. Adding schwa to our diphthong gives you [aʊə] in words with:

<-ower>: *tower, power, flower, glower* (look in an angry way). *"Empowerment of the students",* refers to teaching the students how to learn and help themselves.

<-our>, like *our, hour, flour, devour, scour,* and *scoundrel.*

<-oward>, as in *"Howard the coward",* but note: *toward(s)* [tə¹wɔːd(z)] and *untoward* [ˌʌntə¹wɔːd] *("There was nothing untoward happening")*.

As with the diphthongs, you get smoothing here: [taʊə]→[taːə]. It is perfectly all right for you to stick to the pronunciation with triphthongs, but you should be aware of the smoothing effect or you may have difficulties in working out what some speakers mean by [ˈflaːəˌpaːə].

C 3: Cross-language near-homophones. The English words will be spoken once *without* and once *with* smoothing. Listen and repeat:

1. G. *Bauer* - E. *bower*   2. G. *flauer* - E. *flour*   3. G. *Schauer* - E. *shower*
4. G. *der Tower* - E. *the Tower*   5. G. *Flowerpower* - E. *flowerpower*

E 3: Transcribe the following words. Which word pairs constitute homophones and which are homographs?

a. *our*   b. *hour*   c. *flour*   d. *flower*   e. *wound*   f. *wound*

Foreign words

When you come across a German loanword in English, like *Bauhaus* in the headline *From Bauhaus to that house* (Guardian International, 25 Nov. 1993), you should refrain from showing off your wonderful German. Instead try and pronounce it with an English accent, just like you pronounce English loanwords in German with a German accent, i.e. [ˈbaʊhaʊs], not [ˈbaʊhaʊs]. See chapter VIII. on the pronunciation of foreign words in English.

V.3.5. /ɔɪ/: *English "cowboy" contra German "Cowboy"*

As with the previous diphthongs discussed, the first part of English /ɔɪ/ is fairly long, and the second part barely reaches the region of [ɪ]. So a narrow (more detailed) phonetic transcription of *toy* could be either [tʰɔːɪ] or [tʰɔːə]. It is important for German speakers to take their time with the [ɔː] part of the diphthong, because that tends to be shorter in German, and to ensure that the second part of the diphthong does not go anywhere near the [i] (see fig. 1).

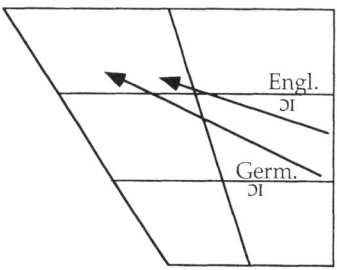

Fig. 1: Vowel chart English and German /ɔɪ/

It should be noted that in conservative English the starting point [ɔː] is lower than indicated in our diagram for present-day English ([ǫ] in fig. 1). The fact that there is a range of possible starting points, one of which coincides with the German [ɔ], is comforting, because you cannot be too far out. Be sure, however, not to go too far up into the region of [i] at the end of *toy*.

C 1: Listen and repeat: *Employers and employees enjoyed a drink at the reception in the foyer at Rolls Royce's new headquarters. The president, Mr. Roy Toynbee, announced a payrise to his loyal members of staff. "Let me make one further point", he said raising his voice above the noise, "Mr. Fitzroy will receive a commemorative gold coin for twenty-five years loyal service to Rolls Royce." Fitzroy was overjoyed.*

C 2/E 1: Cross-language near-homophones. We will now play you only one of the two words that are phonetically similar. Your task is to repeat what you hear and write *a* if you think it is English or *b* if you identify it as German.

English	German	English	German
1a. *ahoy*	b. *ahoi*	4a. *loiter*	b. *Leute*
2a. *cowboy*	b. *Cowboy*	5a. *Freud*	b. *Freud*
3a. *playboy*	b. *Playboy*	6a. *boiler*	b. *Boiler*

The diphthong [ɔɪ] should not cause great difficulties, but we want to point out the dangers of accumulative effects of mistakes. Let us assume you have not quite mastered the pronunciation of *boy*, which in narrow transcription is [bǫːə], but you feel "It's good enough". You then pronounce the plural <s> as

[s] instead of [z], and finally you forget to lengthen the syllable, which would have accompanied the lenis sound [z], if you had not replaced it by [s]. Now your *I like boys* sounds like *I like Beuss.*

In C 1 you heard the word *employee*, which we can use to demonstrate the danger of finishing the diphthong [ɔɪ] with an [i]. In the disyllable [ɔɪiː] you can clearly hear the change of vowel quality from [ɪ] to [iː]: [emˈplɔɪ iː] (N.B., the word can also be pronounced with final stress: [emplɔɪˈiː]).

The spelling of [ɔɪ] is <oi> or <oy>. There are, however, some words where <oi> is not pronounced [ɔɪ]: *tortoise* [ˈtɔːtəs], *porpoise* [ˈpɔːpəs], *Lois* [ˈləʊɪs].

C 3: Listen and repeat

All the schoolboys enjoyed reading Tolstoy, [ɔːɫ ðə ˈskuːɫbɔɪz ɪnˈʤɔɪd riːdɪŋ
ˈtɒɫstɔɪ

which pleased their old teacher named Killjoy wɪʧ ˈpliːzd ðeərəʊɫ ˈtiːʧə neɪmd
ˈkɪɫʤɔɪ

till inside the covers tɪˈlɪnsaɪd ðə ˈkʌvəz
he spotted nude lovers, hi ˈspɒtɪd njuːd ˈlʌvəz
'cause "Tolstoy" was a cover for "Playboy". kəz ˈtɒɫstɔɪ wəzə ˈkʌvə fə ˈpleɪbɔɪ]

V.3.6. /ʊə/, /ɪə/ and /eə/: centring diphthongs: *Journey to the centre of the vowel space*

We borrowed and slightly modified Jule Verne's title *Journey to the Centre of the Earth* to draw your attention to what the three diphthongs [ʊə], [ɪə] and [eə] have in common: It is the movement towards the centre, which is why they are referred to as **centring diphthongs**. As you can see, the respective end point of this tongue movement to the centre is symbolised in each case by schwa [ə]. We can make a few more generalisations in terms of contrastive phonetics if you consider the following cross-language minimal pairs:

1. a. English *sure*   vs. German *Schur*
    b. English *mare, mayor*   vs. German *Meer*
    c. English *beer*   vs. German *Bier*

The two words of each pair are phonetically clearly distinct and should not be pronounced as homophones. In Southern British English there is less of a movement, and the corresponding German diphthongs go to a different place, i.e. to the more open [ɐ], and the first part of the diphthong is slightly longer and more extreme in German: [u]-like instead of [ʊ], [i]-like instead of [ɪ], [e]-like instead of [ɛ].

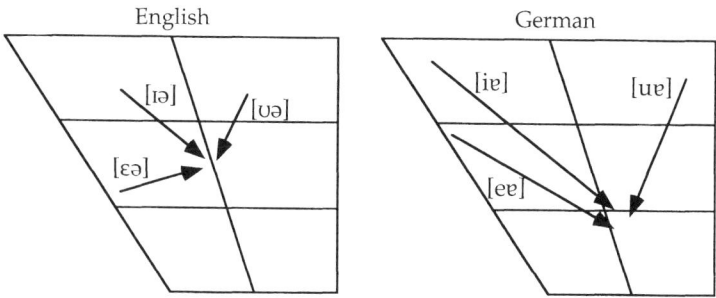

Fig. 1: English and German centring diphthongs

We will demonstrate this with recordings when we deal with these diphthongs individually in the following sections.

V.3.6.1. /ɪə/: _beer_ and _Bier_ taste and sound different

1. A German whose illness was chronic,
Was told that he needed a tonic,
"But Herr Doctor, I fear,
I'd rather have Bier."
"No, no", said the Doc, "that's Teutonic."

[ə ˈdʒɜːmən huːˈzɪɫnəs wəz ˈkrɒnɪk
wəz ˈtəʊɫd ðəti ˈniːdɪdə ˈtɒnɪk
but hɛɐ ˈdɔktɔ aɪ ˈfiːɐ
aɪd ˈraːðə hæv ˈbiːɐ
nəʊˈnəʊ sed ðə ˈdɒk ðæts tjuˈtɒnɪk]

The doctor's remark that this is Teutonic refers (a) to the belief that _Bier_ is the national drink in Germany, and (b) to the fact that it is the German pronunciation and definitely not the English way of saying _beer_. As you saw in fig. 1 in the general discussion of centring diphthongs, the vowel in _Bier_ starts higher than the one in _beer_, which starts not only lower but also more central. There is less of a movement. German goes from the higher [i] to a different place, i.e. the more open [ɐ]. And finally, the first part in German _Bier_ is slightly longer and more extreme than that in _beer_. These differences are reflected in the phonetic transcription [biːɐ] for _Bier_ as opposed to English [bɪə].

C 1/E 1: Discrimination exercise: cross-language near-homophones.

a. Listen and repeat: German: _Bier_, English: _beer_; German: _hier_, English: _here_; German: _Peer group_, English: _peer group_; G: _Piercing_, E: _piercing_

b. Listen to the numbered pairs of words and put a "G" behind the appropriate number if you think you heard the German word, and an "E" if you think it was the English word:
1. _Bier_ vs. beer   2. _hier_ vs. _here_   3. _vier_ vs. _fear_   4. _dir_ vs. _dear_
5. _ihr_ vs. _ear_   6. _Tier_ vs. _tear_   7. _Gier_ vs. _gear_   8. _Pier_ vs. _pier_

C 2: Listen and repeat immediately after each line:

a. I knew a young fellow named Weir,
who hadn't an atom of fear.
He indulged a desire
to touch a live wire. -
Almost any last line will do here.

[aɪ ˈnjuːə jʌŋ ˈfeləʊ neɪmd ˈwɪə
hu ˈhædntəˈnætəməv ˈfɪə
hi ɪnˈdʌɫdʒdə dɪˈzaɪə
tə ˈtʌtʃə laɪv ˈwaɪə
ɔːɫməʊstˈeni lɑːst ˈlaɪn wɪɫ du ˈfɪə]

b. _Two beers_ [bɪəz] _please. Thank you. Here_ [hɪə] _you are, dear_ [dɪə]. - _Thanks John, I really_ [ˈrɪəli] _needed that. Cheers_ [tʃɪəz]. - _The beer's_ [ˈbɪəz] _getting dearer and dearer_ [ˈdɪərəːnˈdɪərə]. _I hear_ [hɪə] _Deirdre_ [ˈdɪədri] _doesn't come here any_ [hɪəreni] _more. - That's right. She prefers going to museums_ [mjuˈzɪəmz] _now. - Deirdre_ [ˈdɪədri] _and museums? You are not serious_ [ˈsɪərɪəs], _are you? - I am. There's a series_ [ˈsɪəriːz] _of lectures on at the moment: Rembrandt's Early Period_ [ˈpɪərɪəd]. - _I bet that was Ian's idea_ [ˈɪənz aɪˌdɪə]. _He's always trying to educate Deirdre_ [ˈdɪədri]. _Another beer, dear_ [bɪə dɪə]? - _No thanks, it's getting crowded in here_ [hɪə]. _Is there another pub near here_ [nɪə hɪə]? - _No, but fancy seeing a film? "Tears for fears"_ [ˈtɪəz fə ˈfɪəz] _is on now._

The pitfalls of spelling

You are used to pronouncing <ee> as a long [iː], and this may tempt you to pronounce *steer* wrongly as * [stiːə] instead of the correct [stɪə], or even worse, *steering* as *[ˈstiːrɪŋ] (rhyming with *keyring*), where Germans tend to use a long [iː] and no diphthong. The correct pronunciation is [ˈstɪərɪŋ]. The same goes for *career*, which incidentally is a homophone of *Korea*, since both are pronounced [kəˈrɪə]. You will now be able to hear and pronounce the different endings of English *pioneer* [ˌpaɪəˈnɪə] and German *Pionier* [pioˈniːɐ].

The ending <-ier> represents a problem, as different pronunciations are possible, for instance as two syllables in the loanword *dossier* [ˈdɒsieɪ], a triphthong in *drier* [draɪə] and a diphthong in *pier* [pɪə]. It is useful to remember that, as a rule, multisyllabic words ending in <-ier> that have the stress on the <-ier> are pronounced with the centring diphthong [ɪə], like *cashier* [kæ ˈʃɪə]. Words stressed on an earlier part of the word are not pronounced with [ɪə]. The <-ier> is either pronounced as two syllables [si.ə] if said slowly, or in rapid speech as a rising diphthong [i̯ə], (with a non-syllabic [i̯] and the schwa as a syllable nucleus): e.g. *financier* [ˌfaɪˈnænsi.ə] or [ˌfaɪˈnænsi̯ə], *courier* [ˈkʊri.ə] or [ˈkʊri̯ə], *frontier* [ˈfrʌnti.ə] or [ˈfrʌnti̯ə].

V.3.6.2. /ʊə/: *Are you sure?*

You may want to follow the trend and ignore the pronunciation [pʊə] for *poor*, in which case, you may turn back to section V.2.6. and apply all the things that were said about /ɔː/ to the /ʊə/ words below! An increasing number of standard English speakers just do not have the /ʊə/ sound any more (except perhaps in the rare and very Scottish word *dour* (pronounced [dʊə]), and in combination with a preceding /j/, in words such as *allure* [ə'ljʊə] and *demure* [dɪ'mjʊə]). For them, *poor* and *paw*, *tour* and *tor*, *moor* and *more*, *sure* and *shore* are homophones. This can be made to sound ludicrous, as the following concentration of /ɔː/ words and potential /ʊə/ words shows:

1.   ['mɔːr ən 'mɔː wɪə 'ʃɔ | tə gəʊ‿ɒn ðə 'tɔː frəm ðə 'ʃɔ: tə ðə 'tɔːr‿ɒn ðə 'mɔː]

Can you decipher the sentence and put it into normal orthography? (see XII)

Of course, sequences of /ɔː/ words and potential /ʊə/ words like this are very rare, and many people are not even aware whether they pronounce words like *sure* and *shore* the same or not.

C 1. The following sentences and expressions are recorded twice to illustrate the acceptable alternatives in present-day English:

> *The Spice Girls are on tour.*
> *Give more to help the poor!*
> *Don't say anything till you're sure.*
> *There's a haunted house on the moor.*
> *She's so demure! That's her allure.*

The following two-verse limerick perhaps sums up the situation:

2.   *The problem with words like assure,*   [ðə 'prɒbləm wɪð 'wɜːdz laɪk ə'ʃɔː
     Is they don't rhyme with dour any more.   ɪz ðeɪ 'dəʊnt raɪm wɪð 'dʊər‿eni 'mɔː
     So, if you ask me,   səʊ 'ɪf ju ɑsk 'mi:
     We're now all at sea,   wɪə 'naʊ ɔl ət 'si:
     And unlikely to get back ashore.   ənd‿ʌn'laɪkli tə 'get bæk‿ə'ʃɔː]

     But conservatives always assure   bʌt kən'sɜːvətɪvz‿'ɔːɬweɪzə'ʃʊə
     You the word rhymes with   ju ðə 'wɜːd raɪmz wɪð
               dour and with tour.   'dʊərən wɪð 'tʊə
     And they're highly incensed,   ən ðeə 'haɪli‿ɪn'senst
     In fact strictly against   ɪn fækt 'strɪktli‿ə'genst
     Any rhyme of "ashore" with "assure".   eni 'raɪməvə'ʃɔː wɪðə'ʃʊə]

If you *do* wish to distinguish the relatively rare /ʊə/ words from the much more common /ɔː/ words, then it is important to avoid using the corresponding German vowel sequence from words like *Tour, stur, pur* or *Spur* because the quality of the [u]-element is too extreme (compare what was said about German and English /uː/ in section V.2.2.). In German the tongue is too retracted, and the lips are too strongly rounded. In fact, these words can best be transcribed with the vowel symbols [uːɐ], indicating the more retracted starting and finishing positions compared to [ʊə] as the diagram in V.3.6. illustrates.

A more acceptable German correspondence to start from is the vowel sequence in the words *Turm* and *Sturm* ([tʊɐm], [ʃtʊɐm]) – though not if you have a Ruhrpott accent, because the quality there is too close to the extreme quality found in standard German *Tour* and *stur*.

Spelling:

One probable reason for the almost complete fusion of the pronunciation of /ʊə/ and /ɔː/ is the non-unique spelling of /ʊə/ words.

Compare: *poor* [pʊə]   *door* [dɔː]   *tour* [tʊə]   *your* [jɔː]

The <ure> sequence is a more reliable indication of a potential /ʊə/ word: *endure, cure, lure, allure, demure, pure* (but *sure* is often [ʃɔː]).

V.3.6.3. /eə/: Open-air für´s Wattenmeer?

Fig. 1: *Open Air für´s Wattenmeer*

You should have by now developed a deep-rooted and perfectly justified mistrust of those language-teaching gurus who try and tell you that you knew many English words even before you started learning the language. What people all over the world know are loanwords, words borrowed from English and turned into words of their own language with appropriate adjustments. Let us give you an example: In some African languages the word for bollards or traffic islands in the middle of a street is *keepilefiti*. What you see on these bollards in England is the words *"keep left"*. If you did not know exactly what they meant you might think that was the name for the thing they were written on. And if your language requires a vowel after consonants you call the bollard *keepilefiti*, which is a loanword, but not an English word any more.

Similarly the loanword *das Open-air* [ˌoːpm ˈeɐ] is not the English word any more, firstly because in the title of this section it is a noun, whereas in English it is an adjective, and secondly because English *open air* does not rhyme with *Wattenmeer*. In German the first part of the diphthong in *Meer* is like the [eː] in *Beet* compared to the lower starting point of English *air*, with an onset quality that is often more open than the vowel in *bet*. Apart from these qualitative differences, in Southern British English there is less of a movement, and the second element is [ə], while the corresponding German diphthong moves to the more open [ɐ].

Since, in this section, we want to draw your attention to the particular phonetic properties, we will use a special symbol – [ɛə] – to distinguish the difference *in both elements* between English and German (see V.3.6. Fig. 1). In the rest of the book, however, we use [eə] like most other books on English pronunciation.

C 1: Cross-language near-homophones. Listen and repeat:

German vs. English		German vs. English	
a. *Meer*	*mare,*	b. *er*	*air*
c. *Bär*	*bear, bare*	d. *Teer*	*tear*
e. *fair*	*fair*	f. *Software*	*software*
g.*Tony Blair*	*Tony Blair*	h. *kehr*	*care*

C 2: Listen and repeat immediately after each line:

Excuse me, where can I find lingerie? - It´s over there, Sir, right under the sign that says "underwear". - Under where? - Yes, that´s right, "lingerie" means "underwear"; "women´s underwear" to be precise. - Oh, uhm, I see. And where´s the sportswear department? - It´s over there. There´s a special offer on: A jersey and two pairs of plimsolls for £10. - That sounds fair enough. I hope the jersey won´t tear easily. You see, my son is a bit of a tearaway, if you pardon the pun. - No, I wear them myself and I swear by them. And we give a six-month guarantee. - Look, I´ve done my fair share of running in marathons: You´ll wear off those soles in under six weeks. - Well, a marathon´s different, but they <u>are</u> guaranteed against normal wear and tear. It´s an honest offer, £10 fair and square.

"Fair Fares", "Tears cause tears" and other problems of spelling /eə/

1. *This conceited young lady from Ham,*   [ðɪs kənˈsiːtɪd jʌŋ ˈleɪdi frəm ˈhæm
   jumped hastily onto a tram.   dʒʌmpt ˈheɪstɪli̯ ˈɒntuə ˈtræm
   As she swiftly embarked,   əz ʃi ˈswɪftli̯ ɪmˈbɑːkt
   the conductor remarked,   ðə kənˈdʌktə rɪˈmɑːkt
   "Your fare, Miss." She said, "Yes I am."   jɔː ˈfɛə mɪs ʃi ˈsed jes̬a̬ɪ̯ˈæm]

Now that you have mastered the tongue movement of this diphthong, we have to point out some problem areas: In 1. the misunderstanding between conductor and passenger is due to the fact that *"Your fare"* and *"You´re fair"* are homophones. There are a number of different spellings for [ɛə], but if you read the following sentence in its carefully articulated version with its seven occurrences of [ɛə] you have nearly all spelling variants in a nutshell:

2.   a. *Mary and Sarah wear their hair there with care.*
      b. [ˈmɛəri ən ˈsɛərə wɛə ðɛə ˈhɛə ðɛə wɪð ˈkɛə]

The words *there* and *their* actually have an alternative pronunciation. If you look at the text of C 2, you will find the following passage: *"It´s over there. There´s a special offer on."* When *there* is used as an adverb of place, as in *"It´s over there."* and *"there and then"*, when it is stressed as in *"There you are. Where have you been?"*, and generally when it occurs at the end of a phrase, as in *"Hello there!"*, it is pronounced [ðɛə]. But as a pronoun in *"Waiter, there´s a fly in my soup."* it is usually pronounced in its so-called weak form [ˈweɪtə | ðəzə ˈflaɪ̯ɪn maɪ ˈsuːp]. (We strongly recommend you read section VI.3 *"Weak /əz/ weak /kən/ be! – The fate of function words"*. The use of strong forms where English speakers use the weak form may have other consequences than just sounding foreign!)

Another pitfall that English spelling has in store for learners with regard to [ɛə] is contained in the following limerick. Read it aloud and make sure you get the rhyme in the last line right:

3. *A Salvation lassie named Claire*
    Was having her first love affair.
    As she climbed out of bed
    "Ah men!" she just said
    As a heartfelt, if rather short prayer.

[ə sæɫˈveɪʃn ˈlæsi neɪmd ˈklɛə
wəz ˈhævɪŋ fɪə ˈfɜːst lʌvəˈfɛə
əz ʃi ˈklaɪmd̮‿aʊtəv ˈbed
ɑːˈmen ʃi dʒʌst ˈsed̮
əzə ˈhɑːtfeɫt l ɪf ˈrɑːðə ʃɔːt ˈprɛə]

The trap here is that you are familiar with words that have the diphthong [eɪ], as *play, player, layer, Dorothy Sayers, grey* and *greyer*, but even though you have *pray* [preɪ], the corresponding noun *prayer* is pronounced [prɛə], and rhymes with the strong form of *there*, as for instance in Madonna´s pop song:

4. *Life is a mystery, everyone must stand alone*
    I hear you call my name
    And it feels like home
    When you call my name it´s like a little prayer
    I´m down on my knees, I wanna take you there ...
    Just like a prayer, your voice can take me there ...
    Just like a prayer
    No choice
    Your voice can take me there.

The other exception to the rule is the word *mayor* [mɛə], which is an exact homophone of *mare*.

E 1: Look up the following words and give the phonetic transcription for the diphthong in each of them:

pear, dear, bear, aerobics, mayor, mare, surveyor, care, bare, Bär, kehr

Having worked your way through this section you will appreciate the inter-lingual pun of the *"Berliner Stadtreinigung"*. It proves that Germans *do* have a sense of humour, and it gives a chance to smile be-nignly at the fact that *"We kehr for you"* is not a homophone of *"We care for you"*.

Fig. 2.

VI. Putting sounds together

In this chapter we come to those aspects of pronunciation that make speaking really speaking, rather than just putting one - word - after - the - other. We would have liked to give the chapter the priority it deserves by placing it at the beginning of the book because it is the rhythmic framework that carries the sounds along. However, there would have been little point in talking about differences between syllables of a word or about changes in the sound structure of words in a phrase until we had told you about the sounds themselves. Thus, it is in chapter VI., not chapter I., where we deal with "utterance phonetics", as it is sometimes called. But you will have noticed that we have anticipated this chapter throughout the previous sections by using examples in context, by using poems, limericks and recorded dialogues to get you into the rhythm of spoken English. So we believe that we have prepared the ground for "Putting sounds together", and that the phenomena which we will make explicit in this chapter will help you to become aware of things you have been doing or trying to do all along anyway.

The different aspects of connected speech are presented in four sections: (i) the linking of words, (ii) questions of stress and accent, (iii) the weakening of unaccented and unstressed syllables, and (iv) changes that can occur at the edges of words as a result of the context.

VI.1. Linking: *Joinitup! A "binding" principle*

Fig. 1: The secret code that native speakers of English use. (*KREK WAITER'S SPEAK BRISTLE*, ed. by D. Robson, Abson Books, Bristol 1988)

Most readers are baffled when they first see the above cartoon. It is this kind of shock that you experiences when, after years of carefully pronounced class-room English, you set foot in the British isles, listen to the natural, casual con-versation of native speakers, do not understand a single word and begin to wonder: Is this the language I have been taught? Or is it a secret code that native speakers use among themselves? The answer is yes and no. We guar-antee that at the end of this chapter you will look at the above cartoon and say: *"Well, it's pretty obvious, isn't it?"* But chapters, like good stories, should begin with the beginning:

1   a.   *I - am - awfully - amazed - at - all - our - articulatory - antics!*
    b. [ˀaɪ ˀæm ˈˀɔːfli ˀəˈmeɪzd ˀæt ˀɔːl ˀaʊə ˀɑːˈtɪkjələtri ˈˀæntɪks]

If you ponder for a moment over the above sentence you will probably be prompted to say that *we do not speak word by word*, we speak in groups of words that run together according to certain rules. Those rules come so natur-ally to us in our native language (whatever that language might be) that we are not aware there *are* any rules. Only by listening to foreigners speaking our language do we realise that there *must* be some because they are breaking them! They are not stringing the words together properly; they have a foreign accent! One of the most useful things to do is to listen to the way English learners of German break these rules. If you can imitate their English accent in German you are halfway there. Typical mistakes are, for instance, *"Woche 'nende"* and *"Nimm den Hu tab"*, or the pronunciation *"Undines Kleid"* when the speaker actually meant *"und Ines' Kleid"*. This English accent in German provides us with important clues as to what we have to aim at in English.

Learner´s Question: "Can I get away without practising linking?"
(a) The learner-listener´s problem

If you are not aware of what the English do when stringing words together, most of their utterances will seem like the above cartoon, or they will give rise to typical conversation snippets like:

2a.   A: *ge taway to sou theas tasia this wee kend!*
      B: *Sorry, what does "tasia" mean and what is a "kend", please?*

In normal writing A´s sentence is easier to understand because you can see the gaps between the words in the right places:

2b.   *Get away to South East Asia this weekend.*

But this should not lead you to believe these gaps on paper should be respected by the English or by you in normal English conversations. If you are not used to linking, you may be puzzled by utterances such as 2a. or – to demonstrate this phenomenon in phonetic transcription – as

3a. [ɪtsə ˈsɔː təˈvəʊp ˈmeərɪ ˈvent],

which may seem just a meaningless chain of sounds to you, unless you hear it in its totally unrealistic unlinked form:

3b. *it-is-a-sort-of-open-air-event.*

For the teacher, or really anybody talking to foreigners with language problems, there is thus always the danger of respecting the word boundaries phonetically, allegedly in order to make the meaning clearer to the learner. Beware of these traps! If the English you teach is a *3b-[ˈsɔːt ʔɒv ˈʔɪŋglɪʃ], your students will experience the shock exemplified by our cartoon at the beginning of this section when they encounter real English.

This chapter is concerned with words that begin with a vowel because the last consonant of a word or morpheme should be linked to the next word or morpheme if that begins with a vowel. In contrast to German, where in these cases the basic rules (with its exceptions of course) are "Separate the words" and "Observe morpheme boundaries", the basic rule in English is "Link the words". This accounts for the tendency of native speakers of English to say *wee kend, take your ha toff, *Woche nende* and *Hu tab*, and the tendency of German speakers to say *week end, take your hat off, Wochen ende* and *Hut ab*.

Some of the things done in English to string words together properly are dealt with in other sections (see VI.2 to VI.4. on stress, weak forms, assimilation and elision). Just to give you a taste of what to expect read the sentence *"Drinka Pinta Milka Day"*, which you may have seen in the advertisement for milk that was used by the Milk Marketing Board in Britain, derived of course from "Drink a pint of milk a day", but exploiting the automatic linking conventions of English. Here the unstressed words "a" and "of" seem to become parts of the preceding words.

(b) The speaker's problem: German separatism?

We can separate a word beginning with a vowel from the preceding word by inserting a "glottal stop" [ʔ] (see IV.3.7. for details). In German it is appropriately called *Knacklaut* and in Standard German you get it in *Ver-ein*. In 1., each word starts with a vowel, and each one has a glottal stop [ʔ] before it. You do not need to be a native speaker of English to hear that it sounds very *un*-English. But a comparable German sentence does *not* sound quite so artificial:

4.   a. *In einem anderen Auto aktivierte ich alle Agenten.*
     b. [ʔɪn ʔaɪnəm ʔandʁən ʔaʊto ʔaktivieɾə ʔɪç ʔalə ʔagentn̩]

Transferring the natural German habit of "defining" the word units by glottalizing the vocalic word onsets makes English utterances sound definitely foreign! Admittedly, the German example above *does* sound rather carefully pronounced. A normal reading of the same sentence would probably not have any glottal constriction between *in* and *einem* or between *aktivierte* and *ich*. Such prepositional and pronominal elements tend to become joined onto the lexical word they belong to. An unfortunate fact about glottal stops in German, is that they are used more frequently in careful speech than in fast speech. And since it is usual to speak a foreign language much more carefully than one's mother tongue, the effects are made even worse .

If you say *"We have gone to the cinema last night"*, the English will know what you mean and think *"Not correct, but a nice try"*. But the most dangerous mistakes to make in a foreign language are the ones that are not interpreted as mistakes by the native speakers. If, e.g., you say: *"Put it in a bag, please."* and pronounce it in an otherwise perfect English accent as: [ˈpʊt ʔɪt ʔɪn ʔə ˈbæg pliːz], then they may not detect it as a German habit, because this is the way an English speaker would say it if he was very pedantic, irritated, and on the verge of losing his temper because his listeners were a bit slow in picking up his message. Let us illustrate this by an excerpt from Winnie the Pooh, in which Rabbit is trying to vent his feelings and to develop a cunning plan with Pooh among his audience who is a bit slow on the uptake:

5.   *"What I don't like about it is this," said Rabbit. "Here are we - you, Pooh, and*
     you, Piglet, and Me - and suddenly ...."
     "And Eeyore, " said Pooh. - "..... and Eeyore - and then suddenly ..."
     "And Owl," said Pooh. - "... and Owl - and then all of a sudden ...."
     "Oh, and Eeyore, " said Pooh. "I was forgetting him."
     "Here - we - are," said Rabbit very slowly and carefully, "all - of - us, ..."

Of course conventional orthography has no symbols for glottal stops, but it does not require a great deal of imagination to hear the glottal stops in the last line with every word beginning with a vowel. It is not a good idea to make this register your standard for normal conversation, in other words, do not treat all your listeners as if they were Winnie the Pooh because it is only when people feel conscious of the process of conversing or when they feel they may not be understood that they pronounce a sentence as if it were a list of words. Germans do not make pauses between words, but phonetically they tend not to cut across word or morpheme boundaries in quite the same way the English do.

You may now say, *"Okay, I may have difficulties in understanding linked English, but surely the English will understand me even if I do not always get the linking right."* Not quite, because firstly, every deviation from what people are used to may impede the communication process. If the English keep asking *"Pardon?"* when you speak you should not automatically assume the whole nation is a bit hard of hearing. Secondly, and more importantly, if somebody says to you, *"Oh dear, I'm awfully sorry, I seem to have spilled ketchup on your shoes. I hope you don't mind."* and instead of saying casually [nɒ tə ˈtɔːɬ], you carefully pronounce the three words *"Not - at - all!"* without linking and with two glottal stops, you will certainly be understood, but you are not playing the situation down and everybody will think, *"What a sarcastic sod!"*

C 1: Compare the two versions of the following everyday phrases in which, first, the words are spoken with a glottal onset separating them, and then in a correct, fluent style with the words linked together. Repeat both versions and pay attention to what you are doing differently:

a. *Put it in a bag, please.*   [ˈpʊt ʔɪt ʔɪn ʔə ˈbæg pliːz] vs. [ˈpʊtɪtɪnə ˈbæg pliːz]
b. *Can I get out of it?*   [ˈkæn ʔaɪ get ˈʔaʊt ʔəv ʔɪt] vs. [ˈkænaɪ geˈt‿aʊtəvɪt]
c. *What an awful idea!*   [wɒt ʔən ˈʔɔːfʊɬ ʔaɪˈdɪə] vs. [wɒtəˈn‿ɔːfʊɬ‿aɪˈdɪə]
d. *Put it on immediately!*   [pʊt ʔɪt ʔɒn ʔɪˈmiːdɪətli] vs. [pʊtɪtɒn‿ɪˈmiːdɪətli]
e. *Take it off again!*   [ˈteɪk ʔɪt ˈʔɒf ʔəgen] vs. [ˈteɪkɪˈt‿ɒfəgen]

Infobox

Our transcription conventions for indicating the sort of linking we are talking about in this section may already be clear to you from the many examples given in previous transcription examples of running text. We feel they are intuitive and rather obvious. The one principle behind them is to signal linking but help maintain word recognizability.

Short unaccented function words are simply attached to the preceding word. Sometimes this may involve more than one word, e.g. *"Put it in a bag"*, [ˈpʊtɪtɪnə ˈbæg]. They are linked to following lexical words with vowel onsets by means of a horizontal brace, e.g., *"an exception"*, [ən‿əkˈsepʃən].

Words beginning with a stressed vowel are linked by placing the stress mark before the final consonant of the preceding word; they are graphically "resyllabified" to help avoid a glottal onset to the stressed syllable. e.g. *"He ate everything"* [hi‿eˈt‿evrɪθɪŋ].

This resyllabification gives the final consonant more weight than it should really have (it should not truly become an initial consonant) but we want to break the glottalizing habit at all costs, and therefore use a radical method!

E 1: Read the following limerick aloud:

Said the fair-haired Rebecca from Klondike,   [sed ðə ˈfeə heəd rəˈbekə frəm
                                               ˈklɒndaɪk

"Of you I'm exceedingly fond, Ike.   əv ˈjuː aɪm ɪkˈsiːdɪŋli ˈfɒnd aɪk

To prove I adore you   tə ˈpruːvaɪ əˈdɔː juː

I'll dye, darling, for you   aɪɫ ˈdaɪ dɑːlɪŋ ˈfɔː juː

and be a brunette, not a blonde, Ike."   ən ˈbiː ə bruˈnet nɒtə ˈblɒnd aɪk]

When German beginners read this limerick it often does not rhyme, because they tend to read *Klon-dike* but *fond-Ike*, pronouncing *Ike* even with a glottal onset. This is essentially a problem of linking: phonetically speaking, the final -*d* of *fond* should be the first sound of the next syllable: *fon-dIke*. So [ˈklɒn-daɪk] rhymes with [ˈfɒn-daɪk]. Apply this principle to the following limerick:

6. *Did you hear of this farmer from Frattonne,*   [dɪd ju ˈhɪərəv ðɪs ˈfɑːmə frəm
                                              ˈfrætɒn

who would go to church with his hat on.   hu wʊd ˈgəu tə ˈʧɜːʧ wɪðɪz ˈhæt ɒn

"If I wake up," he said,   ɪf aɪ ˈweɪk ʌp hi ˈsed

"with my hat on my head,   wɪð maɪ ˈhæt ɒn maɪ ˈhed

I shall know that it-has not been sat on."   aɪ ʃəɫ ˈnəu ðətɪt ˈhæznt bɪn ˈsæt ɒn]

C 2: Linking is about getting into the right rhythm of it. So listen to this song, where *Finnigan* rhymes with *chin again*:

There was an old man called Michael Finnigan,
He grew whiskers on his chinigan,
The wind came up and blew them inigan,
Poor old Michael Finnigan, beginigan.

As a matter of interest: When the French word *naperon* became an English word after the Norman conquest, *"a naperon"* changed to *"an apron"*, because the English could not tell where the word boundary was. The advertisement *Have an Ice day* takes advantage of this phenomenon. N.B., there are two more examples of linking at the bottom of the picture: "WES-TICE and TES-TIT.)

Fig 2: [hævən aɪs ˈdeɪ | ˈwest aɪs | ˈtest ɪt]

In very fast speech in German, too, confusions might arise with words like *Facharbeiterzeugnis*, which might mean *Facharbeit-Erzeugnis* or *Facharbeiter-Zeugnis*, or there might be confusion as to whether somebody said *ein Aktbild* or *ein Nacktbild* (not that it makes a big difference semantically), but by and large these words are kept distinct, or at least disambiguating these words would sound less artificial than doing the same thing in English with, for example:

7a. *They need a lot of support from others.* b. *They need a lot of support from mothers.*
  c. [ˈiːvn̩ə ˈbædiːɫ kəmbiə ˌɡʊdiːɫ ˈbetə ðənə ˌrɒtn̩ ˈfɪʃ] →
  c′. *Even a bad eal can be a good deal better than a rotten fish.*
  c″. *Even a bad deal can be a good deal better than a rotten fish.*
  (Of course the length of /d/ vs. /dd/ is a giveaway in slow speech

If you listen carefully you will detect differences in the way *print* and *out* are linked in the English word *printout* and the German loanword *Printout*. These differences between the two languages in linking words mean that English words borrowed into German take on a German character.

What is important for you is to rethink some utterances, to un-learn to respect word and morpheme boundaries phonetically. It is best to start with rhymes, like *Klon-dike/ fon-dIke, Finnigan/ beginigan* etc. Next it is useful to actually re-think sounds as phonetic, and not semantic or lexical units.

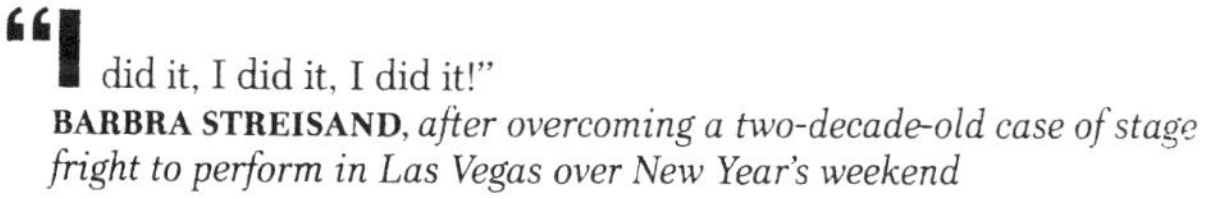

"I did it, I did it, I did it!"
BARBRA STREISAND, *after overcoming a two-decade-old case of stage fright to perform in Las Vegas over New Year's weekend*

Fig. 3: *"I di-dit, I di-dit, I di-dit."*

Ignore for the time being the words and say this aloud as if you were singing a song the words of which you had forgotten: *"di-dit, di-dit, di-dit."* Or look at Sainsbury´s advertisement, start the chain of repetions first the *German* way with *week after week after week* and then rethink it as *wee kafter wee kafter week*.

Fig. 4

Or memorise set phrases like [ɡʊ ˌdɑːftəˈnuːn] and [ˈnɒ tə tɔːɫ], which we have built into the following conversation and which you should keep practising as one unit rather than individual words.

C 3: Listen and repeat: a conversation:

Good_afternoon_everybody. - Good_evening, John. - Yes_I know_I'm late, I'm awfully sorry. You know, we're short_of staff_at the Bank_of_England and we have to work late_hours_and_all that sort_of_thing. - Oh that's quite_all right. Can_I get you_a drink? A glass_of_wine, or_an_orange juice? - Just_a glass_of_water with some_ice_in_it would be fine, thank you. Do you mind_if_I sit here? - Not_at_ all. Short_of_staff, you said? I thought there were thousands_of_unemployed_experts queuing_up_at the job centres. - That's_a bit_of_a myth I'm_afraid, to keep_our salaries_and_wages_as low_as possible. - But how can you do the job_of_others? Aren't they_all_experts_in whatever_it_is they_are doing? - Yes_of course,_in_a way they_are. But_I'm_a bit_of_a Jack_of_all trades, so_I can help_out_in most_of the cases. - Are you the boss_at the Bank_of_England? - Not_exactly, but_I have to keep_an_eye_on people_in my department. - Oh, you're_a sort_of supervisor then. Come to think_of_it, I wouldn't mind_a job_at the Bank_of_England. - You'll end_up_as_a kind_of_underpaid_and_overworked_accountant. - Come_off_it the two_of you. We_are here to have_a bit_of fun. Forget the_office_and_all that sort_of thing. You shouldn't talk_about_it_at_a party. Anybody for_a cup_of tea?

Take these jokes seriously!

There are even jokes that have established themselves as a genre in their own right which rely on the English linking conventions: the *"knock knock"* jokes, where the last line starts with words that sound like the name in the previous two lines:

8a. *Knock knock. - Who's there? - Liza. - Liza who? - <u>Lies are</u> dangerous!*
 b. *Knock knock. - Who's there? - Henrietta - Henrietta who? - <u>Henry ate a</u> piece of cake!*
 c. *Knock knock. - Who's there? - Helen - Helen who? - <u>Hell and</u> high water!*

You may feel that these jokes are below your intellectual dignity. In that case treat them as an exercise in phonetics and remember: phonetics is about speaking, so read these jokes aloud. If you do not get them straight away it may be due to the fact that you still have too high a respect for word boundaries. We will start you off with three jokes plus an explanation.

Fig. 5: *Mountaineers* and *mountain ears* are homophones.

Question: *Where did they keep freshwater fish at the time of the Flood?* Answer: *In a carp Ark. (N.B.: There is of course a slight difference between the pronunciation of "carp Ark" and "car park".* The /p/ in *"car park"* is more aspirated.)

Question: *What is copper nitrate?* Answer: *Overtime for policemen.*
Explanation: *copper nitrate* is a chemical, but a *copper night rate* is the money a copper (= policeman) gets paid for the night shift.

From now on you are on your own. Have fun!

Why do women put their hair in rollers at night? - So they can wake curly in the morning.

I told the solitary pedestrian he had BO (body odour). And he replied: "That´s why I wore Cologne." [wɔːkə'ləʊn]

What do you call a Scotsman with Italian ancestors? - McAroni.

At the vicar´s tea-party for the choir, the vicar´s wife had arranged a super spread with all kinds of goodies. She held out a plate to the smallest choir-boy and said, "Now, then Davey, is there any kind of cake that you don´t like?"- "Yes – stomach ache." said Davey.

Fig. 6: a) *"A nation at ease with itself"* b) *"An Asian at ease with himself."*

Linking r

All the examples so far have had words with a final consonant preceding the vocalic onset. Linking consists of carrying that consonant over to the following vowel. However, if a word ends with an orthographic <r> it is not normally pronounced in standard Southern British English.

9   a. *pour* as in ['pɔː mi: ə 'kʌpəv 'tiː]   b. *car* as in [hi ˌkeɪm baɪ 'kɑː]
     c. *fair* as in ['feə ˌweðə 'frendz]
     (This is not the case in Scottish, Irish and Southwestern accents:
     [pɔr 'bɔɪ], ['kɑr ˌlaɪsn̩s], [fɛr 'weðɚ])

However, if the following word begins with a vowel the [r] reappears and acts as a linking element:

10   a.   *Pour a* cup of tea.   ['pɔrə kʌpəv 'tiː]
      b.   He drove the *car away*   [hi 'drəʊv ðə 'kɑːr̩ əweɪ]

c. *Fair enough!* ['feər‿ə'nʌf]
d. She *wore a* dark costume. ['ʃi wɔrə dɑːk 'kɒstjuːm]
e. The *door opened* slowly. [ðə 'dɔr‿əupmd 'sləuli]
d. It was a *war of* nerves. [ɪt wəz ə 'wɔrəv 'nɜːvz]

Now read the following sentence pairs, noting that the first one has a word where the final <r> is not pronounced, and the second one has the same word in a linking-r context:

11. a. How *far can* you see? How *far is* it to London?
    b. The *tour lasted* three weeks. The *tour of* Italy lasted three weeks.
    c. A *fire broke* out in the school. There was a *fire in* the school.
    d. I don't *care, so* there! I don't *care a jot!*
    e. Can you *spare the* time? Can you *spare a* moment?

Idioms with linking-r that you should memorise: *After‿all; As a matter‿of fact; ...for‿example; Pure‿ and simple; Leave her‿alone.*

Vowel-to-vowel linking

Of course, if a word begins with a vowel and the preceding word *ends* with a vowel, there is no consonant to carry over! However, the principle of linking still applies, and the nature of the English vowels that can occur in an open syllable (and can therefore end a word) determines the nature of the linking that is found. Word-final vowels are either a) close front vowels ([i]-like) or b) rounded close back vowels ([u]-like), or they are c) the same vowels that can have a latent linking-r.

12 a. [iː], [eɪ], [aɪ], [ɔɪ]
    E.g. *fee, sea, Brie; way, whey, weigh; lie, rye, why, sigh; boy*
    b. [uː], [əu], [au]
    E.g. *too, two, shoe, due, lieu, new, so, sew, show, dough, bureau, now, plough*
    c. [ɑː], [ɔː], [ə]
    E.g. *Shah, fah, lah, la-di-da, bra, haha* (but also *bar, star, far, etc); *flaw, awe, Waugh* (but also *floor, ore, wore*); *sonata, pizza, Granada, charter*, etc.)

The fact that the vowels in category 12c.-words and the vowels in words with linking r are the same provides a clue to how they are linked: they are frequently produced with an [r] as if they *were* linking-r words. This is called **intrusive r** in the jargon of pronunication teaching, and there is a *purist* school of thought which maintains that intrusive r is *incorrect* and *to be avoided*. However, the same people that preach avoidance of this r can often be heard producing it themselves when their attention slips, and they speak naturally! So there is no reason why German learners of standard English should not transfer the linking-r to words of the category 12c. type.

13 a. *No need to be la-di-da about it.* ['nəu niːd tə bi lɑːdi'dɑːr‿əbaut‿ɪt]
    b. *There's a flaw in your argument.* [ðəzə 'flɔːrɪn jə'r‿ɑːgjəmənt]

c. *Granada in April is paradise on earth.* [grəˈnɑːdərɪn‿ˈeɪprɪlɪz ˈpærədaɪ-
ş ɒˈn‿ɜːθ]

Of course, any speaker whose variety of English has a natural post-vocalic
/r/ (Scottish, Irish and Southwestern British English were mentioned earlier)
will *never* produce an intrusive r because for them words like *flaw* and *floor*,
fah and *far*, *manna* and *manner* are never homophones. Such speakers are
always conscious of an /r/ in a word, and would therefore never pronounce
one if it was not there. They link these word-final vowels to word-initial
vowels simply by gliding smoothly from one to the other, as the purists
would like us all to do.

In the case of categories 12a. and b. we do in fact glide smoothly to the word-
initial vowel. But due to the [i]-like and [u]-like final element, it sounds as if
there is an intruding consonant – similar to the intrusive r – here too. In the
case of category 12a. vowels the [i]-like end-element allows a weak [j] to intrude as a linking sound, while the [u]-like end-element in category 12b.
vowels allows a weak [w] to intrude. These **intrusive [j]** and **[w] glides** are in
fact the natural articulatory consequence of not separating the words because
[j] and [w] are nothing more than a glide from a close [i]- and [u]-position,
respectively. In the following examples, which you should practise reading
aloud, we shall put a raised "intrusive [j]" and "intrusive [w]" to remind you.

14. Intrusive [j]

    a. *The tree always blooms in June.* [ðə ˈtriːʲ ɔː ɬweɪz ˈbluːmzɪn ˈdʒuːn]
    b. *Her cry alarmed the neighbours.* [hə ˈkraɪ ʲ əˈlɑːmd ðə ˈneɪbəz]
    c. *We were told to weigh all the samples.* [wɪ wəˈtəʊldtə ˈweɪʲ ɔːɬ ðə ˈsɑːmpɬz]
    d. *They accused the boy of cheating.* [ðeɪʲ əˈkjuːzd ðə ˈbɔɪʲəv ˈʧiːtɪŋ]

15. Intrusive [w]

    a. *He took his shoe off because his foot hurt.* [hi ˈtʊkɪz ˈʃuːʷɒf bɪkəzɪz ˈfʊt hɜːt]
    b.*We plough our fields early.* [wɪ ˈplaʊʷaʊə ˈfiːɬdˈz̩ ɜːli]
    c. *Show us the way!* [ˈʃəʊʷʌs ðə ˈweɪ]
    d. *We were due in at eight.* [wɪ wə ˈdjuːʷɪnəˈt‿eɪt]

E 2: Read these phrases aloud with linking as indicated:

    a. *London*
      Hop-on
      hop-off
      service

b. *Get a move on with it.*
c. *It´s a sort of open air event.*
d. *It goes on and on and on.* [ɪt gəʊ'z ɒnə'n ɒnə'n ɒn]
e. *Henry the Eighth made himself the head of the Church of England*

f. ['nəʊʷəvə 'benɪfɪt 'rɪpɒf]
['gɪvəsə 'teləfəʊn 'tɪpɒf]
[kɔːɬ 'biːtə 'ʧiːtɒ'n əʊʷeɪt
dʌb'ɬ əʊ]

Know of a benefit rip-off?
Give us a telephone tip-off.

Call **BEAT-A-CHEAT** on **0800 854 440**

E 3: These titles and authors are taken from a joke book. Rewrite the names of the authors and read column 2 and 3 as homophones. Example:

At the South Pole	by Ann Tarctic	→Antarctic. Now continue:
Swimming the Channel	by Frances Near	→
The Bullfighter	by Matt Adore	→
The Unknown Author	by Ann Onymous	→
The Long Hot Summer	by I. Scream	→
A Cliff-top Tragedy	by Eileen Dover	→
The Cause of Colds	by Mike Robe	→
The Escaping Sheep	by Gay Topen	→
The Return of the Prodigal Son	by Gladys Back	→

(If you still don´t get the cartoon at the beginning of this section turn to XII.)

VI.2. Stress: *Stress can cause headaches*

In this chapter we deal with some of the <u>common mistakes</u> made by German-speaking learners with stress patterns, such as

ˡkitchen sink	*ˡAnimal Farm*	*and so ˡon*
good ˡafternoon	*ˡloud speaker*	*[gʊd ˡiːvənɪŋ]*

NB: **the asterisk * tells you: this is wrong**! We quote these examples as a warning, *not* for you to memorise them. If you are surprised that they are incorrect *read this chapter*. If you know why they are wrong, there may still be aspects of English word stress and sentence accent that you are not completely familiar with, so read this chapter:

We will explain why German *Hongkong* is not like English *Hong Kong* and in what way German *Make-up* differs from British *make-up*;

we will try and explain why some foreigners have the irritating habit of (inadvertently) correcting the English pronunciation of native speakers, as in the following dialogue heard in the London Underground:

> Man at the ticket office: *Two to London ˡRoad?*
> German tourist: *Yes, two to ˡLondn Road.*

We will explain why, depending on the context, it is sometimes *eighˡteen* and *Berˡlin* and sometimes *ˡeighteen* and *ˡBerlin*;

we will explain how the pronunciation of vowels differs in stressed and unstressed syllables; and we will explain the difference between stress, rhythm and accent.

The "why" and the "how": A word of advice on learning strategies

Let us take a break here and deal with learning strategies. First we would like to deal with the question of *why* you should learn these stress patterns, and secondly with the problem of *how* one should try to master the complexity of rules and exceptions.

The "why" may seem obvious to most readers, but there are a surprising number of people who belong to what we call "the excuses brigade":

1   a. *Surely, it doesn´t make such a big difference, does it?*
     b. *If I get it wrong, they will still understand me, won´t they?*
     c. *If I can´t even hear the difference, it can´t be that important.*

Would you accept those excuses in German? Let us look at a possible example, because in your own language you can certainly judge how serious mistakes are:

2   a. *Dem Polizisten sagten wir, wir wollten die alte Frau umFAHren.*
     b. *Dem Polizisten sagten wir, wir wollten die alte Frau UMfahren.*

Do you really want to stick to excuse 1a? Admittedly, stress patterns are not always a question of life and death, so let us turn to excuses 1b and c:

A foreigner, speaking German, talked about *FerinSÄÄN* and nobody understood him. He was a native speaker of a language that does not allow for consonant clusters, so he tended to insert a vowel between German consonants, so *fern* became *ferin,* and since he felt that *sehen* was the important part of the word he stressed it (after all, it is teleVISION in English, televisiON in French etc.). Unfortunately the vowel was rather too open ([ɛ:] rather than [e:]), a frequent mistake with foreign learners of German. When this dawned upon the Germans they exclaimed: "Oh, you mean *Fernsehen.*", to which he replied: "That´s what I said, isn'it?"

You may protest that he made other mistakes, not just a stress error, and that *they* caused the misunderstanding. Of course, mistakes combine to make understanding harder, but the rhythmic pattern of a word or phrase is the *framework* for understanding. It has been shown to be even more important for correct understanding than completely accurate segmental quality because it is the auditory space within which the segments are arranged. The segmental decoding is dependent on the rhythmic structure of the utterance.

If you find that people in England keep asking "Pardon?" when you talk to them, they may not *all* be hard of hearing! Sometimes a little distortion of the the stress pattern with the wrong adjustment of vowels makes a word sound awfully strange. The witch in *The Hundred and One Dalmations* is called *Cruella de Ville,* which pokes fun at those foreigners who shift the stress pattern and pronounce *cruel devil* like *cruˈelle deˈveal* [kruˈelə dəˈvi:l]

Let us now turn to the question "*How* can I memorise all these rules?" Well, of course the aim is not to "remember rules" but to internalise the regularities so that the words are produced correctly without you having to think about rules. But that is probably what you meant, and it is a real problem, so your concern is justified. And if you teach or are going to teach English you need to understand the regularities (rules) anyway. We suggest, therefore, the following learning strategies:

Step One: Raise your language awareness. Read this chapter and force yourself to read the examples aloud. You will become aware of the differences without – at this stage – being able to apply all the rules. Simply try and hear the difference between, e.g., the wrong **ˈkitchen sink* and **ˈPrime Minister* and the correct *ˌkitchen ˈsink* and *ˌPrime ˈMinister.* Focus on the correct pattern. Once you are aware of the difference, you are halfway there, because the most effective way of learning a language is by imitating. But you have to give the native speakers a chance to act as your models. Remember our example at the beginning of this section: "*Two to London* ˈ*Road?*" - German tourist: "*Yes, two to* ˈ*Londn Road.*" (Note that the German tourist has not only "corrected" the stress pattern but also made a second "correction"at the segmental level.)

Imitating native speakers of English is better than "correcting" them:

Smiley:

Waiter: *And what will you have, sir?*   Man: *Steak and kiddly pie, please.*
Waiter: *You mean steak and <u>kidney</u>, sir.*   Man: *I said kiddly, diddle I?*

Step Two: Master one rule at a time. You can start with the reassuring rule that says, most English and German compounds have similar stress patterns, namely stress on the first constituent of the compound: 'bottleneck* has a pattern like 'Flaschenhals* and 'trouser leg* one like 'Hosenbein*. This is not always the first syllable of course: gui'tar string* and Gi'tarrenseite* have the stress on the second syllable of the first constituent because that is where the stress falls on *guitar* and *Gitarre*. But you will undoubtedly also register the fact that not all English compounds are actually written together as one word.

The next step is to tackle some noun-noun compounds with the main stress on the *second* noun. The most important group is the *Oxford* 'ROAD* type (see the rule below). Practice it until it "comes out of your ears" or rolls off your tongue. When you feel perfectly at ease with this rule, you might become a little bit more ambitious and tackle a third rule.

Step Three: When the rules seem too complex, just memorise a few compounds that are important to you. For example: The geographical term *Treasure* 'Island* is an exception to the rule of stress on the first constituent, 'Channel Islands* is an exception to the exception as opposed to *Channel* 'Tunnel*. "Clear as ditch water", as the saying goes. In these cases it is often easier to select words and write them into a vocabulary book, marking the stress patterns, until you feel you are ready for more rules. The criterion for selecting these words should be:

(a) choose the words that are likely to cause problems for German learners. Of the above examples chose *Treasure* 'Island*, because it contrasts with the stress pattern of German 'Schatzinsel*. And if you come across *evening* 'paper* and '*evening dress*, jot down the stress pattern only of the former, because it differs from its German equivalent 'Abendblatt*, whereas 'evening dress* and 'Abendkleid* have similar stress patterns and you are not likely to make a mistake.

(b) Choose a subclass of the troublemakers selected under (a) on the basis of what is important to <u>you</u>. If you are planning a culture trip to London, write down ,Globe 'Theatre*, ,Drury 'Lane*, and, say, the musical ,Kiss me 'Kate*, if that´s what you are interested in.

We wrote the following limerick to illustrate a stress-pattern phenomenon which might puzzle you now that you have become more sensitive to stress. And there is nothing like a bit of confusion to get the little grey cells going, is there?

Fig. 1: Afternoon tea in Rangoon

3.　*An Englishman based in Rangoon*　　[əˈn̩ ɪŋglɪʃmən ˈbeɪstɪn ræŋˈguːn　1
　　Sipped his afternoon tea much too soon.　sɪptɪˈz ɑːftənuːn ˈtiː mʌtʃ tuː ˈsuːn　2
　　He declared late at night,　　hi dɪˈkleəd leɪtət ˈnaɪt̠　　3
　　As the moon shone so bright:　　əzðə ˈmuːn ʃɒn səʊ ˈbraɪt　　4
　　"But in England it's now afternoon."　　bʌtɪˈn̩ ɪŋgləndɪts ˈnaʊʷˌɑːftəˈnuːn]　5

C 1: Listen to and repeat 3., comparing *afternoon* in lines 2 and 5.

Firstly, the limerick may cause confusion, because a common mistake made by Germans is to say *[gʊd ˈɑːftənuːn] with a stress pattern like *der Nachmittag*. But let yourself be guided by the rhythm of the above limerick and you will observe that if *afternoon* in the last line is to rhyme with [ræŋˈguːn] and [tuː

ˈsuːn] in lines 1 and 2, it must be pronounced with the main stress on the last syllable, and this is exactly how you should greet people in Britain after midday and before evening (and don't forget the linking): [gʊˌdɑːftə ˈnuːn].

And now we come to the second part that may cause confusion: if you read the limerick aloud, tapping the rhythm on your knee, you will find that the two occurrences of *afternoon* get different beats, or stress patterns. In line 5 the stress pattern is AF ter NOON (*dam-di-daahm*), but in line 2 it is AF ter noon, (*dam-di-di*). Admittedly, we just told you that *[ˈɑːftənuːn] was a common mistake, but you have to pronounce it differently here because it is part of AF ter noon TEA (*dam-di-di-daahm*). If you ask native speakers of English: "What is *Nachmittag* in English?", they will say: AF ter NOON, or in phonetic transcription: [ˌɑːftəˈnuːn]. This is what is called the **citation form** of the lexeme *afternoon*, because here you do not <u>use it in context</u>, but only <u>mention the word</u>: you only talk about it, or: you only *cite* it. Classroom conversations about words that typically start with *What do you call ...* are statements about the language, that is they are **metalinguistic statements**. After the word has been mentioned, you proceed to use it. In *good afternoon*, pronounced [gʊˌdɑːftə ˈnuːn], the citation stress pattern is retained, and luckily this is the case in the vast majority of words. But in *afternoon tea* [ˌɑːftənuːn ˈtiː] the simple **transition from mention to use** does not work. The change from [ɑːftə ˈnuːn] to [ˌɑːftənuːn ˈtiː] is called **stress shift** (and will be discussed in detail further down). Good pronouncing dictionaries warn you about this possibility. Learning the stress pattern of a word in its citation form is a good starting point, but for advanced learners of English it is not the whole story.

As there are a number of things you can do phonetically to put greater emphasis on a syllable, it is useful to introduce a neutral term for that unit: the **prominent syllable**. In the sentence: *"And then he had the cheek to put his hand on her thigh"*, you could make the last word sound particularly nasal or even whisper it to make it the prominent syllable. Here, however, we will concentrate on the more usual phonetic devices that make a syllable prominent. Take the following string of words:

4.   *But you should have seen her face.*

All seven words consist of only one syllable each, i.e. they are **monosyllabic**. So looking up the stress patterns in the dictionary would not help you to decide which one or which ones should be prominent. Let us first have a look at this clause in the following context:

5.   *The young girl <u>said</u> she liked whisky, but you should have seen her <u>face</u>.*

We asked a speaker to pronounce it, and as the most important linguistic way of achieving **prominence** in English is to make the word longer and to change the pitch, we recorded the way in which his voice went up and down. Fig. 2 shows the pitch curve.

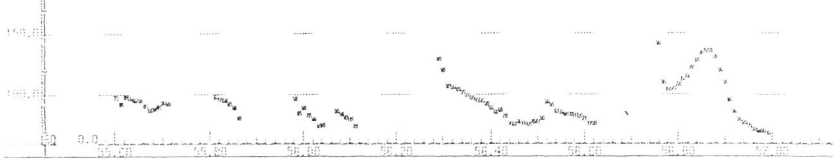

Fig. 2: The pitch curve of 5.: ... *but you should have seen her face.*

On the word *face* the **pitch** of the speaker´s voice goes up a bit and then down. Of all the devices we use to make a syllable prominent in spoken English, a **change of pitch** is the most important one. As our speaker read *but you should have seen her face* in one go we say that this stretch of his utterance constitutes a **tone unit**. In our example *face* bears the **accent** [ˈæksənt], or, put differently, is the **accented syllable** [ækˈsentɪd ˈsɪləbɬ]. It is important to remember that this is not something you can look up in a dictionary or lexicon, because it is not an inherent or lexical feature of the word *face*, but rather a phonetic feature of tone unit 4. in the context of 5. The *accent* is the prominent syllable of a tone unit. It can be recognised by the change of pitch, and it focuses the listener´s attention on this item as the most important part of the message.

If you put the seven words of our example into a different context, as in:

6. *He liked the whisky, but you should have seen her face.*

then – because of the new contrast between the two persons (male and female) – *her* is the important part of the message. It is pronounced with a change of pitch (in this case it is probable that you raised the pitch of your voice from *seen* to *her* and lowered it again afterwards, so that *her* stands out and thus represents the accent of the tone unit.

If you play around with the clause *but you should have seen her face*, you will easily create four new tone units by finding contexts that would make *but, you, should* or *seen* the accented syllable. It will, however, be almost impossible to find one where *have* receives the accent. This is because in this phrase *have* is a word that does not contrast with anything else. In the predicate *should have seen, should* may be replaced by another modal verb and thus potentially contrasts with, for example, *must*, and *seen* may be replaced by *observed*. In the context *but you should ... seen his face* you do not have a choice: it´s got to be *have*, which can then be pronounced only in its weak form. In a personal letter, for instance, this would be reflected in the written form, too:

7. *but you should´ve seen her face.*

So not all syllables are candidates for the accented syllable of an utterance. This observation eases us into another aspect of prominent syllables. If we change our example to:

8. *but you should have seen the expression on her face,*

then the second syllable of *expression*, but not the syllables *ex-* and *-sion* would be potential places for accent. The reason for this can be found in a lexical feature of this word. The dictionary gives the following phonetic information:

9.   *expression*, n. [ɪks 'preʃən].

The dictionary cannot possibly predict the importance you wish to attach to this word in context. It can only give you lexical information on the pronunciation of this particular noun in isolation, i.e. not in terms of its information content or importance in an utterance or tone unit. The word [ɪks 'preʃən] has three syllables, the second of which is marked by the symbol ['] to indicate the lexically stressed syllable. We can simplify this information by adopting the following notation: [- ˡ - -]. This **stress pattern** is called **word-stress** or **lexical stress**. As the dictionary cannot predict whether *expression* in 8 will be chosen as the word with the accented syllable, the symbol ['] does not say anything about the change of pitch.

Other phonetic ways of marking a syllable as the prominent one is to **stress** it by making it longer and louder. In order to increase **loudness** we use greater muscular effort, but keeping a syllable going for a longer time also requires greater effort. So it is perhaps not surprising that greater duration and greater intensity (these are acoustic, i.e. **physical** attributes) work together to make us hear a syllable as louder, i.e. more prominent (that is not a physical but a an **auditory** property of the syllable, something we experience but which cannot be measured objectively). The notation [ɪks'preʃən] or [- ˡ -] tells you to pronounce the syllable in the middle with greater effort to make it more prominent than the other two.

In the dictionary, the phonetic transcription of a word with more than one syllable gives you information on its **stress pattern** in terms of the **relative prominence**. *Relative prominence* simply means "prominence *in comparison* with the other syllables": you may scream or whisper the word *expression*, as long as the second syllable is more prominent than the others.

If you make *face* the accented syllable in 8, the second syllable of *expression* is stressed, i.e. more prominent than the other two of this word, but there is no change of pitch. If, on the other hand, you wish to focus on the word *expression* (as opposed to "the make-up on her face"), the second syllable is still stressed in terms of length and loudness, but at the same time it reveals a change of pitch, because it is now both the stressed syllable of this word and the accented syllable of the tone unit. Under normal circumstances only a stressed syllable can serve as a candidate for accent. So [ʃən] in [ɪks'preʃən] cannot be accented. But let us take an extreme example, just to illustrate and underline the basic difference between stress and accent again. Let us assume somebody was not quite sure which prefix you had used and wanted confirmation on this. She might then ask you:

10.   *Sorry, did you say depression or expression?*

Only when talking <u>about</u> the language and the choice of prefixes is it possible to put emphasis on "ex-" in *expression*, i.e. put the accent on a syllable that is not the lexically stressed one.

Of course the dictionary does not give you pointless information on the stress pattern of a monosyllabic word, so you will not get *['feɪs], as a monosyllabic word cannot have a stress pattern. Words of more than one syllable are called **polysyllabic** (from Greek *poly* for *more than one*). Let us choose a word that really and truly deserves this label: *indecipherability*. With its eight syllables it is a bit of a mouthful (and if you come across it for the first time, your reading of it may be an illustration of its meaning!). In cases like these it is best to aim at one syllable, make it your target, go for it and neglect the rest:

indecipharaBILity. [ˌɪndɪˌsaɪfərəˈbɪlɪti].

The symbol: [ˈ] means **primary stress** (or main stress), i.e. the loudest syllable in this word should be [ˈbɪl]. The symbol: [ˌ] means **secondary stress**, i.e. you give the syllable that it precedes less emphasis than [ˈbɪl] in our example, but a little bit more emphasis than the **unstressed** syllables [dɪ] and [fərə] and [ɪti].

The inverse of prominence

We have now dealt with two means of achieving prominence: change of pitch and loudness (as a result of greater length and energy). In order to draw your attention to another, complementary aspect of prominence we would like you to read the following limerick aloud:

11. *A poet from distant Japan*   1
     wrote verses that never could scan.   2
     When I said: "But the thing   3
     doesn't go with a swing"   4
     he said: "<u>Yes</u> but I always try to get as many words into the last line as I <u>p_o_ss</u>ibly <u>can</u>. 5

When we read poetry, in particular the sort of thing that we have concocted ourselves in a great hurry for Aunt Mabel´s eightieth birthday, we usually try and make up for the wrong number of syllables by keeping up the beat and by speeding up if there is a syllable too many in one line. A line like 5 in the above limerick, however, is so ridiculous that even Aunt Mabel would be disgruntled with her favourite nephew and would-be poet. Our excuse for presenting it here is a didactic one; what we have encouraged you to do is what happens in English all the time. It is claimed that native speakers of English have quite a regular beat of accented syllables – even in prose – and the more unstressed syllables there are between the beats, the more they are compressed. We trust that this is what you were trying to achieve in the last line of the limerick.

If you want something more realistic than that, read the first four lines again, tapping the beat on your knee. You will observe that the rhythm does not change irrespective of the number of syllables. The lines of all limericks start with at least one unstressed syllable, like line 1: [ə ˈpəʊt] and line 2: [rəʊt ˈvɜːsɪz], but if they start with two unstressed syllables, you simply squeeze them into the same amount of time, as in line 3 [wenaɪ ˈsed] and line 4 [dʌznt ˈgəʊ]. Even if we reduced line 3 to five syllables and increased the number of syllables in line 4 to eight, you would still tend to give them the same amount of time because we have not changed the number of beats:

12.   I <u>said</u>: "But the <u>thing</u>   3´
      doesn't really <u>go</u> with a <u>swing</u>"   4´

Let us think of line 5 as a stretch across a frozen river with thin ice and only three stepping stones represented by the syllables *Yes, pos,* and *can.* After *Yes* you gingerly race across the thin ice with quick, small steps, trying not to put your full weight down before getting to *pos,* then two more tiny little steps (*sibly*) and now you can rest with your full weight on *can.* This phenomenon is called **stress-timing**, and English is said to be a **stress-timed language**, with the tendency to have roughly the same amount of time between stressed syllables irrespective of the number of unstressed syllables between them. Of course this is an oversimplification, and in everyday prose there is no need to keep the beat as rigorously as in music and poetry, but in English it is always there, at least as a tendency. By comparison, the rhythm in French sounds very different because French is considered a **syllable-timed language** with more of a tendency to allocate each syllable a more equal amount of time.

We have seen that syllables can be made prominent by change of pitch, loudness and duration, and this prominence is made even clearer by the inverse change to unstressed syllables, namely their compression in time, and a reduction of effort (loudness) when producing them. This reduction in effort, however, results in one more feature that helps to distinguish between prominent and non-prominent syllables. Stress-timing, specifically the reduced effort on unstressed syllables, has important consequences for the articulation of English. In order to appreciate what is going on here, put yourself in the position of a waiter who is supposed to take orders from guests of the bowling club, all sitting round the beautifully trimmed bowling green. One guest at the far end raises his hand and – as you do not want to damage the lawn – you walk carefully round the edges to take the order. You do that a few times, but more and more guests are waving their hands, claiming to be dying of thirst. So you walk faster and you decide to cut corners. More guests arrive, impatiently trying to give their orders, you are rushed off your feet and find yourself in the middle of the lawn, and while you are taking orders you simply take a few steps in their direction, swivelling round to move in the opposite direction, but never getting far away from the centre.

Now think of the lawn as the vowel diagram, and the waiter as the highest point of the tongue. At first you have plenty of time, so sentence number 8 comes out carefully articulated as

8´ [bʌt juː ˈʃʊd hæv ˈsiːn ði ɪksˈpreʃən ɒn hɜ ˈfeɪs]

But people do not talk like that: they do cut corners, turning 8´ into

8´´ [bətjə ʃədəv ˌsiːn ði̯ ɪksˈpreʃn̩ ɒnə ˈfeɪs].

The schwa-sound [ə] is the most central vowel, and in the natural speech version of 8´´ it is used five times as compared with its single occurrence in 8´, where each word was so carefully pronounced that it was identical with its citation form. The schwa-sound is often referred to as the **reduced vowel**, and the process of change from other vowels to schwa is called **vowel reduction**. Schwa can never occur in stressed syllables. The process of reduction of unstressed syllables is particularly noticable in the case of *have* and *her*, where you do not only get vowel reduction but also the loss of initial [h].

The implications of the notions of stress-timing and vowel reduction to learners of English will be dealt with in detail in the next section (VI.3.).

Stress patterns of noun+noun compounds

Compounding is a process of word formation that sticks words together to form a new word, i.e. a **compound**. So you take *fire* as the **first constituent** and *wood* as the **second constituent** to form the compound *firewood*.

First the good news:

stress on the first constituent / initial stress

English *firewood* and German *Feuerholz* have the same stress pattern, and so do *beer garden* [ˈbɪə gɑːdn̩] and *Biergarten*. With most compounds of the noun+noun type, the stress is on the first constituent. So you get the following compound nouns with **initial stress**:

13. ˈsafety belt, ˈshoestring, ˈgym shoes, ˈbread crumbs, ˈearring, ˈraincoat, ˈbookmark, ˈmountain top, aˈlarm clock, ˈlawn mower, ˈchatterbox, reˈmoval van, Mˈ'A course

The two nouns *symphony* and *orchestra* are polysyllabic nouns with the lexical stress pattern: [ˈ– – –], pronounced [ˈsɪmfəni] and [ˈɔːkɪstrə]. If you now wish to form the compound *symphony orchestra*, you have to apply the rule of initial stress, but [ˈsɪm] would not be followed by an unrhythmic sequence of five unstressed syllables. *orchestra*, like all polysyllabic second constituents of initial stress compounds, retains its original pattern on a reduced scale: the first syllable remains long but only receives secondary stress: [ˈsɪmfəni ˌɔːkɪstrə]. The same principle applies to the compounds:

14. ˈteacher ˌtrainer, comˈputer ˌsalesman, ˈmanagement conˌsultant, ˈsafety ˌhelmet

As a stranger – almost by definition – you have to ask for directions. So you approach someone (who will then turn out to be a stranger himself) and ask in your best English:

15   a. *Excuse me please, could you tell me the way to Park Street?*
15   b. [ɪkˈskuːzmɪ pliːz | kʊʤʊ teɫmiðəwəɪtʊ ˈpɑːkstriːt]

So far the good news, *and now the interesting news:*

Stress on the last constituent

If you consult the *London AZ* [ðə ˈlʌndən eɪtəˈzed], you will see that even though it is called *street atlas* it also contains other words in this semantic field, such as *Road, Avenue* and *Crescent.* If the second constituent is not *Street* itself but any other name, for instance *Park Road*, the stress pattern is different: the stress is on the second constituent, so you get

16   a. *PARK Street*, but
16   b. *Park ROAD, Park DRIVE, Park CRESCENT* etc.

This is important and worth remembering for two reasons: firstly, as we said, you will hardly have set foot in the United Kingdom before you find yourself lost. Being able to talk about place names must be part of your survival kit abroad. And secondly, stubbornly sticking to the stress pattern of *PARK Street* for all place names is one of the most common mistakes even among advanced German learners of English.

Before we go on to give you more examples, we have to explain the rule of **stress shift** we mentioned earlier. *Oxford* is pronounced [ˈɒksfəd], and the compound *Oxford Street* retains the main stress on the first syllable:

17a. [ˈɒksfəd] → [ˈɒksfəd striːt]

In *Oxford Road*, however, it is the second constituent that must receive the main stress, and as a consequence of this the first syllable of *Oxford* is reduced from primary to secondary stress; but the stress does not disappear completely, nor does it move onto another syllable; it merely shifts down a level in prominence.

17b. [ˈɒksfəd] → [ˌɒksfəd ˈrəʊd]

In order to get used to these two different stress patterns read the list of street names with *Oxford* as the first constituent aloud:

17c. [ˈɒksfəd striːt], but: [ˌɒksfəd ˈrəʊd], [ˌɒksfəd ˈsɜːkəs], [ˌɒksfəd ˈgɑːdn̩z], [ˌɒksfəd ˈkləʊs], [ˌɒksfəˈdævənjuː], [ˌɒksfəd ˈdraɪv], [ˌɒksfəd ˈleɪn], [ˌɒksfəd ˈskweə], [ˌɒksfəd ˈkreznt]

This can be extended to many cases where the second constituent is a geographical term:

17d. ˈSalisbury   →   ˌSalisbury ˈPlain;
     ˈNottingham →   ˌNottingham ˈForest,
     ˈLiverpool   →   ˌLiverpool ˈBay;
     ˈYorkshire   →   ˌYorkshire ˈDales

A different and more radical type of stress shift occurs in words like *Waterloo* when they are in compounds like *Waterloo Station*. In the sentence

18a. *Wellington defeated Napoleon at Waterloo.*

the stress pattern of the place name is

18b. [ˌwɔːtə ˈluː]

Waterloo Station is a compound where the main stress must fall on the second constituent. To be more precise, in this case it must be on the first syllable of *Station*. This poses a problem, because there is a rule which says that in English compounds you should avoid two syllables with primary stress adjacent to each other. This means that you should not simply stick the two nouns together with their original lexical stress patterns:

18c. * [ˌwɔːtə ˈluː ˈsteɪʃən]

Hence the syllable [-luː], which bears the main stress in 18a, is reduced to an unstressed syllable in *Waterloo Station*:

18d. [ˌwɔːtə ˈluː] → [ˌwɔːtəlu ˈsteɪʃən]

It is important to become aware of this process: As a learner of English you have to learn the English stress pattern WaterLOO and *unlearn* the German stress pattern 'WAterloo. And when you have mastered this, you have to *unlearn* it again and destress the last syllable of it when you use it in the compound. Under those conditions you have to use the pattern you have so carefully suppressed!

Now, let us come back to other compounds with stress on the second constituent. This stress pattern is the correct pronunciation of many other important sights and places. Some of the most frequent mistakes may be due to the differences between German and English because some of these famous places have become household names in German, and have consequently been given the German stress pattern.

19. So if you speak **German**,
    it is perfectly acceptable to say:

    BUCKingham Palast,
    WESTminster Abtei, or, if you like,
    [ˈvestminstə ˌebi],
    ALbert Hall,
    STONEhenge,

but if you switch to **English**,
they should be pronounced:

[ˌbʌkɪŋəm ˈpæləs]

[ˌwesminstəˈr̩ æbi]
[ˌæɫbət ˈhɔːɫ]
[ˌstəʊnˈhendʒ].

Note also the different stress patterns of the following English compounds and their German equivalents:

20. | German | English |
     |---|---|
     | *NORDsee* | *North SEA* [ˌ– ˈ–] |
     | *OSTsee* | *(the) Baltic SEA* [ˌ– – ˈ–] |

NORDpol　　　　　　　*North POLE* [ˌ‐ ˈ‐]
NiaGAra Fälle　　　　　*Niagara FALLS* [naɪˌægrə ˈfɔɫz]

E 1: Read the following dialogue out loud, paying particular attention to the stress pattern as it is indicated here:

"Excuse me please, is this ˌLeicester ˈSquare?" - "No, this is ˌOxford ˈCircus. For ˌLeicester ˈSquare you can take the tube, but change at ˌPiccadilly ˈCircus. Is it the cinemas you want?"- "No, actually it´s ˌNelson´s ˈColumn we wanted to see." - "Ah, in that case you want go to Traˌfalgar ˈSquare. Have you done much sight-seeing in London?" - "Yes, we´ve been to ˌHyde ˈPark, to St. ˌPaul´s Caˈthedral, to ˌWestminster ˈAbbey [ˌwesmɪnstəˈræbi] and to ˌBuckingham ˈPalace."

So much for finding your way round the ˌEnglish speaking ˈworld. Of course, compounds are not restricted to geographical names, and we will now deal with a few others. To whet your appetite, we have prepared the following passage.

E 2: Read the passage out loud. Mark the stress pattern of all compounds with a pencil as you go along:

"I read an article in our morning paper about the first hearing at <u>Birmingham Crown Court</u>. Apparently a gang had been trying to steal the <u>crown jewels</u>, but got away with only a few <u>gold coins</u>. The Queen and the <u>Prime Minister</u> were wakened up at 4 a.m. and were informed immediately." - "Good Lord, it can´t have been that important. I mean it´s not like a revolution or a civil war breaking out." - "Well, it´s caused a <u>government crisis</u>. The <u>backbenchers</u> demand a full enquiry." - "Dear oh dear, the country´s going to the dogs. Let´s think of something more cheerful. How about going out tonight?" - "No, the <u>kitchen sink</u> is still full of dirty dishes from last night." - "Oh c´mon. Fancy going to a <u>country dance</u>?" - "Thanks, but no thanks. Have a look at the <u>Manchester Evening News</u>, I´ve marked the things I´wouldn´t mind going to with a <u>ballpoint pen</u>." - "Okay, let´s see: '<u>Midsummernight´s Dream</u>' is on at the <u>Globe Theatre</u> and '<u>Calamity Jane</u>' at <u>Drury Lane</u>. Oh, listen, the <u>Battlefield Band</u> will be giving autographs at the <u>Hilton Hotel</u>."

All the compounds in E 2 have the main stress on the second constituent. Luckily, this is statistically very odd, because – as we have already said – the majority of compounds have the main stress on the first constituent: ˈshirt sleeve, ˈlawn mower, ˈfingernail. Since these do not normally cause problems for German learners of English, we devote more space to the compounds that do, and these are, for example, the ones in the above passage:

21.　ˌBirmingham Crown ˈCourt, the ˌcrown ˈjewels, ˌgold ˈcoins, ˌPrime ˈMinister, ˌgovernment ˈcrisis, ˌbackˈbencher [ˌbækˈbentʃə], ˌkitchen ˈsink, ˌcountry ˈdance, the ˌManchester Evening ˈNews [ðə ˌmæntʃəstəɾ iːvnɪŋ ˈnjuːz], ˌballpoint ˈpen, ˌMidsummer-night´s ˈDream, ˌGlobe ˈTheatre, Caˌlamity ˈJane, ˌDrury ˈLane, ˌBattlefield ˈBand, ˌHilton ˈHotel

You can now judge for yourself whether you are in need of a little bit of revision. If so, we give you a list of compounds that many German learners get wrong in English (given here with the correct stress patterns):

22. *a ˌpound ˈnote* (G.: ˈ*Pfundnote*), *a ˌten-pound ˈnote, a ˌfive P ˈstamp* (G.: *eine 50-* ˈ*Pfennig-Marke*)*, the ˌevening ˈstar* (G.: *der* ˈ*Abendstern*)*, the ˌMiddle ˈAges* (G.: *das* ˈ*Mittelalter*)*, the ˌMidland ˈBank, the ˌBattlefield ˈBand* (G.: *die* ˈ*Bettelfielt* ˌ*Bent*)*, Neanderthal man* [– ˌ– – – ˈ–]*, ˌChristmas ˈEve, ˌChristmas ˈDay, five o´clock* [ˌ– –ˈ–] → *five o´clock tea* [ˌ– – –ˈ–]*, ˌapple ˈpie, head´quarters,* (as opposed to the regular pattern for ˈ*headlights,* ˈ*headhunter,* ˈ*headset,* ˈ*headline*).

E 3: stress shift:
1. Give a phonetic transcription of the following lexemes and their compounds. Example:

> *Midsummer* → *Midsummer Night* → *Midsummer Night's Dream*
> [mɪdˈsʌmə] → [ˌmɪdsʌmə ˈnaɪt] → [ˌmɪdsʌməˌnaɪts ˈdriːm]
>
> *Tottenham* → *Tottenham Court* → *Tottenham Court Road*
> *Golden* → *Golden Gate* → *Golden Gate Bridge*
> *Manchester* → *Manchester Evening News*
> *Manchester* → *Manchester Airport*
> *nine years old* → *a nine-year-old girl;*
> *fifty* → *fifty miles* → *a fifty-mile walk*
> *fifteen* → *fifteen miles* → *a fifteen-mile walk*
> *Saint* → *St. Paul* → *St. Paul's Cathedral*

2. Transcribe the following limerick and explain the stress patterns of "sixteen" in lines 2 and 5.

> *An old girl on the train to Loch Sheen*
> *claimed to be three months under sixteen.*
> *So she got the cheap fare,*
> *but when she got there*
> *Sixteen boys cried: "Mum where have you been?"*

C 2: Listen and repeat: At the post office: *Excuse me please, could you change a 20 pound note for me please? - I´m sorry, we don´t change money. - Alright, fair enough, in that case I´d like a 30 p stamp please, and ... what´s the postage for a postcard to Germany? - 25 p, how many do you need? - Just one, please. - That´s 55 p please. So you get £19-45 change. So, here´s a ten pound note and ... - Could I have that in fives please, if you don´t mind. - Okay, so here are three five pound notes and fifty-five pence. - Actually, I want to make a few phone calls and I would like to have that in five 10 p pieces, please. - Here you are. Is the five p piece okay or would you rather have two two p pieces and one one p piece or five one p pieces. - No, the five p piece is fine. I´m sorry I´ve been such a nuisance. Thank you very much for your patience. - You´re welcome. Actually, I was only kidding. Next please. - Excuse me please, could you change a 20 pound note for me please? - I´m sorry, we don´t change money, but the gentleman who´s just left has plenty of small change.*

Fig. 3: The evening star

C 3: Listen and repeat.

A beautiful girl from Dunbar	1
said she worshipped the bright evening star.	2
"Such a wonderful sight,	3
I adore a good (k)night	4
every evening in the back of my car."	5

E 4. Transcribe this limerick and explain the stress patterns of *evening* in lines 2 and 5.

Adjective + Noun vs. Compounds

In *adjective +noun* constructions the main stress in English and German is on the noun, as in

23.   ˌblue laˈgoon and ˌblaue Laˈgune

Simple enough, but Germans sometimes make mistakes here, because they think of a German equivalent that is not a straightforward noun phrase consisting of an adjective plus noun, as for instance *Kurzgeschichte* and *Kurzarbeit* with the stress on the first syllable. In English, however, their equivalents retain the normal pattern: ˌshort ˈstory and ˌshort ˈtime .

24.	English: adjective + noun	German: compound
	ˌshort ˈtime	ˈKurzarbeit
	ˌshort ˈstory	ˈKurzgeschichte
	ˌloudˈspeaker	ˈLautsprecher
	ˌfull ˈmoon	ˈVollmond
	ˌcivil ˈwar	ˈBürgerkrieg

In German you could say: *"Nicht jede kurze Geschichte ist eine Kurzgeschichte"*, which you would have to translate as *"Not every short story is a short story in the technical sense"*, because the stress pattern remains the same. You could, however, say: *"Not every* [ʃɔːt ˈlɪst] *is a* [ˈʃɔːtlɪst]*."* If you have a list that is short, it is, of course, a ˌshort ˈlist. But when people apply for a job you select only some of the applicants you want to interview, i.e. you shortlist them or put them on your shortlist, pronounced [ˈʃɔːtlɪst]. When this happens these constructions are then treated as one noun, which – luckily – is often reflected in spelling it as one word, and phonetically in treating it as a regular compound with the stress on the first constituent.

25.	adjective + noun	compound
	ˌblack ˈbird	ˈblackbird
	ˌblue ˈprint	ˈblueprint
	ˌblue ˈbottle	ˈbluebottle: a common fly
	ˌshort ˈbread	ˈshortbread: a type of biscuit
	ˌdark ˈroom (dunkle ˈKammer)	ˈdark-room (ˈDunkelkammer)
	ˌmore best ˈcellars [ˌmɔː best ˈseləz]	ˈbestsellers [ˈbestseləz]
	a ˌwhite ˈhouse	the ˈWhite House (in Washington)

We find that German learners of English rarely experience problems with the compounds under 25, but find the items under 24 difficult to learn. So concentrate on these and leave the others to your intuiton. *Blue Jeans*, however, is a problem case: Germans often say *Meine* ˈBlue Jeans, but in English the stress pattern is ˌblue ˈjeans, though mainly because the generic item has been reduced simply to *jeans*, and the former compound is more likely to be an adjective + noun combination, since jeans come in a variety of colours nowadays.

"Cleaning ladies can be such fun."

When the present participle of a verb functions as an adjective modifying a noun (as in *"an amusing tale"*), it has the same appearance in writing as a gerund modifying a noun, as in *planning permission* (*Planungserlaubnis*). Just by looking at *dancing girls* you cannot tell whether these are girls who happen to be dancing or whether their status as professional dancers is being referred to. The different stress patterns disambiguate the phrase in the same way as 25, where the compounds take the usual stress pattern with stress on the first constituent. We leave it to you now to ponder about the two possible interpretations of the sentence: *"Cleaning ladies can be such fun."*

26. adjective+noun	gerund+noun (compound)
ˌdancing ˈgirls	ˈdancing girls
ˌcleaning ˈladies	ˈcleaning ladies
	ˈdriving licence

Compound adjectives of the type "adjective + past participle"

E 5: Read the following passage loud and pencil in the stress pattern of *absent-minded* and *absent-mindedly*:

> *Are all professors absent-minded? The absent-minded professor of biology told his first-year students in the lab: "I will now introduce you to a galvanic experiment on a dead frog. I have brought you a lovely specimen here." He took a small parcel from his briefcase, unwrapped it and stared at a sandwich. "Well, well," he said absent-mindedly, "I could have sworn I had had my sandwich for lunch."*

All compounds of the type *absent-minded* have the stress on the second constituent when used in predicative position, i.e. in the verb phrase after the noun, as in: *Professors are absent-minded.* [ˌæbsənt ˈmaɪndɪd]. This causes problems for German learners of English for two reasons: firstly, because German equivalents have the stress on the first constituent:

27. adj. + past participle in predicative position: *That´s rather old-fashioned.*			
ˌold-ˈfashioned	ˈaltmodisch	ˌblue-ˈeyed	ˈblauäugig
ˌshort-ˈlived	ˈkurzlebig	ˌoverˈpaid	ˈüberbezahlt
ˌshort-ˈsighted	ˈkurzsichtig	ˌthick-ˈskinned	ˈdickhäutig

And secondly, it causes problems, because all these English constructions are subject to stress shift when they appear in attributive position (i.e. preceding the noun), and then, of course, they take on a form that corresponds to the German stress pattern, which is misleading: When you hear a joke about [ðiˌæbsənt maɪndɪd prəˈfesə] you might jump to the wrong conclusion that this stress pattern of *absent-minded*, where *minded* is destressed, is also the citation form. This wrong interpretation is reinforced by the fact that with a number of these compounds you are more likely to hear them in the attributive position (i.e. after the application of stress shift), as for instance in:

28. ˌshort-term ˈcontract, a ˌfair-sized ˈgarden, the ˌblue-eyed ˈboy vs.
it's only ˌshort-ˈterm; *his garden is* ˌfair -ˈsized; *the boy is* ˌblue-ˈeyed.

Read the above joke again, tell it to everybody you like or – perhaps more suitably – to everybody you *do not like,* until you are familiar with the difference between *Are all professors absent-minded?* [ˌæbsənt ˈmaɪndɪd] and [ðɪˌæbsənt maɪndɪd prəˈfesə]. Then learn the words under 27. to 29., and do E 6.

29. ˌred-ˈhanded (*He was caught red-handed.* G: *Er wurde auf frischer Tat ertappt.*)
   ˌleft-ˈhanded ˌhigh-ˈhanded ˌheavy-ˈhanded ˌover-ˈqualified
   ˌshort-ˈstaffed ˌover-ˈstaffed ˌlight-ˈhearted ˌhalf-ˈhearted
   ˌopen-ˈended ˌgood-ˈnatured ˌlily-ˈlivered [ˌlɪli ˈlivəd] = ˈhasenfüßig

E 6: Read the following passage aloud and mark the stress patterns of all constructions of the type "adjective + past participle":
*"Our boss is so old-fashioned and his methods of maintaining discipline are so
heavy-handed that everybody in the office is low-spirited." - "That approach
seems rather shortsighted. How can he expect to motivate you if he does not rely
on self-discipline?" - "He's got this deep-seated belief that people work hard
only under pressure. But his attempts to monitor our output are only half-
hearted. And he's not even fair. With some of us he is short-tempered, but with
this new yuppy he is ever so lenient. That young chap was appointed to the sales
department even though they were over-staffed." - "Sounds like he's the boss's
blue-eyed boy." - "Rumour has it he is the boss's wife's blue-eyed boy." - "I see.
And I've been told she's such a high-minded person telling everybody else what
is right and what is wrong." - "That's true, but none of these lily-livered creeps
has the courage to stand up to her." - "But you have kept silent, haven't you?
Doesn't that mean you too are lily-livered?"*

NB. Make sure you do not confuse these compounds with adjectives of the
type "noun + past participle", because they usually have the stress on the first
constituent, like ˈhen-pecked, ˈdiamond-shaped, ˈferet-faced (but ˌham-ˈfisted).

As you may have guessed, you get the same stress pattern with adjective +
present participle: *One mother to another: "What a pretty little girl you have. Is
your husband ˌgood-ˈlooking?*

English [ˈmeɪk ʌp] vs. German [meɪk ˈʔap]

Make-up is a household word in German and since every learner recognises it
as a loanword from English, they think they know it. *"Why should I look it up?
I've been using it all my life!"* In terms of pronunciation, however, there are at
least two differences: firstly, (as indicated in the above phonetic transcription)
the linking of the [k] to the following syllable, as opposed to the German loanword, where the second syllable is often even pronounced with a hard onset:
[meɪk ˈʔap]. It helps if you recognise the principle at work here. This noun is
obviously *made up* of the verb *make* and the ... the ... yes? No, it is not a
preposition here, so let us call it the "particle" for the time being.

Quite a number of nouns with the pattern of *make-up* have found their way
into the German language, and we can always observe a kind of English →
German stress shift rule - but strangely reversed compared to the usual Ger-

man pattern – where the stress is moved from the verb in the English compound to the particle in the German loanword:

30a. **English**   **German loanword**

the countdown [ˡ‿ ‿]   *der Countdown* [‿ ˡ‿]
the comeback [ˡkʌmbæk]   *das Comeback* [kamˡbek]
the pullover [ˡpʊləʊvə]   *der Pullover* [pʊˡloːvɐ]
the know-how [ˡnəʊhaʊ]   *das Knowhow* [noː ˡhaʊ]
the knock-out [ˡnɒkaʊt]   *der Knockout* [nɔkˡaʊt]
the showdown [ˡ‿ ‿]   *der Showdown* [‿ ˡ‿]
the sit-in [ˡ‿ ‿]   *das Sit-in* [‿ ˡ‿]
the drive-in [ˡ‿ ‿]   *das Drive-in* [‿ ˡ‿]
the cover-up [ðə ˡkʌvrʌp]   *das Cover-up* [das kave ʔap]
the check-in [ˡʧekɪn]   *das Check-in* [ʃek ˡɪn]
the layout [ˡleɪaʊt]   *das Layout* [leːˡaʊt]/[ˡleːʔaʊt]

Fig. 4: The differences between German airport English and English English:

30b.   English English: [ˌbrɪtɪˡʃeəweɪz | ˡhæmbægəʤ ˡʧekɪn]
        German English: [ˌbʁɪtɪʃ ˡʔeɐveis | ˡhentbegəʧ ʃek ˡʔɪn]

It is interesting to note that some of the more recent loans do not seem to have had enough time to acquire the German stress pattern, as for instance *workout* in the international world of sport, which – if it is used in German – retains its English pattern [ˡ‿ ‿]. With some other loanwords German allows for both patterns, as with *Blackout*, pronounced either [ˡblek ʔaʊt] or [blek ˡʔaʊt], but in English it is always [ˡblæ kaʊt].

30c. Read these nouns aloud and make sure you put the stress on the verb and link the final consonant of it to the first vowel of the particle:
Example: *a break-in* [ə ˡbreɪ kɪn]

> *left-overs; grown-ups, walk-over, take-over, stop-over, shake-up, sit-in, the car is a complete write-off*

31.   *SHEIKH-UP*

> *Maktoum pull-out warning. British racing reeled last night after an astonishing attack by Sheikh Mohammed.*

> *The world´s leading owner threatened to pull out the Maktoum dynasty´s 500*
> *blueblood horses.*

The headline in 31 is one of those puns British newspapers are so fond of: a *shake-up* staged by a *sheikh* becomes a *"sheikh-up"*. The sub-headline contains a noun of the "verb + particle" constructions we are dealing with in this section, and in *pull-out* we see that stress-shift is not necessary even when the compound modifies another noun:

32. *A 'pull-out → a 'pull-out ₁warning.*
    The race was a simple 'walk-over for Johnson → Johnson´s ₁walk-over 'victory.
    Let´s go to a ₁Chinese 'take-away → a Chinese 'take-away ₁bar

In the last paragraph of 31., *pull out* is used as a verb, and we promised to come back to the question of the particle after the verb. Note that in *pull-out* as a noun the *out* is unstressed, but in *pull out* as a verb the particle is stressed. This makes *out* something other than a preposition, because prepositions are normally unstressed, as in the prepositional phrases *in the house* and *at the weekend*. Look at the sentence

33a. *We´ll go on Sunday.*

This is ambiguous, as it could be the answer either to *"When will you go?"*

33b. *We´ll ₁go on 'Sunday.*

or the answer to *"When will you go on?"*

33c. *We´ll go 'on 'Sunday.*

In 33b *on Sunday* is a prepositional phrase, and the prepostion is unstressed.

Let us briefly go back to the verb *pull out* in the final paragraph of 31. The reason for having the verb (*pull*) and its particle (*out*) side by side here is a stylistic one: In English the noun phrase functioning as the object in this sentence is considered too long to be put between verb and particle: **"to pull the Maktoum dynasty´s 500 blueblood horses out."* If, however, you reduced the noun phrase to its head *horses*, both positions of *out* would be possible:

34a. *He threatened to pull out the horses.*
34b. *He threatened to pull the horses out.*

Now compare *to pull ʼout the horses* with *to ʼpoint at the corrupt politicians*:

34c. *He threatened to point at the corrupt politicians.* but not
34d. **He threatened to point the corrupt politicians at.*

Concerning the last paragraph of 31. you might ask: *"Sorry, what did he threaten to do with the horses?"*, and the answer might be:

35a. *He threatened to pull them out.*

After having heard 34c. you might ask: *"Sorry, what did he threaten to do with the politicians?"* And here the answer would have to be:

35b. *He threatened to point at them.* but not
35c. **He threatened to point them at.*

This simple test helps to distinguish between two types of "verb + particle" constructions: **phrasal verbs** and **prepositional verbs,** where *pull out* belongs to the former category and *point at* to the latter.

Fig. 5:   **verb plus particle**

           phrasal verbs   **prepositional verbs**

Stress

The particle of the phrasal verb is usually stressed:	the preposition is usually unstressed:
The show must go ¹on.	*We can´t charge him yet, we have nothing to ¹go on.*
Those are the politicians he threatened to point ¹out.	*Those are the politicians he threatened to ¹point at.*
I gave it ¹up *I gave ¹up smoking* *He ran ¹up a bill.*	*He ran up a ¹hill.* *The play is worth ¹going to.*

Word order

verb + personal pronoun + particle:

He pulled them ¹out	* ~~He pointed them at.~~

verb+noun phrase+particle:

He pulled the horses ¹out.	* ~~He pointed the politicians at.~~

verb+particle+noun phrase:

He pulled ¹out the horses.	*He ¹pointed at the politicians.*

"We can´t compete with the Jones´s." contains a prepositional phrase. If you replace *compete* by the phrasal verb *to keep up,* you combine the two types and get a **phrasal-prepositional verb** (*to keep up with*), where the stress rule concerning the two types of verbs still holds, because it is the particle of the verb that carries the stress, and the preposition remains unstressed.

36. *We can´t keep UP with the ¹Jones´s.*

Summary of "verb+particle" constructions:

The particle of the phrasal verb is stressed (*come* ˈ*back*). In the corresponding noun it becomes unstressed (ˈ*comeback*). The corresponding German loanword is a noun, but has the stress pattern of the English phrasal verb.

37. | phrasal verb | English noun | German noun |
|---|---|---|
| *drive* ˈ*in* | ˈ*drive-in* | *das Drive-*ˈ*in* |
| *cover* ˈ*up* | ˈ*cover-up* | *das Cover*ˈ*up* |

E 7: Read aloud and mark the stress patterns of "verb+particle" constructions.

a. *They never come back*

"*I told you, George Foreman wouldn´t be able to keep up with the young boxers. As the saying goes: They never come back.*" - "*Well, Muhamed Ali staged an impressive comeback, didn´t he?*" - "*I admit, his first major bout was a walk-over, and as a young fighter he certainly caused a shake-up of the boxing world. But his last fights were a bit of a let-down, weren´t they.*" - "*It looks like these walk-over victories are a thing of the past then.*"

b. *A lovers´ tiff*

"*Last Tuesday, Susan and Peter had a row and broke up. He was in a hell of a state and nearly had a nervous breakdown. He jumped into his Jaguar and drove off into the dark night.*" - "*Yes, I know, he´s such a show-off, isn´t he? The whole thing is a farce: he hit a lamp post and the car was a complete write-off. And instead of laughing it all off she then has a guilt hang-up, walks out on her new boyfriend, and since then she and Peter have made up.*" - "*How do you know?*" - "*I saw her make-up on his collar.*" - "*Ah yes, that´s a give-away. So the great tragedy turned out to be just a little lovers´ tiff. And I was certainly taken in by this would-be Romeo. I simply couldn´t put up with his childish behaviour. I think they should start behaving like grown-ups.*" - "*Yes, but she was so impressed by his roaring off and the scratch on his face. She embraced him like a war hero.*" - "*Well, well, whatever turns you on, baby.*"

c. *Workers strike for better pay*

After a take-over bid by a Japanese car manufacturer had failed, 500 workers were laid-off. In a showdown between employers and employees, the trade unions first staged a sit-in and later on even a walk-out to put pressure on the manage-ment. The directors promptly reacted with lock-outs at two branches of the Ford company and the demand to call off the strike immediately.

Nouns

The majority of English <u>nouns</u> with two and three syllables have stress on the first one. This is particularly true of simple words like *window, woman, finger* and *paradise*, which do not have prefixes or suffixes. Historically this is due to the fact that this is where – a long time ago – Germanic languages had the stress in all words, as opposed to French, where most words are stressed on the final syllable. Please bear in mind that we are only talking about statistics here, or trends and tendencies. Think of a car whose wheels are badly aligned and that does not keep track. In French your car would constantly pull you to the right, i.e. towards the end of a word, as in *alba'tros*, whereas your **stress carrying** English and German cars would pull you to the left and place the stress of *'albatross* on the first syllable. Now these two Germanic languages have absorbed words of Greek, Latin and French origin, and here English has been slightly more consistent in keeping its original Germanic stress pattern even for non-Germanic words. So we get quite a number of pairs like English *instinct* vs. German *Instinkt*, or English *la*byrinth vs. German *Labyrinth*. This tendency in English is often referred to as **leftward pull** or **backward stress**. We have distinguished here between pairs that do not cause problems (38a) and those that – according to our data – sometimes do (38b&c):

38. Contrastive analysis to demonstrate the "leftward pull" of English stress.

38a. Pairs that do not normally cause problems:

English stress on the first syllable	German stress on the last syllable
'student	Stu'dent
'metal	Me'tall
'general	Gene'ral
'paradise	Para'dies
'camel	Ka'mel

38b. Pairs that learners may have problems with:

'instinct	In'stinkt
'oboe	O'boe
'amateur	Ama'teur
'convoy	Con'voy
'record (noun)	Re'kord
'ballet (not USA)	Ba'llett
'catapult	Kata'pult
'Odeon	O'deon
'Andrea	An'drea
prospect ['prɒspekt]	Pros'pekt

The last item is interesting in so far as semantically English *prospect* (*Zukunfts-perspektiven*) is not the same as German *Prospekt*, which in English is *prospectus* [prəs'pektəs] or *leaflet*. In contrast to English *prospectus*, German *Prospekt* does not have vowel reduction in the unstressed first syllable.

The same trend can be observed in many French loanwords and names:

38c. French loanwords and French proper names in:

English	German
'gourmet	Gour'met
'rendezvous	Rendez'vous

ˈcafe	Caˈfé
ˈcliché	Kliˈschee
ˈchauffeur	Chauˈffeur
ˈPeugeot	Peuˈgeot
ˈRenault	Reˈnault

The difference in leftward pull can also be observed where the German noun does not have the stress on the final syllable, as with

38d. English   German

ˈcalender	Kaˈlender
ˈcylinder	Zyˈlinder

Geographical names

There are some places and countries for which English and German have completely different names, like *Venice/Venedig* or *Germany/Deutschland*. For the others, a look at the stress patterns is quite rewarding, as – in writing, at least – the words are so similar they are easy to compare. We do not wish to make matters unnecessarily complicated here, so it is comforting to note that – despite the different sounds they contain (we give you the phonetic transcription of the English versions) – the stress patterns are mostly the same:

39. English and German place names with the same stress pattern:

Hamburg [ˈhæmbɜːg],   *Palermo* [pəˈlɜːməʊ]   *Oslo* [ˈɒzləʊ]
Chicago [ʃɪˈkɑːgəʊ]   *Copenhagen* [ˌkəʊpmˈheɪgn]   *Marseille* [mɑːˈseɪ]
Madrid [məˈdrɪd]   *Barcelona* [ˌbɑːsɪˈləʊnə]   *Tel Aviv* [ˌteləˈviːv]

There are, however, a number of important place names where you get different stress patterns because the German names do not reveal a left-hand pull. You are, of course, familiar with English *Paris* [ˈpærɪs] and German *Paris* [–ˈ–], but many Germans mispronounce the London district of Soho, putting the stress on the last syllable. So look at the examples under 40:

40. Geographical names that may cause problems because of leftward pull in English but not in German:

English	German	English	German
ˈHanover	Hanˈnover	ˈStockholm	Stockˈholm
ˈMonaco	Moˈnaco	ˈFlorence	Floˈrenz
ˈHebrides	Heˈbriden	ˈSoho/Soˈho	Soˈho
ˈNewfoundland	Neuˈfundland	ˈCanberra	Canˈberra
[ˈnjuːfənlənd]			

41. Proper names, where the trend of leftward pull in English is reversed.
(We have restricted this list to words that seemed important to us, and where the stress patterns of English and German differ. So names like *Madrid* and *Sudan* have not been included.)

41a. Europe

English	German	English	German
Water'loo	*'Waterloo*	*Dun'dee*	*'Dundee*
Bel'fast	*'Belfast*	*Belgrade* [bel'greɪd]	*'Belgrad*
Bucharest	*'Bukarest*	*Budapest*	*'Budapest*
[ˌbjuːkəˈrest]		[ˌbjuːdəˈpest]	

41b. Overseas

English	German	English	German
Illi'nois	*'Illinois*	*Montreal*	*'Montreal*
		[mɒntriˈɔːɬ]	
Ja'pan	*'Japan*	*Singapore* [sɪŋəˈpɔː]	*'Singapur*
Hong 'Kong	*'Hong Kong*	*Bang'kok*	*'Bangkok*
Bom'bay	*'Bombay*	*Nepal* [nɪˈpɔːɬ]	*'Nepal*
Tibet [tɪ 'bet]	*'Tibet*	*Su'matra*	*'Sumatra*
Bagh'dad	*'Baghdad*	*Tehe'ran*	*'Teheran*
Paki'stan	*'Pakistan*	*Katmandu*	*Kat'mandu*
		[ˌkætmænˈduː]	

41c. Names

Mu'hammed	*'Mohammed*	*Mon'roe*	*'Monroe*

E 8: Work with a partner. Take it in turns to ask the following questions. Write the answer in phonetic transcription. Compare results at the end.

Example: *A: What´s the capital of Norway?* B: says *Oslo* and writes ['ɒzləʊ].

Student A:
What´s the capital of Spain?
Which actress starred in Some like it hot*?*
What´s the capital of Finland?
What´s the capital of Irak?
Which London area is famous
for its night clubs?
What is the capital of Germany?
What´s the capital of Northern Ireland?

Student B:
Which country is Islamabad the capital of?
Who is the most famous boxer of all times?
What´s the capital of Rumania?
Where did Wellington beat Napoleon?
Which town is situated on Montreal
Island?
What´s the capital of the Netherlands?
Which British colony was given back to
China in 1997?

Choose your answers from this list:
Muhammad Ali, Helsinki, Pakistan, Baghdad, Berlin, Marilyn Monroe, Belfast, Hongkong, Montreal, Bucharest, Madrid, Soho, Waterloo, Amsterdam

VI.3. Weak and strong forms:
Weak /əz/ weak /kən/ be! – The fate of function words

When learning and teaching the words of a foreign language, we tend to treat them as if they existed in isolation, and often neglect to learn *how they adapt to context*, how they change when they are used in a longer utterance. We have several chapters in this book which we devote to various aspects of this problem (see also the sections on linking, assimilation, stress and "The sounds of Grammar"). This chapter is concerned with what happens to *function* words when they are fitted in between the informationally more important *content* words (verbs, nouns, adjectives, adverbs).

Fig. 1: *Frank'n'Stein* and *Fruit'n'Veg*

C1: a. Listen to the text spoken by the English speaker in the recording. b. Listen to the same speaker reading a short selection of words from the text.

a. *Saturday January 29th*
Bert Baxter rang to ask why I hadn't been round. I said I'd been too busy. Bert said, 'Yes, too busy to visit an old lonely widower.' I promised to go round tomorrow after dinner. Bert said, 'Dinner? What's that?' I said, 'You remember, Bert, it is meat and three veg and gravy and stuff'. Bert said that it was so long since he had eaten properly that his vocabulary was suffering. I asked him round for dinner tomorrow and told him that my father would give him a lift. But when I told my parents they went mad, and said that they'd arranged to visit some properties tomorrow and were planning to get a Chinese take-away.
(Sue Townsend *The Growing Pains of Adrian Mole*)

b. Word selection: *to, for, an, him, his, some, was, were, that, and, not, is, had, but*

How does the speaker's pronunciation of the words in the context of a sentence differ from their pronunciation in the list? Try and describe the differences you hear.

You should have noticed the following differences:
(i) the vowel qualities are very different. The vowels in *for, but, some, was, were* and *that* all have different vowel qualities when spoken in the list. In the text, however, they all have much the same vowel, a central vowel somewhere in the region of [ə].
(ii) some of the words have lost their vowels altogether (**vowel elision**) and in extreme cases only a consonant is left, e.g. *an, and, is, had* and *not*.
Read the text aloud and try to imitate the features we have just been talking about. If necessary listen to C1 again.

Communicative (un)importance and (lack of) prominence
The words with these extreme differences in vowel quality and from which vowels and consonants are **elided** are the **function words** we mentioned in the opening paragraph. Function words are the words that help to link the content words together, to relate them to each other, like prepositions, pronouns, relative conjunctions, auxiliary verbs etc. They carry the grammatical structure of the utterance and are highly predictable because, compared to the limitless choice of content words, there are only a limited number of forms from which to choose. *Since they do not normally carry the main message of an utterance, they are not made prominent by accenting.* This means not so much time or effort is spent articulating them fully, and their form is **reduced**. Consider the following short sentences:

1. a. *Drink a pint* of *milk a day!*   b. *What* do you *think?*   c. *See* for *yourself!*
   d. *We* have *already finished.*   e. *She* is *softer* than *butter.*   f. *Come* and *see.*

The de-italicised words are examples of function words (sorry, we couldn't think of a better way of indicating something without giving it the emphasis it doesn't deserve!). Say the phrases to yourself, and consider whether you change the pronunciation of the de-italicised words compared to their pronunciation in isolation. You might like to check your version against a range of possible reduced forms, from minimal to extreme:

2. *of*:   [əv], [ə] *"a bit of luck"*
   do you: [dəjʊ], [djə], [tʃə] *"what do you want?"*
   and: [ənd], [ən], [n̩] *"fish 'n chips"*
   have: [həv], [əv], [v] *"I've read it"*
   is: [z], [ʐ] *"it's late"*
   than: [ðən], [ðn̩] *"Better late than never"*
   for: [fə], [f] *"it was all for nothing"*

"Speak more clearly! Don't swallow your words!"
The pronunciation of a grammatical item that you are most likely to use when speaking is the weak or reduced form and it is important that you master this pronunciation. Sometimes you will see the strong form referred to as the careful pronunciation, but do not allow yourself to be misled into thinking that the

other form is the opposite of careful, i.e. sloppy or such like, and therefore to be avoided. Of course you do not want to be accused of speaking in a slovenly manner. But using weak forms is *not* slovenly; you are *not* speaking badly when you use them. In fact *not* using them makes you sound strange, possibly pedantic and pompous and certainly accentuates any other traces of a foreign accent you might have. *"I'll help you if you'd like me to"* is much better than *"I vill help you if you vish"*! Weak forms of grammatical items are an important part of a good, idiomatic pronunciation and it is by no means easy to acquire them, as is witnessed by the recordings of the C 1 text by a German speaker.

C 2: Listen to a German speaker reading the same text that you listened to above (C 1). Pay particular attention to the way in which he pronounces the underlined words.

You should be able to hear that the German speaker pronounces the words from the list using vowel qualities similar to those we would have expected had she read them in isolation. There are a number of reasons why German speakers have problems pronouncing weak forms correctly. The first was mentioned briefly in the opening paragraph: When we begin to learn a new language we often pay a great deal of attention to the pronunciation of words in isolation and not to the pronunciation of sentences. Secondly, we often talk <u>about</u> words: So when answering the question "Which relative pronoun can refer to things and people?" a native speaker of English would say "that", using the strong form [ðæt], but when giving an example she would automatically switch to the weak form: [ðə ˈgɜːɫ ðət lefˈtɜːli]. This means that [ðət] we can pick up bad habits at the start which are hard to get rid of later. Another reason has to do with differences between German and English. Although German also has words which have strong and weak forms, they are less numerous. So, although pronouns, such as *es, du, sie* and various forms of the indefinite article have forms with [ə], none of the modal verbs (e.g. *kann, will, muss, soll*) have a weak form at all.

Of course, the degree to which function words are weakened depends on the style of speaking you are using, something that depends on the particular situation you are in and who you are talking to. One situation in which weak forms would probably be avoided completely is, for example, in the corridor of an express train in summer, with the windows down! Chatting at home with a good friend about something you have experienced together would provide a situation in which the most extreme weakening is likely. So learning to use weak forms means learning to use them flexibly. As you become more fluent in English, your style of speaking should become more adaptable to different communicative situations, and if you practise the deaccenting of function words sufficiently the weak forms will adapt accordingly.

What are the most important weak forms? Of course all weak forms are important because an unaccented word that is pronounced in its full form

sticks out like a sore thumb. The following sections group the main categories
and give you short example phrases to practise and remember:

Prepositions

to:	[tə]	*We went to the shops*
	[tʊ], [tu]	*He gave his money to others.*
for:	[fə]	*Time for tea.*
	[fər]	*For ever and ever.*
from:	[frəm], [frm̩]	*From here to eternity.*

Clause linkers

because:	[bɪkəz], [kəz]	*We did it because we wanted to.*
that:	[ðət]	*We knew that it could happen.*
as:	[əz]	*He watched as the building collapsed.*
but:	[bət]	*We wanted to but couldn't.*

Comparative structures

than:	[ðən]	*It is better than nothing.*
as .... as:	[əz] ... [əz]	*She´s as good as gold.* [ʃiːzəz ˈgʊdəz ˈgəʊɫd]
(not) so .. as:	[sə].. [əz]	*These are not so good as the others.*

Personal and possessive pronouns

he:	[hi],	*He helped me to understand.*
	[i]	*What did he say?* [wɒt dɪdi ˈseɪ]
him:	[hɪm],	*We'll see him tomorrow.*
	[ɪm]	*I'll tell him this evening.*
his:	[hɪz],	*His son's a missionary.*
	[ɪz]	*What's his idea?*
she:	[ʃi]	*Why did she say that?*
we:	[wi]	*Can we help?*
us:	[əs]	*Tell us what to do.*
our:	[aə], [a]	*That's our great strength!*
	[ar]	*It's our own fault* [ɪtsaˈrəʊn ˈfɔːɫt]
you:	[ju], [jʊ], [jə]	*What do you mean?* [wɒt˺djə ˈmiːn]
your:	[jə], [jə]	*How's your father?*
	[jər], [jər]	*Press here and Bob's your uncle.* (= it´s very easy)
they:	[ðə]	*Do you know what they think?*
them:	[ðəm]	*Tell them to watch it!*
their:	[ðɛ]	*That's their slogan.*
	[ðɛr]	*It's their other daughter.*

Auxiliary and modal verb constructions

is:	[z]	*The idea is a good one.* [ðiaɪˈdɪəzə ˈgʊd wʌn]
	[s]	*The cup is broken.* [ðə ˈkʌps ˈbrəʊkn̩]
has:	[həz], [əz], [s]	*What has he done?* [wɒtsi ˈdʌn]
	[ɦəz], [əz], [z]	*Why has he done it?*

have:	[həv], [əv], [v]	*What have they done?*
	[ɦəv], [əv], [v]	*Why have they done it?*
can	[kən],	*What can you tell me?*
	[kŋ]	*How can they do it?*
was:	[wəz]	*What was the reason?*
had:	[həd], [əd]	*I knew the cat had eaten it.*
	[ɦəd], [əd], [d]	*I knew the boy had eaten it.*
would:	[wəd], [əd], [d]	*We thought he would choke!*
should:	[ʃəd]	*He said we should go for it.*
could	[kəd]	*How could you do such a thing?*

N.B. Of course there are also combinations of auxiliaries in the more complex verbal structures, but in general they follow the same weakening principles: E.g.: *Children* could have *stumbled over it.* [ˈʧɪɫdrən kədəv ˈstʌmbɫd͜əʊvərɪt]

C 3: Listen and repeat. Here are some sentences with weak forms in their ˋnatural surroundingsˊ. The words we think would be pronounced with their weak form have been de-italicised in the orthographic version. The accented words have been marked with ˡ in the transcription. Try to pronounce the grammatical items in the way the speaker does. These examples have again taken from Sue Townsend´s *The Growing Pains of Adrian Mole.*

1. *My mother says* that *my father will* do anything to avoid working *for Man-power Services as a canal bank renovator.*
[maɪ ˈmʌðə sez ðət maɪ ˈfɑːðərəɫ du͜ˈeniθɪŋ tu͜əˈvɔɪd ˈwɜːkɪŋ fə ˈmæmpaʊə ˈsɜːvɪsɪz͜əzə kəˈnæɫ bæŋk ˈrenəveɪtə]

2. *My mother found* them; *they were hidden under a crumb* of *fruitcake.*
[maɪ ˈmʌðə faʊnd ðəm | ðeɪ wə ˈhɪdn͜ʌndərə ˈkrʌməv ˈfruːtkeɪk]

3. *I* was shocked *at his* sexist attitude *and* told *him* that *I* was *in love with Pandora* because of *her* brains *and* compassion *for* lesser mortals.
[aɪ wəz ˈʃɒktətɪz ˈseksɪsˡt͜ætɪtjuːdən təʊɫdɪm ðətaɪ wəzɪn ˡlʌv wɪð pænˈdɔːrə bɪkəzəv hə ˈbreɪnzən kəmˈpæʃn̩ fə ˈlesə ˈmɔːtɫz]

4. *I* hoped *that* this *would* mean *she would* cook some dinner *but* no, *she* went into *the* kitchen *and* read The Guardian *from* cover *to* cover, *so I* opened a tin of tuna again.
[aɪ ˈhəʊpt ðət ðɪs wəd miːn ʃid ˈkʊk səm ˈdɪnə bət ˈnəʊ | ʃi wentɪntə ðə ˈkɪtʃɪn͜ ən red ðə ˈgɑːdɪən frəm ˈkʌvə tə ˈkʌvə | səʊ͜aɪ ͜ˈəʊpəndə tɪnəv ˈtjuːnəˡəgen]

5. *I have* written Pandora a short note.   [aɪv ˈrɪtn̩ pænˈdɔːrə͜ə ˈʃɔːt ˈnəʊt]

6. There were lots of visitors *at* Pandora's house.
[ðə wə ˈlɒtsəv ˈvɪzɪtəzət pænˈdɔːrəz ˈhaʊs]

7. *They* should be made *to* take the Hippocratic oath, *like* doctors *and* nurses.
[ðeɪ ʃədbi ˈmeɪd tə ˈteɪk ðə ˌhɪpəˈkrætɪˡk͜əʊθ | laɪk ˈdɒktəzən ˈnɜːsɪz]

8. ´If I *don't* see you *in* school tomorrow, Mole, *I* shall be severely displeased!´
[ɪfaɪ ˈdəʊnt siː ˡju͜ɪn ˈskuːɫ təˈmɒrəʊ ˈməʊɫ | aɪ ʃəɫ bi sɪˈvɪəli dɪsˈpliːzd]

9. *Why* do *people wait* to *do* their *shopping until* there are *only two days left before Christmas?*
[ˈwaɪ də ˈpiːpɫ ˈweɪt̮‿tə ˌduː ðeə ˈʃɒpɪŋ əntɪɫ ðəɹ‿əɹ əʊnli ˈtuː deɪz left bɪfɔː ˈkrɪsməs]

10. *How* could *any English person want* to *live abroad?*
[haʊ kəˈd‿eni‿ˈɪŋglɪʃ pɜːsn̩ wɒnt tə lɪv‿əˈbrɔːd]

11. *Pandora* has been *round* but *I declined* to *see* her.
[pænˈdɔːrəz bɪn ˈraʊnd bət̮‿aɪ dɪˈklaɪnd tə ˈsiː ə]

12. We are *both in a lower social class* than our *loved ones.*
[wɪə ˈbəʊθɪnə ˈləʊə səʊʃɫ ˈklɑːs ðən‿aə ˈlʌvd wʌnz]

13. *The nation* has been *told* that *Britain* and *Argentina* are *not at war,* we are at *conflict.*
[ðə ˈneɪʃn̩z bɪn ˈtəʊɫd ðət ˈbrɪtn̩ən‿ɑːˈdʒn̩tiːnəˈə ˈnɒtət ˈwɔː | wɪəɹət ˈkɒnflɪkt]

14. *The vicar forced* us to *pray* for *the Falkland Islanders.*
[ðə ˈvɪkə ˈfɔːstəs tə ˈpreɪ fə ðə ˌfɔːklənˈd‿aɪləndəz]

15. *After Crossroads* had *finished I asked my father why* he had *married my mother.*
[ɑːftə ˈkrɒsrəʊdzəd ˈfɪnɪʃt‿aɪ‿ɑːskt maɪ ˈfɑːðə waɪ hid ˈmærɪd maɪ ˈmʌðə]

Fig. 2: Newspaper pun that depends on the weak form of *and*

You might have noticed while working through the last exercise that some grammatical items have more than one weak form. This usually depends on whether what follows begins with a vowel or not. For many items with two weak forms (e.g. *for, her, their*) the second form is due to linking-r which we dealt with earlier in IV.3.2. But although *the, do, to,* and *you,* have [ə] before words that begin with consonants, the quality of the vowel before words that begin with a vowel is similar to that of the strong form, only shorter:

3.   a. *I'll do it for* you; *nobody else will.* [ˈaɪɫ du ɪt fə ˈjuː | ˈnəʊbədɪ ˈeɫs wʊd]
     b. *The good, the bad and the ugly.*   [ðə ˈgʊd ðə ˈbædən ði‿ˈʌgli]

Many auxiliary verbs have a form which consists of a single non-syllabic consonant, which is then stuck onto the end of the previous syllable. In the vast majority of cases this contracted form consists of a pronoun and an auxiliary verb. In most less formal styles of writing contracted forms are often written:

4. a. *They'd better do it.*   [ðeɪd ˈbetə ˈduː ɪt]
    b. *We've finished.*   [wiv ˈfɪnɪʃt]
    c. *There'll be trouble.*   [ðeəɫ bi ˈtrʌbɫ]

But contracted forms often have a pronunciation in which the long vowel or diphthong is replaced by the short vowel which is closest in quality. In fact, *they're* is pronounced [ðɛə] (rhyming with *there*) and should never be allowed to rhyme with *player*. Here are examples with the short vowel qualities:

5. a. *They'd better do it.*   [ðed ˈbetə ˈduːˌɪt]
    b. *They're doing it for us.*   [ðe ˈduɪŋɪt fəˈrˌʌs]
    c. *There'll be trouble.*   [ðeɫ bi ˈtrʌbɫ]

The contracted forms *there's*, *there'll* and *there've* can even go one step further and have their own weak form in which the vowel is [ə]:

6. a. *There's nobody there.*   [ðəz ˈnəʊbədɪ ˈðeə]
    b. *There's none left.*   [ðəz ˈnʌn ˈleft]
    c. *There'll be trouble.*   [ðəɫ bi ˈtrʌbɫ]

Fig. 3: [ð ð ðəzə ˈspaɪdər̩ ɪn ðə ˈbɑːθ] (Priestley & Riddell: Bestiary)

Contracted forms of auxiliary verbs + *not* have a pronunciation all of their own. Fortunately the pronunciation is reflected in the way they are written:

7. a. *That can't be right.*   [ðæt ˈkɑːnt bi ˈraɪt]
    b. *I won't do it.*   [aɪ ˈwəʊnt ˈduː ɪt]
    c. *We shan't come then.*   [wi ˈʃɑːnt ˈkʌm ðen]

After a word-final [t] the contracted forms of *has*, *does* and *is* are identical: the voiceless alveolar fricative [s]. Fortunately, ambiguities are usually avoided by the rest of the sentence. Look at the following examples:

8. a. *What's he doing now?*   [ˈwɒtsi duɪŋ ˈnaʊ]   *(is)*
    b. *What's he done that for?*   [ˈwɒtsi dʌn ˈðæt fɔː]   *(has)*

c. *What's he do at the weekend?*   [ˈwɒtsi ˌduː‿ət ðə wiːˈkend]   *(does)*

You should now be able to appreciate the caption accompanying the following photograph.

What's a tuna
fisherman urn?
This 4th-century
BC Graeco-Sicilian
vase shows
precisely how tuna
should be sliced

Fig. 4: [ˈwɒtsə ˈtjuːnə ˌfiʃəməˈn̩ ɜːn]

Not accented but unreduced!

Although weak, contracted forms are the most likely pronunciation of grammatical items in a sentence, there are a number of cases where the strong form is required. The exact conditions under which a strong form is required are quite complex. The following five rules should help to account for most of the examples you will encounter. Always compare the a. examples with b. ones:

(i)   The strong form of a preposition is used when it is not directly followed by its object (this is often phrase-final position).

   a. *He's the last person I'd have given it to.* [hiz ðə ˈlɑːs pɜːsn̩ aɪdəv ˈgɪvn̩ɪt tuː]
   b. *I gave it to Kevin.*   [aɪ ˈgeɪvɪt tə ˈkevɪn]
   a. *What on earth did you do that for?*   [wɒtɒˈn̩ ɜːθ dɪd jə du ˈðæt fɔː]
   b. *I only did it for you.*   [aɪ ˈəʊnli dɪdɪt fə ˈjuː]

We said "directly followed by its object". We might have said "immediately followed by its object", because when a speaker hesitates on *to* as a preposition or an infinitive marker, he automatically changes [tə] into [tuː], since the one thing you must not do is to have an extended weak form with a schwa. So the fluent "*I would like to go to London.*" [aɪd ˈlaɪk tə gəʊ tə ˈlʌndən] becomes "*I would like to ... to ... go to ... to ... London*"[aɪd ˈlaɪk tuː tuː gəʊ tuː tuː ˈlʌndən]. This is of special interest to learners, because as a learner one is bound to hesitate at these junctions: *"I would like to ... to ... (now what was the word for `stornier-en´ again?)."* So <u>un</u>learn to say: *[aɪd ˈlaɪk təː təː gəʊ təː təː ˈlʌndn̩].

(ii) The strong form of an auxiliary verb is usually used if the main verb is missing (making the auxiliary phrase-final). If the subject and auxiliary verb are inverted, the weak form can still be used.

    a. *I can.* [ˈaɪ kæn]
    b. *Who can go tomorrow?* [ˈhuː kən gəʊ təˈmɒrəʊ] and: *So can I.* [ˈsəʊ kəˈnaɪ]

    a. *What a clever girl I am!* [wɒtə ˈklevə gɜː ˈɭ aɪ æm]
    b. *So am I.* [ˈsəʊəˈmaɪ]

(iii) In a sequence of two auxiliary verbs without a main verb (a) the strong form of the first is used. With a main verb, both auxiliaries may be weak (b).

    a. *I would have.* [ˈaɪ ˌwʊdəv]
    b. *I'd have gone as well if you'd waited.* [ˈaɪdəv gɒnəz ˈwelˌɪf jud ˈweɪtɪd]

(iv) The strong form must always be used for stressed grammatical items.

    a. *London's <u>the</u> place to be.* [ˈlʌndənz ˈðiː pleɪs tə ˈbiː]
    b. *<u>That</u>'s the way to do it.* [ˈðæts ðə weɪ tə ˈduːˌɪt]

    a. *Why did they give her a second chance?* [ˈwaɪ dɪd ðeɪ ˈgɪvərə ˈsekənd ˈtʃɑːns]
    b. *Why did they do it to <u>her</u> of all people?* [ˈwaɪ dɪd ðeɪ duːˌɪt tə ˈhɜːrəvˌɔːɫ ˈpiːpɫ]

(v) With the auxiliary *do*, the strong form is used as an emphatic strengthener (example a. i.) or to `carry´ *not* if there is no other auxiliary verb (a. ii.). Used as an unnegated question auxiliary (example b. i.), it is used in its weak form, unless a clear emphasis of the question is required, and there is no other question element to place the emphasis on (b. ii.):

    a. i. *They <u>do</u> make a lot of fuss.*   [ðeɪ ˈduː meɪkə lɒtəv ˈfʌs] and
       ii. *They don't make a lot of fuss.*   [ðeɪ ˈdəʊnt meɪkə lɒtəv ˈfʌs]
    b. i. *Do they make a lot of fuss?*   [də ðeɪ ˈmeɪkə lɒtəv ˈfʌs]
       ii. *<u>Do</u> they have malaria? (I doubt it)* [ˈduː ðeɪ hæv məˈleəriə]

C 4/E 1: Pair work. Read through the following excerpt from an interview. N.B. this is genuine English, i.e. an unedited passage of what the speaker actually said, including *ums `n´ ahs* and hesitations. Try to mark the weak and contracted forms, which we have intentionally written in full. Try to work out whether any of the grammatical items in the excerpt might be in their strong form and why. Compare your findings with your neighbour trying to come to an agreement on any discrepancies before listening to the recording. When you check the solutions at the end of the book you will see that there are often several possibilities. To give you an example: At the end of the passage the speaker says *"looking at"* three times. Whether she uses the strong or the weak form is not a question of correctness, it is determined partly by aspects of tempo: When she hesitates she tends to use the strong form, but when she knows what she wants to say she races on and uses the weak form.

> *Likewise we have always been uhm r-really concerned that e that the language support teachers, our language support teachers out in school are as knowledgable as they can possibly be. So we have always run a training course for them and and that is quite unusual; there's not many places left who get the resources to do that and we have been very lucky in Redbridge that the council have actually given us the money to to run this, and it is a year-long course that they do for an afternoon and an evening a week and uhm it covers all sorts of areas from ... English ... teaching English as an additional language, looking at issues around bilingualism, looking at racism and an anti-racist curriculum, looking at the needs of black pupils ...*

E 2: After that rather serious interlude, take a look at the dialogue in the following cartoon. Although English words are being used, you will probably not understand a thing at first. But read the dialogue aloud to yourself or to the person next to you, and try to work out what is said. The faster you read, the easier it gets. If you still cannot make any sense of it all, check the solution in chapter XII.

(from: KREK WAITER'S SPEAK BRISTLE, ed. by D. Robson, Abson Books, Bristol 1988)

VI.4. Assimilation and elision: *Can a leopard change its spots?*

In III.4. we talked about distinctive sounds, whose only function was to distinguish meaning. Notice the word "distinguish". These phonological units have no meaning in themselves (the smallest linguistic unit that *carries* meaning is the *morpheme*), but they have the function of distinguishing meaningful units. Minimal word pairs like *bat* and *bad* and like *tense* and *dense* are immediately recognized as different words because /t/ and /d/ are distinctive sounds. The question we want to ask in this section is: Do these distinctive sounds always retain their phonetic identity? Or put differently, is it true to say: once a phoneme, always a phoneme?

We say that "a leopard *cannot* change its spots" when we want to stress that people cannot really change their nature. Speech sounds are not leopards, of course, and that could be the reason why, unlike leopards they *can* change! At first, it may seem like a contradiction in terms to you. Speech sounds are different from one another so that words can be kept distinct. That is why the concept of the phoneme developed. We can communicate our news, observations, thoughts and feelings to one another because sounds are different and distinguish words. So, the natural thing to assume is that if one sound can change into another, the words will lose their identity, and communication will become even more difficult than it already is.

But what about phrases like:

1   a. *Come and get it!*   b. *Stand back!*   c. *What has happened?*
     d. *Pull the plug.*   e. *Close the door!*   f. *But of course!*
     g. *I can do it!*

Say them slowly and distinctly and the words have the sounds you would expect when you look them up in the pronouncing dictionary. But say them in the normal fluent way that befits the situation in which they might occur, and some of them take on a different form:

2   a. [ˈkʌmənd ˈgetɪt] → [ˈkʌməŋ ˈgetɪt]   b. [ˈstænd ˈbæk] → [ˈstæm: ˈbæk]
     c. [ˈwɒt həz ˈhæpənd]→[ˈwɒts ˈhæpmd]
     d. [ˈpʊɫ ðə ˈplʌg] → [ˈpʊɫ̪ ðə ˈplʌg]   e. [ˈkləʊz ðə ˈdɔː] → [ˈkləʊz zə ˈdɔː]
     f. [bʌt ʔəv ˈkɔːs] → [bʌtəf ˈkɔːs]   g. [aɪ kən ˈduː ɪt] → [aɪkŋ ˈduːˠɪt]

Of course, *and, stand, the* or *of* cannot be pronounced [əŋ], [stæm:], [zə] and [əf] in isolation, but as soon as you add context, the changes of phonetic shape are "explained", and the brain accepts them as contextual variants of the fully formed words. In fact, the brain *notices* if the articulatorily normal economy of movement does *not* occur; the result sounds over-precise.

As we explained in section VI.2 and 3., this is because languages tend to use the difference between accented and unaccented words to direct the listeners' attention to the informationally important parts of the utterance. That is why most of the examples given above are weak forms that are not only reduced – in duration, or timbre, or by losing a sound (elision) – but also *assimilated* to their contexts; i.e. they *mould* themselves into their contexts:

In 2a., the /n/ of the reduced *and* changes from an alveolar to a velar nasal ([ŋ]) in preparation for the velar onset consonant /g/ of the informationally more important *get*.

Has can be reduced by the elision of /hæ/ to a single fricative sound because there can be no confusion between *is* and *has* in 2c., and the fricative is pronounced as voiceless [s] after the voiceless plosive [t] of *what*.

After the word *close* in 2e., the /ð/ of *the* can assimilate to the alveolar [z] because there can be no doubt about the identity of the definite article before the noun *door* (and in this case there is a word *clothe* which would make the phrase sound strange if the assimilation went the other way!).

Assimilation can go the other way, as we see in 2d. *Pull the plug.* The /l/ in *pull* is articulated as an interdental [ɬ] before *the* because an /l/ sounds no different whether it is dental or alveolar, so there is no danger of the important word *pull* being distorted.

As this last example shows, it is not only the weakly pronounced function words that modify their form to fit in with their contexts. There is an overall need for an utterance to be produced smoothly, and with the avoidance of unnecessary articulatory effort. This means that the same principles of articulatory economy apply to content words. The modified form of *happened* in 2c. shows that the principle applies within words as well as at the boundaries between words. However, it is vital that the informationally more important words can still be recognised from their phonetic form because they are not predictable from their context in the same way that function words are. In *happened*, the unstressed <en> syllable can be reduced (schwa elision) to a syllabic nasal that is assimilated to the preceding /p/ without any risk at all of the word being misidentified. In 2b., the change in the word *stand* to [stæmb] before the /b/ of the stressed word *back* cannot cause any confusion because there is no such word as **stamb*. In a sentence such as *"You can only sin consciously"*, however, we might predict that the assimilation of /n/ in the word *sin* to the initial /k/ of *consciously* is less likely because the word *sing* also exists. As a verb it fits the syntactic context, and it could plausibly fit that semantic frame.

You may have noticed that nearly all the assimilatory changes to place of articulation that we have discussed have affected the alveolar sounds, and the only one that was not alveolar (the change of [ð] to [z]) also involved the tongue tip. This is no coincidence. The alveolar place of articulation is recognised as being particularly susceptible to modification, and that applies not only to English but also to German (as in *"Hast Du einen Moment Zeit?"* in the pronunciation [ˈhasd̥ʊəməˈmɛnˈtsaɪt]). The other regularity that you may have noticed is that a large proportion of the changes have been *word-final assimilation* to the initial consonant of the next word.

Interdental /t, d, n, l/: [ˈʃʌt̪ðə ˈdɔ:] vs. [ˈkləʊzə ˈdɔ:]

As you will recall from 2e., [ˈkləʊzə ˈdɔ:] is acceptable, but *[ˈʃʌtzə ˈdɔ:] certainly not. So the most important assimilation phenomenon for you to practise – because it occurs in stressed words as well as unstressed ones, and because it involves a non-German combination of word-final and word-initial consonants – is the adaptation of word-final alveolars to word-initial interdental fricative (/θ/ and /ð/). This is one of the cases where you cannot hear when it is done *correctly*, because dental /t, d, n, l/ sound like normal alveolars. But you *should* notice if they are not pronounced dentally preceding /θ/ and /ð/ because the transition from the alveolar to the interdental place of articulation would not sound so smooth. That is why many German speakers of English either find <th> difficult, or they produce a smooth transition by staying in the alveolar position and consequently produce a sort of /z/, which is not acceptable except after /z/ (see the *close* example) and in *months*, where [mʌnθs] is often replaced by [mʌns] in fast speech. Practice the following poem to condition yourself to pronouncing interdental [t̪, d̪, n̪, l̪] before /θ/ and /ð/:

E 1: *A talented thinker in Thrace*
Had thought that the whole human race
Should throw all their riches
To the tramps in the ditches,
With the thought that they'd then have more space.

"Labial" and "velar" /t, d, n/

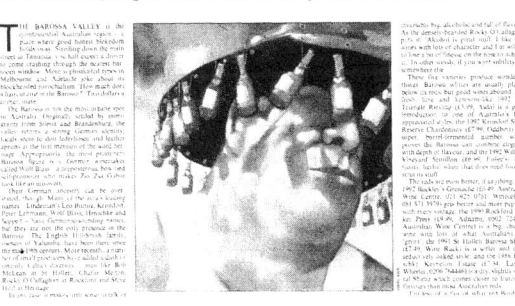

Grape blokes

Far from being as rough as their surroundings, the wines of the Barossa Valley are among Australia's finest, and like their makers, have great character. TIM ATKIN wouldn't give a XXXX for anything else

Fig. 1: *Grape blokes* are *great blokes*

/t, d/ and /n/ only become assimilated to labial and velar places of articulation if the degree of unstressing and the rate of articulation is sufficient. We
find evidence that such changes have always occurred in words like *impossible*, where the negative particle *in* has been orthographically frozen in its
assimilated form. Of course, in words like *incorrect* [ɪŋkəˈrekt], the nasal is also
permanently assimilated to the following plosive (though orthographically
orientated purists may claim that the spelling pronunciation [ɪnkəˈrekt] is
what we ought to say), but the spelling remains <n> instead of the incorrect
<ingcorrect>.

Under the same influence, many words ending in /n/ are assimilated in
fluent speech, so *on course* becomes [ɒŋ ˈkɔːs], and *in part* becomes [ɪm ˈpɑːt].
Also, /t/s and /d/s can assimilate to a labial or velar place of articulation if
the speech rate is favourable. It is important to realise that such assimilations
are not *incorrect* and a sign of the *decay of the language*, but that there is a style
and a place for the different degrees of accommodation.

C 1/E 2: Read the following phrases aloud in different styles; starting with a
careful rendering, *without* assimilation, and then progressing to a fairly fast,
fluent version *with* the full assimilation indicated in the transcription. Compare your own production with the recordings.

a. *He has gone missing.*   [hiz gɒm‿ˈmɪsɪŋ]
b. *They soon capitulated.*   [ðeɪ suːŋ‿kəˈpɪtjəleɪtɪd]
c. *She always rode carefully.*   [ʃiʲ ˈɔːɬwɪz rəʊg‿ˈkɛəfli]
d. *We did not find many.*   [wi dɪdn̩ faɪm‿ˈmeni]
e. *Let go if you can.*   [lek‿ˈgəʊʷɪf jə ˈkæn]
f. *They soon hit back.*   [ðeɪ ˈsuːn hɪp‿ˈbæk]

Gotcha!

You may have noticed an extreme form of assimilation that is fairly widespread in colloquial English, which turns a word-final /t/ and a word-initial
/j/ into a [tʃ]. What happens is a fronting and devoicing of the palatal glide
/j/ under the influence of the /t/. It has been stylized in games of tag, when
the person chasing the others catches one of them, and announces *"Gotcha!"*
([ˈgɒtʃə]). But it may be heard in the casual question "Whatcha doing?", which
can be derived from the sequence of reductions and assimilations:

3.   *What are you doing?* [ˈwɒtə ju ˈduːɪŋ] →*What ye doing?* [ˈwɒt jə ˈduːɪŋ] →
     Whatcha doing? [ˈwɒtʃə ˈduːɪŋ]

It is not essential to learn to speak with this degree of assimilation, but you
may find it amusing to shift the register of your pronunciation and use it on
occasions. The following phrases (4a-e) may be useful if a suitable opportunity arises:

4   a. *Have you brought your handbag?*   [ˈbrɔːtʃə]
     b. *Where did you get your nose-ring?*   [dɪdʒə ˈgetʃə]

c. *Put your money where your mouth is!*   [pʊtʃə]
d. *Sit yourself down, mate!*   [ˈsɪtʃəseɬf]
e. *Get yourself a drink.*   [ˈɡetʃəseɬf]

The shift of register just mentioned is in fact an important reason for you to familiarise yourself with these assimilations even if you do not use the extremer forms actively in your own speech. If you are not familiar with them, you may well have difficulty understanding everyday English conversation. All levels of English can occur, and unfamiliar forms can interrupt your understanding, just like the early beginnings in English, when you probably wondered "Is this the same language I have been taught at school?" when you first heard English people talking to one another.

VII. Morphology and morphophonology: The internal make-up of words

E 1: To whet your appetite, we have written a short dialogue between two male chauvinists for you to read aloud (and record it, if you can):

> *A: The minutes from our last meeting were very elaborate down to every minute detail, and certainly not comparable with the slovenly records that Deborah kept.*
> *B: Absolutely, and she was unfriendly with the customers, too. I think the prevalent opinion amongst us top executives is that badly-trained personnel is the recipe for desaster...*
> *A: ... a catastrophe. After all, we are not a benevolent institution, that´s why I had to make the proposal of dismissing her...*
> *B: ... and that´s why I seconded it. She could have been seconded to the stock taking department, but she doesn´t know how to make an inventory. Of course we had to reconcile our views with those of the shop-stewards, but in the end the decision was unanimous.*
> *A: They even wanted to upgrade her!*
> *B: That´s when you came up with that brilliantly equivocal remark: "She can´t go far enough." Admirable rhetoric.*

Now turn to chapter XII. and check your pronunciation against the solution suggested there. We assume you will be up against a number of surprises because E 1 is a nasty concoction with our students´ favourite mistakes as ingredients. We did not give it to you in order to show you up, but because we wanted to raise your language awareness. You may have thought, e.g., that *unanimous* consisted of the prefix *un-* plus *animous*. The *un-* in this word is, however, derived from *united*, and *unanimous* is pronounced [juˈnænɪməs] and means *einstimmig*. In this jungle of words that use mimicry to look like other words, it is important to become aware of the ploys used by the English language to trick poor foreigners. To drive home this message we have written another skit that makes fun of people who find that *morphophonology* is not exactly a household term

1. *Morphophonology: a bit of a mouthful*

> *Excuse me, sir, will we get more phonology in this course? - No, morphology. - What´s "phology"? - No, that word doesn´t exist. I didn´t say "more phology", I said "morphology" - Sorry? - You know, as opposed to morphophonology. Right? - Oh please, not more phophonology when we haven´t even fully understood nology. - What´s a nology? - A nology? Surely you mean "analogy".*

Confused? Okay, let us take a break here. The problem with the above conversation is that these two people have different ideas as to where the word boundaries are and what constitutes the individual elements these words are made up of. These are **morphological** criteria: **Morphology** is the study of the internal make-up of words in terms of grammatical analysis. The word *kitchen* consists of two phonetically defined syllables, but neither [kɪ] nor [tʃən] nor any other portion of *kitchen* constitute grammatical elements. But if you now look at *kitchens* or hear [ˈkɪtʃənz], you recognise the letter <-s> and the sound [z], respectively, as the plural ending, which means that the form *kitchens* consist of two morphological units: the noun *kitchen* and the plural ending. These two units are called morphemes. **Morphemes** are the smallest units in a word that can be analysed in terms of grammar.

There are different kinds of morphemes. First, we can distinguish between free and bound morphemes. **Free morphemes** are units that may or do form a word without any other morphemes, and **bound morphemes** are units that cannot constitute a word in its own right. Take *kitchen-sink*, which consists of two free morphemes, i.e. the words *kitchen* + *sink*; or *kitchenette*, which consists of the free morpheme *kitchen* and the bound morpheme *-ette*, which you add to a noun to derive a new word with the meaning *a small one of those*. When you add grammatical endings like plural <-s> or past tense <-ed> to a word, you do not form a new word but only inflect the noun or verb respectively. Bound morphemes may thus be divided into **inflectional morphemes** like <-s> and **derivational** morphemes like <-ette>.

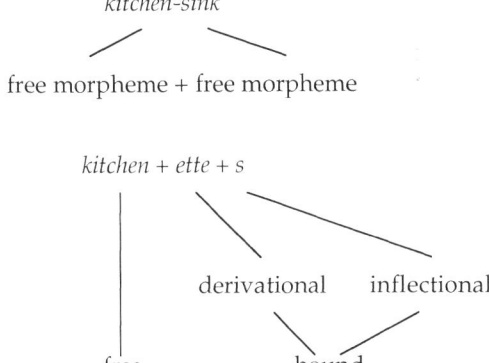

Fig. 1: derivational and inflectional, free and bound morphemes

In VII.1.1.&2. we will discuss various ways of <u>pronouncing</u> inflectional morphemes like plural <-s> and past tense <-ed>. Since this deals with both phonological and morphological units, this is referred to as **morphophonology**.

VII.1. The sounds of grammar

VII.1.1. Regular past tense and past participle endings: *Have you ever wished you were better informed?*

Fig. 1: A sundial in pouring rain: [hæv ju‿ˈevə ˈwɪʃt ju wə ˈbetər‿ɪnˈfɔːmd]

What the above advertisement teaches us is that dark clouds are the wrong medium for sundials. And letters are the wrong medium for teaching sounds. It is the old story: the young and inexperienced teacher walks briskly into the classroom and informs his students: "The regular past tense and past participle in English is formed by adding `-ed´. That's easy, so let's have a go. Karen, the past tense of `I wish you a Merry Christmas´ is?" - "I wished you a Merry Christmas." "Good. Now Sven, the past tense of `I inform you´ is?" - "I informed you." – Everybody is happy, but you cannot teach somebody what the colour *mauve* looks like by informing them how the word is spelled. By analogy, you cannot expect Sven to know how *informed* is pronounced by telling him that you add <u>the letters</u> <-ed>. Had we given you the above conversation in phonetic transcription, you would have <u>seen</u> that Karen pronounced *wished* correctly as [wɪʃt] and Sven pronounced *informed* incorrectly as *[ɪnˈfɔːmt]. How were either of the two to know how to pronounce <-ed>?

The lesson to be learned from this sketch is embarrassingly simple: If you want your students to be able to pronounce the grammatical units you are talking about, use the spoken medium to demonstrate how to pronounce these units.

Let us assume, for the sake of argument, that your class consists of intelligent but completely illiterate German-speaking students. You could start by saying: *"Today, children play with computers, but in 1950, children played with toys."*

The students only hear [pleɪ] and [pleɪd]. You then devise similar pairs of sentences with present and past tenses of the verbs

1a.   ['træv̩], [plæn], [əd'vaɪz], [fɪə], [stæb], [klaɪm] and [lɒŋ].

You could then draw the students' attention to what these (carefully selected) verbs have in common: they all end in a voiced sound. You can demonstrate this by artificially prolonging the last sound of each verb, holding the fingers against the larynx so you can feel the vibration of the vocal folds as you say

1b.   [træv̩ɬɬ], [plænnn], [əd'vaɪzzz], [fɪə::], [klaɪmmm] and [lɒŋŋŋ].

And then you tell the students about assimilation: since you have the vocal folds vibrating anyway, keep them going and add the voiced plosive [d] to get

1c.   ['træv̩d], [plænd], [əd'vaɪzd], [fɪəd], [stæbd], [klaɪmd] and [lɒŋd].

It is true that this plosive is usually devoiced, but from a didactic point it is not a good idea to labour the fact at this stage. Remember that with all the verbs under 1a.-c. the danger with native speakers of German is to shorten the vowel and to replace the final lenis sound by a fortis one to get * [hɪ 'klaɪmt ə tri:] and *[ðeɪ 'lɒŋt fə 'pi:s]. This is particularly irritating if you get an accumulation of mistakes, i.e. the shortening of the syllable, the replacement of a final lenis sound by a fortis sound, and then, for example, the typically German replacement of [æ] by [e], so that the intended

2a.   *He was stabbed to death.* [hi wəz 'stæbd tə deθ]

will be interpreted by a native speaker of English as

2b.   *He was stepped to death.* [hi wəs 'stept tə deθ]

And this brings us to the next rule for the pronunciation of past tenses. You now use examples like

3.   *Today typists work with computers, in 1970 they worked with typewriters.*

As you did not write down these verb forms the students only hear: [wɜ:k] and [wɜ:kt]. You then go on with similar present tense/past tense oppositions using the verbs

4a.   [heɬp], [stɒp], [həʊp], [pɑ:s], [wɪʃ], [sæk], [kɒf] and [dɑ:ns]

What all these words have in common is a final voiceless consonant. If you now apply the principle of assimilation, the voiced plosive [d] gets replaced by its homorganic voiceless counterpart [t] with the past tense forms

4b.   [heɬpt], [stɒpt], [həʊpt], [pɑ:st], [wɪʃt], [sækt], [kɒft] and [dɑ:nst]

As German speakers are not used to voiced stops (or plosives) at the end of a word (remember that German *Bund* and *bunt* sound the same), it is best to start teaching the 1c past tense forms. Once the learners have mastered these they will find the 4b past tense forms easy. The wrong application of [d] after, say, [pɑ:s] or [wɪʃ] is never a problem with German learners.

Let us once again remind you of the "Let´s pretend" game that every teacher teaching the spoken medium first should play: We pretend the class is illiterate. For these learners the verb *climb* ends with the sound [m], because that is all the information they have. And the verb *decide* ends in the sound [d]. As every learner will readily see, it would be decidedly odd to pronounce the past tense form as *[dɪˈsaɪdd]. So we need a third past tense rule: for ease of pronunciation you add [ɪd] to the stem of verbs ending in an alveolar plosive, i.e. in either [d] or [t]. So you get

5.   [dɪˈsaɪd] and [dɪˈsaɪdɪd]; [fɪt] and [fɪtɪd]

> **Infobox**
>
> In English there is an exponent for *regular* past tense forms. This is called a past tense **morpheme** and it is an abstract unit. In terms of the spoken medium, this morpheme is represented by the three **allomorphs** [d], [t] or [ɪd]. In terms of the written medium the *regular* past tense form is <*-ed*>. To illustrate the difference we can say for the written medium that in terms of the rule "Add <*-ed*> to the infinitive", the following verbs are exceptions: *decide, hope, dance, love, hurry, pity, die, argue* and *plan*, because in none of these cases can you form the past tense by simply adding `-ed`. In terms of morphophonology they are regular.

A word of warning: should you ever wish to buy *corned beef* in England, avoid the pronunciation of the English loanword in German. It is not * [ˈkɔːnet ˌbiːf], which most Englishmen would find either amusing or incomprehensible. The correct pronunciation is the regularly formed [kɔːnd ˈbiːf].

E 1:   a. Rewrite [ðə ˈpɑːstəv ˈpɑːsɪz ˈpɑːst] into normal spelling

b. Which of the past tense forms *burnt, scorched, charred, singed, toasted* in the above cartoon is not regular in terms morphophonology?

E 2:   a. Give a phonetic transcription of: *We discussed the problem, argued about possible solutions, and decided that we wanted more information.*

b. Analyse the past tense forms of this passage in terms of phonetics and morphology and explain the rules for the pronunciation of regular simple past tense endings.

VII.1.2. Plural, simple pres. tense 3rd pers. sing., and genitive: *How to kill three birds with one stone*

The inexperienced teacher walks briskly into the classroom and informs her students: *"The regular plural is formed by adding an `s`."* Does that sound familiar to you? We used a similar example in the previous section to illustrate the impossibilty of teaching the spoken medium through the written medium. Look at two illustrations that were used in a textbook for the practice of plural forms. Fig. 1a was published in 1970, and figs. 1b&c in a revised edition 1975. What we want you to think about is: why was the first illustration changed?

Fig. 1b

Fig. 1a   Fig. 1c

Einführungskurs zu ENGLISH H1 1970&1975. By permission of Cornelsen-Velhagen&Klasing Berlin

The answer is that if you want pupils to do written exercises 1a is sufficient, if, on the other hand, you want the pupils to talk about these things, you need to take morphophonology into account, which is the whole point of having two groups of things in 1b and 1c. The ones in 1b all end in voiced sounds, the ones in 1c in voiceless sounds. (1a contains a mixed bunch.) As you are familiar with the principle of assimilation you will be able to predict the rules:

1   a. after a voiced ending of the stem, as in [bɜːd], you add [z] to get [bɜːdz]
     b. after a voiceless ending, as in [stɪk], you add [s] to get [stɪks].
     c. after [s], [z], [ʃ], [ʒ], [tʃ] and [dʒ] you add [ɪz] to get [ˈbʌsɪz], [ˈbʌzɪz], [ˈbuʃɪz], [məˈsɑːʒɪz], [ˈmætʃɪz] and [ˈbrɪdʒɪz].

From a didactic point of view it is best to start with rule 1a., because firstly German does not have a voiced [z] at the end of words, and secondly there are many loanwords that have become germanised in terms of phonetics, like the slogan *Hits für Kids* (as pointed out in IV.1.), where the two nouns rhyme in German, but not in English: [ˈhɪts fə kɪdz].

Fig 2: These words do not rhyme in English: [ˈbetə ˈʤɒbz ˈfjuːə ˈflɒps]

Fig. 3:

[ˌprɪti ˈmeɪdz]

or [ˌprɪti ˈmeɪts]?

If – as a man – you said *my mates*, then *mates* would refer to males, to which the term *pretty* can only be applied with an accompanying innuendo about their sexual preference. With a foreign accent you might not just communicate that you are German but also other unintended messages.

[ˈjuərəu ˌsnæk bɑː:
ˌəupmfə
ˈtiː ˈkɒfiː ˈsæmwʤəz
rəuɫz
ˈbrekfəst
ˌhɒt ˈpaɪz ˈsælədz
ˈhɒt ˌʤækɪt pəˈteɪtəuz
keɪks ˌkænd ˈdrɪŋks
iːˈtɪnɔ: teɪkəˈweɪ]

Fig. 4 Examples of all three rules of 1a.-c. on one and the same board

E 1: Transcribe the nouns in these sentences phonetically and analyse the plural forms in terms of phonetics and morphology explaining the rules for the pronunciation of regular plural endings:

　　a. *After the two phoneticians had won many prizes in several competitions they were able to afford the prices for new tapes to record speeches.*

　　b. *The students crossed the bridges of both rivers to visit the churches on the southern hills.*

E 2: give a phonetic transcription of the following proverb:

　　Sticks and stones will break my bones, but words will never hurt me.

E 3: read aloud:

This listener from radio Devizes,	[ðɪs ˈlɪsənə frəm ˈreɪdiəʊ dɪˈvaɪzəz
had ears of two different sizes;	hæˈdɪəzəv ˈtuː dɪfrənt ˈsaɪzəz
one was so small	ˈwʌn wəz səʊ ˈsmɔː⁺
it heard nothing at all,	ɪt hɜːd ˈnʌθɪŋəˈtɔː⁺
but the other won several prizes.	bət ðiˈʌðə wʌn ˈsevərə⁺ ˈpraɪzəz]

In the title of this subsection we suggested that it was possible to kill three birds with one stone, and indeed, the morphophonological rules for the three morphemes for (a) plural, (b) simple present tense third person singular, and (c) genitives are identical. You may like to apply the rules of plural allomorphs to those of the third person in the following advertisement:

E 4: give a phonetic transcription of this text that advertised a concert.

　　"Where the spirit of rock speaks to you, sings to you, plays for you, moves and touches you."

E 5: Give a phonetic transcription of the nouns in the genitive and in the plural.

　　If Harrison´s, Woodcock´s and Fudge´s videos are removed from the shops they will appeal to the judges.

E 6: Read this traditional limerick aloud, making sure you pronounce the plural allomorphs in *methods, gallons,* and *i´s,* and also the present tense allomorphs of *there´s, tries, says,* and *saves* as [z]:

There´s a clever old miser who always tries	[ðəzə ˈklevərəʊ⁺d ˈmaɪzə huˡʷɔː⁺weɪz
	ˈtraɪz
different methods and ways to economize.	dɪfrənt ˈmeθədzən ˈweɪztuˡʷiˈkɒnəmaɪz
So he says with a wink,	səʊi ˈsez wɪðə ˈwɪŋk
"One saves gallons of ink	wʌn seɪvz ˈgælənz‿əˈvɪŋk
by simply not dotting one´s i´s."	baɪ ˈsɪmpli nɒt ˈdɒtɪŋ wʌnˈz‿aɪz]

(The last line refers to the expression *"to dot one's i's and cross one's t's"*, meaning *"to pay attention to every detail"*. We apologize for the originator's awkward rhythm!)

VII.1.3. /ŋ/ <ng>: Why doesn't "finger" rhyme with "singer"?

In Harry Belafonte´s song, the lines *"... don´t linger, put that wedding ring on your finger"* contain four occurrences of the letter sequence <ng>. All word-final <ng>s, like the ones of *wedding* and *ring*, are pronounced just like the final sound in German *Ring*. This sound is a **velar nasal** represented by the phonetic symbol [ŋ] (see section IV.3.6.).

Belafonte could not have sung: *"Fall in love with the handsome young singer, put a wedding ring on his finger"*, because *singer* ['sɪŋə] and *finger* ['fɪŋgə] do not rhyme: in the second word the nasal [ŋ] is followed by the plosive [g]. As both sounds have the velum as their place of articulation they are said to be homorganic. The articulation of the sound sequence [ŋg] should not cause any problems, because many German speakers pronounce *Tango, Ingo* and *Känguruh* with [ŋg], and you certainly hear the [ŋ] followed by a [g] in *Ingrid*. The problem arises because Germans know that neither *Sänger* nor *singer* have the velar plosive [g], and then tend to wrongly extend the analogy from German *Finger* ['fɪŋɐ] to English *finger* ['fɪŋgə]. How do native speakers of Southern British English know when to add a [g]? There *must* be rules, or else they would not be able to remember how to pronounce the hundreds of words with <ng>. The rules are based on morphology: *singer* consists of the free morpheme *sing* [sɪŋ], which happens to be a verb, and the bound morpheme *-er* [ə], which is used to derive nouns from verbs. The morphophonological rule is: you simply stick those two morphemes together to get [sɪŋə]. *finger* on the other hand is **monomorphemic**, i.e. it consists of only one morpheme, as there is no free morpheme **fing*. If <ng> occurs within a morpheme it is pronounced [ŋg].

Let us now apply this rule. You may not be familar with the word *wringer*, but if you know that there is a verb *wring*, you know how to pronounce the derived noun: ['rɪŋə] (an old-fashioned contraption with two rollers for pressing water from clothes). *clanger*, as in the idiomatic phrase *"He really dropped a clanger there"* (*"Da hat er richtig in den Fettnapf getreten"*), is derived from *clang* and is therefore pronounced ['klæŋə]. *monger*, as in *fishmonger, scaremonger* and *warmonger*, seems to have the suffix *-er*, but as there is no verb **to mong* from which you might derive them, the nouns are treated as monomorphemic and are pronounced with [ŋg]: ['fɪʃmʌŋgə].

wrangler consists of two morphemes, but the verb *wrangle* has the <ng> in the middle of the morpheme and is pronounced ['ræŋgɫ], to which you then simply add [ə], yielding ['ræŋglə]. *banger* refers to a cheap old cars and is derived from *bang*, allowing us to predict the pronunciation ['bæŋə], which is different from the monomorphemic name of the Welsh town *Bangor*, pronounced ['bæŋgə]. *hunger, single, anger* and *angle* are all monomorphemic words and contain the sounds [ŋg].

The easy-to-learn words are the ones where both English and German have the [ŋg], as *flamingo, mango, kangaroo* and their German equivalents. The difficult-to-learn words are the ones where the equivalents in the two languages are different; [ŋg] in English, but only [ŋ] in German. This is particularly true in the case of loanwords, because one thinks of these as English words, as in the case of German *Singles* ['sɪŋəls], and then often forgets to translate this "English" word phonetically into English when using it in that language: ['sɪŋɫz]. (Please note that the German loanword displays three phonetic differences: the clear [l], the omission of [g], and the plural [s]. Only the initial voiceless [s] makes a phonetic allowance for its origin.)

E 1: Read aloud: *Female German* ['sɪŋl] *wishes to meet male* ['ɪŋglɪʃ ˌsɪŋɫ]

German [ŋ]	English [ŋg]	German [ŋ]	English [ŋg]
Singles	*singles*	*Dschungel*	*jungle*
Hunger	*hunger*	*Finger*	*finger*
Englisch	*English*	*Jingle Bells*	*Jingle Bells*

Exceptions

So far we have carefully selected our examples so as to exclude **comparative and superlative constructions**, because in terms of morphophonology they are the exceptions. If you have the free morpheme *strong* [strɒŋ] and wish to form the comparative, you do not apply the above rule, but add [g] to get ['strɒŋgə], and ['strɒŋgəst] for the superlative. For *young* you get: *younger* ['jʌŋgə] and *youngest* ['jʌŋgəst], but as this applies only to the comparative and superlative morphemes *-er* and *-est*, but not to other bound morphemes, you simply add [-ɪʃ] to [jʌŋ] to get *youngish* ['jʌŋɪʃ]. (Another exception is the word *hangar*. As it is monomorphemic, you would expect [ŋg], but it is pronounced just like the regular *hanger* (as in *coat hanger*): ['hæŋə].)

E 2: a. Give a phonetic transcription of the following passage, paying particular attention to the words containing the letters <ng>:

Two anglers were fishing off the East Anglian coast. They were getting hungry and tired because they hadn't caught a single fish all day. Suddenly they saw a man, clinging to a plank and shouting: "Hiiilfe". After a while, the younger of the two anglers, who could hardly conceal his anger, because the splashing and shouting scared all the fish away, asked his older mate: "What does that mean: hiiilfe?" - "That's not English, it's German and means 'help'." - Ten minutes later the first chap turned to his friend and suggested: "He should have learned to swim instead of learning foreign languages."

b. Transcribe this sentence phonetically:
I had been longing for a longer holiday, but as the storm grew stronger and stronger we decided to leave Anglesey and go back to Bangor on the mainland.

C 1: listen and repeat:

Tell me, why have you come to England for a holiday? - I'm studying English Language and Literature and I want to improve my spoken English. - Is this your first visit to Inglewood? - No, I've been here before, but this is my longest stay here. Unfortunately I can't afford to attend the summer school because the pound is stronger than I thought. - Ah, once we get the single-currency Europe, that won't be a problem any more. - But there seem to be so many scaremongers, perhaps that will never come. - So what are you doing now? Just mingling with the English and picking up our language? - Yes, and I also watch films on TV, some of the old classics, like "Goldfinger" and "The Longest Day". - What do you consider typically English? - Well, Shakespeare, Buckingham Palace, bingo, fish fingers, and many pop singers. - Oh you mean like Ringo Starr? - No, I belong to a younger generation.

Avoid singin' in the rain.

A word of advice: in pop songs and films you will often hear the ending *-ing* pronounced [-ɪn], orthographically represented as *"Singin' in the rain"*. That is just perfect for your next karaoke presentation of Gene Kelly, but presumably you will not always wish to impersonate Kelly or the Spice Girls. Remember that your English pronunciation should be fairly consistent, and slang, specific dialect or sociolect forms very rarely come across convincingly from foreigners. *"So look 'ere, mate, stop usin' them -in' forms for the time bein' and keep learnin' how to speak English proper, righ'?"*

<ng>, <nk>, <nc> and [ŋ], [ŋg], [ŋk], [nʤ]

The basic rule for <ng> is, as you will recall, [ŋ] at the end of a morpheme (as in *ring* and *singer*), but [ŋg] inside a morpheme (as in *finger* and *anger*). <nk> and <nc> are always pronounced [ŋk]: so it is *ring* [rɪŋ] but *ice rink* [ˈaɪs rɪŋk]; *bring* [brɪŋ], but *on the brink of extinction* [ɒn ðə ˈbrɪŋkəv‿ɪksˈtɪŋkʃn].

<ngl> is pronounced [ŋɫ] (with a "dark" l), as in *single, bungle, angle, dangle, tangle, shingles* and *mingle*, where the /l/ does not precede a vowel, but it is pronounced [ŋgl] in those cases where it does: *bungling, dangling*.

There are some words where the <ng> is pronounced [nʤ]. These just have to be learned, but there are not many and most should be familiar to you any-way because they are high-frequency words, like *danger, endanger, passenger* and *messenger*. But note also: *manger* (G. *Krippe*), *ranger, harbinger* (lit., G. *Bote*), *ginger* (G. *Ingwer*), *the river Ganges* [ˈgændʒiːz], and *Schlesinger* and *Kissinger*.

Smileys:

Dad, can I read in bed until I fall asleep? - Alright, but not a minute longer.

Answer the phone. - It's not ringing. - Why leave everything till the last minute?

What do you call a mushroom who takes you out to dinner? - A fun-gi to be with. (*fungus, fungi* [ˈfʌŋgaɪ]: German *Pilz, Pilze; a fun guy* [ˈfʌnˈgaɪ] or [ˈfʌɲˈgaɪ]

VII.2. Stress and morphology: *More stress!*
contrast "contrast" with "kontrast"

Fig. 1: Wolf learning a foreign language (Punch, Feb 8-14, 1997)

Luckily it is possible to formulate rules about whether bound morphemes affect the stress pattern of the words they are attached to, and if so, how.

Inflectional morphemes do not cause problems: most of them do not even form a syllable, so both *jump* and *jumps* are monosyllabic; and if the inflecting bound morpheme constitutes a syllable in its own right, like *-ing*, for example, it does not change the stress pattern of the word it is added to: both *e'valuate* and *e'valuating* are stressed on the second syllable. There is also a number of derivational suffixes that do not shift the stress of the original word to another syllable, like *-hood* in *motherhood*.

Bound morphemes that do not move the stressed syllable of the original word are called **stress-neutral morphemes**. English examples are the inflectional morphemes *-s, -ed, -ing, -er, -est* and some derivational morphemes, like *-ful* as in [sək'ses] → [sək'sesfʊɫ]. The others are:

Non-neutral morphemes

a. Stress-carrying suffixes

We argued in VI.2. that most English nouns have stress on the first syllable and that this was certainly true of the monomorphemic ones. And we also explained the leftward pull, which favours early stress in words. Let us now assume you want to talk about *cigarettes* but are not quite sure whether the English leftward pull is in operation or not. This would not be surprising, because you may well have heard <u>both</u> stress patterns from native speakers, as Americans tend to put the stress on a different syllable of this word. It helps to know that *cigarette* is not a monomorphemic word and that *-ette* is a bound morpheme which is attached to nouns and means "*a small one of those*". This suffix attracts the main stress of the newly formed word. So for British English you start with *cigar* [- ˡ-], add *-ette* and get [- - ˡ-]. You now have the correct stress pattern, but before you pronounce the word make two further adjustments: firstly, the long [ɑː] of the stressed syllable in [sɪˡgɑː] becomes a reduced vowel in the unstressed second syllable of *cigarette*, and secondly, you must link the <r> to the following vowel to get [sɪgəˡret].

Equipped with this morphophonological knowledge you can now start with the verb *launder* and derive *launderette* from it with a linking "r": [ˡlɔːndə] → [ˌlɔːnˡdret]; or you can talk about a small kitchen [ˡkɪtʃɪn] and call it a *kitchenette* [ˌkɪtʃɪˡnet], or call a small statue [ˡstætʃuː] *statuette* [ˌstætʃuˡet]. You can coin new words and say: "*I had to give a lecture in front of 20 people, well, it was only very informal and a very short one. Only a lecturette, really.*" Manufacturers like to call their new products *Moulinette, Computerette,* etc. This type of word formation takes advantage of the fact that everybody knows what they mean and how to pronounce them. We may have problems with the morphological analysis, when we ask, for instance: "What is the root of *serviette* or *roulette?*" (*servi? roul?*), but we can still safely assume that all nouns ending in *-ette* have the stress on this, i.e. the final syllable, as in *marionette, gazette, cassette,* and also in those formations where *-ette* is not used as a diminutive, but as a feminine suffix, as in *brunette, suffragette* [ˌsʌfrəˡdʒet] (i.e. a woman fighting for suffrage [ˡsʌfrədʒ], the right to vote) and also the names *Colette* and *Paulette.* Advanced students may like to note the two exceptions: *etiquette* [ˡetɪˌket], *palette* [ˡpælət].)

A selection of stress-carrying suffixes for nouns with final stress

-oo: We will concentrate here on words that native speakers of German tend to get wrong, like *kangaroo.* This might be a case of interference with the mother tongue (or a case of negative transfer), as the German word *Kängeruh* has the stress on the first syllable. In English, however, words ending in *-oo* have the stress on this final syllable: *kangaroo* [ˌkæŋgəˡruː], *shampoo, bamboo, ballyhoo* [ˌbæliˡhuː] (where *ˡigloo* is an exception).

-ee: In the above paragraph we deliberately said that putting the stress on the first syllable of *kangaroo* <u>might</u> be due to negative transfer. But the mistake of putting it on the first syllable of *chimpanzee* is harder to explain, because the German word *Schimpanse* is stressed on the second syllable. So perhaps a more plausible explanation is that these speakers have learned that English as a Germanic language tends to put the stress on the first syllable. In the case of these stress bearing suffixes they would now have to unlearn this rule of thumb and say *chimpanzee* [ˌtʃɪmpənˡziː], *dungarees* [dʌŋgəˡriːz] and *settee* [seˡtiː] (German: *Sofa*). This rule also applies to active/passive pairs of nouns like *trainer* [ˡtreɪnə] (as in *teacher trainer,* i.e someone who teaches other people) and *trainee* [treɪˡniː] (i.e. someone who is being taught something), and *interviewer* [ˡɪntəvjuə] vs. *interviewee,* [ˌɪntəvjuˡiː].

-aire: millionaire [ˌmɪljəˈneə] *legionnaire* [ˌliːdʒəˈneə]
-ade: lemonade [ˌleməˈneɪd] and *stockade* [-ˈ-], but remember *marmalade*, which is
the exception: [ˈmɑːməleɪd].
-eer: volunteer, mountaineer, engineer, career
-ese: Chinese [ˌtʃaɪˈniːz] with stress shift in [ˌtʃaɪniːz ˈrestəˌrɒnt], *journalese*
-ess: stewardess [ˌstjuːəˈdes]
-ine: magazine [ˌmægəˈziːn], *submarine*

b. Stress-repelling morphemes

Now let us assume you want to see the film "Titanic" and have a similar
problem as the one described with *cigarette*. The rule you have to learn here is
that the ending *-ic* is used to form adjectives and that it puts the stress on the
syllable preceding it. The titans [ˈtaɪtənz] in Greek mythology were gods of
great size and strength, and somebody or something like them can be called
[taɪˈtænɪk]. So the ending *-ic* changes the stress of the noun it is attached to, but
does not attract stress itself. It is like a water-repellent chemical that cannot
actually stop the water getting closer, but that will not combine with it. This
morphophonological rule says, if a word ends with the bound morpheme *-ic*,
the syllable immediately preceding it must be stressed. And since the schwa
vowel [ə] can never occur in a stressed syllable, you automatically have to
make the vowel adjustment from [ˈtaɪtən] to [taɪˈtæn] before *-ic* to get [taɪˈtænɪk].
The Greek poet´s name Homer [ˈhəʊmə] has the stress on the first syllable, but
the derived adjective *Homeric* moves the stress to the right. To be precise, the
suffix *-ic* moves the stress to the last but one syllable, and this is precisely
where the original word has the schwa vowel, which needs to be adjusted to
the full vowel [e] to get [həʊˈmerɪk]. Other adjectives with stress on the syllable
before *-ic* are: *apologetic, barbaric, fantastic, gigantic*. (An exception is *catholic*
[ˈkæθlɪk]).

Other nouns with the stressed syllable before the suffix are, for instance, the
ones ending in *-ion*: *incomprehension* [- ˌ - ˈ- -], *medallion* [- ˈ- -], *pavilion* [- ˈ- -],
introversion [ˌ- - ˈ- -].

Without an awareness of these principles you would have to learn each word
individually. Let us compare the German suffix *-ismus* with English *-ism*:
German *-ismus* is a non-neutral morpheme, and to be more precise, it is
stress-carrying. In *Alkohol* the stress is on the first syllable and has to be
shifted to [ˈlɪsmʊs] in *Alkoholismus* [ˌ- - - ˈ- -]. The rules for English are as
follows: If the form that *-ism* is added to is a free form, that is a word in its
own right, *-ism* is a stress-neutral morpheme: As the word *alcohol* [ˈæɫkəhɒɫ]
exists the stress remains on the first syllable in [ˈæɫkəhɒlɪzm]. If, however, the
form before *-ism* is not a free form, *-ism* becomes a stress-repellent morpheme
that pushes the stress two syllables to the left. You can now predict the stress
patterns of *Neologismus* and *neologism*. As German *-ismus* is autostressed, the
stress pattern of *Neologismus* has to be [- - - ˈ- -]. As *neolog* does not exist as a

free form, rule two applies, i.e. *-ism* is a stress-repellent morpheme that pushes the stress two syllables to the left to give us [niˈɒlədʒɪzm].

One of the most important rules to remember is that *un-* in English is a stress-neutral prefix and that *un-* in German is a stress-carrying prefix, so you get [ˈfrendli] and [ʌnˈfrendli], but in German you have [ˈfrɔɪntlɪç] but [ˈʊnfrɔɪntlɪç] with a stress shift. *dis-*, too, is a stress-neutral prefix, so you get *appoint* [əˈpɔɪnt] and derive from this [ˌdɪsəˈpɔɪnt] and [ˌdɪsəˈpɔɪntɪd] but not, repeat NOT *[ˈdɪsəpɔɪntɪd], which is a frequently heard mispronunciation.

Infobox

Summary: Morphemes that do not change the stress of the word they are added to are **stress-neutral morphemes** like-*hood*. The ones that do affect stress are called **non-neutral**. There are two types of non-neutral morphemes: 1. Bound derivational morphemes that attract stress – like *-ette* – are called **stress-carrying** (or **autostressed**) **morphemes**. 2. Bound morphemes that move the stress of the word they get attached to, but that do not attract stress to themselves, like *-ic*, are called **stress-repelling morphemes**.

What does a rebel without a cause rebel against?
[ˈwɒt dʌzə ˈrebɫ wɪðautə ˈkɔːz rɪˈbel̩ əˈgenst]

The two occurrences of <*rebel*> are pronounced differently depending on whether it is a verb [rɪˈbeɫ] or a noun [ˈrebɫ]. As you see, the changing of the stress patterns requires further adjustments: The vowel of the prefix changes, and when you put the stress on the second syllable there cannot, of course, be a schwa sound, as schwa never occurs in stressed syllables. Our rather unconventional use of fonts in the title of this section was an attempt to draw your attention to another such pair: the verb *contrast* [kənˈtrɑːst] and the noun [ˈkɒntrɑːst]. Here is a list of such pairs that you need to know:

With change of vowels:

verb	noun		verb	noun
[ɪkˈspɔːt] *export*	[ˈekspɔːt]		[ɪmˈpɔːt] *import*	[ˈɪmpɔːt]
[rɪˈkɔːd] *record*	[ˈrekɔːd]		[səsˈpekt] *suspect*	[ˈsʌspekt]
[kənˈdʌkt] *conduct*	[ˈkɒndʌkt]		[kənˈtest] *contest*	[ˈkɒntest]
[kənˈflɪkt] *conflict*	[ˈkɒnflɪkt]		[kənˈtrɑːst] *contrast*	[ˈkɒntrɑːst]
[kənˈtrækt] *contract*	[ˈkɒntrækt]		[kənˈvɪkt] *convict*	[ˈkɒnvɪkt]
[prɪˈzent] *present*	[ˈpreznt]		[prəˈdjuːs] *produce*	[ˈprɒdjuːs]
[prəˈdʒekt] *project*	[ˈprɒdʒekt]		[prəˈtest] *protest*	[ˈprəʊtest]
[əˈdɪktɪd] *addict(ed)*	[ˈædɪkt]		[prəˈsiːd] *proceed(s)*	[ˈprəʊsiːd(z)]

Without a change of vowels

[daɪˈdʒest] *digest*	[ˈdaɪdʒest]		[dɪsˈkaʊnt]*discount*	[ˈdɪskaʊnt]
[trænsˈfɜː] *transfer*	[ˈtrænsfɜː]		[ɪnˈsʌɫt] *insult*	[ˈɪnsʌɫt]

With *suspect* you also have the adjective, which is pronounced like the noun: [ˈsʌspekt], whereas the adjective *content* is [kənˈtent] (G.: *zufrieden*), as opposed to the noun *content* (G.: *Inhalt*): [ˈkɒntent].

Fig. 2: Suspect packages [səsˈpekt ˈpækədʒɪz] or [ˈsʌspekt ˈpækədʒɪz]

E 1: a. Indicate the stress patterns of English *institute, institution* and German *Institut, Institution* and classify the suffixes *-ion* in English and German.

b. Indicate the stress pattern of the underlined words and explain the rules: *Lord Reith on the best form of government: "Despotism tempered by assassination.*

c. Which is the odd-man-out?: *crocodile, tiger, elephant, kangaroo, leopard, penguin, dolphin, tortoise.*

d. Why might you be less successful if you said as a door-to-door salesman or saleswoman: [kænaɪ ˈɪntrest ju ɪn‿aʊə ˌmægəˈziːn ˌriːdəz daɪˈdʒest] instead of [ˌriːdəz ˈdaɪdʒest]? Translate both versions.

Smileys:

[ˈkwestʃən | ˈwɒt du ju ˈget ɪf ju krɒsə ˈʃiːp wɪðə ˌkæŋgəˈru: ˈɑːnsə | ə ˈwʊli ˈdʒʌmpə]

How many multi-millionaires does it take to change a light bulb? - Multi-millionaires don´t change light-bulbs, they change apartments.

VIII. Foreign words in English

As a non-native speaker of English you probably have a soft spot for foreign words, by which we mean non-English words imported into the language, because they tend to lighten the vocabulary learning load. They may be words actually taken from German, like *kindergarten, rucksack* and *abseil*, but there are many more from French, like *restaurant, ballet* and *au pair*, some common ones from Latin, like *de facto, carpe diem*, and *quid pro quo*, and the many science- or illness-linked ones from Greek, like *psychology, philosophy, pneumonia*.

The advantage is that they are often loanwords in German too, and consequently have the same internationally defined meaning. But the disadvantage is the established German pronunciation for them, which is likely to intrude when you are using the words in English.

But how do you know how to pronounce them in English? The quick answer is *as English as possible*! Unlike the German use of nasalised vowels in French words like *Genre*, there are no pronunciation compromises in the form of special sounds as a gesture towards the language of the word's origin. Admittedly, sometimes the letters are given a non-English interpretation as a gesture to the word's foreign origin: e.g. *ballet* without a final [t]. But however the *letters* are decoded, the *sounds* are always standard English phonemes.

Let us look at some French words first. The *silent 't'* rule of *ballet* applies to other French words and expressions too; *au fait, filet, Dubonnet, Bizet*, etc. When the [t] is dropped, the vowel in the final open syllable ([e] or [ɛ] in French) has to be pronounced long, and the only English vowel anywhere near these French vowels is the diphthong [eɪ] (as in *lay*). So we are left with:

1. *ballet*   [ˈbæleɪ]   *I love classical ballet.*
    au fait   [ˈəʊ ˈfeɪ]   *I'm afraid I'm not au fait with it.* (= *not familiar with*)
    filet   [ˈfɪleɪ]   *That was a lovely tender filet.*
    Dubonnet [duːˈbɒneɪ] *I'd like a Dubonnet before the meal.*
    Bizet   [ˈbiːzeɪ]   *I like Chopin and Bizet/ And the songs of yesterday.*
                                          (cf. p.153)
    buffet   [ˈbʊfeɪ]   *I prefer a buffet to a sit-down meal.*
    foyer   [ˈfɔɪeɪ]   *Shall we meet in the foyer after the performance?*

French words ending in <é, et, er> are pronounced [eɪ]. Notice too, that in some cases the stress pattern has been changed from the word-final syllable, which would accentuate the Frenchness of the word, to the first syllable. Only *au fait* keeps a stress on the final syllable, as does the similar phrasal expression *au pair* ([ˌəʊ ˈpɛə]). The American pronunciation of French words tends to retain the final-syllable stress, however (compare [bæˈleɪ], [fiˈleɪ], and Eartha Kitt's *Bizet* actually requires a second-syllable stress in the song to fit rhythmically with the following line.

Like the [e] or [ɛ], the French monophthong [o] in the *au* of *au pair* and *au fait* is also changed to a diphthong, this time to [əʊ]. Logically, the same vowel is used in *bureau* [ˈbjuːrəʊ] and *eau de cologne* [ˌəʊ də kəˈləʊn].

The French nasal vowels are replaced by the nearest oral vowel, so *Chopin* is pronounced [ˈʃəʊpæn]. The French [ɑ̃] as in *en, dans*, etc. becomes English [ɒ], so *en suite* and *encore* are realised as [ˌɒn ˈswiːt] and [ˈɒŋkɔː].

C 1/E 1: To see how well you have absorbed the regularities in English pronunciation of French loanwords and expressions, read the following phrases out loud once without listening to the recording, and then read them again and compare your reading of them with the recording.

    a. *Poirot noticed a bottle of eau de vie standing on the bureau.*
    b. *All the rooms in the hotel had en suite bathrooms.*
    c. *They contained free samples of shampoo and eau de cologne.*
    d. *The young student was not au fait with the finer points of silver service.*
    e. *The retired colonel savoured his Dubonnet and then ordered a filet of beef.*
    f. *After a Chopin sonata, Bizet's toreador song made a strange encore.*
    g. *They asked the au pair to babysit while they went to the ballet.*
    h. *All the lamps in the foyer were from the art nouveau period.*

Most French loanwords have permeated to all social groups, which, in these times of affluence and DIY home improvements, has even led to the complete anglicisation of *en suite* as *on suite*. By contrast, many Latin expressions retain an air of intellectualism about them. The principle of using only English phonemes applies just as much to the Latin loanwords as to the French ones. So you get *ad hoc* [ˈæd ˈhɒk] and *quid pro quo* [ˈkwɪd prəʊ ˈkwəʊ]. English pronounces *ad* with a [d] rather than the [t] that German "final devoicing" has imposed on *its* Latin expressions. The same applies to the expression *quid pro quo*, so that the first word is the same as the slang word for a pound, as in *"That'll cost yer ten quid, mate!"*. There is only one pronunciation for the more commonly used *'post mortem'* and *'de facto'*: [ˈpəʊst ˈmɔːtəm], [ˈdeɪ ˈfæktəʊ].

With German words you may feel on safe ground, but you will have to learn the pronunciation of German loanwords in English just like the French ones:

Porsche [pɔːʃ], pl.: [ˈpɔːʃɪz], *Mercedes* [məˈseɪdɪz], pl.: [-iːz] (so it is treated like *species* and *series*), *Volkswagen* [ˈvɒɫkswægŋ], sometimes [ˈvəʊkswægŋ], *abseil* [ˈæbseɪɫ], *rucksack* [ˈrʌksæk]. But note the allowances made for <z> and <w> in *Mozart* [ˈməʊtsɑːt] and *Wagner* [ˈvɑːgnə].

IX. Extralinguistic sounds with meaning: *tut-tut, tsk, ugh, phew, uhm, arrgh!*

C 1/E 1: Read this short dialogue, which contains some of the nonverbal elements that we regularly use in our everyday interactions, and then listen to the recording to check whether your interpretation was correct:

Holiday Plans
A: Uhm, those holiday plans of ours - B: Uh huh. What about them? - A: I think they've gone phut. - B: Huh? - A. Yeah, told you so. - B: But why? - A: Oh for Christ's sake, you know bloody well ... - B: Tut-tut. Language! - A: All right, all right: I'll spell it out for you: not enough funds. - B: Is that all you are worried about? - A: Yup. - B: Pshaw! - A: What do you mean "pshaw"? After all this toiling and saving and me sacrificing my ... - B: Diddums. - A: Well, ehm, I was thinking, ehm, we may just have enough for Blackpool. - B: No, the wife wants to go to Cheltenham Spa. - A: With that la-di-da friend of hers? Whatever next. Posh restaurants where they only serve escargot and that sort of thing? Yuck. - B: Well, she thinks its yummie. And you can always have a cheap burger, since that is what you prefer anyway. - A: Ha! Ha! Very funny.

There may have been a number of surprises for you in E 1 and you will have noticed that the most obvious area of written communication where the relationship between the orthography and the sounds produced breaks down is in the representation of non-verbal, often emotional reactions. We will take you through the most important of these for two reasons. Firstly, because one tends to think that laughing, sneezing and producing noises of surprise, hesitation, admiration, disgust etc. are universal: Nothing could be further from the truth. And secondly, because you will find written representations of these noises in novels and you may like to know how to pronounce them.

Hesitations correspond to a number of phonetic variants [ə::], [əm::], [ʌ::], [ʌm::] and can appear in many different spellings – *er, eh, ehm, uh, um, uhm*. The problem with hesitation forms is that they differ from language to language, that in a foreign language one tends to use them more often than in one's mother tongue because one is constantly pausing to search for the right expression, but that they are never taught. So please recall what we said about hesitation in the section on schwa (V.2.9.) under "Does your `eh´ betray your origins?" We drew your attention to a French speaker's tendency to hesitate with rounded lips – something which would be very unusual for an English speaker. And we said that if you listen to different people hesitating, particularly people from different language backgrounds, there seems to be a link between that neutral vocalization and their language. And what we find very amusing in French or Chinese learners of English, i.e. the hesitation sounds sticking out like a sore thumb because they do not fit in with the rest of the articulatory basis, sounds so natural to us when we use German hesitations in English, that we fail to see the funny side of prolonged "ääääh"s and "öööõh"s sprinkled into our English conversation. To native speakers of English this sounds very exotic, as they find these sounds difficult to produce even when something very similar to them is required within the phonological system of words like the initial sound in *Öffnung*. And just as we advised you in section V.2.1. not to use German paralinguistic lip rounding in English to signal "I don´t have strong feelings on this" as in **yöööös, füsh and chüps wüll do*, we advise you now not to take it for granted that these extralinguistic sounds are universal. Listen carefully to the drawn out monotone schwa or nasal of the hesitation of English speakers and try to copy it.

Of course, hesitation phenomena are much too varied within a language, and variable within a speaker for us to want to claim that schwa = hesitation = relaxed vocal tract. People do not have to hesitate with a schwa-like sound. [əm::], [m::], [a::], [i::], [e::] are all possible transcriptions of different hesitation sounds, and you can probably think of other, quite idiosyncratic hesitation phenomena.

But even with the apparently simple hesitations we can soon run into trouble in the written medium because the form *eh* is homographic with the indignant *eh?* found in contexts such as *What do you think you're doing, eh?* or the *eh?* uttered to prompt a repetition or explanation when you have not understood or cannot accept something that was said. The phonetic realisation of both these homographs is different: The indignant *eh?* is something like [ʔeɪʔ] (a diphthong with an abrupt onset and offset spoken on a high rising tone), very different from the d r a w n o u t monotone schwa of the hesitation. The enquiring *eh?* is not abrupt, but retains the diphthongal [eɪ] with a high rising tone.

Infobox		
Hesitation spellings and sounds:		
er [ə::]	*um* [əm::], [ʌm::]	*u h m* [əm::], [ʌm::]
uh [ə::], [ʌ::]	*eh* [ə::]	*e h m* [əm::]

Before demonstrating further paralinguistic sounds and their significance in English we will explain how they are produced and represented in writing.

There are a number of exclamations and interjections which, in contrast to the hesitation sounds, bear no relationship to the usual sounds of English. Naturally, these are even more difficult to convey in writing, though conventions have established themselves over the centuries. However, this demands a special reading strategy, because the sequence of letters cannot be interpreted according to the normal sound-to-letter rules. The result is often – both for less practised native speakers and for foreign learners – a reading which bears no resemblance to the sounds that were actually being expressed by the writer.

Infobox

Clicks are small *implosions* that are produced by, first, simultaneously forming a closure at the front of the mouth (tongue tip/blade or lips) and at the back of the mouth, between the tongue dorsum and the soft palate (velum). Then the space is increased, and the pressure in the mouth thus reduced, by lowering the middle part of the tongue and/or moving the velar closure point backwards. Finally the closure is released at some point, causing the implosion as the air rushes in to equalize the pressure. Probably the most common case is the ***tut-tut*** or ***tsk-tsk*** expression. These two very different letter sequences actually represent exactly the same sound, namely the **disapproving click**. It is an *alveolar* or tongue-tip click [ǀ] that is produced by releasing the tongue-tip closure.

The **"kiss" sound** is a **bilabial click** used to convey affection, or in combination with a preceding [m] and a following nasalized [w̃ãː] ([mʘw̃ãː]) to indicate effusive approval of something – often accompanied by a kiss of the bunched fingers of one hand, which is then drawn away from the mouth. There seems to be no orthographic representation of this interjection. The click [ʘ] arises when the front closure is formed and released at the lips.

For the *postalveolar* click [ǃ] and the palato-alveolar click [ǂ] (sometimes used to imitate the clip-clop of horses' hooves) the front closure is formed, and released, by the blade of the tongue against the back part of the alveolar ridge or the front part of the hard palate.

The lateral **"gee-up" click** [ǁ] (often used to encourage horses to speed up) is an alveolar + velar closure, but here (as opposed to the alveolar click) the side(s) of the tongue dorsum are drawn inwards to release the closure.

C 2: Listen and repeat:

1. a. *She was ... eh ... how shall I put it? ... eh ... a very cool customer! So I had to ... uhm ... had to ... be on my er guard, if you see what I mean.*
   b. *What do you think you're doing, eh?*
   c. *Eh? I don't think I can believe what you're saying!*

2. clicks

   a. Disapproval: [ǀ]: *Tut tut! That's not a very good example for the others!*
   b. [mʘw̃ãː]! That's the best soufflé I've had in years.
   c. "gee-up" click [ǁ] used to encourage horses to speed up.

3. Disgust
    a. *ugh!*   [ɯ::] a sort of [u:::] with spread instead of rounded lips.
    b. *yuck*   [jʌk]

4. Horror/Fear
    arrrgh!   [ɑ̣::]

5. Contemptuous dismissal
    pshaw [p̥ʙ̥ə][p̥ɸə] a [pʰə] produced with loose lips, so that there is friction or even a roll of the lips on release. It is often read as (spelling pronunciation): [pʃɔ:]

6. Communication prompts
    ahem: roughly [ʔm̥mʔm̥m]; a cough to bring something to someone's notice: Also used sometimes for writing a signal of continued attention to what is being said: [m m̥m:] with a low rising tone on the second element.

7. Relief
    phew [ɸiу̥] but also the spelling pronunciation [fju:]

8. Approval
    a. *yeah*   [jɛʔ]
    b. *yup/yep:* [jʌʔp̚]/[jeʔp̚]. Note the unreleased /p/.
    c. *yuh:*   [je]. Almost like the German unemphatic *ja*.

X. Concluding remarks

We believe that the teaching of phonetics should not be exclusively devoted to articulatory exercises (important though they are), because learning a foreign language, in particular the pronunciation of it, is a multi-faceted issue, depending on aspects of attitude, motivation, personality, age, social environment of learner groups and teachers, teaching materials, teaching aims, learning strategies etc. The ideal type of learner for us is an intelligent, highly motivated, inquisitive and communicative person who enjoys acting and impersonating others and has a great sense of humour coupled with the ability to laugh at herself/himself. We do hope you recognise yourself in this description because it is for you, our favourite reader, listener and speaker that we have compiled this course book with a theoretical background for language awareness, with practical exercises for eartraining, speaking and phonetic transcription, with some real life English and some passages that we concocted to make you think, and also with jokes to keep your spirits up. We are convinced that it is the interaction of cognitive, emotional and social aspects that is required for adult learners of a foreign language to progress.

Some learners (and indeed some teachers) believe that imitating is sufficient. Let us remind you of our example of *"the ˌabsent-minded proˈfessor"*, which may induce you to believe that now you have mastered the stress pattern of *absent-minded* once and for all. But without knowledge about the language you would come up with utterances like *"In everyday life professors are often ˈabsent-minded."* without ever becoming aware of your mistake because you claim to have imitated native speakers. On the other hand, one should not take it for granted that abstract knowledge about phonology coupled with some articulatory drills in the language lab alone will suffice to make learners communicate successfully. We recommend a lifelong spiral of language awareness raising, practice, experiments in real life communication combined with observation assisted by knowledge of how languages work, then back to new studies, practice, real life communication and so on.

What we mean by making an "observation assisted by knowledge of how languages work" is that you need to develop the linguistic skills for collecting data. One important exercise on the way to becoming a language learner-cum-linguist, i.e. becoming your own teacher, is to practice phonetic transcription, not because these skills may be required in a test, but as a means to an end. A ventriloquist tries to pretend that not he but the dummy is talking, and he does so by not moving his lips. As this is impossible with bilabial sounds he does not use them. Instead of saying *"To get to the Houses of Parliament you just cross this bridge."* they say *"To get to the Houses of Karlianent you just cross this gridge."*, and the audience actually "hear" *Parliament* and *bridge*. It is important to understand this phenomenon: We hear what we have been led to expect, either on the basis of our own native language or of our teaching or of what we have seen in writing. This explains mistakes like *celery* for *salary*, **Do it AS soon AS possible*, and **[ˈsæɫmən]* for *salmon*.

Phonetic transcription helps you to understand the speech habits of ventriloquists and native speakers of English. Listening carefully to a recorded text and comparing notes with others afterwards will teach you that native speakers do not say *This is the house that* [ðæt] *Jack built* but rather *This is the house that* [ðət] *Jack built*, that they often say [aɪɫ hævə ˈsæmwɪtʃ pliːz] rather than the very careful [aɪɫ hævə ˈsændwɪtʃ pliːz]. By analogy with the idiom "that's an eye-opener" we can say "Phonetic transcription is an ear-opener". And by reversing the process, i.e. by learning to read phonetic transcription out loud, you can force yourself to counteract the silly things that your brain keeps telling you, like *"But if the word is spelled s-a-n-d as in* [sænd] *then I really ought to pronounce it like that in `sandwhich´ and `sandpit´ too."* or *"If I pronounce `that´ as* [ðæt] *then I can´t go wrong."* We strongly recommend you to keep going back to the dozens of transcription exercises in this book until it becomes a habit to pronounce the symbol [ɫ] as a velarised lateral rather than telling yourself *an <l> is an <l> is an <l>*. And should you decide to memorise a limerick to strengthen your understanding of the linguistic point we were trying to make with it, read the phonetic transcription of it out loud, instead of perpetuating the spelling pronunciation by sticking slavishly to the orthography.

We would also like to encourage you to create situations in which you can practise your newly acquired knowledge. After having worked your way through the /v w/ section, celebrate your achievement by inviting an English speaker over for a drink: "We were wondering, Vickey, whether you would like to come round for a drink tonight. We have a bottle of fine old vintage wine that we would like to share with you." And after your perusal of the section on stress shift you take an English speaker to you local and say casually: "Have you heard the one about the ˌabsent-minded proˈfessor? Well, this professor, he was really absent-ˈminded, ..."

Academic studies, having a bit of fun and communicating in real life do not have to be mutually exclusive. [ɪt kəmbi ˈhaɪli ˈməʊtɪveɪtɪŋ tə kəmˈbaɪn ðiːz ˈθriː ˌˈæspeks ǀ əz ˈlɒŋəz ju ˈteɪk ðə ˈdʒəʊks ˈsɪərɪəsli].

XI. Additional exercises for advanced students and teachers

To give you additional practice we have concentrated on transcription exercises. These are of two kinds, transcription from recorded texts and transcription of written texts.

The transcriptions we have provided throughout the book offer another type of exercise, of course: Transcription reading. We are not suggesting that this is an essential exercise, but it does give you a graphic form without the orthographic features which reinforce any bad pronunciation habits you may still have. Of course, it also tests your familiarity with the IPA system to the limit.

1. Transcription from recorded texts.

We start the exercises in transcription of spoken texts with a couple of short read utterances, first a pithy saying, then a little ditty written by that productive and long-lived writer Anon:

C 1/E 1: Folk wisdom. Listen and transcribe, first orthographically then phonetically.

C 2/E 2: Poem by Anon. Listen and transcribe as for C 1/E 1.

Interviews

In E 1 and E 2, as in the previous chapters we have aimed to familiarize you with, and given you practice in recognizing phrase-level, contextually induced features of English pronunciation. We have, perhaps paradoxically, tended to use a slightly idealised version of "real" spoken English (in fact mostly texts that have been read) in that we have used linking, assimilation and weak forms whenever these were possible and made sense. We have done this partly for didactic reasons because learners, in particular German learners, tend to err in the other direction. In this chapter we confront you with spoken English from some live TV-interviews. You will recognise all the features of putting sounds and words together that we have advocated, but you will also find that native speakers of English sometimes deviate from these "rules", i.e. sometimes they use a hard onset, occasionally they do not link words (sometimes they do not even use linking r), sometimes they use strong forms when you would expect weak ones. You will find, however, that the deviations can usually be explained in terms of hesitations, in terms of being "lost for words", lack of verbal planning strategies etc. But as soon as they have made up their mind and know what they want to say they will speed up and apply the contextual rules of spoken English.

Listening to these recordings very carefully and transcribing them phonetically is excellent ear training. But do not expect it to be easy! You will continually have to fight against listening to "what" they are saying and concentrate on "how" they are saying it. So you will tend to transcribe a bit more phonemically than is warranted. We find the observation of what people actually articulate quite fascinating; we hope you will too. Have fun!

C 3/E 3: Alan Clark in an interview. Listen carefully and transcribe what you hear, first orthographically and then phonetically, using a fairly narrow notation, i.e., trying to capture phonetically any deviations from the phonemic structure of the words.

C 4/E 4: Hugh Grant in an interview. Listen and transcribe what you hear, first orthographically and then phonetically .

C 5/E 5: Interview with Princess Diana. Again, listen and transcribe what you hear, first orthographically and then phonetically.

You will find our suggested transcriptions and a discussion in chapter XII.

2. Transcription of written texts

Putting orthographic texts into phonetic transcription according to the principles of pronunciation that we have been advocating in this book is a more theoretical exercise. It requires introspection as to how you would pronounce the text (although there is nothing to stop you actually speaking the texts out loud and transcribing what you say).

To test your command of English pronunciation rules, we suggest you work your way from limerick to limerick through the previous chapters. Cover up the transcriptions we have given you and produce your own, then compare them with our's. The well-known poem below is in fact the only new text we give you for this type of transcription. Here too you should cover up the right side of the page while you transcribe the orthographic text – or cover up the left side if you wish to practise your transcription reading.

E 6: Transcribe the following orthographic text, keeping the transcription on the right side of the page covered.

I take it you already know	[aɪ ˈteɪkɪt juᵂɔ-ɫˈredi ˈnəʊ
Of tough and bough and cough and dough?	əv ˈtʌfən ˈbaʊᵂən ˈkɒfən ˈdəʊ
Others may stumble but not you	ˈʌðəz meɪ ˈstʌmbɫ bət ˈnɒt ˈju:
On hiccough, thorough, laugh and through.	ɒn ˈhɪkʌp ˈθʌɹə ˈlɑːfən ˈθɹu:]
Well done! And now you wish perhaps,	[weɫ ˈdʌn əˈn‿naʊ ju ˈwɪʃ pəˈhæps
To learn of less familiar traps?	tə ˈlɜːnəv ˈles fəˈmɪljə ˈtræps
Beware of heard, a dreadful word	bɪˈweəɹəv ˈhɜːd ə ˈdredfəl ˈwɜːd

That looks like <u>beard</u> but sounds like <u>bird</u>,

ðət ˈlʊks laɪk ˈbɪəd bət ˈsaʊndz laɪk
ˈbɜːd]

And <u>dead</u> - it's said like <u>bed</u>, not <u>bead</u> –
For goodness' sake don't call it <u>deed</u>!
Watch out for <u>meat</u> and <u>great</u> and <u>threat</u>
(They rhyme with <u>suite</u> and <u>straight</u> and <u>debt</u>).

[ən ˈded ǀ ɪts sed laɪk ˈbed nɒt ˈbiːd
fə ˈɡʊdnɪs ˈseɪk dəʊntˉ ˈkɔːlɪt ˈdiːd
wɒˈʧ‿aʊt fə ˈmiːtən ˈɡreɪtən ˈθret
ðeɪ ˈraɪm wɪð ˈswiːtən ˈstreɪtən ˈdet]

A <u>moth</u> is not a <u>moth</u> in <u>mother</u>
Nor <u>both</u> in <u>bother</u>, <u>broth</u> in <u>brother</u>,
And <u>here</u> is not a match for <u>there</u>
Nor <u>dear</u> and <u>fear</u> for <u>bear</u> and <u>pear</u>,

[ə ˈmɒθɪz ˈnɒt ə ˈmɒθɪn ˈmʌðə
nɔ ˈbəʊθɪn ˈbɒðə ǀ ˈbrɒθɪn ˈbrʌðə
ənd ˈhɪərɪz ˈnɒtə ˈmæʧ fə ˈðeə
nɔː ˈdɪərən ˈfɪə fə ˈbeərən ˈpeə]

And then there's <u>dose</u> and <u>rose</u> and <u>lose</u> –
Just look them up - and <u>loose</u> and <u>choose</u>,
And <u>cork</u> and <u>work</u> and <u>card</u> and <u>ward</u>,
And <u>font</u> and <u>front</u> and <u>word</u> and <u>sword</u>,

[ən ˈðen ðəz ˈdəʊsən ˈrəʊzən ˈluːz
ʤʌst ˈlʊk ðəˈmʌp ǀ ənd ˈluːsən ˈʧuːz
ən ˈkɔːkən ˈwɜːkən ˈkɑːdənd ˈwɔːd
ən ˈfɒntən ˈfrʌntənd ˈwɜːdən ˈsɔːd]

And <u>do</u> and <u>go</u> and <u>thwart</u> and <u>cart</u>–
Come, come, I've hardly made a start!
A <u>dreadful</u> language? Man alive!
I'd mastered it when I was five!

[ən ˈduːʷən ˈɡəʊʷən ˈθwɔːt ən ˈkɑːt
kʌm ˈkʌm‿aɪv ˈhɑːdli meɪdə ˈstɑːt
ə ˈdredfʊ‿ˈlæŋgwɪʤ ǀ ˈmæn‿əˈlaɪv
aɪd ˈmɑːstədɪt weˈn‿aɪ wəz ˈfaɪv]

XII. Solutions to exercises

III. Sound Examples

p. 9, E 1:
a. Name the vowels of English and German.
Monophthongs: English: /iː ɪ   e   æ ɑː ɒ ʌ ɔː ʊ uː ɜː ə/
                   German: /iː yː ɪ ʏ eː øː ɛ ɛː œ a aː ɔ   ʊ uː   ə ɐ/
There are also diphthongs like /aɪ aʊ ɔɪ/, but these will be dealt with in V.3.
b. How do you pronounce <ng> in English and German?
[ŋ] or [ŋg] in English, e.g. *singer* vs. *finger*;
only [ŋ] in German, e.g. *Sänger, Finger* (with the inevitable exceptions like
Ingo and *Tango*)
c. How do you form the regular plural in English? By adding <s> or <es> in the
orthography; e.g. *cat - cats, home - homes, rose - roses, bush - bushes.* By adding
/s/, /z/ or /ɪz/ when speaking; e.g. [kæts] [həʊmz][ˈrəʊzɪz] [ˈbʊʃɪz].

III.1. /l/

p. 16f., C 6/E 1:
a. [ˈkl̩ɪntən], [pl̩æn], [lɔː], [ˈpaʊəfʊɫ], [ˌnæʃnəɫ ˈheɫθ bɔːd], [wɪɫ], [ˈdiːteɪɫz],
[ˌmedɪkəl‿ɪnfəˈmeɪʃn̩], [elekˈtrɒnɪk] [ˈheɫθ], [wʊd], [ɪˈneɪbɫ ˈriːʤənəɫ ˈheɫθəˈlaɪənsəz],
[ˈfedərəɫ], [ˌləʊkəɫ ˈheɫθ‿əˈfɪʃɫz], [əˈsemblən‿ɪksˈʧeɪnʤ], [ðə ˈpl̩æn wɪˈl‿ʌɫtɪmətl̩iʲ
ɪŋˈkl̩uːd], [wɪˈl‿ɔːɫsəʊ], [pl̩æstɪk], [kʊd], [ˌnæʃnəl‿aɪdentɪfɪˈkeɪʃn̩], [ˈsɜːtnli], [ˈheɫθ
‿ɪnfəˌmeɪʃn̩], [kl̩ɪə], [kəmˈpelɪŋ], [kl̩ɪˈnɪʃn̩z kʊd ˈkwɪkl̩i], [ˌmedɪkɫ ˈtests kʊd], [ˈheɫθ
kl̩eɪmz kʊd].

b. [ˈstrʌɡɫd], [ˈʃædəʊˌlændz], [smɔːɫ], [weɪɫz], [ˈraʊɫ ˌmɒdlənɪz ˈfæntəm ˌraɪvɫ],
[ˈɔːɫweɪz‿ɪˈklɪpst], [ˈnæʃnəɫ], [əˈlɪvieɪz], [ˈbɒtɫ], [ˈlʌndən], [wʌnˈseɫf], [hɪmˈseɫf], [ˈlaɪtn̩
hɪmˈseɫf‿ʌp], [tə teɪk ˈlaɪf les ˈsɪəriəsli], [ˈresləs], [wɪɫ ˈwɔːk‿əˈraʊnd].

p.17, E 2:   The cl̲oisters of L̲incol̲n Cathedral̲.
                  [l̩]   [l]   -   [ɫ]

III. 3. Letters & sounds

p. 27, E 1: Identify the "silent" letters in the following words:
a. <b>: [bɒm] [wuːm] [tuːm]   b. <gh> [bɔːt] [fɔːt]
c. <p> [saɪˈkəʊsɪs] [njuːˈməʊniə]; <p,l> [sɑːm]   d. <k, gh> [naɪt] <k> [nəʊ] [nɪt]
e. <g> [nəʊm] [næʃ] [nɑː ɫd]   f. <l> [pɑːm] [ˈɑːmənd] [ɑːmz]
g. <c> [siːn] [sent] [ˈsaɪɒn]

p. 28, E 2: The statement is phonetically wrong because the <oo> in *room* stands
for the vowel sound /uː/.

p. 29, E 3: They are all "spelling pronunciations", where letters are pronounced which should not be (the star symbol: * = wrong!):

carriage	*[ˈkærɪədʒ]	instead of [ˈkærɪdʒ]
basically	*[ˈbeɪsɪkæli]	instead of [ˈbeɪsɪkli],
shepherd	*[ˈʃephɜːd]	instead of [ˈʃepəd],
casualty	*[ˈkæʒʊæɫti]	instead of [ˈkæʒɫti]
every	*[ˈeveri]	instead of [ˈevri]
gnome	*[gnəʊm]	instead of [nəʊm]
gnaw	*[gnɔː]	instead of [nɔː]
extraordinary	*[ˌekstrə ˈɔːdɪnəri]	instead of [ˌeksˈtrɔːdn̩ri]

p. 29, E 4: The correct spellings of the rhyme words in the limericks are:
a. *colonel* [ˈkɜːnɫ] rhymes with <infernel> [ɪnˈfɜːnɫ] *and* <journal> [ˈdʒɜːnɫ]
b. *Slough* rhymes with <cow> and <now>, and *off* rhymes with <cough>
c. *Gloucester* rhymes with <Foster> and <lost her>, and *Leicester* rhymes with <arrest her>

IV.1. /t/ - /d/

p. 42, C 2/E 1: The speaker produced the following sentences:
a. *Excuse me, <u>Fort Street</u> is supposed to be around here somewhere?*
b. *Excuse me, how do I get to <u>Radcliffe Road</u>, please?*
c. *Excuse me, is this <u>The Mound</u>?*
d. *Excuse me, I'm looking for <u>Meat Road</u>.*
e. *Excuse me, you don't happen to know where <u>Wates Grove</u> is, do you?*
f. *Oh no, I think you want <u>Ridgemound Gardens</u>.*

IV.2.2. /p/ - /b/

p. 55, E 1/C 1: Spot the foreign accent. The order of presentation was as follows:
a. *He grabbed the money and ran.*   F/E
b. *She certainly has the gift of the gab but sometimes I wish she'd shut her gob.*
                                                                            F/E
c. *Let's take a cab and go to a pub and have a drink or two.*   E/F
d. *When my son joined the cubs they taught him to wash his cups himself.* E/F
e. *I still like fairy tales like "The Wolf and the Seven Little Kids" and "Little Red Riding Hood".*   F/E
f. *He was stabbed to death.*
  E/F

p. 56 no. 5, fun exercise with orthographical nonsense. It does make sense after all: *The new suit was far more than he could pay. Tony sighed; he knew he was doomed to serve, and never to know fame or fortune.*

IV.2.3. /s/ - /z/

p. 59-60, E 1:
a. *That buzzing noise means something. You don't get a buzzing noise like*
           [z]   [z]   [z̤ s]   [z]   [z]

that, just buzzing and buzzing, without its meaning something. If there's a
  [s]   [z]   [z]   [s]   [s]   [z]

buzzing noise, somebody is making a buzzing-noise, and the only reason for
  [z]   [z]   [s]   [z]   [z]   [z]   [z]

making a buzzing noise that I̲ know of is because you're a bee."
      [z]   [z]   [z]   [z]

b. *If a man has ten sons and each son has a sister, how many children has h e*
    [z̦]   [s] [z]   [s]   [z̦ə sis]   [z‿i]

altogether? - Eleven, because the daughter is each son's sister.
        [z]   [z]   [s] [z̦ sis]

IV.2.4. /ʃ/ - /ʒ/ - /tʃ/ - /dʒ/

p. 66, C 1/E 2: Pronounced <u>correctly</u> (C) with /dʒ/ or <u>incorrectly</u> (I) with /tʃ/:
a. *John*   I   **b.** *cage*   I   **c.** *raging*   C   **d.** *jury*   C
e. *stagecoach* I   **f.** *alleged*   I   **g.** *German* C   **h.** *refuge*   I
i. *germain*   I   **j.** revenge   C

IV.3.1 /v/, /w/ and /f/

p. 75, E 3: Phonetic transcription of each word containing <v>:
Man: *I'll have apple-pie without custard please.*
           [hæˈv‿æ]
W:*Sorry, sir, we don't serve it with custard. You'll have to have it without*
             [ˈsɜːvɪt]   [ˌhæftə ˈhævɪt]
    cream.

IV.3.3 /j/ (yod)

p. 86, C 4/E 3: The words were read in the following order:
1. G,   2. E,   3. G,   4. E,   5. E,   6. G,   7. G,   8. E

IV.4.4. /θ/ vs. /ð/ (plus /s/ and /z/ revisited)

p. 93, E 3: Exercise for *seize, sees, seas, cease, seethe.*
a. *seize, sees, seas* [siːz]
b. *cease*
c. *Real sailors seize every opportunity to travel the seven seas, where one sees, in*
    [s]   [z̦ siːz]   [s]   [siːz]   [siːzɪn]

dark and stormy nights, how the waves seethe, and where, in the deep blue sea,
    [s]   [s]   [z̦ siːð]   [s]

wonders will never cease.
    [z]   [siːs]

p. 93, E 4

a. *October* [tʰ] *is the tenth month* [ˈtʰenθ ˌmʌnθ] *of the year.*
b. *Could I borrow your Shakespeare anthology.*[ˌʃeɪkspɪər‿ æn̩ˈθɒlədʒi]

c. *It's not in the interest of the public.* [ɪts ˈnɒtɪn̩ðiˈɪntrəst̬əv ðə ˈpʌblɪk]

d. *Does the National Health Service apply to all Commonwealth countries?*
[dʌz ðə ˌnæʃnəɬ ˈheɬθ ˌsɜːvɪs̬əˈp̬laɪ tu ˈɔːɬ ˌkɒmənweɬθ ˈkʌntrɪz]

e. *At the moment* [ət̬ðə ˈməʊmənt]

p. 95, E 6:

a. *seize/sees/seas* [siːz] vs. *sis* [sɪs] vs. *cease* [siːs] vs. *seethe* [siːð]

b. *breath* [breθ] vs. *breeze* [briːz] vs. *breathe* [briːð]

c. *size/ sighs* [saɪz] vs. *scythe* [saɪð]

d. *teeth* [tiːθ] vs. *teething* [ˈtiːðɪŋ], *teethe* [tiːð] vs. *tease* [tiːz]

e. *wreath* [riːθ] vs. *wreathe* [riːð]   f. *loath* [ləʊθ] vs. *loathe* [ləʊð]

g. *close (adj.)* [kləʊs] vs. *close (vb)* [kləʊz] vs. *cloze* [kləʊz] vs. *clothe* [kləʊð]

h. [ðə ˈnɔːsmənɪn̩ðə ˈnɔːθəv ˌskændɪˈneɪvɪə əbˈzɜːvd ˌnɔːðən ˈlaɪts | wɪtʃ ðə ˈsʌðənəzɪn ðə ˈsaʊθəv ˈswiːdn̩ nevə ˈsiː]

V.1. Vowels

p. 106, E 1: The poem in normal orthography and in phonetic transcription:

<swan swam over the sea	[ˈswɒn ˈswæm ˈəʊvə ðə ˈsiː
swim, swan, swim.	ˈswɪm ˈswɒn ˈswɪm
swan swam back again	ˈswɒn ˈswæm ˈbækəgən
well swum swan>	ˈweɬ ˈswʌm ˈswɒn]

V.2.1. / iː /

p. 113, C 1/E 1: The words that you heard are underlined:

1. *Biest.*   2. *Beat*   3. *flee*   4. *she*
5. *nie*   6. *bieten*   7. *fee*   8. *lieh*

V.2.2. / uː /

p. 118, E 3:

/ uː /		/ ʊ /	other
tomb		*wool*	(also [ˈfɔːtʃən])
fortune		*brook*	*brooch* [brəʊtʃ]
tribute			
menu	[ˈmenjuː]		
canoe	[kəˈnuː]		

V.2.3. / ʊ /

p. 121, E 1: [ʌ]   [ʊ]   [ʌ]   [ʊ]   [ʌ]   [ʌ]   [ʊ] [ʌ]   [ʌ]
     puddle, pudding, budding, pulpit, culprit, putt, put, custard, lucky,

[ʊ]   [ʌ]   [ʌ]   [ʌ] [ʊ]   [ʊ]   [ʊ]
cushion, gushing, bud, pus, puss, courier, Fulham

V.2.5. / ɒ /

p. 126, C 2/E 1: The order of the languages was:

1. *otter* vs. *Otter*   E/G   2. *dock* vs. *Dock*   E/G
3. *got* vs. *Gott*   G/E   4. *flock* vs. *Pflock*   E/G

5. *block* vs. *Block*   G/E   6. *pop* vs. *Pop*   G/E
7. *shot* vs. *Schott*   E/G   8. *plotter* vs. *Plotter*   G/E
9. *shock* vs. *Schock*   E/G   10. *Oppenheimer* vs. *Oppenheimer*   G / E

p. 126, C 3/E 2: Order of languages and analysis of English/German differences

1. *stock* vs. *Stock*   G/E; E [st-] vs. G [ʃt-]; E [ɒ] vs. G [ɔ]
2. *nonstop* vs. *Nonstop*   E/G; E [ᵣ ˡ-] vs. G [ˡ- ᵣ-]; E [ɒ] vs. G [ɔ]; E [st-] vs.
                                G [ʃt-];
3. *Hongkong*   E/G; E [ᵣ ˡ-] vs. G [ˡ- ᵣ-]; E [ɒ] vs. G [ɔ]
4. *Concord*   G/E; E [ɒ] vs. G [ɔ]; E [ɔ:] vs. G [ɔɐ]; E [-d] vs. G [-t];
5. *Pavarotti*   G/E; E [ˌpævəˈɹɒti] vs. G [ˌpavaˈʁɔti]
6. *job* vs. *Job*   E/G; E [ɒ] vs. G [ɔ]; E [-b] vs. G [-p];
7. *hot pants* vs. *Hot Pants* G/E; E [ɒ] vs. G [ɔ]; E [æ] vs. G [ɛ];
8. *logbook* vs. *Logbuch*   G/E; E [ɒ] vs. G [ɔ]; E [-g] vs. G [-k]; E [ʊ] vs. G [u:];
                                E [-k] vs. G [x];
9. *Tom Stoppard*   G/E; E [ɒ] vs. G [ɔ]; E [ɑ:] vs. G [aɐ]; E [-d] vs. G [-t];
10. *Oliver Cromwell*   G/E; E [ˌɒlɪvə ˈkɹɒmweɫ] vs. G [ˌɔlivɐ ˈkʁɔmvel]

V.2.7. / ʌ /

p. 133, C 2/E 1: Identify the language. The word you heard is underlined:

1. *luck* vs. *Lack*.   5. *but* vs. *Bad* (North German pronunciation! [bat])
2. *hut* vs. *hat*   6. *puck* vs. *Pack*
3. *putt* vs. *patt*   7. *mutton* vs. *Matten*
4. *bun* vs. *Bann*   8. *done* vs. *dann*

p. 133, C 3/E 2: "E" or "G" marks what you heard. The features that should have helped you identify the status of the word are specified in each case:

1. *bubble gum*   G   (G [a] for E [ʌ]; G [l] for E [ɫ])
2. *curry*   E   (E [ʌ] and E [r]; G [ˈkari] or [ˈkœri])
3. *comeback*   G   (G [a] for E [ʌ], G [ɛ] for E [æ], stress on "*-back*")
4. *button*   E   (E [ʌ])
5. *pub*   G   (G [a] for E [ʌ], [p] for [b])
6. *ketchup*   G   (G [a] for E [ʌ])
7. *butler*   E   (E [ʌ])
8. *punk*   E   (E [ʌ])

p. 136, E 4: Phonetic transcriptions of a. and of the underlined words in b.:

a. *one* [wʌn]; *won* [wʌn]; *wan* [wɒn]; *wandering* [ˈwɒndərɪŋ];
wondering [ˈwʌndərɪŋ];
donkey [ˈdɒŋki]; *monkey* [ˈmʌŋki]; *monk* [mʌŋk]; *monetary* [ˈmʌnətri];
commonwealth [ˈkɒmənweɫθ];
ironmonger [ˈaɪənmʌŋgə]; *scaremonger* [ˈskeəmʌŋgə]; *mongrel* [ˈmʌŋgrəɫ];
yoghourt [ˈjɒgət]; *waddle* [ˈwɒdɫ]; *waffle* [ˈwɒfɫ]; *The Grapes of Wrath* [ðə
ˈgreɪpsəv ˈrɒθ]; *trough* [trɒf]; *scones* [skəʊnz] / [skɒnz]; *tons* [tʌnz];
mongoose [ˈmɒŋgu:s]; *monastery* [ˈmɒnəstri].

260 *Solutions*

b. *"The boat was chock-a-block* ['ʧɒkə'blɒk] *with people, all of them English. I spent the first quarter of an hour wandering* ['wɒndərɪŋ] *around wondering* ['wʌndərɪŋ] *how they had got* [gɒt] *there without getting filthy ..."*

V.2.8. /ɜː/

p. 139, C 3: You heard the words in this order.
1. *Terminal.*	G	2. *Flirt*	E	3. *Churchill*	E
4. *Birmingham*	G	5. *Guernsey*	G	6. *Girls*	E
7. *Safety first*	E	8. *Wordsworth*	E	9. *Gershwin*	G
10. *Surfer*	E	11. *Server*	G	12. *Surfboard*	E

V.2.9. Schwa

p. 142, E 1: The two sentences behind the transcriptions are:
a. *An apple a day keeps the doctor away.*
b. *The man who lay in the road was not sick but drunk.*

p. 145f., C 1/E 2: The marked letters are pronounced as schwa.
a. *apparently*   **b.** *suggestively*   **c.** *resurrection*   **d.** *contagious*
e. *surgeon*   **f.** *remorseless*   **g.** *conspiracy*   **h.** *competition*
i. *parachute*   **j.** *conflagration*   **k.** *phonetics*   **l.** *semantic*

p. 147, C 2/E 3: The words you heard as English or German are underlined.
	i. E	**ii. G**	**iii. G**
a.	*bitter*	*bitte*	*bitter*
b.	*clipper*	*Klippe*	*Klipper*
c.	*locker*	*Locke*	*locker*
d.	*Linda*	*Linde*	*linder*
e.	*clever*	-	*clever*
f.	*fitter*	-	*fitter*
g.	*setter*	-	*Setter*

V.3.2. /əʊ/

p. 155, C 1/E 1: English or German? You heard the following words:
lope E;   *toast* E;   *coat* E;   *folk* E;   *Coke* G;   *Choke* G;   *Dope* G;   *hob* G

V.3.3. /aɪ/

p. 158, C 2/E 1: You heard the following words:
1. *eye* vs. *Ei*	E	2. *my* vs. *Mai*	G	3. *lime* vs. *Leim*	G
4. *mine* vs. *mein*	E	5. *shine* vs. *Schein*	E	6. *nine* vs. *nein*	E
7. *fine* vs. *fein*	G	8. *tiger* vs. *Taiga*	G	9. *lice* vs. *leis*	E
10. *mice* vs. *Mais*	G	11. *light* vs. *Leid*	E	12. *might* vs. *Maid*	E

p. 159, E 2: The last word of each line: [strɪkt], [naet], [prə'dɪkt], [ɪn'daet]

p. 161, E 3: Phonetic transcription:
[mɑe 'brʌðə 'klɑev wəz 'trɑeɪŋ tə bɑeə mægə'ziːnɒn ðə jə'semiti næʃnəl 'pɑːk fə ði'ɑːkɑevzəvɪz 'lɑebrəri | bɪkəzɪz 'sɪstəz 'pɔːliːn | 'ɑeriːnə'n‿ɪzəbeɫ wɒntɪd

tə ˈklɑem ðə ˈspaeəzəv ðə ˈfaev ˈʧɜːʧɪz ðeə | wɪððə ˈfaen ˈkɑːvd ˈkwaeəz]

V.3.4. /aʊ/

p. 162f., C 1/E 1: You heard the following words:
1. E. *how*   2. G. *Haus*   3. G. *Maus*   4. E. *louse*
5. G. *Clown*   6. G. *laut*   7. E. *clout*

p. 163, E 2: The last word of each line are: [braʊ], [rəʊ], [raʊ], [ʃəʊ]

p. 165, E 3: Homophones or homographs?
a. *our*   [aʊə]   b. *hour*   [aʊə] (homophones)
c. *flour*   [flaʊə]   d. *flower*   [flaʊə] (homophones)
e. *wound*   [wuːnd] (*Wunde*) f. *wound*   [waʊnd] (as in: *She wound*
him round her little finger.) (homographs but not homophones)

V.3.5. /ɔɪ/

p. 166, C 2/E 1: What you heard was:
1b. *ahoi*   2a. *cowboy*   3b. *Playboy*   4a. *loiter*   5a. (English) *Freud*   6a. *boiler*

V.3.6.1 /ɪə/

p. 169, C 1/E 1b: You heard:
1. *Bier* G   2. *here* E   3. *fear* E   4. *dir* G
5. *ear* E   6. *Tier* G   7. *gear* E   8. pier E

V.3.6.2 /ʊə/

p 171, no. 1 in normal orthography: *More and more, we are sure to go on the tour from the shore to the tor on the moor.*

V.3.6.3. centering diphthong /eə/

p. 175, E 1: pear [pɛə], dear [dɪə], bear [bɛə], aerobics [ɛərəʊbɪks], mayor [mɛə], mare [mɛə], surveyor [səˈveɪə], care [kɛə], bare [bɛə], Bär [beːɐ, *kehr*, [keːɐ].

VI.1. Linking:

p. 177, Fig. 1: Cartoon text: *"There's no end to it! The minute you're out of yesterday's news, you're up to your eyes in today's." - "It's the way life is, isn't it?"*

p. 187, E 3: Read column 2 and 3 as homophones.

At the South Pole	by Ann Tarctic	→ Antarctic. Now continue:
Swimming the Channel	by Frances Near	→ France is near
The Bullfighter	by Matt Adore	→ matador
The Unknown Author	by Ann Onymous	→ anonymous
The Long Hot Summer	by I. Scream	→ ice cream
A Cliff-top Tragedy	by Eileen Dover	→ I leaned over
The Cause of Colds	by Mike Robe	→ microbe
The Escaping Sheep	by Gay Topen	→ gate open
Return of the Prodigal Son	by Gladys Back	→ glad he's back

VI.2. Stress

p. 201, E 3: Stress shift:

1. *Tottenham* → *Tottenham Court* → *Tottenham Court Road*
   [ˈtɒtnəm] → [ˌtɒtnəm ˈkɔːt] →   [ˌtɒtnəm kɔːt ˈrəʊd]

   Golden → *Golden Gate* → *Golden Gate Bridge*
   [ˈgəʊɫdn̩] → [ˌgəʊɫdn̩ ˈɡeɪt] → [ˌgəʊɫdn̩ ɡeɪt ˈbrɪʤ]

   Manchester → *Manchester Evening News*
   [ˈmænʧestə] → [ˌmænʧestəriːvnɪŋ ˈnjuːz]

   Manchester → *Manchester Airport*
   [ˈmænʧestə] → [ˌmænʧestəˈr‿eəpɔːt]

   nine years old → *a nine-year-old girl;* (but N.B. *nine-year-olds*)
   [ˌnaɪn jɪəˈzəʊɫd] → [əˌnaɪn jɪər‿əʊɫd ˈɡɜːɫ] (but: [ˈnaɪn jɪəˌrəʊɫdz])

   fifty → *fifty miles* → *a fifty-mile walk*
   [ˈfɪfti] → [ˌfɪfti ˈmaɪɫz] → [ə ˌfɪfti maɪɫ ˈwɔːk]

   fifteen → *fifteen miles* → *a fifteen-mile walk*
   [fɪfˈtiːn] → [ˌfɪftiːn ˈmaɪɫz] → [ə ˌfɪftiːn maɪɫ ˈwɔːk]

   Saint → *St. Paul* → *St. Paul's Cathedral*
   [seɪnt] → [sənt ˈpɔːɫ] → [sənt ˌpɔːɫz kəˈθiːdrəɫ]

2. *An old girl on the train to Loch Sheen*   [ənəʊɫd ˈɡɜːɫ ɒn ðə ˈtreɪn tə lɒx ˈʃiːn
   claimed to be three months under sixteen. kleɪmd tə ˈbiː θriː mʌnθˈs‿ʌndə sɪksˈtiːn
   So she got the cheap fare,   soʊʃi ˈɡɒt ðə ʧiːp ˈfeə
   but when she got there   bʌt ˈwen ʃi ɡɒt ˈðeə
   Sixteen boys cried: "Mum where have   sɪkstiːn ˈbɔɪz kraɪd mʌm ˈweərəv
   you been? "   ju ˈbiːn]

In line 2, the word *sixteen* is accented and phrase-final, therefore it retains the standard stress pattern [- ˈ-]. In line 5, the word is not only unaccented to fit the rhythm, but it is followed immediately by the accented monosyllable *boys*, which blocks any stress prominence on the *-teen* of *sixteen*.

p. 202, E 4:

A beautiful girl from Dunbar   [ə ˈbjuːtɪfʊɫ ˈɡɜːɫ frəm dʌnˈbɑː
Said she worshipped the bright evening star. sed ʃi ˈwɜːʃɪpt ðə ˈbraɪt‿iːvnɪŋ ˈstɑː
"Such a wonderful sight,   sʌʧə ˈwʌndəfʊɫ ˈsaɪt
I adore a good (k)night   aɪ‿əˈdɔːrə ɡʊd ˈnaɪt
Every evening in the back of my car."   evri‿ˈiːvnɪŋɪn ðə ˈbækəv maɪ ˈkɑː]

In their citation forms the stress patterns of *evening* and *evening star* are [ˈ- -] and [ˌ- - ˈ-], respectively. The rhythm of the limerick, however, requires the first *evening* to be unaccented, which is possible because it is only the secondary stress of the citation form of [ˌiːvnɪŋ ˈstɑː] that gets suppressed, whereas the second time the word *evening* is used it is accented.

p. 204, E 5: The stress pattern of *absent-minded* and *absent-mindedly*:
*Are all professors absent-ˈminded? The ˌabsent-minded proˈfessor
"Well, well," he said absent-ˈmindedly...*

p. 205, E 6: The stress patterns of the type "adjective + past participle":
*"Our boss is so ˌold-ˈfashioned and his methods of maintaining discipline are s o
ˌheavy-ˈhanded that everybody in the office is ˌlow-ˈspirited." - "That approach
seems rather ˌshortˈsighted. How can he expect to motivate you if he does not rely
on ˌself-ˈdiscipline?" - "He's got this ˌdeep-seated beˈlief that people work hard
only under pressure. But his attempts to monitor our output are only ˌhalf-
ˈhearted. And he's not even fair. With some of us he is ˌshort-ˈtempered, but with
this new yuppy he is ever so lenient. That young chap was appointed to the sales
department even though they were ˌover-ˈstaffed." - "Sounds like he's the boss's
ˌblue-eyed ˈboy." - "Rumour has it he is the boss's ˈwife's blue-eyed ˌboy." - "I see.
And I've been told she's such a ˌhigh-minded ˈperson, telling everybody else what
is right and what is wrong." - "That's true, but none of these ˌlily-livered ˈcreeps
has the courage to stand up to her." - "But you have kept silent, haven't you?
Doesn't that mean you, too, are ˌlily-ˈlivered?"*

Remember that the standard stress pattern [ˌ ˈ] is modified if an accented word
follows the compound. Thus: *ˌdeep-seated beˈlief; ˌblue-eyed ˈboy* (but: *ˈwife's blue-
eyed ˌboy* because the contrast accent on *wife* reduces the following stress
prominences); *ˌhigh-minded ˈperson; ˌlily-livered ˈcreeps.*

p. 209, E 7: The stress patterns of "verb+particle" constructions.
a. *They never come ˈback* "I told you, George Foreman wouldn't be able to keep
ˈup with the young boxers. As the saying goes: They never ˌcome ˈback." - "Well,
Muhamed Ali staged an impressive ˈcomeˌback, didn't he?" -"I admit, his first
major bout was a ˈwalk-ˌover, and as a young fighter he certainly caused a ˈshake-
ˌup of the boxing world. But his last fights were a bit of a ˈlet-ˌdown, weren't they."
- "It looks like these ˈwalk-ˌover victories are a thing of the past then."*

Additional comments: Compare the stress pattern of the verb + adverbial particle
"come back" and the compound noun consisting of the same morphemes:
"comeback"

b. *A lovers' tiff* "Last Tuesday, Susan and Peter had a row and ˌbroke ˈup. He was
in a hell of a state and nearly had a nervous ˈbreakˌdown. He jumped into his
Jaguar and ˌdrove ˈoff into the dark night." - "Yes, I know, he's such a ˈshow-ˌoff,
isn't he? The whole thing is a farce: he hit a lamp post and the car was a complete
ˈwrite-ˌoff. And instead of ˌlaughing it all ˈoff she then has a ˈguilt ˌhang-up, ˌwalks
ˈout on her new boyfriend, and since then she and Peter have ˌmade ˈup." - "How
do you know?" - "I saw her ˈmake-ˌup on his collar." - "Ah yes, that's a ˈgive-
aˌway. So the great tragedy ˌturned ˈout to be just a little lovers' tiff. And I was
certainly ˌtaken ˈin by this would-be Romeo. I simply couldn't put ˈup with his
childish behaviour. I think they should start behaving like ˈgrown-ˌups." - "Yes,
but she was so impressed by his ˌroaring ˈoff and the scratch on his face. She*

embraced him like a war hero." -"Well, well, whatever ₁turns you ᵇon, baby."

Additional comments: In the main, the <u>noun</u> compounds consisting of "verb + particle" have the expected [ᵗ- ₁-] pattern (e.g. *a nervous ᵗbreak₁down*) while the <u>verbal</u> constructions with "verb + particle" have a [₁- ᵗ-] pattern (as in *she ₁broke ᵗdown*) even when there is something between the verb and the particle (e.g., *laughing it all ᵗoff*), or the verbal construction serves a nominal function in the sentence (*his ₁roaring ᵗoff*). The stress pattern of the compound (*ᵗhang-up*) can change, however, if it is modified by a preceding stressed word (e.g. *a ᵗguilt ₁hang-up*).

c. <u>*Workers strike for better pay*</u> *After a ᵗtake-over ₁bid by a Japanese car manufacturer had failed, 500 workers were ₁laid ᵗoff. In a ᵗshow₁down between employers and employees, the trade unions first staged a ᵗsit-₁in and later on even a ᵗwalk-₁out to put pressure on the management. The directors promptly reacted with ᵗlock-₁outs at two branches of the Ford company and the demand to ₁call ᵗoff the strike immediately.*

Additional comments: The semi-stressed second element of the compound *take-over* is destressed before the word *bid*, which takes over the stress. The three-word combination is itself a compound.

p. 212, E 8:.

Student A:	Student B:
What's the capital of Spain?	*Which country is Islamabad the capital of?*
Madrid [məˈdrɪd]	Pakistan [ˌpækɪˈstɑːn]
Which actress starred in <u>*Some like it hot?*</u>	*Who is the most famous boxer of all times?*
Marilyn Monroe [ˌmærɪlɪn mənˈrəʊ]	Muhammad Ali [məˌhæməd‿ɑːˈliː]
What's the capital of Finland?	*What's the capital of Rumania?*
Helsinki [ˌheɫˈsɪŋki]	Bucharest [ˌbukəˈrest]
What's the capital of Irak?	*Where did Wellington beat Napoleon?*
Baghdad [ˌbægˈdæd]	Waterloo [ˌwɔːtəˈluː]
Which London area is famous for its night clubs?	*Which town is situated on Montreal Island?*
Soho [ˌsəʊˈhəʊ] or [ˈsəʊhəʊ]	Montreal [ˌmɒntriˈɔːɫ]
What is the capital of Germany?	*What's the capital of the Netherlands?*
Berlin [ˌbɜːˈlɪn] or [bəˈlɪn]	Amsterdam [ˌæmstəˈdæm]
What's the capital of Northern Ireland?	*Which British colony was given back to China in 1997?*
Belfast [ˌbeɫˈfɑːst] or [ˈbeɫˌfɑːst]	Hongkong [ˌhɒŋˈkɒŋ]

VI.3. Weak Forms

p. 221, C 4/E 1: <u>Before</u> listening to the tape, mark the weak and contracted forms, which we have intentionally written in full. Work out whether any of the grammatical items in the excerpt might be in their strong form and why.

Likewise we have [wɪv] *always been* [bɪn] *uhm r-really concerned* at [ə?] *that* [ðə?]*the language support teachers, our language support teachers out in school* are as [ɑːrəz] *knowledgable* as they can [əz ðeɪ kəm] *possibly be. So* we have [wiːhəv] *always run a training course <u>for</u>* [fɔː] *them* [ðəm] *and* [æn] *and* [ən] *that* is [ðæ?s]*quite unusual;* there's [ðəz] *not many places left* who [u] *get the resources* to [tə] *do that,* and we have been [ŋwɪvbɪn] *very lucky in Redbridge that* [ðə?] *the council* have [əv] *actually given us the money <u>to</u>* [tuː]*to* [tə] *run this,* and it is [ənɪts] *a year-long course* that [ðə?] *they do* for an [frən] *afternoon* and [ən] *evening a week and uhm it covers all sorts* of [əv] *areas <u>from</u>* [frɒm]... *English ... teaching English* as an [əzn̩] *additional language, looking* at [ə?] *issues around bilingualism, looking* at [æt?] *racism* and an [ænən] *anti-racist curriculum, looking* at the [ə?ðə] *needs of black pupils ...*

p. 222, E 2: The dialogue in the cartoon is: *"Why do you have to get plaice again? Why didn't you get us a nice bit of cod?"* - *"There wasn't any cod left. It was all sold out. Why don't you buy it next time?"*

VII. Morphology

p. 228, E 1: Check your pronunciation against the solution suggested here:

A: The minutes from our last meeting were very elaborate down to every minute detail, and certainly not comparable with the slovenly records that Deborah kept.

[ðə ˈmɪnɪts frəmaʊə ˈlɑːst ˈmiːtɪŋ wə veriˈiˈlæbərət daʊn tuˡʷevri maɪˈnjuːt ˈdiːteɪɫ ǀ ən ˈsɜːtn̩li nɒt ˈkɒmpərəbɫ wɪð ðə ˈslʌvn̩li ˈrekɔːdz ðət ˈdebərə kept]

B: Absolutely, and she was unfriendly with the customers, too. I think the prevalent opinion amongst us top executives is that badly-trained personnel is a recipe for disaster...

[ˈæpsəluːtli ǀ ənˌʃi wəzˌʌnˈfrendli wɪð ðə ˈkʌstəməz ˈtuː ǀ ˈaɪ θɪŋk ðə ˈprevələntˌəˈpɪnjənˌəmʌŋstˌʌs tɒpˌɪgˈzekjətɪvz ɪz ðət ˈbædli treɪnd pɜːsəˈnelɪzə ˈresɪpi fə dɪˈzɑːstə ...]

A: ... a catastrophe. After all, we are not a benevolent institution, that's why I had to make the proposal to dismiss her...

[ə kəˈtæstrəfi ǀ ɑːftəˈrɔːɫ ǀ wiə ˈnɒtə bəˈnevələntˌɪnstɪˈtjuːʃn̩ ǀ ˈðæts waɪˈaɪ hædˌtə ˈmeɪk ðə prəˈpəʊzɫ tə dɪsˈmɪʃə]

B: ... and that's why I seconded it. She could have been seconded to the stock-taking department, but he doesn't know how to make an inventory. Of course we had to reconcile our views with those of the shop-stewards, but in the end the decision was unanimous.

266 *Solutions*

[ən ˈðæts waɪˈaɪ ˈsekəndɪdɪt | ʃi ˈkʊdəv bɪn səˈkɒndɪd tə ðə ˈstɒkteɪkɪŋ dɪˈpɑːtmənt bət ʃi ˈdʌznt nəʊ ˈhaʊ tə meɪkəˈn‿ɪnvəntri: | əf kɔːs wi ˈhæt‿tə ˈrekənsaɪl‿aʊə ˈvjuːz wɪˈðəʊz‿əv ðə ʃɒp ˈstjuːədz | bət‿ɪn ðiˈend ðə dəˈsɪʒn̩ wəz juˈnænɪməs]

A: *They even wanted to upgrade her!*

[ðeɪ ˈˌiːvn wɒntɪd‿tuʷʌpˈɡreɪd‿hə]

B: *That's when you came up with that brilliantly equivocal remark: "She can't go far enough." Admirable rhetoric.*

[ˈðæts wenju keɪˈm‿ʌp wɪð‿ðæt ˈbrɪliəntliˈˌkwɪvɪkəɫ rɪˈmɑːk | ʃi ˈkɑːnt ɡəʊ ˈfɑːr‿ɪˈnʌf | ˈædmɪrəbɫ ˈretərɪk]

VII.1. Regular past tense

p. 232, E 1 :

a. [ðə ˈpɑːst‿əv ˈpɑːs‿ɪz ˈpɑːst]: *The past of "pass" is "passed".*

b. *burnt* [bɜːnt] is irregular. (*burned* [bɜːnd], an alternative form, is regular.)

p. 232, E 2:

a. [wi dɪsˈkʌst ðə ˈprɒbləm | ˈɑːgjuːd‿əbaut ˈpɒsɪbɫ səˈluːʃn̩z | ən dəˈsaɪdɪd ðət wi wɒntɪd ˈmɔːr‿ɪnfəˈmeɪʃn̩]

b.i. The past tense of *discuss* is regularly formed with <-ed>, and is also phonetically regular. The alveolar stop is realised as [t] after fortis [s].

b.ii. Since *argue* ends with <e> the past tense is formed with <-d>, not <-ed>. However, phonetically it is regular, since the alveolar stop is assimilated to the preceding voicing and is realised as [d].

b.iii. *Decide* ends with <e>, so the past tense is again formed with <-d>. Phonetically, an alveolar stop cannot be pronounced after a final [d] without an intervening vowel. Therefore the past tense is realised phonetically with [-ɪd].

b.iv. The past tense of *want* is formed regularly with <-ed> but, like *decide* it also ends with an alveolar stop, so the past tense is again realised phonetically with [-ɪd] .

VII. 1.2. Plural forms

p. 235, E 1:

a. [ˈɑːftə ðə ˈtuː fəʊnəˈtɪʃnz‿əd ˈwʌn meni ˈpraɪzɪz ɪn ˈsevrəɫ kɒmpəˈtɪʃnz | ðeɪ wəˈr‿eɪbɫ tuʷəˈfɔːd ðə ˈpraɪsɪz fə njuː ˈteɪps tə rəˈkɔːd ˈspiːʧɪz]

b. [ðə ˈstjuːdn̩ts ˈkrɒst ðə ˈbrɪʤɪz‿əv ˈbəʊθ ˈrɪvəz tə ˈvɪzɪt ðə ˈʧɜːʧɪz‿ɒnðə ˈsʌðən ˈhɪɫz]

p. 235, E 2: [ˈstɪksən ˈstəʊnz wɪɫ ˈbreɪk maɪ ˈbəʊnz | bət ˈwɜːdzɫ ˈnevə ˈhɜːt miː]

p. 235, E 4: [weə ðə ˈspɪrɪt‿əv rɒk ˈspiːks tə juː | ˈsɪŋz tə juː | ˈpleɪz fə juː | muːvz‿ən ˈtʌʧɪz juː]

p. 235, E 5: [ɪf ˈhærɪsənz | ˈwʊdkɒks‿ənˈfʌʤɪz ˈvɪdiəʊz‿ə rɪˈmuːvd frəm ðə ʃɒps | ðeɪɫ‿əˈpiːɫ tə ðə ˈʤʌʤɪz]

VII.1.3. [ŋ] vs. [ŋg]

p. 237, E 2:

a. [ˈtuːᵂæŋgləz wə ˈfɪʃɪŋ‿ɒf ðiˈiːsˈtæŋgliən ˈkəʊst | ðeɪ wə getɪŋ ˈhʌŋgriˈən ˈtaɪəd bɪkəz ðeɪ ˈhædn̩t kɔːtə ˈsɪŋɫ ˈfɪʃ‿ɔːɫ ˈdeɪ | ˈsʌdn̩li ðeɪ sɔː‿ə ˈmæn ˈklɪŋɪŋ tuˏə ˈplæŋk‿ən ˈʃaʊtɪŋ | hɪːːːlfə | ˈɑːftər‿ə ˈwaɪɫ ðə ˈjʌŋgər‿əv ðə tuːᵂæŋgləz | hu kəd ˈhɑːdli kənˈsiːlʅˈzæŋgə bɪkəz ðə ˈsplæʃɪŋ‿ən ˈʃaʊtɪŋ ˈskeəd‿ɔːɫ ðə ˈfɪʃ‿əweɪ | ˈɑːskt‿ɪz‿əʊɫdə ˈmeɪt | ˈwɒt‿dʌz ðæt ˈmiːn | hɪːːːlfə | ˈðæts nɒˈt‿ɪŋglɪʃ‿ɪts ˈʤɜːmən‿ən miːnz ˈheɫp | ten mɪnɪts ˈleɪtə ðə ˈfɜːstʃæp ˈtɜːnd‿tu‿ɪz ˈfrend‿ən səˈʤestɪd | hi ˈʃud‿əv lɜːntə ˈswɪm‿ɪnstedəv ˈlɜːnɪŋ ˌfɒrən ˈlæŋgwəʤɪz]

b. [aɪd bɪn ˈlɒŋɪŋ fər‿ə ˈlɒŋgə ˈhɒlɪdeɪ | bət‿ˈæz ðə ˈstɔːm gruː ˈstrɒŋgər‿ən ˈstrɒŋgə ˈwi dɪˈsaɪdɪd‿tə ˈliːv‿ˈæŋgɫsiːˈən gəʊ ˈbæk tə ˈbæŋgər‿ɒn ðə ˈmeɪnlænd]

VII.2. Stress and morphology

p. 243, E 1:

a. E: ˈinstitute, ˌinstiˈtution. G: ˌInstiˈtut, ˌInstituˈtion

English -*ion* is a bound derivational morpheme and a stress-repelling suffix.
German -*ion* is a bound derivational morpheme and a stress-carrying suffix.

b. [ˈdespətɪzm] because the word [ˈdespɒt] exists, and <-ism> is a stress-neutral morpheme when added to this free form.
[əˌsæsiˈneɪʃn̩] – <-ation> is a stress-carrying morpheme, so the primary stress of [əˈsæsɪn] is reduced to secondary stress in [əˌsæsiˈneɪʃn̩].

c. Phonetically speaking *kangaroo*, because it is the only one with a final syllable bearing stress.

d. [ˈriːdəz daɪˈʤest] means "Leser verdauen (alles)", whereas [ˈriːdəz ˈdaɪʤest] means something like "Leseauswahl".

XI. Additional exercises for advanced students and teachers

Not all of our phonetic symbols will be the standard symbols used for SBE, but we shall explain to you what they signify.

In fact, we shall comment on the pronunciation phenomena that clearly deviate from the sort of standard that we have been explaining and giving you to practise throughout the book. We expect them to be slightly problematical for you, either because you are listening at too high a level (influenced by the words you know underlie the utterance you hear) or because you hear the deviation and it raises questions in your mind as to how to transcribe them.

Although we consider it an invaluable tool for holding onto the sound patterns of spoken language, we would also like you to be aware of the imperfections of phonetic transcription as a tool for capturing pronunciation in writing. The principle of putting the continual flow of articulatory movement into a sequence of discrete symbols is – of course – a basic flaw. However, it rests on the assumption that acoustic changes resulting from the movements allow us to perceive the quasi-segmental structure of the syllables we hear.

We provide the orthographic text of the recordings and our suggestion for a moderately narrow phonetic transcription. We would stress, however, that our transcription can never be considered the *only* correct version.

C 1/E 1: Folk wisdom

When all is said and done, much more is said than done.

[wen‿ɔːɫ^z sedn̩ˈdʌn | ˈmʌʧ ˈmɔːrɪz ˈsedðən ˈdʌn]

Comments: This reading follows all the conventions we have introduced. A small refinement in the transcription here – the small raised [ᶻ] after the dark l – signals that we do not have a full [z] followed by a full [s] across the word boundary, but that only a weak reflex of the reduced *is* remains.

C 2/E2: Poem by Anon

I always eat peas with honey;	[aɪˈjɔːweɪz‿iːtˀ ˈpiːz wɪð ˈhʌni	1
I've done it all my life.	aɪv ˈdʌnɪˈt‿ɔːɫ maɪ ˈlaɪf	2
It makes the peas taste funny,	ɪʔ ˈmeɪks maɪ ˈpiːz teɪs ˈfʌni	3
But it keeps them on my knife.	bəɾɪt ˈkiːpsəˈm‿ɒmːaɪ ˈnaɪf]	4

Comments: Again the reader has conformed to the conventions we describe. However, his style is a bit less formal than purists would like – though they would probably not notice. Did you? He did not produce an /l/ after /ɔː/ in *always* in line 1; the /t/ of *it* (line 3) was replaced by a glottal stop, and the word-final /t/ in *taste* on the same line is elided before /f/; in line 4 the word-final /t/ in *but* is reduced to a tapped [ɾ], the [ð] of *them* is completely elided, and the /n/ of *on* is assimilated into the /m/ of *my*, resulting in a rather longer [m].

C 3/E 3: Interview with Alan Clark

To control one´s media image is is very very difficult uhm because don´t forget
[tə kənˈtɾʌʊ wʌnz ˌmiːdjəˈʳɪmɪʤ‿ɪz ɪz ˈveri veri ˈdɪfkʊɫt | ʔəːm | bəˈkʊz ˈdəʊn fəge?

   1   2   3   4   5

the media try and resist that. Er they want to ... they like to typecast you and they
ðə ˈmiːjə trɑən rɪˈzɪs ðæs | <breath> | əˈðeɪ wɒnteu | ˈðeɪ laɪkˀtə ˈtaɪpˀkɑːstʃu | əneɪ

   6   7   8   9   10   11

want to put you in situations which reinforce the way that they see you or the
wɒntə ˈpʊtʃuʷɪn ˌsɪtʃəˈleɪʃnz wɪʧ ˌriːɪnˈfɔːsːə weɪ | <breath> | ðət̯ ˈðeɪ ˈsiː ju‿ʊ ðʊ

   12   13   14   15   16

way they are projecting you.
weɪ ðɛə prəˈʤektɪŋ juː]

   17

Comments:

1. [kən'tɹəʊː wʌnz]: Final dark /l/ is frequently realised as a vocoid. Here the lengthened second part of the diphthong signals the /l/ slot rhythmically.

2. [ˌmiːdjəˤʳɪmɪʤ ɪz]: an example of intrusive [r]. <media> has no /r/, but it ends in /ə/, and is treated as if the /ə/ was spelt <-er>.

3. ['dɪfkʊɬt]: The vowel of the second syllable is elided. A possible explanation is the relative mass of the tongue dorsum which has to be raised – helped by a high jaw position – to form the closure for /k/. This is a relatively slow operation, and the high jaw works against the opening of the lips, thus maintaining the labial friction until the velar closure is formed. And even if a very short vocalic opening does occur, the switch from voiceless /f/ to voiced /ɪ/ and back to voiceless /k/ is an uneconomical series of gestures which can be avoided without endangering the identity of the word.

4. & 5. [dəʊn fəgeʔ ðə]: /t/ dropping word-finally in cross-word clusters is common in Southern British English. The loss of /t/ between /n/ and /f/ is not very salient perceptually, but avoids the careful timing to raise the velum for the /t/ closure phase. It must be raised for /f/ too, of course, but the transition is much less critical. The glottal replacement of /t/ seen in 5. is a common articulatory "economizing" strategy (although it is not considered standard. Compare also the Hugh Grant and Princess Diana interviews below). The glottal closure simulates the closure phase of the /t/, and here the fine adjustment from a tongue-tip closure to a tongue-tip fricative constriction can be avoided.

6., 7. & 8. [ðə 'miːʝə trɑən rɪ'zɪs ðæs̄]: This phrase shows the consequences of rapid speech: /iːdjə/ is reduced to a palatal fricative (probably a combined palatal and lamino-prepalatal fricative (tongue blade behind the alveolar ridge = [ʑ]) resulting from the palatal vowel+glide context and the incompletely raised tongue-tip for the /d/. In *try and* there is smoothing of [ɑɪən]; *resist* loses its final /t/ (compare 4. & 5. above), and in the phrase-final *that*, the final /t/ is articulated weakly so that an alveolar fricative results. We use the [s̄] transcription for this type of **fricativization**, as we do not wish to imply that it is a standard grooved /s/.

9. [wɒntəʊ]: The cross-word geminate /tt/ is clearly reduced to a single [t], and the /uː/ shows clear diphthongization (compare V.2.2.). Notice the strong form of the function word *to* (compare VI.3.). Alan Clark hesitates, indicating his search for what to say next. Hence the *to* is not in a rhythmically weak position and remains strong.

10. ['taɪpˀkɑːstɕu]: The final /t/ of *typecast* is not dropped before the /j/ of *you*, but forms an affricate (compare section VI.4.). Note the [tɕ] transcription, rather than the standard [tʃ]. We wanted to draw your attention in this advanced exercise to the difference between this sound and the one in *chew*.

11. [əɲeɪ]: The /ndð/ of *and they* is reduced to a single, dental [n̪] in this combin-

ation of unaccented function words. In the exercises we have standardly reduced *and* to [ən] and [n] but we have not mentioned before that the release of the dental closure in [n̪] is sufficient to signal the /ð/.

12., 13. & 14. [wɒntə ˈpʊtçuʷɪn ˌsɪtçəˈeɪʃnz]: The /tt/ of *want to* is simplified (see 9. above); the [tç] in *put you* and *situation* is comparable to 10. above.

15. [ˌriːɪnˈfɔːsːə weɪ]: Here we have a good example of the loss of dentality in initial /ð/ following /s/ or /z/ (compare section IV.3.4.). Notice that the [s̄] is longer than normal to signal *reinforce the* rather than *reinforce a*.

16. [ˈðeɪ ˈsi: juˍʊ ðʊ weɪ]: The vowels in *or* and *the* are "harmonized" with the preceding /uː/ *you* and the following /w/ of *way*. They remain <u>rounded</u> and in the <u>close back</u> region rather than opening to /ɔː/ and then moving to the mid-central region and becoming unrounded for /ə/, The "economy" factor in this should be clear.

17. [ðɛə prəˈdʒektɪŋ juː]: The putative triphthong /eɪɑː/ in *they are* is smoothed to a diphthong [ɛə].

C 4/E 4: Hugh Grant in an interview

I. *It can be slightly self-conscious making ehm to have eh people, you know, do*
[ɪʔkəmbɪ ˈsl̩aɪʔli ˌseʌf ˈkɒnʃəs ˌmeɪxɪŋ | əːm | tsə hæf: | ɜː | ˈpiːpʊ jəˈnøː du
  1   2   3   4   5   6   7   8*
that again but ehm it's it's odd 'cause eh, eh for as many days as it's self-
ˈðæsəgən | bʌtəm: | <breath>| ɪʔɪtsʔɪtˈsɒd kəz ɜː | əʊʌ | fɹːəz ˈmeni ˈdeɪzːːts ˌsʌf
  9   10   11   12*
conscious making there are others when I suppose if I'm being honest it's quite
ˈkɒnʃəsˌmeɪxɪŋ   ðərə   ˈʔʌðəz   wənˍʌɪ   ˈspøːzˍɪfˍəm   bɪˈŋɒnɪstˢ   ˌkwaɪt⌐
         13   14   15   16   17 18   19   20*
titillating as well especially if you've ah had years of absolute obscurity
ˈtɪtɪleɪtɪŋˍəz weː | sˈpeʃɪf jyf | <breath> ɜː | hæd ˈjɪəznˈjɪəzəv ˈæpsəluːt əbˈskjɹːəti
        21   22 23   24   25*
you know ehm so it's a double-edged coin.
jəˈnøː | ɜː m | søːs | <breath> | ʔɪts ɪtsə ˈdːʌbələdʒd ˈkɔɪn]
  26   27

Comments:

1. & 2. [ɪʔkəmbɪ ˈsl̩aɪʔli]: The syllable-final /t/ in *it* and *slightly* are replaced by a glottal stop. This is a common feature in Hugh Grant's (HG) speech (compare also Alan Clark above and Princess Diana below)

3. [ˌseʌf ˈkɒnʃəs]: This vocoid realisation of /l/ in postvocalic position is typical of HG's speech (see below also).

4. [ˌmeɪxɪŋ]: The fricativisation of /k/ as [x] is indicative of a rather lax articulation. HG's repetition of this form shows it to be more than a one-off event.

5. & 6. [tsə hæf: ɜ:]: The affricated rather than aspirated initial /t/ in *to* again shows a rather lax articulation. The voiceless final consonant ([f]) in /hæv/ is an interesting possible indicator of HG's hesitation mannerism, which may not have anything to do with a hesitation for planning what to say. Normally, /hæv/ would be realised [hæv] before a hesitation sound like [ɜ:]; [f] represents an assimilation to a following voiceless consonant (see section IV.3.1., p. 74). In this example, we see that the first word after the hesitation pause, *people*, begins with a voiceless plosive! Could it be that the contextually sensitive planning for *have* was established, and the hesitation mannerism inserted later?

7. & 8. [ˈpiːpʊ jəˈnøː]: Compare 3. above for vocoid /l/. HG has interesting idio-syncratic cases of smoothed diphthongs (see sections V.3.3. and V.3.4. for smoo-thing of /aɪ/ and /aʊ/). Here and in quite a number of other words (see below), he smooths the /əʊ/ diphthong to [øː]; i.e. he combines the liprounding expected in the (missing) second element with a strongly fronted first element.

9. [ˈðæs̄əgen]: This time, the final /t/ of *that* is not glottalised (compare 1. & 2. above), it is very laxly articulated as a fricative. It is without a groove in the tongue tip, a sort of non-dental lisped [s], indicated by the diacritic [¯] (see also C 3/E 3 above and C 5/E 5 below).

10. & 11. [fɹːz ˈmeni ˈdeɪz:::ts]: The reduced function word *for* in *for as many* is linked to *as* with a linking r. The more complex tongue shape required for the approximant [ɹ] dominates the preceding and following (reduced) vowels, resulting in a lengthened r-like sound. We have transcribed it as a single long [ɹː] with a syllabic function, but it clearly changes its quality as the tongue tip moves forward to the [z] from its retracted r position.
In the sequence *days as it's*, HG's lax articulation again manifests itself. He avoids the rapid lowering and raising of the tongue tip which is required to move from the /z/ to /ə/ to /z/ to /ɪ/ to /t/, resulting in an extended [z:::] followed by [ts].

12. & 13. [ˌsʌf ˈkɒnʃəsˌmeɪxɪn]: See 3. for vocoid /l/ and 4. for fricativized /k/ realisation. Note that *-making* ends with [n] instead of standard [ŋ] in preparation for the following [ð].

14. & 15. [ðərə ˈʔʌðəz]: *There are* is maximally reduced (compare VI.3), and as a re-sult of the [ərə] sequence, no linking r is possible between *are* and *others*. Conse-quently, there is – logically – a slight glottal onset to *others* even though the word is not emphasized.

16., 17., 18., 19. & 20. [wən‿aɪ ˈspøːz‿ɪf‿am bɪˈŋɒnɪstˢ ˌkwaɪt]: This word sequence shows a number of interesting deviations from expected vowel qualities. *When* has a reduced vowel in keeping with the unaccented production, although *when* is not normally quoted as a word which is commonly reduced. *Suppose* loses its first vowel, which is not unusual, resulting in a [sp] cluster onset, and the /əʊ/ is realised as [øː] again (compare 8. above). /aɪ/ is smoothed to [ɑ] in *I'm* and the two syllables of *being* are reduced to one by smoothing the /iːɪ/ sequence to [ɪ]. Notice how the sequence *honest it's* loses a syllable.

21., 22. & 23. [əz wɐ: | sˈpeʃɪf jyf]: Two different cases of vocoid /l/ are heard here, dependent on their context, one word-final in *well* as [ɐ], the other word-medially in *(e)specially* between close front vowels as [j]. *You have* is reduced maximally, even though it precedes a hesitation pause, and the final consonant is [f] rather than [v] despite the pause (compare 6. above). The /uː/ of *you* is extremely strongly fronted ([y]) following the palatal glides and vowel combination.

24. & 25. [ˀæpsəluːt̪əb̥ˈskjɹːəti]: The vowel onset of the emphasized word is glottalized. In *obscurity*, we again have a lengthened r sound carrying a syllable (compare 10. above).

26. & 27. [jəˈnɵ: | ɜ: m | sɵːs]: See 8. above.

II. *If you go to a dinner party now and you tell your normal indiscreet kind of*
[fjy ˈgɜːˀ tʊə ˈdɜnʌˌpɑːsi naʌ | ˀændʑy ˈtel jɔ; ˈnɔːmʊ ˀɪndəsˈkriːˀ kaɪ nə
    1   2   3   4   5   6   7   8
stories ehm for a laugh uhm, whereas in the old days that was the end of it and it
ˈstɔːrɪʐ | ɜːm fərə ˈlɑːf | <breath> | ˀɜːm wəɹzniˌˀəʊɫdez ðæˀ wəziˌˈendəvɪˀnɪ
                                                          9   10   11   12   13
was quite fun, although none of the people you are with will ring up
wəz ˌkwaɪˀ | ˈfʌn | ˀɔːˈðəʊ ˈnʌnəðə ˈpiːpʊɫjɔː ˈwːɪð | wɪʊᵗ | ɹːːːːˈŋʌp
        14   15   16   17
the Evening Standard and say "Oh I've got a great story about Hugh", they
ðiːvnɪŋ ˈstændədn̩ ˈseɪˌɔˌˈav gʌdə ˌgreɪˀ ˈstɔːriˌəbaʊˀ ˈçɵː | <breath>| ˈðɜðə
18   19   20   21   22   23
might tell their friend who might tell their friend and eh...
ˈmaɪˀ teɫ ˈðeə frend hu maɪtːeɫ ˈðeə frendənə]
  24   25

Comments:

1., 2., 3. & 4. [fjy ˈgɜːˀ tʊə ˈdɜnʌˌpɑːsi naʌ]: By dropping the initial /ɪ/ of *if*, the rhythm changes to a single "upbeat" before the accent on *go*. The vowels in *go*, *dinner* and *now* are <u>more open</u> than the SBE standard we have been advocating, and reflect a certain social style, associated perhaps with cultured Upper Middle Class. Note too the strongly fronted /uː/ (compare HG I. 23. above) and the fricativized /t/ in *party* (compare HG I. 9. above).

5., 6. & 7. [ˀændʑy ˈtel jɔ; ˈnɔːmʊ ˀɪndəsˈkriːˀ]: Note the glottal onset to *and* after the pause, the fusion of /d/ and /j/ (*and you*) to [dʑ], and the strongly fronted /uː/ again. The /l/ in *normal* is realised as a vocoid (compare HG I. 3., 7., 12. & 21. above), despite the fact that it could act as a link to *indiscreet*, which now begins with a glottal constriction.

8. [kaɪ nə]: *Kind of* loses /d/ and /v/ in this unaccented form. The loss of /d/ is the consequence of not raising the velum until the apical closure (shared by /n/ and /d/) is released; i.e., it is a matter of timing, not of reducing the number of

articulatory gestures. This can easily occur in prosodic contexts where the duration of the /nd/ cluster is reduced. The loss of /v/ is a reduction in the number of gestures; the labio-dental gesture is simply omitted.

9. & 10. [wəɹzni‿ˈəʊɫdez]: We offer an extreme version of the possible transcription versions here to underline the discrepancy between top-down perception, where we hear 4 syllables for *whereas in the*, roughly [wəɹəzɪni], and what is produced, which is an r-coloured schwa merging into [ɹ], and the [n] following immediately on the [z] without dropping the tongue tip for a vowel. A slightly less extreme version could acknowledge the syllables perceived because we "know" the underlying units are *as* and *in*: [wəɹzni̩].
The diphthong /eɪ/ in *days* has been reduced to a short monophthong in this unaccented part of a fast stretch of the utterance.

11., 12. & 13. [ðæʔ wəzi‿ˈendəvɪʔn̩ wəz]: Compare I. 1 & 2 for glottal replacement of /t/ in *that* and *it*; the /ð/ is dropped completely in *was the* (see section IV.3.4.); the /t/ is dropped in *it was*. This is not uncommon in fast speech, and it is to be expected here, following so closely on the previous glottaly replaced /t/ in the first *it*. Note the reduction of *and* to a syllabic /n/.

14. [kwaɪʔ]: Glottal /t/ replacement (cf. I. 1. & 2.).

15., 16. & 17. [ʔɔːˈðəʊ ˈnʌnəðə ˈpiːpuɫjɔː ˈwːɪð]: /l/ elision in *although*; /v/ elision in *of*. Both cases can be seen as an economy of articulatory effort under time pressure at negligible communicative cost. Perceptually, dark l is close to the quality of [ɔː], and a [v] is very similar to [ð]. In addition, /l/ is redundant in the context /ɔː_ˈðəʊ/ and *of* is redundant between *none* and *the*.
[jɔː] as the reduced form of *you are* [jʊə] is an interesting illustration of how strongly the /ʊə/ diphthong has been replaced by /ɔː/ (cf. section V.3.6.1.). In this case the replacement is by analogy; the underlying form is not phonemic /ʊə/ but /uːɑː/.

18. - 23. [ði:vnɪŋ ..... ˈseɪ‿ɔ‿ˈav gʌdə ˌgreɪʔ ˈstɔːri‿əbaʊʔ ˈçɔː ..... ˈðӡəə]: Here we see a number of examples of vowel modification: /iː/ + /iː/ is reduced to a single [iː] in *the evening*; /əʊ/ and /aɪ/ are both smoothed to monophthongs; *Oh I* /əʊ aɪ/ becomes [ɔɑ]. /uː/ is pulled forward by the /j/ and pronounced with a more open quality [øː] in *Hugh*; in *they*, also, the vowel quality is more open.
Note the two glottal replacements of /t/ in *great* and *about*, where the /t/ precedes an apical /s/ or front dorsal [ç] fricative, vs. the [d] realisation of /t/ preceding a vowel (*got a*).

24. & 25 [ˈmaɪʔ teɫ...... maɪtːeɫ ˈðeə]: Another case of glottalized vs. non-glottalized word-final /t/ as a function of context: Accented *might* before *tell* has glottal replacement (or possibly a glottally reinforced cross-word geminate /t#t/), whereas unaccented *might* before *tell* has the geminate reduced to a single [t].

C 5/E 5: Interview with Princess Diana

I.

Interviewer: *Your Royal Highness, how prepared were you for the pressures that*
[ju ˌrɔə ˈhaɪnəs ˈhaʊ | prəˈpɛəd wɜː ju: | fɔː ðə ˈpreʃəz ðə?
                 1   2   3
came with marrying into the Royal Family?
ˈkeɪm wɪð | ˈmæriŋ‿ɪntə ðə ˌrɔː ˈfæmɪlɪ]
                                    4
Diana: *At the age of nineteen you always think you are prepared for everything*
[ət̪ðɪ ˈeɪʤəv naɪnˈtiːn | juːwəs ˈθɪŋkjɔ ɸrɪˈpeə̄s fə ˈevrɪθɪŋ |
                                          5   6   7   8
and you think you have the knowledge of what's coming ahead. But although I
ænjy ˈθɪŋkçyæv ðə ˈnɒlɪʤəy̆ wɒts ˈkʌmɪŋ əˈhed̪ | <breath> | bɜt | ʔɔːɫðəʊe
 9   10
was daunted at the prospect at the time I felt I had the support of my husband to
wəz̪ ˈd̪ɔːnˈsɪz̄əʔðə ˈprɒspeçəʔðə ˈtaɪm | ʔaɪ feɫt‿aɪ ɦæd̪ðə səˈpɔːsəv maɪ ˈhʌzbən tə
      11   12   13   14
be.
ˈbiː]

Comments:

1. [rɔə ˈhaɪnəs]: The /ɔɪ/ in *royal* is smoothed, the second element fusing with a vowelized dark l; only a weak schwa vowel is left.

2. [fɔː ðə]: After the pause, the interviewer uses the strong form of *for*.

3. [ðə?]: Another case of glottal replacement of /t/, this time preceding /k/.

4. [ˌrɔː ˈfæmɪlɪ]: Even more extreme smoothing of /ɔɪ/ than in 1. above.

5. [juːwəs]: Extreme reduction of unaccented and rapidly produced *you always*. The long, lax rounded high back vowel allows the interpretation of two syllables.

6. & 7. [ˈθɪŋkjɔ ɸrɪˈpeə̄s]: The reduced *you are* is realized as [jɔ]. *Prepared* shows very lax articulation in the (unstressed) initial /p/ and the final /d/, both of which are realized as fricatives.

8. [fə ˈevrɪθɪŋ]: The expected linking r is not used here, giving *everything* more emphasis.

9. & 10. [ænjy ˈθɪŋkçyæv]: Two different realizations of *you*, both with a very fronted /uː/, though the second less extreme under the opening influence of following /æ/. The first one has [j] for /j/ following [n], whereas the second has [ç] following the fortis /k/ plosive. Note the "sub-standard" h-dropping in the full verb *have*.

11. & 12. [d̪ɔːnˈsɪz̄əʔðə ˈprɒspeçəʔðə]: two further cases of glottal /t/ replacement in *at the*. Lax articulation is apparent in the non-glottalized plosives; in *daunted* the

medial /t/ and the final /d/ are fricativized, as is the /kt/in *prospect*. Interestingly, the quality of the fricative reflects the fusion of velar and alveolar.

13. & 14, [sə'pɔːs̄əv maɪ 'hʌzbən tə 'biː]: More indication of lax articulation: Fricativized /t/ in *support*, and /d/ elision in *husband* preceding /t/, without any compensatory lengthening of the [n].

II.

Interviewer: *What were the expectations that you had for married life?*
     ['wɒt wɜː | ði ˌekspek'teɪʃn̩z ðə? ju 'ɦæd fə ˌmærɪd 'laɪf]
                        1   2

Diana: *I think like any marriage, especially when you've had eh divorced parents*
     [?aɪ θɪŋk laɪ'x̣_eni 'mærɪʤ | <breath> | 'speʃli wen juɣɦæd̠_ə: | dɪ'vɔːs 'pearn̩ts
             3   4   5
like myself, you'd want to try even harder to make it work and you don't want to
laɪ? maɪ'self jud wɒntš 'tɹaɪ_iːvən 'hɑːdə | tə̣ meɪxɪt 'wɜːk? | ən ju 'dəun'wɒntu
   6   7   8   9
fall back into a pattern that you've seen happen in your own family.
 | <breath> | fɔːᵗ 'bækɪntu ə: 'pæ?n̩ | ðəɣv siːn 'ɦæpənɪn jɔrəuŋ 'fæmlɪ | <breath> |
                             10   11   12
I desperately want it to work, I ... I desperately love my husband and I
?aɪ 'despɹ̩li 'wɒns̄iˌs̄ə 'wɜːk? ?aɪ | ?aɪ 'despɹɪ?lɪ 'lʌv ma' 'ɦʌzbənd̠ | <breath> | ænd ?aɪ
       13   14   15   16   17
wanted to share everything, together, and I thought that we were a very good
'wɒntˢɪtˢə 'ʃɛː 'evrɪθɪŋ | tə'geðə | ænaɪ 'θɔːˀs̄ | <breath> | ?ðəwi wərə 'veri ɡʏd̚
   18   19   20   21   22
team.
'tiːm]

Comments:

1. [wɒt wɜː]: Full form of *were* preceding a pause.

2. [ðə?]: Glottal replacement of word-final /t/.

3. [laɪ'x̣_eni]: Weakened articulation of word-final /k/ as a velar fricative in an unaccented word.

4. ['speʃli]: Presumably the more colloquial *specially* is intended rather than the standard *especially* in this context. Despite the emphasis on the word, it is reduced to two syllables: ['speʃəli] → ['speʃli] → ['speʃli].

5. [dɪ'vɔːs 'pearn̩ts]: Loss of word-final /t/ between consonants; note also the reduction of *parents* to <u>almost</u> one syllable. The loss of schwa between [r] and [n] is an obvious "economy" in terms of tongue tip movement (raised and slightly retracted for [ɹ], lowered for [ə], raised again for the alveolar closure of [n]). Despite being no more suited than /r/ to taking over the role of syllable nucleus,

the /n/ appears to be syllabic because /r/ can only occur in syllable onsets or ambisyllabically between vowels.

6. - 9. Variants of /k/ and /t/. [laɪˀ maɪˈseɬf]: A rare glottal replacement in *like* of word-final /k/, occurring in this unaccented position because the glottal reinforcing gesture is quicker than the tongue dorsum raising gesture. Later, in *work*, we have a glottally reinforced prepausal /k/, where there is time for the dorsal closure to be formed. In *make it*, there is a case of fricativized, intervocalic /k/ ([meɪxɪt], compare 3. above).
A similar variation in /t/ can be observed: In *want to try* (7) the realisation [wɒnt͡s ˈtɹaɪ] can be interpreted as a) a fusion of the final /t/ in *want* with the initial /t/ of *to*, b) an articulatory weakening of the /t/ to an affricate [t͡s] before the vowel of *to*, where the fricative segment also takes over a quasi-syllabic function of the deleted [ə]. In 9, on the other hand, the final /t/ of *don't* is glottalized before the consonantal onset of *want* ([ˈdəʊnˀwɒnt]).

10. [ˈpæˀn̩]: Despite the <ern> spelling, the unstressed vowel is elided and the /n/ becomes syllabic. This would normally call for precise timing of the velum lowering gesture to give the nasal release of /t/. However, glottalizing the /t/ allows an interesting economy of articulatory effort: Neither the alveolar closure for the /tn/ closure nor the velum lowering for /n/ have to be carefully timed because the on- and offset of /t/ are defined glottally.

11. [ðəçɣʋ]: The final /t/ in unaccented and reduced *that* is fricativized preceding /j/ in contrast to the final /t/ of accented *don't* before /w/ (compare 9. above). Under the influence of the palatal glide /j/ the frication becomes palatal, and the following deaccented /uː/ is fronted to [ɣ].

12. [jɔrəʊŋ ˈfæmlɪ]: The alveolar /n/ of *own* is assimilated to the following labiodental /f/.

13. & 16. Two renderings of *desperately*: [ˈdespɹli] and [ˈdespɹɪˀlɪ], both reduced to 3 syllables. In the first (13.), the two medial unstressed vowels (/despərətliː/) are not realised and the approximant /r/ takes over as the nucleus of the second syllable. The /t/ is also elided. In 16. the second syllable is realised more conventionally, but the syllable-final /t/ is glottally replaced. This avoids the complex tongue-tip and -blade combination where the complete [t] closure is formed and then released laterally for the [l].

14. & 15. [ˈwɒnsˌ͡sə ˈwɜːkˣ]: Further examples of weakened plosive articulation. The intervocalic /t/s in *want it to* are fricativized (compare 7. and 11. above). In the accented monosyllable *work*, the final /k/ is slightly affricated to [kˣ].

17. [ænd ˀaɪ]: Strong forms of function words after a pause, produced without linking. Possibly an indication of continued 'planning' of what is to come.

18., 20. & 21. Three different degrees of /t/ weakening: In the accented *wanted to* ([ˈwɒntˌ͡sɪtˢə]) we have <u>affrication</u>, i.e. a short /t/ closure with apical fricative release; in *and I thought* ([ænaɪ ˈθɔːˀs]) where *thought* is accented, we find <u>fricati-</u>

<u>vized</u> /t/ with the closure phase simulated by laryngealization (creak); in the totally unaccented function word combination *that we* ([ʔðəwi]), the /t/ is completely elided.

19. [ˈʃɛː ˈevrɪθɪŋ]: The smoothing of /eə/ before /e/ is a plausible ˋeconomy' of movement.

22. [ˈveri ɡʏd]: The strongly fronted /ʊ/ in *good* is a typical younger generation Southeastern pronunciation. It is an indication that the fronting of the back close vowels is not *just* a product of the palatal context (compare 11. above).

III.

<u>Diana</u>: *I wasn´t daunted, and uhm I´m not daunted by the responsibilities*
   [<sigh; breath> | aɪ wɒzn̩ ˈdɔːntis̄ | ænʌm ʔæm nɒtⁿˈdɔːntɪd baɪ ðə rɪˌspɒnsˈbɪlɪtɪz̰
                    1   2
th' that that role creates. ehm It was a challenge, it is a challenge, ehm,
ð°ðəˀðæˀ ˈrəʊɫ krɪˈeɪts | <breath> | ɜm ˀɪˀwəzə ˈʧælɪndʒ | ɪˈtɪzə ˈʧælɪndʒ | <breath> ɜːm
     3   4
as for becoming Queen it´s was never eh at the forefront of my mind when I
ˈæz fɔː bɪˈkʌmɪŋ ˈkwiːn‿ɪtsː | wəz ˈnevəːɹːːːˀəːːːˀæt̪ðə ˈfɔːfrʌntəmaɪ ˈmaɪnz̄ weⁿai
     5   6   7
married my husband, it was a long way off that thought.
ˈmærɪz̄ maɪ ˈhʌzbənz̄ | wəzə ˈlɒŋ weɪˈlɒːf ðæˀ ˈθɔːts̄]
  8   9   10   11

Comments:

1. [aɪ wɒzn̩ ˈdɔːntis̄]: Fricativized and devoiced word- (and phrase-) final /d/.

2. [ænʌm ʔæm]: The unaccented personal pronoun in *I 'm* is smoothed to a monophthong. Note the fronted quality of the vowel, an indication of the fronted starting point of the diphthong, which is characteristic of the speaker's social group.

3. & 4. Three glottal replacements for /t/: Twice in (3.) *that that role* ([ðəˀðæˀ ˈrəʊɫ]), again in (4) *it was a challenge* ([ɪˀwəzə ˈʧælɪndʒ]).

5. [ˈæz fɔː bɪˈkʌmɪŋ]: A full form of *for*, possibly following the hesitation, and a reflection of a fairly slow speech rate. A similar full form for *at the* follows a later hesitation in the same line.

6. [ˈfɔːfrʌntəmaɪ]: The lenis fricative /v/ is elided before /m/ in *of my*.

7., 8. & 9. Three cases of word-final /d/ fricativization: (7) in *my mind* ([maɪ ˈmaɪnz̄]), (8) in *when I married* ([weⁿai ˈmærɪz̄]), and (9) in *my husband* ([maɪ ˈhʌzbənz̄]).

10. [ˈlɒŋ weɪˈlɒːf]: The word *off* shows an interesting phonetic mixture of <u>long vowel</u>, associated with more conservative RP speakers pronunciation, and the

standard <u>open quality</u>.

11. [ðæ⁷ ˈθɔːts̄]: Two variants of word-final /t/, differing with context. The deictic *that* shows glottal replacement preceding the consonantal onset of *thought*. In that word the /t/ is affricated, a common occurrence (together with fricativization) in phrase-final position.

IV.

The most daunting aspect was the media attention because my
ðə məʊs ˈdɔːntiˈŋ‿æspeʔk wəz ðəːːˀˌmiːdjəˀəˈs̄enʃən | <breath> | bɪˈkʌʒː | maɪ
  1   2   3   4

husband and I we were told when we got engaged that the media would go
ˈfiʌzbənːaɪ wɪwə ˈtəʊɬz̄ | wem wi gɒˀs̄‿ɪŋˈgeɪʒ ðəʔt | <breath> | ðə ˈmiːdjɪə wʊʔ | ʷᵃgəʊ
  5   6   7   8   9   10

quietly and then it didn´t, and then when we were married they said it would go
ˈkwaɪətli | <sniff> | ənðeʔn ˈdɪdn̩t | æn ˈðen wem wi wə ˈmæriːs̄ | ðeɪ ˈsedɪʔ wʊgəʊ
                11   12   13   14

quietly and it didn´t, and then it started to focus (of) very much on me; and I
ˈkwaɪəʔli ɪnɪʔdɪdn̩ts̄ ən ˈðenɪʔ | ˈsˈɑː s̄ɪts̄ə ˈfəʊkəs ᴰⱽˈveˀə mʌtʃɒn ˈmiː | <sniff> | ændaɪ
        15   16

seemed to be on the front of a newspaper every single day, which,
ˈsiːmtə̰ ˈb̰j̰iɒn ðə ˈfrʌntəvə ˈnjyːspeɪpˀ ˈevri sɪŋʲɬ ˈdeɪ | <breath> | wɪtʃ | <breath> |
  17   18

eh is isolating experience and the higher the media put you, place you, is the
əʔɪˈzaɪsəleɪsɪŋ‿ɪksˈpɪrɪəns | ɜnɜˈfiaʒ ðəˈmiːʒjə ˈpʊʔtʃju | ˈpleɪsju | <breath> | ɪz ðə
                19   20   21

bigger the drop. And I was very aware of that.
ˈbɪɣə ðə ˈdɟɒʔp̚ | ənaəz ˈverɪ əˈweərəv ˈðæs̄]
  22   23   24

Comments:

1. & 2. [ðə məʊs ˈdɔːntiˈŋ‿æspekʔ wəz]: 'Standard' /t/ elision in word-final cluster preceding /d/ in *most daunting*. The /t/ is also elided from the /kt/ cluster in *aspect*. However, the accompanying glottalization may either be glottal reinforcement of /k/ or glottal replacement of /t/ - or both!

3. & 4. [ˌmiːdjəˀəˈs̄enʃən]: Intrusive [ɹ] between the final [ə] of *media* and the initial [ə] of *attention*. In *attention* the initial /t/ of the stressed middle syllable is fricativized. This shows extremely lax articulation.

5. [ˈfiʌzbənːaɪ]: Schwa elision and twofold /d/ elision in *husband and*. The only reflex of *and* is in the lengthened nasal. An alternative transcription could be [nn] to indicate that the lengthened nasal has a coda function in *husband* and a syllabic function as *and*.

6. [ˈtəʊɬz̄]: Another case of fricativized word-final /d/.

7. [wem wi]: Assimilation of /n/ to [m] before /w/.

8. & 9. [wi gɒ²s̰‿ɪŋ'geɪʒ ðə²t]: Fricativized /t/ word-finally in *got*. As in an earlier case (B. 20 above), the /t/ closure is simulated by laryngealization (creak) at the end of the preceding vowel, triggering the percept of an affricated /t/. In *engaged* the final /d/ is elided preceding the consonantal word onset of *that*. In *that* the final /t/ is glottally reinforced before the pause. This is probably not a case of free variation between fricativization and glottaling, but a hesitation gesture. In completed phrases before a pause, this speaker regularly affricates or fricativizes.

10. [ðə 'mi:dʒɪə wu² | ʷəɡəʊ]: The apparent glottal replacement of /d/ in *would* preceding a pause is a second example of articulatory interruption, similar to 9. above. This is supported by the very weak, reduced *would* after the pause.

11. [ənðeˀn 'dɪdn̩t]: Here is a fascinating example of loss of synchronization between glottal and supra-glottal gestures. The sequence /nɪt/ in *then it*, which we could expect to be realized as [nɪ²] before *didn't*, loses its phonetic identity because the laryngeal constriction for /t/ occurs too early relative to the apical closure and velum lowering for /n/.

12. [wem wi]: A second case of /n/ assimilated to [m] before /w/ (see 7. above).

13. ['mæri:s̄]: Fricativized final /d/ phrase-finally.

14. A series of glottal replacements for /t/ in *said it*, in *quietly* and in *and it*: ['sedɪ² wʊɡəʊ 'kwaɪə²li ɪnɪ²dɪdn̩ts̄]. In each case the /t/ is followed by a heterosyllabic consonant. In *would go*, on the other hand, the final /d/ is completely elided.

15. [ɪ²dɪdn̩ts̄ ən 'ðenɪ² 's̩ᵗɑ: s̄ɪts̄ə]: The final /t/ in phrase-final *didn't is*, is, as expected, affricated; also as expected, the word-medial intervocalic /t/ in *started* and the fused intervocalic apical /dt/ cluster in *started to* are fricativized and affricated respectively. Note, however, that the preconsonantal final /t/ of *it* (*then it*) is glottally replaced.

16. ['veʳə mʌtʃ]: A rather weak /r/ in *very*, with the vowel in the second, unstressed syllable very open and central, presumably in anticipation of the /ʌ/ in *much*.

17. ['si:mtə 'b̥jɒn]: Loss of final /d/ in *seemed to*. An interesting sequence of two devoiced syllables in *to be*.

18. ['njy:speɪpˀ 'evri]: In *newspaper* as in similar contexts the /u:/ is strongly fronted under the influence of /j/. In contrast to the intrusive [r] observed in 3.&4., we here have a case of schwa-to-vowel linking without linking [r].

19. [ɜnɜ'ɦaɜ]: *and the higher* is radically reduced: *and the* loses two of the three intervocalic consonants, retaining only [n]. The /aɪ/ in *higher* is smoothed to a fronted open vowel. The central vowels are realized with a rather open quality; therefore we use [ɜ] instead of [ə].

20. & 21. [ðə'mi:ʑjə 'pʊ²tʃju]: Two cases of fricativized /j/. In *media*, the /d/ fuses with /j/ and results in a voiced alveolo-palatal fricative [ʑ] followed by a palatal

glide. In *put you*, we find a complex mixture, with a glottally reinforced first affricate element, again with a trace of the palatal glide following the fricative element.

22. ['bɪɣə]: The intervocalic /g/ in *bigger* is fricativized ([ɣ]) despite the word being accented. This weakening of /g/ to a fricative might be considered more likely than the fricativization of /k/, which we have observed several times (see I. 12., II. 3. & II. 8.), because /k/ is a 'fortis' plosive, i.e. it has more inherent articulatory force. The relative frequency is, however, a chance product of the text; there have been no other candidate words or phrases for /g/ weakening.

23. [ənaəz]: Similar to 19. (*and the higher*) above, the phrase *and I was* is very strongly reduced. Again it is the consonantal structure which is most affected: the final /d/ of *and* together with the initial /w/ of *was*. In addition, the /aɪ/ of *I* is smoothed. None of these changes are remarkable in themselves, but together they change the structure from a normal degree of reduction – [əndaɪwəz] – to a structure which is incomprehensible out of context.

24. ['ðæs̄]: One more case of fricativized phrase-final /t/ in *that*.

Further reading

English Pronouncing Dictionaries

Wells, J. C.: (latest edition) *Longman Pronunciation Dictionary*
Jones, D.: (latest edition) *English Pronouncing Dictionary*, CUP

General phonetics and phonology

Carr, P. (1993): *Phonology*. Macmillan, London
Clark, J. and Yallop, C. (1990): *An Introduction to Phonetics and Phonology*.
 Blackwell, Oxford
Laver, J. (1994): *Principles of Phonetics*. CUP, Cambridge

Phonetics and phonology of English

Arnold, R. und Hansen, K. (1995): *Englische Phonetik*. Langenscheidt, Leipzig
Bowen, T. and Marks, J. (1992): *The Pronunciation Book*; Longman, Harlow
Cruttenden, A. (1994): *Gimson's Pronunciation of English*, Revised by A.
 Cruttenden. Edward Arnold, London
Davies, J. (1998): *Phonetics and Phonology*. Klett, Stuttgart
Dretzke, B. (1998): *Modern British and American Pronunciation*; UTB Schöningh
Giegerich, H. J. (1992): *English Phonology; An Introduction*. CUP
Hollingsworth, K. and Martin, E. (1994): *Sounds good! Ein unterhaltsames
 Aussprachetraining*; mit Cassette. Max Hueber Verlag, Ismaning
Roach, P. (1983): *English Phonetics and Phonology. A Practical Course*. plus
 Tutor's Book and 2 Cassettes, CUP

English stress and intonation

Berg, T. (1997): Lexical Stress Differences in English and German: The Special
 Status of Proper Nouns. In *Linguistische Berichte 167*, pp 3-22
Couper-Kuhlen, E. (1986): *An Introduction to English Prosody*, Edward Arnold
Cruttenden; A. (1986): *Intonation*, plus cassette; CUP
Fudge, E. (1984): *English Word-Stress*, Allen&Unwin, Hemel Hempstead

Teaching English phonetics and pronunciation

Brown, A., ed. (1991): *Teaching English Pronunciation; A book of readings*,
 Routledge, Lo & N.Y.
Brown, A., ed. (1992): *Approaches to Pronunciation Teaching*, Macmillan, London
Celce-Murcia, Marianne; Brinton, D.M.; Goodwin, J. M. (1997): *Teaching
 Pronunciation. A Reference for Teachers of English to Speakers of Other
 Languages*. CUP
Dalton, C. and Seidlhofer, B. (1994): *Pronunciation*, OUP/Cornelsen
Fitzpatrick, F. (1995): *Teacher's Guide to Practical Pronunciation*, Macmillan
Laroy, C.(1995): *Pronunciation* (Resource Books for Teachers), OUP
Underhill, A. (1994): *Sound Foundations*, Heinemann, Oxford

INDEX:

Page numbers in bold print refer to definitions of this term.
Page numbers in brackets refer to pages where the topic is dealt with but the
particular term is not mentioned explicitly.

THE INTERNATIONAL PHONETIC ALPHABET (revised to 1993, corrected 1996)

CONSONANTS (PULMONIC)

	Bilabial	Labiodental	Dental	Alveolar	Postalveolar	Retroflex	Palatal	Velar	Uvular	Pharyngeal	Glottal
Plosive	p b			t d		ʈ ɖ	c ɟ	k g	q ɢ		ʔ
Nasal	m	ɱ		n		ɳ	ɲ	ŋ	N		
Trill	ʙ			r					ʀ		
Tap or Flap				ɾ		ɽ					
Fricative	ɸ β	f v	θ ð	s z	ʃ ʒ	ʂ ʐ	ç ʝ	x ɣ	χ ʁ	ħ ʕ	h ɦ
Lateral fricative				ɬ ɮ							
Approximant		ʋ		ɹ		ɻ	j	ɰ			
Lateral approximant				l		ɭ	ʎ	ʟ			

Where symbols appear in pairs, the one to the right represents a voiced consonant. Shaded areas denote articulations judged impossible

CONSONANTS (NON-PULMONIC)

Clicks	Voiced implosives	Ejectives
ʘ Bilabial	ɓ Bilabial	ʼ Examples:
ǀ Dental	ɗ Dental/alveolar	pʼ Bilabial
ǃ (Post)alveolar	ʄ Palatal	tʼ Dental/alveolar
ǂ Palatoalveolar	ɠ Velar	kʼ Velar
ǁ Alveolar lateral	ʛ Uvular	sʼ Alveolar fricative

OTHER SYMBOLS

ʍ Voiceless labial-velar fricative   ɕ ʑ Alveolo-palatal fricatives

w Voiced labial-velar approximant   ɺ Alveolar lateral flap

ɥ Voiced labial-palatal approximant   ɧ Simultaneous ʃ and x

ʜ Voiceless epiglottal fricative

ʢ Voiced epiglottal fricative

Affricates and double articulations can be represented by two symbols joined by a tie bar if necessary. k͡p t͡s

ʡ Epiglottal plosive

VOWELS

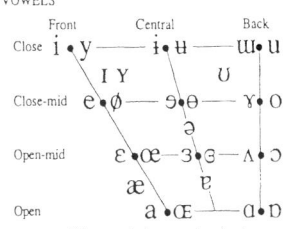

Where symbols appear in pairs, the one to the right represents a rounded vowel.

SUPRASEGMENTALS

ˈ Primary stress

ˌ Secondary stress ˌfoʊnəˈtɪʃən

ː Long eː

ˑ Half-long eˑ

˘ Extra-short ĕ

| Minor (foot) group

‖ Major (intonation) group

. Syllable break ɹi.ækt

‿ Linking (absence of a break)

DIACRITICS   Diacritics may be placed above a symbol with a descender, e.g. ŋ̊

Voiceless	n̥ d̥		Breathy voiced	b̤ a̤		Dental	t̪ d̪
Voiced	s̬ t̬		Creaky voiced	b̰ a̰		Apical	t̺ d̺
Aspirated	tʰ dʰ		Linguolabial	t̼ d̼		Laminal	t̻ d̻
More rounded	ɔ̹		Labialized	tʷ dʷ		Nasalized	ẽ
Less rounded	ɔ̜		Palatalized	tʲ dʲ		Nasal release	dⁿ
Advanced	u̟		Velarized	tˠ dˠ		Lateral release	dˡ
Retracted	e̠		Pharyngealized	tˤ dˤ		No audible release	d̚
Centralized	ë		Velarized or pharyngealized	ɫ	
Mid-centralized	e̽		Raised	e̝ (ɹ̝ = voiced alveolar fricative)
Syllabic	n̩		Lowered	e̞ (β̞ = voiced bilabial approximant)
Non-syllabic	e̯		Advanced Tongue Root	e̘
Rhoticity	ɚ a˞		Retracted Tongue Root	e̙

TONES AND WORD ACCENTS

	LEVEL			CONTOUR	
e̋ or ˥	Extra high	ě or ˩˥	Rising
é ˦	High	ê	Falling
ē ˧	Mid	e᷄	High rising
è ˨	Low	e᷅	Low rising
ȅ ˩	Extra low	e᷈	Rising-falling
↓	Downstep	↗	Global rise
↑	Upstep	↘	Global fall

Vocal Tract (sagittal section)
with places of articulation (and corresponding adjectives in italics)

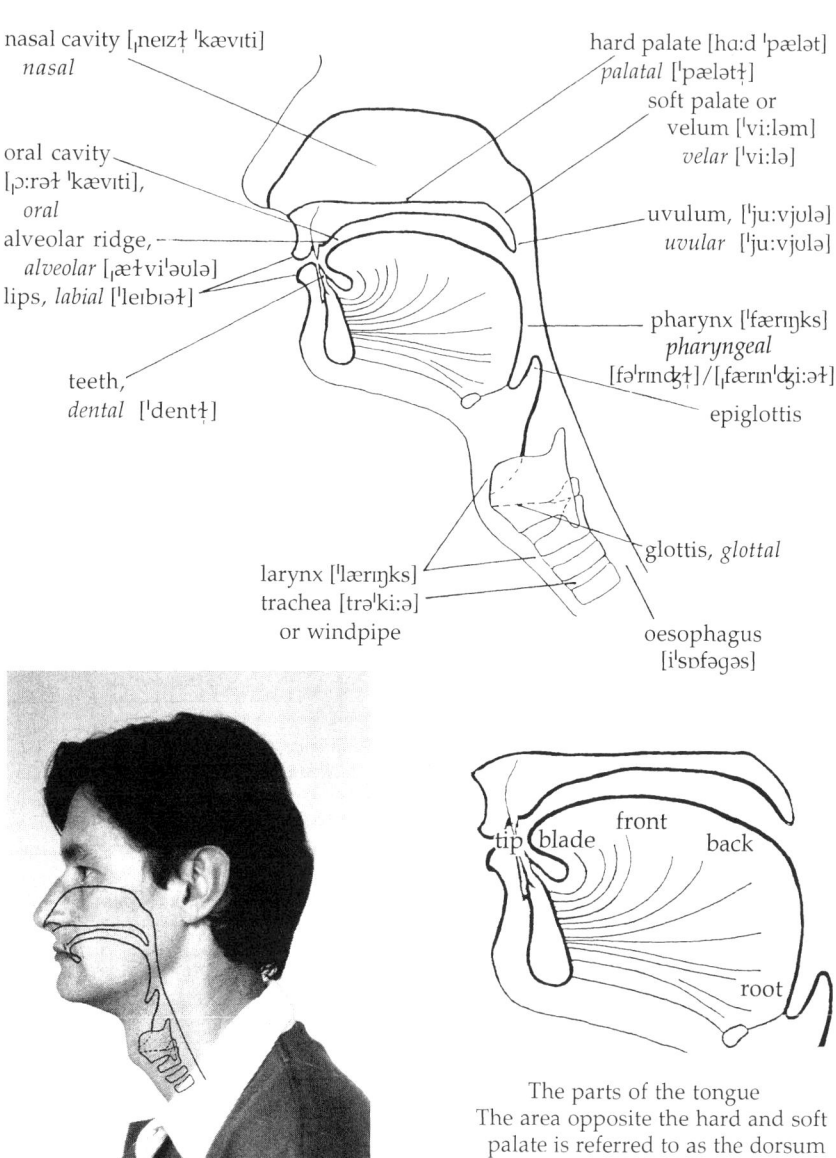

nasal cavity [ˌneɪzɫ ˈkævɪti]
nasal

oral cavity
[ˌɔːrəɫ ˈkævɪti],
oral
alveolar ridge,
alveolar [ˌæɫviˈəʊlə]
lips, *labial* [ˈleɪbɪəɫ]

teeth,
dental [ˈdentɫ]

hard palate [hɑːd ˈpælət]
palatal [ˈpælətɫ]
soft palate or
velum [ˈviːləm]
velar [ˈviːlə]

uvulum, [ˈjuːvjʊlə]
uvular [ˈjuːvjʊlə]

pharynx [ˈfærɪŋks]
pharyngeal
[fəˈrɪndʒɫ]/[ˌfærɪnˈdʒiːəɫ]
epiglottis

larynx [ˈlærɪŋks]
trachea [trəˈkiːə]
or windpipe

glottis, *glottal*

oesophagus
[iˈsɒfəgəs]

The parts of the tongue
The area opposite the hard and soft
palate is referred to as the dorsum

The Use of Phonetic Symbols

English Consonant symbols

/p/ [pʰ] *pin*; [p] *spin, happy, nip*; [p̚] *lipmark*
/b/ [b] *about; chubby, nib*; [b̥] *offbeat, clubfoot*
/t/ [tʰ] *tin*; [t] *step, batter, bit*; [t̚] *letdown*
/d/ [d] *ado; caddy, bad*; [d̥] *cashdesk, godson*
/k/ [kʰ] *kin*; [k] *Scot, lucky, sick*; [k̚] *pockmark*
/g/ [g] *ago; soggy, log*; [g̊] *popgun, dogcart*

/f/ [f] *fin, toffee, cough*
/v/ [v] *vine, savour, dive*; [v̥] *Latvia, dovecote*
/θ/ [θ] *thin, cathode, wrath*
/ð/ [ð] *thine, bother, lithe*; [ð̥] *stop that! lithesome*
/s/ [s] *sin, racy, loose*
/z/ [z] *zoom, lousy, lose*; [z̥] *ice-zone, buzzcock*
/ʃ/ [ʃ] *shine, usher, leash*
/ʒ/ [ʒ] - *leisure, beige*; [ʒ̊] *beige coat*
/h/ [h] *sit here*; [ɦ] *ahead, come here*

/m/ [m] *mine, summer, some*
/n/ [n] *next, funny, bin*
/ŋ/ [ŋ] - *singer, long*

/l/ [l] *let, alive, feel it*; [ɫ] *feel, help*
/r/ [ɹ] *red, hurry, share it*; [ɾ] *three*
/j/ [j] *yellow*; [ç] *Hugh, cue*
/w/ [w] *wind*, [ʍ] *queen*

English Vowel symbols

/iː/ [iː] *beat*; [i] *happy*
/ɪ/ [ɪ] *bin, before*
/e/ [e] *bet, any*
/æ/ [æ] *bat*
/ɑː/ [ɑː] *cart*; [ɑ] *partake*
/ɒ/ [ɒ] *shop*
/ʌ/ [ʌ] *shut*
/ɔː/ [ɔː] *caught*; [ɔ] *portend*
/ʊ/ [ʊ] *put*;
/uː/ [uː] *shoot*; [u] *rubella*
/ɜː/ [ɜː] *shirt*
/ə/ [ə] *about, bitter*

/eɪ/ [eɪ] *late*
/əʊ/ [əʊ] *coat*
/aɪ/ [aɪ] *kite*
/aʊ/ [aʊ] *shout*
/ɔɪ/ [ɔɪ] *coin*

/ɪə/ [ɪə] *fear*
/eə/ [eə] *fair*
/ʊə/ [ʊə] *tour*

Transcription of running speech

Stress and accent marks:

Primary: [ˈxxx] [hiz ˈkʌmɪŋ təˈnaɪt]   Secondary: [ˌxxx] [aɪ ˈtəʊɫdɪm ˌtuː]
[ˈɒbvɪəsli]   [ˌmɪsˈfʌŋkʃən], [ˈkɒmplɪ̩keɪt]

Linking conventions:

Clitics joined to lexical word: [ˈpʊtɪt ˈðeə]; [ˈgetɒnət ðə ˈsteɪʃən]
Linking bar between words: [teˈl‿evrɪwʌn]; [hi ˈfaʊndɪt‿əmʌŋ‿aʊə ˈpeɪpəz]
Raised linking sounds:
  linking [r]   [ˈteəʲɪˈt‿ɒf]; [ˈweəˡʲɪzɪt]
  linking [j]   [aɪ ˡʲ iːzli fəˈget]; [ˈwiːˡ ɔːlweɪz ˈlaɪkɪt]
  linking [w]   [ˈhuːʷɑːskt ˈjuː]; [haʊˡʷɑː juː]
Brackets: phonemic / /; phonetic [ ]; orthographic < >